CHILDHOODS IN CONTEXT

CHILDHOOD: THE SERIES

This book is the second of four which have been prepared as the core teaching texts for the Open University course U212 *Childhood*. The growing field of childhood and youth studies provides an integrative framework for interdisciplinary research and teaching, as well as analysis of contemporary policy and practice in, for instance, education, health and social work. Childhood is now a global issue, forcing a reconsideration of conventional approaches to study. Childhood is also a very personal issue for each and every one of us – scholars, policy-makers, parents and children. The books therefore include children's and parents' voices as well as academic discussion of childhood in diverse societies and points in history. The recognition of childhood and youth as a focus of study, debate and personal reflection provides the starting point for this introductory series.

Book 1 *Understanding Childhood: an interdisciplinary approach* asks 'What is a child?' and introduces a range of perspectives within childhood and youth studies. Topics in this book include the history of beliefs about childhood, the growth of scientific approaches to studying children, the significance of gender, debates around children's rights and how far children are seen as innocent or knowing.

Book 2 *Childhoods in Context* examines the interplay between family, work, schooling and other influences in the daily lives of children and young people. Topics include changing family patterns, debates about school versus work, and current concerns about child labour. Issues in early childhood are discussed, as well as the transition from child to adult.

Book 3 *Children's Cultural Worlds* looks at the distinctiveness of children's cultural worlds by exploring the everyday activities of young children through to teenagers. Topics include friendships and the significance of play, how children use language to construct relationships and identities, the role of print literature, other media and information technology in children's lives, and their growing power as consumers.

Book 4 *Changing Childhoods: local and global* considers the status of children in society, and the significance of children's rights. Topics include the effects of poverty, ill-health and violence on children's well-being. Finally, the book illustrates the ways in which children and young people become engaged with social issues, including issues surrounding their status as children.

Further details on The Open University course U212 Childhood and other courses in the BA Hons *Childhood and Youth Studies* degree can be obtained from the Course Information and Advice Centre, PO Box 625, The Open University, Walton Hall, Milton Keynes, MK7 6YG, United Kingdom. Telephone +44 (0)1908 653231, e-mail general-enquiries@open.ac.uk, web site http://www.open.ac.uk/courses.

WILEY

The Open University

CHILDHOODS IN CONTEXT

edited by Janet Maybin
and Martin Woodhead

Copyright © 2003 The Open University

First published 2003 by John Wiley & Sons Ltd in association with
The Open University

Reprinted 2007

The Open University
Walton Hall
Milton Keynes MK7 6AA
United Kingdom
www.open.ac.uk

John Wiley & Sons Ltd
The Atrium
Southern Gate
Chichester PO19 8SQ
www.wiley.com

Other Wiley editorial offices

John Wiley & Sons Inc., 111 River Street, Hoboken, NJ 07030, USA

Jossey-Bass, 989 Market Street, San Francisco, CA 94103-1741, USA

Wiley-VCH Verlag GmbH, Boschstr. 12, D-69469 Weinheim, Germany

John Wiley & Sons Australia Ltd, 42 McDougall Street, Milton,
Queensland 4064, Australia

John Wiley & Sons (Asia) Pte Ltd, 2 Clementi Loop #02-01, Jin Xing
Distripark, Singapore 129809

John Wiley & Sons Canada Ltd, 6045 Freemont Blvd, Mississauga, ONT,
L5R 4J3

Library of Congress Cataloging-in-Publication Data

A catalog record for this book is available from the Library of Congress.

British Library Cataloguing in Publication Data

A catalogue record for this book is available from the British Library.

ISBN 978 0 470 84693 3

Edited, designed and typeset by The Open University.
Printed in Malta by Gutenberg Press Limited.

1.3

Contents

Contributors

Rachel Burr is a lecturer in Childhood Studies at The Open University. She has worked as a social worker and trainer in England, Ireland and Vietnam. Between 1996 and 1998 she lived in Vietnam where she did child-focused research for a doctorate in anthropology at Brunel University. Her research interests are in child-focused human rights, the role of child-focused international aid agencies, and children of the streets and orphanages in Vietnam (she is currently investigating the effects of HIV/AIDS on the lives of those children). She has taught anthropology in the US. Her recent publications include 'Global and local approaches to children's rights in Vietnam', *Childhood*, vol. 9(1) and 'Ethics of doing anthropological fieldwork', *Anthropology Matters*, vol 3.

Hugh Cunningham is the Professor of Social History at the University of Kent at Canterbury. He has published widely on the history of childhood, in particular on child labour, and is the author of *The Children of the Poor* (Blackwell, 1991) and *Children and Childhood in Western Society since 1500* (Longman, 1995). He has recently completed a volume in the New History of Britain, entitled *The Challenge of Democracy: Britain 1832–1918* (Longman, 2001), and is currently working on popular memory and national identity in nineteenth-century Britain.

Donald Mackinnon is a lecturer in the Faculty of Education and Language Studies at The Open University. He studied sociology and philosophy at Glasgow University and taught in a junior secondary school just outside Glasgow before joining the OU in 1971, not long after its foundation. He has contributed to many OU courses, written books on education in the UK and Europe, and done research into primary education in India.

Janet Maybin is a senior lecturer in the Centre for Language and Communications at The Open University. She has contributed to courses on children and young people's language and learning, particularly from a cross-cultural perspective, and has edited a number of books on research and practice in this area. Her research interests include children's informal peer-group talk and children's and adults' uses of literacy to manage relationships with other people and to construct identity. Recent publications include 'Children's voices: talk, knowledge and identity' in *The Sociolinguistics Reader*, vol. 2, (edited by Cheshire and Trudgill, Edward Arnold, 1998), ' "What's the hottest part of the Sun? Page 3!" Children's exploration of adolescent gender identities through informal talk' in *Gender Identities and Discourse Analysis* (edited by Litosseliti and Sunderland, Benjamins, 2002).

Linda Miller is a lecturer in Childhood Studies at The Open University. Prior to joining The Open University in 1999 she was principal lecturer in early years education at the University of Hertfordshire. Her main research interests are in young children's literacy development and policy and practice in early literacy. Published books include *Towards Reading: Literacy Development in the Pre-School Years* (Open University Press, 1996), *Moving Towards Literacy with Environmental Print* (United Kingdom Reading Association, 1998). She is co-editor of *Looking at Early Years Education and Care* (David Fulton, 2000) and *Exploring Issues in Early Years Education and Care* (David Fulton, 2002).

Heather Montgomery is a lecturer in Childhood Studies at The Open University. She is an anthropologist who has conducted fieldwork in Thailand among young prostitutes and is the author of *Modern Babylon? Prostituting Children in Thailand* (Berghahn, 2001). She has held post-doctoral positions in the USA, Norway and Oxford and is the author of several articles on children's rights, abuse and the anthropology of childhood including 'Imposing rights? A case study of child prostitution in Thailand' in *Culture and Rights* (edited by Cowan, Dembour and Wilson, Cambridge University Press, 2001) and 'Abandonment and child prostitution in a Thai slum community' in *Abandoned Children* (edited by Panter-Brick and Smith, Cambridge University Press, 2001).

Virginia Morrow is Research Lecturer, Department of Health and Social Care, Brunel University. Children and young people have been the primary focus of her research activities since 1988. She has focused on English teenagers' involvement in work, transitions to adulthood in the UK and children's conceptualizations of family. *Understanding families: children's perspectives* (1998) was published by National Children's Bureau/Joseph Rowntree Foundation. She has also published papers on ethical and methodological issues related to social research with children. Her most recent research explored the relationship between social capital and health in relation to children and young people, published as *Networks and Neighbourhoods: children's and young people's perspectives* (2001) Health Development Agency, London.

Janet Soler is a lecturer in Curriculum and Teaching Studies at The Open University. Before she joined The Open University in 1999 she was a lecturer at the School of Education, Otago University in New Zealand. Her interest in the curriculum arose from her experiences as a teacher and school based researcher. Recent publications include *Literacy in New Zealand: Practices, Politics and Policy since 1900* (with Smith, Addison Wesley Longman, 2000), *Teacher Development: exploring our own practice* (as editor with Craft and Burgess, Paul Chapman Publishing in association with The Open University, 2000), *Contextualizing Difficulties in Literacy Development: exploring politics, culture, ethnicity and ethics* (as editor with Wearmouth and Reid, Routledge in association with The Open University, 2002).

Martin Woodhead is a senior lecturer in the Centre for Childhood, Development and Learning at The Open University. He has contributed to courses in child development and education, as well as carrying out research in child development, early education, sociology of childhood, child labour and children's rights. He has been a Fulbright scholar in the USA as well as a consultant to international organizations including Council of Europe, Save the Children and OECD. His publications include *Cultural Worlds of Early Childhood* (with Faulkner and Littleton, Routledge in association with The Open University, 1998), and 'The value of work and school: a study of working children's perspectives' in *Child Labour: policy options* (edited by Lieten and White, Aksant, 2001). He chaired the course team for The Open University course U212 *Childhood*, for which this book is one of the core texts.

Introduction

What are the most significant influences in children's lives? How has children's experience changed over the past two centuries? What does family mean in contemporary societies? Are the early years a time for play or for education? Is school necessarily the best place to learn? Is working always harmful to children's development? How do young people experience the transition from child to adult? These are some of the questions examined in this book. It has been prepared within the interdisciplinary framework of Childhood Studies, drawing on insights from anthropology, developmental psychology, history, philosophy, educational studies and sociology.

The title of this book conveys two central themes – the plurality of childhoods and the power of context. The first theme has already been explored in volume one of this series, which emphasized diversity in children's lives as well as the ways childhood is variously understood – within everyday beliefs, scientific theories, and cultural images (Woodhead and Montgomery, 2003). This second book takes the study of diversity a stage further, drawing on numerous accounts of childhood, ranging from children growing up in fishing communities in nineteenth-century Sweden, childhoods in rural Bolivia and in Zimbabwe, children working in sweatshops in Bangladesh, as well as children in England, Japan and India facing the pressures of formal school learning and competitive examinations. Studying childhoods *in context* is a way of making sense of diversity, of recognizing patterns of social change affecting children's lives, and of evaluating trends towards more globalized expectations for childhood.

The chapters in this book examine some major factors that shape the experience of childhood – social practices in children's homes, neighbourhoods, schools and communities, within the contexts of economic and political forces which shape their prospects. They also consider changing beliefs about childhood which at any given time lead some contexts to be seen as normal, natural and desirable, while others are seen as abnormal, unnatural and harmful.

Throughout the book the authors draw on children's own activities and perspectives as key resources in this analysis. Rather than starting with pre-conceived ideas about 'family', 'work' and 'school' as social institutions shaping childhood, we prefer instead to ask about their meaning to individual children. So we ask how young people themselves experience their home, their workplace or their classroom as key sites in their lives, each of which is associated with specific social practices, related to expectations of children's activities and behaviour. Our approach reflects current thinking within the social sciences, as the developmental psychologist Rudolph Schaffer explains:

> The story of the study of social development in recent years is ... very much a matter of increasing awareness of the importance of *context*, that is, the realization that the behaviour of individual children is given meaning by the relationships in which the child is embedded, that these relationships in turn are embedded in systems such as families, and that these too can only be fully understood within the context of the society of which they form a part.

(Schaffer, 1996, p. 12)

Socialization is understood as a reciprocal process, built on the interactions between children, parents and others, which in turn are embedded in specific social and cultural contexts. Children are not represented – as in the past they sometimes were – as if they were passive objects of nurture and protection, teaching and training, research and experimentation. As the sociologist Anthony Giddens puts it '... Socialization is not a kind of "cultural programming", in which the child absorbs passively the influences with which he or she comes into contact. Even the most recent new-born infant has needs or demands that affect the behaviour of those responsible for its care' (Giddens, 1993, p. 60).

There is another reason for drawing extensively on the voices of young people themselves. Despite increasing attention paid to children's active role in their development and socialization, in other respects children themselves have remained relatively invisible. The anthropologist Charlotte Hardman was amongst the first to note (in the early 1970s) that children were a 'muted group' within the social sciences, and to call for an 'anthropology of children, concerned with ... interpretation of their viewpoint, their meaning of the world' (Hardman, 2001, pp. 502 and 503).

The inclusion of children's voices within research into socialization involves more than a shift in theoretical orientation. It also recognizes their rights to participate in socialization processes, especially in day-to-day decisions that shape their lives. A central tenet of Childhood Studies is that children are not merely adults-in-the-making, the largely powerless objects of adult concern, adult action and adult agendas. Allison James and her colleagues argue that we need to think about children as people-in-themselves, and from a perspective which places their concerns and interests (rather than merely those of adults) at the forefront. In short, the implication is for 'children to be understood as social actors shaping as well as shaped by their circumstances' (James, Jenks and Prout, 1998, p. 6). Issues surrounding children's activity and agency, their perspectives and their rights are at the forefront of Childhood Studies.

The chapters in this book put childhoods into context in another sense too. The questions we began with are charged with controversy, for example about which family structures best support children's development, when children should begin formal schooling, or whether child labour should be outlawed. While schooling has become a dominant setting for the childhoods of many of the world's children, the teaching approaches and assessment systems used are hotly debated, as are the functions of schooling in shaping young people's prospects. Several chapters in this book address contemporary issues directly, but the authors also draw on broader historical and anthropological perspectives, recognizing that in different times and societies, debates about childhood are informed by quite different beliefs and expectations about what childhood is for. Additional perspectives are provided in the short readings at the end of each chapter, which are written from a range of academic perspectives, and include extracts by public figures like Nelson Mandela and Edward Said.

Chapter 1 'Socializing children' introduces some of the dimensions of diversity in children's lives, as these are shaped by social, cultural and economic context. The chapter begins with examples from three contrasting locations, Cape Town in South Africa, Chittagong in Bangladesh and Oakland in California. These examples are taken from the audio-visual case studies associated with this book. They illustrate the variety of different influences on children's lives across a range of cultural settings. Treating children very much as social actors in their own right, the chapter examines the significance of these influences for children's socialization and learning and the ways in which they become skilled and knowledgeable social participants in a particular cultural setting. The authors also look at change and discontinuity in children's lives, as these affect their sense of identity. Chapter 1 lays the groundwork for one of the central arguments of the book: that children's experiences are best understood by examining actual sites and social practices in all their diversity and complexity, rather than dealing with abstractions about the influence of institutions like the family, work and school.

Chapter 2 'Family, kinship and beyond' takes this argument a step further, concentrating on the diverse meanings of 'family' and the implications of these for children, across a range of different cultural contexts. Drawing particularly on anthropological sources, the chapter examines key and often emotive questions to do with what makes a family, who counts as a parent, and the complex relationship between biological and social factors. Covering themes as diverse as spirit children, assisted conception, adoption and institutional care, the authors discuss idealizations about the family as well as the diversity and fluidity of family structures in contemporary societies. The active role of children themselves in claiming kin and shaping the dynamics of the family is central to the chapter.

Chapter 3 'Children's changing lives from 1800 to 2000' shifts the focus to take a historical perspective. Hugh Cunningham considers some of the radical changes in Britain, Western Europe and the United States during the nineteenth and twentieth centuries which have had far-reaching influences on children's lives, and arguably also helped shaped modern Western conceptions of childhood as a period of dependency and learning. In particular, the chapter traces changes in the role of work and education in children's lives over the past two hundred years and the closely connected changes in their role in the family and in broader social conceptions about what childhood should be. Two hundred years ago children played an important role in the economy and often made a key contribution to the income of the family. Their schooling was intermittent, brief or non-existent. Today in Western Europe and the United States, children's productive contribution to the family is rare and schooling is lengthy and compulsory. Drawing on a range of historical evidence including contemporary examples and children's own voices, the chapter examines the key debates and reforms which transformed children's lives during this period.

Chapters 4 and 5 bring these debates up to date through a detailed account of the role of work and school in contemporary children's lives across different cultural contexts.

Chapter 4 'Children and school' examines the very different forms which schooling may take, including a review of available statistics about the nature and amount of schooling for boys and girls in different parts of the world. It then takes a fresh look at the intended, and unintended, functions of schooling, raising issues about cultural identity, students' future participation in society, testing, selection and differentiation. Finally, the chapter examines possible reasons behind the disaffection with schooling among teenagers, especially boys, in societies in the North.

Chapter 5 'Children and work' starts out by defining different kinds of child work and reviewing its prevalence in different parts of the world today. It then introduces the often heated arguments about the advantages and disadvantages of various kinds of work for children, and about whether they should work at all. These arguments are carefully examined in relation to two contrasting case studies: children employed in workshops in Dhaka, Bangladesh, and children engaged in domestic and agricultural work in rural Zimbabwe. The chapter concludes by asking how far research into children's own views about work and school can shed light on these issues.

Chapter 6 'Shaping early childhood education' draws out a theme which has run through earlier chapters: the ways that children's lives are shaped by expectations of their needs, learning and development which are held by parents, teachers and others around them as well as by more general cultural conceptions of what childhood should be about. It examines how competing visions for young children's play and learning underpin systems of early childhood education, examining three influential examples of curriculum and pedagogy, from England, New Zealand and Italy. Focusing on key questions about what and how children should learn, and who decides these curriculum and pedagogy issues, it explores how professional beliefs and more widely driven political agendas shape children's earliest experiences of education and schooling.

Finally, *Chapter 7 'Moving out of childhood'*, takes us to the other end of the age group. The chapter explores transitions which take place in later childhood as children begin to move towards adulthood, arguing that these can be experienced as gradual or very sudden, and that they are frequently fragmented. These transitions are influenced by a range of factors such as gender, class, sexuality, disability, religious practice and traditional customs and the chapter explores how these differences are experienced by young people themselves. Traditional and contemporary rites of passage are examined in relation to social and economic change, and the social shaping of biological processes is explored through historical and contemporary accounts. The chapter covers a wide range of topics such as identity, sexuality and transitions to work, and includes consideration of notions of independence and interdependence.

In preparing these chapters, the authors aimed to draw on examples from a wide range of geographical locations and periods in history. Making comparisons between childhoods according to economic context, cultural tradition or world location is fraught with difficulties. Numerous terms are in circulation, notably Third World, industrialized countries, developing countries, or most recently minority world and majority world. Chapter authors vary in their preferred use of terms, but (as for other books in the series) we use the labels 'North' to denote the richer, more industrialized countries, and 'South' to denote the poorer, less industrialized ones. Also, we use the label 'Western' to denote the cultural beliefs and practices associated with highly industrialized societies, which have their roots in the philosophy that developed in Europe and North America during the seventeenth and eighteenth centuries – the historical period sometimes called the 'Age of Enlightenment'.

Preparation of this book (and the others in the series) has been linked to the production of audio-visual case studies of childhoods in three locations – Cape Town (South Africa), Chittagong (Bangladesh), and Oakland (California). The books and audio-visual material make up The Open University course U212 *Childhood*. Many of the themes of the book were explored with children, parents and communities in these three locations, and quotations are included in several of the chapters.

We would like to thank all those who contributed at each stage in the preparation of this book, especially Professor Berry Mayall (University of London, Institute of Education), Dr William Myers (University of California, Davis), and Dr Allison James (University of Hull).

Janet Maybin and Martin Woodhead
The Open University, 2002

References

GIDDENS, A. (1993) *Sociology*, Cambridge, Polity Press (second edition).

HARDMAN, C. (2001) 'Can there be an anthropology of children?', *Childhood*, **8**, pp. 501–517 (originally published 1973).

JAMES, A., JENKS, C. and PROUT, A. (1998) *Theorizing Childhood*, Cambridge, Polity.

SCHAFFER, H. R. (1996) *Social Development*, Oxford, Blackwell.

WOODHEAD, M. and MONTGOMERY, H. K. (2003) *Understanding Childhood: an interdisciplinary approach*, Chichester, Wiley/The Open University.

Chapter 1
Socializing children

by Janet Maybin and Martin Woodhead

CONTENTS

LEARNING OUTCOMES

When you have studied this chapter, you should be able to:

1   Appreciate and begin to analyse how socialization is occurring all the time in children's diverse experience of daily life.

2   Compare different theories of socialization.

3   Consider how these theories may be reflected in the ways children are actually socialized in different settings.

4   Recognize the significance of children's role in socialization, for example as expressed through their critical reflections on their own experience.

5   Understand the role of language and communication in socialization and the process of guided participation.

6   Recognize that children often experience inconsistency, disruption and dislocation, which affect their sense of identity.

1 INTRODUCTION

Socialization is the process through which a child becomes an active competent participant in one or more communities.

In this chapter we introduce the study of children's daily lives and their experience of socialization in a range of cultural settings. You will read the accounts of children in diverse socio-economic and cultural contexts exploring their own perspectives on their daily lives. Through these examples we hope to identify some of the issues for the chapter (and the book), such as:

- How can we begin to understand the different influences on children's lives, and the significance of these for their learning and development?

- How do children become skilled and knowledgeable participants in social life in a particular cultural setting?

- How do they cope with change and dislocation?

- How far do children themselves influence their own socialization?

In the past, socialization has sometimes been seen as kind of cultural programming of children by adults, through social institutions like the family, school or church. More recently, interest has shifted to what people actually do, their attitudes and interactions with others, how these both reflect and contribute to beliefs and values, and the active role of children in this process. Rather than talk about the influence of abstract institutions, we are going to focus on children's activities and experience in different parts of their lives, and examine how through these they gradually become self-aware, knowledgeable and skilled in particular kinds of ways. It is with children's experiences that we begin.

2 STUDYING DAILY LIVES

Allow about 30 minutes

ACTIVITY 1   How children spend their time

As part of the preparation for this book we interviewed children in Bangladesh, the United States and South Africa about their daily lives. We asked them a series of questions about how they spent their time, the people and places that were important to them. We were interested in the structure of their daily lives, as well as what they felt were the main influences. We were also interested in their feelings of freedom and of being controlled, as well as their sense of their long-term futures.

The edited quotations on pages 4–6 illustrate some of the things the children told us. As you study these examples, pay particular attention to the people, places and activities mentioned by each child and to the contrasts between their lives. We have provided an outline table below that you can use to summarize what the children say. We've put in our notes for the first child, to illustrate what we want you to do.

	Bilkis	Tinco	Chet	Cathy	Wilfred
Places	Home, employer's house, school				
People	Mother, little sisters, employer, Monica				
Activities	Chores, play, reading and writing				
Other	Wants an education so she can get a job in the garment factory				

Children talking about their activities

[Quotations from Bilkis and Tinco are translations]

Bilkis (about eleven years old) lives in one of the poorest and most densely populated communities in the city of Chittagong. Much of her day is spent either doing chores in the one-room shack she shares with her family, or working as a domestic at their landlord's house in a more affluent neighbourhood nearby. She also attends school for two hours each day.

I do the housework first, then I go to play. I stop if I have other chores to do. My mother tells me to look after the house and look after my little sister. Nowadays I can wash the dishes, the clothes, make the beds, everything. But when I was younger I didn't know how to do these things and my mother used to do all the housework ... Usually nobody tells me what to do. Sometimes my mother will tell me, but mostly I do things on my own. I've been doing the housework since I was very young. If I don't do it, who else will?

I like working in [my employer's] house ... When I haven't any work to do I play with Monica [her employer's daughter] and I like to play with her toys ... When I hear the call to prayer I go back home from my landlord's house. I get washed, have my lunch and then go to school.

If I come to school I will learn to read and write. So if somebody needs help reading a letter I can read that letter for them and they will think highly of me and think how clever I am.

With an education I can get a job in the garment factory. When I'm older I want to get a job and I want to achieve three things. I want to buy clothes and presents for my mum. Then I'm going to buy a tape recorder and tapes. And the third thing I want to do is to do something for my little sisters to show them that I love them.

Bilkis.

Tinco (about twelve years old) is from a large family living in a fishing community on the outskirts of Chittagong. Their traditional lifestyle is under threat as the city grows. Tinco spends his time fishing and selling fish in the market, as well as playing with his friends. He doesn't go to school:

It's hard work fishing. If I catch a lot of fish, I feel really good ... the more I catch ... I can make more money selling it ...

When I was smaller my mother and father would tell me to go and collect firewood and fuel for the cooking, and if I didn't go they would scold me or not give me any food. But now if I say that I won't go and collect firewood, they don't say anything to me. So I feel I have more freedom now. The money I make helps my family. We're in debt ... I don't have a lot of responsibilities now. I can go and play. The part of the day I like most is the time when I play 'danguli' [a type of rounders] with my friends ...

I will carry on catching fish for now. But when I'm older I'll get a job and support my parents and my family. I'll have many more responsibilities. I will have to look after my younger brothers and sisters.

Tinco.

Chet (fourteen years old) lives in Oakland, California, with his parents and sister and attends a private high school.

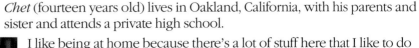

I like being at home because there's a lot of stuff here that I like to do ... because I've got a lot of the things in my room and stuff. So that I get to listen to music or draw or play video games.

Usually when I go to Tony's house we'll play video games or go on-line or we'll walk to Lakeshore (shopping mall) ... We go to the record store ... they have lots of used records they're hard to find – that you can get for fairly cheap cos they're used ...

I think that my friends' parents are a bit more uptight about letting people stay home alone or go out walking by themselves than my parents. My parents will usually let me go pretty much anywhere ...

I like the school cos the teachers are a lot better I think and the stuff we cover is better and we have electives which we didn't have in public school. Electives are classes that we get to choose ourselves.

Chet.

Cathy (fifteen years old) is a Chinese American girl who also lives in Oakland with her parents and sister and attends the local state high school.

... Everything in my life starts in this house. I mean I go out from this house every morning, I come into this house every day ... I have three rooms in my house and one room is me and my sister's room. And she's really messy but I should have taken the front room ... I have a study room in the front ...

For a guy it's easier to go out and then usually people don't mess with guys. For girls especially, walking out late at night is really really bad. And my mum has always told us we have to act like girls and be more careful like girls ...

I think I have a pretty diverse school, cos there's people from all over the world really. The majority of the people there are Asians, kind of like us. There are some kids who just hang around trash cans and do smoke bombs and stuff. The majority of these kids go to class but they don't really want to learn because they don't like the teacher.

I tutor after school. I help kids with their homework. I was trying to save for college.

Sharon and Cathy.

Wilfred (thirteen years old) lives for part of the time on the streets in the centre of Cape Town with other street children. Sometimes he stays at his friend Shane's adopted family home in a township outside the city, from where they catch the train downtown in the morning in order to earn money from begging and parking cars.

Steven, Wilfred and Shane.

In the morning when we wake up we put (the mattress) where we sleep on behind the bed, then we go to the station. First we eat something then we drink tea. Then we run to the station. The security guards are the people with the yellow jackets on. Then they grab us, they beat us, or they keep us the whole day till six o'clock. Then they leave us and we can't go any more to Cape Town, it's too late. And then we go back home and we will have no money. And the other friends come and they are all laughing at us, they are lucky when they have money. And I tell Steven and Shane, 'Don't worry about that money, tomorrow we can get that money double.' And when we go the next day we go to Cape Town, we survive and we struggle* and ask the tourists there by the Greenmarket Square. The tourists give us money and all that, then we are lucky too. Then I go to Long Street and I struggle with another friend ... And then when my stomach is full and I like to sleep then I sleep. When I feel to sleep then I sleep. When I feel to be wake up then I wake up ... In Cape Town, in Long Street sometimes I feel it's dangerous. When you park cars they come, other bad guys you see. They have knives and they walk together, they come around. When you sleep they search you. They get no money and they beat you up.

When I struggle in the day, about 40 rand (around £3) or 30 rand or 35, it all depends what the people give you and how many cars you park.

I decide what to do because my parents tell me they are not taking care of me. That's why I decide every day what to do. I can even smoke. They make nothing. When I come drunk in the house they make nothing.

* 'struggle' is a general term used by street children in Cape Town to describe making a living and surviving on the streets.

COMMENT

One of the most striking features of these accounts is the differences between the children's lives. But there are recurring themes within the three categories of places, people and activities. In terms of *places*, children talk about their home life, although home means very different things in terms of the space available and access to personal possessions. Some of them also talk about the importance of school, although school is a much more significant part of daily life for the two young people in Oakland than for Bilkis in Chittagong, and Tinco and Wilfred don't attend school at all. For Bilkis and Tinco, work is a major part of life – not just doing chores but as a contribution to family income. And Wilfred spends a large part of the day and night 'struggling' to get money to survive. Cathy works part-time in an after-school club, but is saving this money for her further education.

Each of the important places in children's lives are associated with particular kinds of *activities* – studying, doing chores, playing video games, begging – and involve different sets of *people* – parents and siblings at home, teachers and other students at school, friends in the neighbourhood, friends, tourists and bad guys on the streets. Notice the importance of friends of their own age in these children's lives, and the mention of relationships with younger siblings. Note also that there isn't always a clear link between place and activity. For instance, Bilkis talks about combining doing chores with playing with Monica, her employer's daughter, a reminder that many different kinds of activity may happen in one setting or place.

There are contrasts in the kinds of *spaces* that are significant for children and the extent to which they have any private space to call their own. Look at the difference, for instance, between Cathy and Wilfred or between Chet and Tinco. There are also differences between the ways and extent to which the children's days are regularly scheduled. In Oakland, children follow a regular timetable between home and school and within school. By contrast Tinco's daily life is less clearly structured in terms of the clock. The right time to go fishing is governed by the seasons and tides. Bilkis follows a daily routine, divided between home, her employer's house and her school, but rather than using a clock or watch to regulate her daily life she uses the mosque: 'When I hear the call to prayer I go back to our house from my landlord's place, and then I wash, have my lunch and go to school.' Wilfred's days and nights are less predictable; they are often structured around the best times and places to get money. He may sleep at night or during the day, in the township or on the street: 'When I feel to sleep then I sleep. When I feel to be wake up then I wake up.'

This activity illustrates the variety and complexity of children's daily lives. It also introduces some of the major themes for this chapter, and the rest of the book. The central theme is that children's lives can best be understood in their social context. Put simply, the process of growing up doesn't happen in a vacuum. Understanding childhoods means paying attention to the significance of 'sites' (places) and the social practices associated with them.

Social practices are made up of activities and relationships, together with associated beliefs and values.

There are glimpses of different kinds of child–parent, child–employer, student–teacher, child–friend and child–sibling relationships associated with particular sites in the accounts above. There are also hints at the beliefs and expectations that are shaping these relationships. For example, child–parent relationships may be guided by beliefs about how children should be reared, child–employer relationships by expectations about what children are capable of at different ages, and student–teacher relationships by professional theories about teaching and learning. Notice also that it isn't just parents, employers and teachers who have beliefs and expectations. The children in Activity 1 actively evaluate their activities and relationships. Think of Bilkis's comment about liking to work at her employer's house, the way Tinco feels good when he gets a good catch, Cathy's criticism of other students at her school, and Chet and Wilfred's comments about their parents' treatment of them. These evaluations are influenced by how the children believe things should be, in other words, by cultural norms and expectations. One of the most apparent contrasts in children's activities and the meanings they attach to these is between the children who have to work in order to survive, or help their family to survive, and the children who don't.

These examples of children commenting on the activities and relationships in their daily lives link to another major theme of the chapter, which is about children's role in the process, especially how much control they have over their day to day activity as well as their long term destiny. Issues of authority and discipline, freedom and autonomy are central to any discussion of socialization, but they are not at all straightforward. Take the example of Bilkis in Activity 1. Growing up in a slum community in Chittagong, Bangladesh, her life and prospects appears strongly circumscribed. Much of her time is spent doing chores for her mother, or taking directions from her employer, as well as lessons from her teacher. She is living in a community where children are expected to respect authority, and scoldings are part of daily life. Her prospects are strongly constrained by her poverty, her gender and the expectations placed upon her. In all these respects, from an outside perspective, Bilkis has very little agency, in the sense of the freedom to make choices and take control over her destiny. But Bilkis doesn't experience herself as passively shaped by forces of socialization. We already noted that she actively evaluates her activities and relationships, like the other young people in Activity 1. She also experiences herself as having a degree of autonomy: 'Usually nobody tells me what to do. Sometimes my mother will tell me, but most of the time I do things on my own. I go and do the cleaning and everything else on my own ... ' Bilkis's experience of autonomy, despite the many constraints in her life, is a reminder of the complexities and subtleties within any child's experiences of socialization, as well as their active role in the process.

SUMMARY OF SECTION 2

- There is considerable diversity both between and within children's lives. One way of examining this diversity is to consider the significant sites in their lives and the social practices connected with each of these.
- Social practices are complexes of activities and relationships related to particular assumptions about the world, moral values, ideas about behaviour, claims to authority and the exercise of power.
- Children themselves draw on particular beliefs and values in reflecting on and evaluating their individual experience. They actively make sense of their experiences and situation, even where they have limited control over it.

---

3 WHAT IS SOCIALIZATION?

3.1 Socialization in the community

Socialization happens in the course of children's activities in the different places that are important in their lives, for instance at home, at school, on the street, in friends' houses. It occurs in the course of interactions with siblings and other children, and with parents and other adults. Cultural values and beliefs permeate through children's environment and social practices, shaping their activities, their relationships and their emerging sense of self. And, in their turn, children have an effect on their environment, and contribute to continuity and change in their social world.

In this section we introduce you to some examples of ways that social scientists have approached the study of socialization, beginning with an anthropological account of childhood. Anthropologists have been particularly interested in the ways in which the patterns of children's socialization fit them for specific cultural settings. In Reading A, two American anthropologists, Robert and Yolanda Murphy, describe children's lives based on fieldwork carried out in the 1960s amongst the

Mundurucú, South American Indians who lived in small villages in the Amazon basin. At that time a Mundurucú village included four or five extended family households of females, each headed by a senior woman. Their husbands visited the households frequently, but slept at the village communal men's house. The women spent much of their time tending small vegetable gardens and preparing farinha (flour) from manioc (their main source of carbohydrate) while the men hunted and fished in the surrounding forest and savannah. The Mundurucú were matrilocal. In other words, men move to their wives' villages when they marry.

READING

Read Reading A, 'Socialization among the Mundurucú', an extract from Yolanda and Robert Murphy's book.

1   What strikes you most strongly about the Mundurucú children's socialization?

2   In what ways do the Murphys suggest that the Mundurucú children's lives are preparing them for adulthood?

We were particularly struck by the communal nature of children's development and socialization and the way in which they used the whole village and, in the case of the boys, the surrounding local area for play and learning and practising skills in hunting and food production. It reminded us of the African proverb, 'It takes a village to rear a child.' The gendered nature of children's activities and social life from age four

onwards is also very clearly marked, preparing them, the Murphys suggest, for their rather separate adult roles. The boys prepare for adult hunting and fishing activities and their eventual separation, not just from their maternal home, but also from their place of birth when they move to their bride's village at marriage. Between the ages of eight to thirteen, boys seem to have little adult supervision, but are socialized partly through activities and relationships with boys in the same age group, who roam through the village and forest together. (This is a good example of peer socialization, which is an important part of most children's lives. Think back to the children's accounts in Activity 1.) In contrast, girls stay within the village, learning from an early age to help with child care and farinha making, and become part of the co-operative female family productive unit where they will stay throughout their life.

A Mundurucú boy photographed by the Murphys.

While many of the features of childhood described by the Murphys are special to the Mundurucú, their account also illustrates a universal feature of human social life, the expectation that children will exhibit different skills and socially approved behaviour at different stages of their childhood. These stages are often linked to physical development, for instance weaning, cutting teeth, learning to speak, attaining a certain amount of physical strength and entering puberty. But they are always socially defined, with some milestones marked more prominently than others and considerable differences between societies in the kinds of behaviour which are expected in the different stages through which the child passes. Consider the significant stages and milestones in your own childhood. What is important is that these cultural expectations exert a strong influence on adults and children and are an intrinsic part of children's socialization.

Finally, note that the Murphy's description of Mundurucú child rearing as 'laissez-faire' is a value judgement: they judged Mundurucú childhoods against childhoods they were familiar with in the United States. It is most unlikely Mundurucú parents had a sense that they were being 'laissez-faire'. This reminds us that judgements about how children are socialized are rarely entirely objective or neutral. They are always made from a particular perspective, with its own associated theories and values, which can frequently be traced to enduring cultural beliefs about childhood. 'Laissez-faire' is a French phrase meaning 'let do'. Originating in the eighteenth-century doctrine that the economy functions best when there is no interference by government, it has been widely applied to the philosophy of child-rearing proposed by Jean-Jacques Rousseau (1712–78). The influence of laissez-faire alongside other Western discourses of child-rearing is our next topic.

3.2 Socialization theories and child-rearing practices

In this section we introduce the study of child-rearing beliefs and practices. These are about the ways children are treated – cared for, nurtured, trained, and disciplined. They also involve expectations, often implicit, about how children develop and learn and what kinds of skill, knowledge and behaviour they should be acquiring. They may be reflected in proverbs and sayings, for instance 'spare the rod and spoil the child'. A key question is how far children themselves are believed to play an active part in their socialization – one of the themes we introduced in Section 1. Some perennial questions include:

- Is a child's personality pre-formed, unfolding as they grow older? In which case, are they socialized simply through joining in with adult activities?

- Or is a child like a lump of clay which adults can mould into any shape they decide on, which will then 'set' at a specific age?

- Do children have inbuilt instinctive wishes and desires which have to be curbed and tamed in order to turn them into social beings?

- Or is child rearing more of a process of negotiation between children and their carers?

The British psychologist Rudolph Schaffer calls these four ways of conceptualizing socialization the '*laissez-faire*', '*clay moulding*', '*conflict*' and '*mutuality*' models. Each can be traced to long-standing cultural beliefs about the nature of the child (Montgomery, 2003). But these ideas don't just exist as models and theories. Schaffer suggests that each model has been linked to particular ideas about how children should be treated. For instance, a laissez-faire model suggests young children should be allowed to develop at their own rate. In industrialized societies laissez-faire educationalists favour a more child-centred form of pedagogy, at its most extreme giving children free expression in school to follow their spontaneous interests and activities. In contrast, people who adopt a clay-moulding model of socialization will do much more explicit training and teaching, and will favour a more instruction-centred approach to schooling (see Chapter 6). The third model emphasizes the conflictual aspects of bringing up children. Children are depicted as selfish, aggressive, fearful and essentially anti-social and requiring strong discipline. Finally, the fourth 'mutuality' model emphasizes mutual adaptation between children and their care-givers. Children are born with an inbuilt drive for social interaction, and play an active part in their own learning and development. This model is invoked by adults who fall somewhere between the laissez-faire and the moulding and disciplining positions, believing that socialization will proceed best if it includes talk and negotiation. In Table 1, Schaffer shows the links between the models, concepts of the child, parental practices and research traditions within psychology.

Table 1 Models of child rearing.

Model	Concept of child	Parental practices	Ensuing research
Laissez-faire	Preformed	Leave alone	Plotting norms of development
Clay moulding	Passive	Shaping and training	Effects of rewards and punishment
Conflict	Anti-social	Discipline	Parent–child conflicts
Mutuality	Participant	Sensitivity and responsiveness	Reciprocity in social interaction

Source: Schaffer, 1996, p. 233.

Allow 30 minutes

A C T I V I T Y   2   Parents' views of child-rearing

1   (i)   Which model do you see as being dominant in your own approach to child rearing, or that of other people around you?

    (ii) How does this compare with how you were treated when you were a child?

2   Consider the quotations below which come from parents interviewed during 2001 as part of the preparation for this book. The parents were asked to comment on the way they treat their children by comparison with how they experienced their own childhood. They live in very diverse circumstances in terms of cultural context and material poverty/affluence – in the United States of America, Bangladesh and South Africa.

How do the comments of these parents (all mothers) relate to the models in Table 1?

Parents talk about childhoods

PARENT 1   'I'm not a traditional parent. I try to give Maya all the freedom she can have.' (*Bangladesh*)

PARENT 2   'When my children were born I decided that I shouldn't be as distant as my parents were with me. I thought my children should be close to me so I can share all my feelings with them.' (*Bangladesh*)

PARENT 3   'People don't punish children the way we used to be punished. Our parents were too strict with us...When we were children if we interrupted a conversation between our parents and a visitor we would be punished....I don't want to do that with my children.' (*US*)

PARENT 4   'I think their idea of parenting is that you mould a person ... I had lots of pressure on me academically ... So I think with Sophie I've tried have her be, and nurture some of that sense of inner drive, you know doing things because you're personally motivated to, and to allow her to do as best she wants to ... ' (*US*)

PARENT 5   'Now you can't say to your neighbour's child "No, don't do this, that is very wrong," but in the olden days my mother's neighbours were allowed to smack me when I did something wrong. But now you can't ... now we're not smacking any more because we're talking. If he's not listening to you. I don't know.' (*South Africa*)

COMMENT

The first thing to note is that when parents were asked to comment on their approach to child-rearing, most had self-consciously adopted a different (and they felt) better approach compared to their own experience as children. Parent 1 distances herself from what she views as a traditional approach and refers to giving her daughter more freedom, which might be seen as closer to a laissez-faire model. Parent 3 rejects physical punishment (perhaps hinting at 'clay-moulding' and 'conflict' models) in favour of a model built around verbal communication (perhaps closer to a 'mutuality' model). Parents 2 and 4 also emphasize their wish to move to a more intimate, responsive approach, built around talking and sharing, perhaps by contrast with the more authoritarian child rearing they experienced. Parent 5 talks about a similar change in child-rearing style, but seems less convinced that this change is positive. She also raises a different issue, about who has the right to be closely involved in the management of children, which we will return to in Chapter 2. Of course, these comments need not necessarily be always reflected in the way children are actually treated. Nor would it be right to assume that Parents 1–4 share a similar approach to child-rearing, despite (on the face of it) sharing similar views. For example, when Parent 1 speaks of giving her daughter more freedom in the context of traditional attitudes in Bangladesh, this probably means something quite different from 'freedoms' that a boy like Chet enjoys in Oakland (see Activity 1). It is interesting that parents in such diverse economic and cultural contexts draw on very similar discourses when replying to a white British interviewer's questions about their child-rearing beliefs. How did your reflections about your own experience compare with the parents' comments above?

Beliefs may not always translate directly into practice, but they provide an important reference point against which both parents and children evaluate their own experience. For instance in Activity 1 Chet comments favourably that his parents are less uptight and restrictive than other adults: 'My parents will usually let me go pretty much anywhere.' In contrast, Wilfred sees his parents as too laissez-faire: 'I decide what to do because my parents tell me they are not taking care of me. That's why I decide every day what to do. I can even smoke. They make nothing. When I come drunk in the house they make nothing'. You may feel that your own experience as a child, and that of children around you, reflect a mixture of the socialization models described above.

How far should child-rearing be a process of mutual negotiation?

People of all ages are influenced by cultural discourses about socialization (that is, ways of talking about it which encode particular beliefs and values), and may incline more or less strongly towards laissez-faire, clay moulding, conflict and mutuality models in order to guide, make sense of and evaluate their own experiences.

3.3 Children's views on parents

Child researchers have become increasingly interested in studying children's own thoughts about their upbringing and about the experience of being a child. In a study in Geneva, Switzerland, a sociologist Cléopâtre Montandon interviewed 67 girls and boys (aged eleven to twelve years) about what they expected from their parents, their views on child-rearing practices, and their feelings about their status as children in relation to adults. Almost all the children placed great emphasis on the importance of emotional support from parents. One girl said, 'I expect affection. They must take care of me and not only of their work. They must also stay at home a little bit. And also that they have understanding: we are still children, we can't understand everything they say.' While many children wanted to be guided: 'They must tell me if I do something wrong. They must reprimand me and tell me that I shouldn't do this or that,' they also wanted their parents to help them become more autonomous, ' ... not to do too many things for me, so that I start getting along by myself' (Montandon, 2001, p. 58). Sixty per cent of children had been punished by their parents in the previous year and three quarters of these felt that their punishment was justified. One girl said, 'For me, those who are never punished it means that their parents don't care about their child,' and another added, 'I'm never happy when I'm punished, but we must learn and if we don't follow the rules it's normal that we get punished. And when we go visiting people say 'your children are very well educated ... ' Of the children who had not been punished, most felt that it was better for parents to explain to children why they had done wrong rather than to punish them. A few saw lack of punishment as unhelpful: 'Sometimes they should punish us for certain things we do. Perhaps that way we wouldn't repeat so easily,' or as signifying lack of parental interest: 'They should punish sometimes because otherwise we think they don't care.'

These children were very aware of the power asymmetry between themselves and adults, but they could also find many creative ways of opposing their parents. Montandon asked the children questions about familiar situations, for example, 'What do you do when your parents: a) don't let you dress the way you want; b) don't let you go out with your friends on Saturday afternoon; c) don't let you watch the TV programme you want; d) don't give you the money for you to buy something you want?' The strategies described by the children in response to these questions are summarized in Box 1.

Box 1 Children's responses to parental control

1 *Conformity:* A common first reaction was to submit without any discussion. This response however still involved the child's evaluation of the situation or of the importance of the issue. One girl, whose parents would not allow her to go out with her friends, said: 'Well, I obey, because I would be punished even more if they see that I go out secretly. So I prefer to obey.' Similarly, a boy whose parents kept him under strong control said: 'I give up, because if I insist in talking about it, then it's likely I get punished, so … About clothes I do what they tell me, I can't do anything else.'

2 *Circumventing parental orders* was another popular strategy. Children invented alternative ways to get what they wanted. If their parents censored a film, they got a friend to make a video copy or they hid behind a piece of furniture to see the film: 'If I really want to see a film they don't want me to watch, than I do some zapping, leaving it the longest possible on the film I want to see.' When they were not given the money to buy something they saved up or borrowed: 'Well if I have some pocket money I buy, but otherwise I ask my friends to lend me some money, or I ask my brother, or things like that.'

3 *Wearing down* parental resistance was also quite a common strategy. 'I keep on asking, I wear them out, perhaps they'll give way, but if they don't then I have to obey,' admitted a boy. A girl added: 'I have this method of getting them to say yes: I insist, I insist and I insist… And then, in the end, they say OK. Well, it doesn't work every single time, but when they're in a good mood, it works!'

4 *Vociferous defeat.* Many children complied with what was asked of them but clearly communicated their frustration. 'Well, when I'm irritated, I bang the doors and then I go and argue with them.' A girl described a similar reaction: 'I go to my room, I bang the door. I lie on my bed and read and I try to forget and tell myself, "It's always the same thing with my parents." And sometimes this makes me so mad that I throw my erasers all over the place. Then I go to my mother and say, "Explain this to me!"'

5 *Negotiation* was mentioned by some children. They were sensitive to the family situation and prepared to negotiate: 'I try to understand why they don't want me to go out and if they don't because of some family reason, then I give up on seeing my friends and I stay home. And if the reason is money I try to talk with them.' 'I try to convince them to start with and if they say it's no, because of their responsibility, etcetera, if something happens to me, etcetera, I understand, they are worried about me, I understand.'

6 *Argument.* The reactions of some children were more combative. They tried to prove to their parents they were right and sometimes, if this didn't work, or if their parents did not provide valid reasons for refusing them something, they went on doing what they wanted. A boy whose parents didn't like the way he dressed said: 'I reject their answer, I tell them that when they were young they wore these wide trousers too. If they continue to refuse, then as soon as I get out of the house I take my

shirt out of my trousers.' A girl did not give up when her parents wanted to prevent her from joining her friends: 'I try nevertheless to convince them. If for example we have no plans I try to tell them, I also have the right to go out, I am big enough.'

Less frequent strategies:

7   *Bargaining:* Children agreed to do something for their parents in return for permission to go out. 'I do a chore at home and she lets me go sometimes.'

8   *Substitution* was used by a few children. If one activity was forbidden, they chose another; if they are not allowed to go out, they watch a video, if they cannot see a film, they listen to music.

9   *Fait accompli.* Anticipating their parents would refuse their requests, particularly in matters of clothing, some children didn't ask for permission, even if they knew they would be reprimanded later.

10 *Terrorism* was employed by one boy who attacked his parents when they refused his request: 'I shout at them, that they are rotten, not nice, that they have no heart, I sulk, I become bad, I pester them and sometimes I hit them a little, I push them; one time I pushed my mother against a cupboard, I gave her a fright!'

(adapted from Montandon, 2001)

Allow about 10 minutes

ACTIVITY 3   Responses to parental authority

How far do the children in Box 1 experience agency in their lives? What underlying models of socialization do the children's strategies suggest?

COMMENT

That children recognize the importance of their parents' affection, support and discipline doesn't mean that they are always compliant. While adults' reactions to the strategies documented by Montandon were that these children seemed to have a lot of agency and could avoid doing unwelcome tasks, manipulate their parents, and pursue activities against their parents' wishes, Montandon found that the children themselves felt 'more supervised than surrounded with care, more controlled than listened to' (Montandon, 2001, p. 65). The children seem to be operating a child-centred version of the conflict model of socialization, where parents have to be taught that they are unreasonable, over-restrictive and lacking in understanding. Of course, we need to remember that the children's responses were shaped by particular questions posed by the researcher. For this part of the research, they were asked about situations where there might be conflict. Arguably, however, challenging parental authority is part of the process through which these eleven to twelve-year-old children become more independent and autonomous. Independence and autonomy are highly valued within the cultural context studied by Montandon.

SUMMARY OF SECTION 3

- Socialization refers to the processes through which a child becomes an active and competent participant in one or more communities. These processes shape children's behaviour, skills, ways of thinking and communicating and their identity, especially through activities and interactions with other people, including other children.

- Expectations and provision for children's behaviour and activities within the broader community are central factors in their socialization. Activities and relationships with other children are important influences.

- Child-rearing practices are shaped by, and contribute to, different beliefs and theories about the nature of the child and how they can best develop and learn.

- Children have their own views about their treatment (which also reflect cultural beliefs) and may resist or influence the actions of adults around them.

4 HOW DOES SOCIALIZATION HAPPEN?

In the previous section, we introduced several approaches to the study of socialization, explored the power of child-rearing beliefs and practices and considered children's perspectives on some of these themes. In this section we look in more detail at how socialization happens, based on studies of interactive social processes through which children are drawn into ways of thinking and behaving in particular cultural settings. The section will focus on what happens between children and other people in different contexts, thereby emphasizing that children's intellectual development and their socialization within cultures are closely intertwined. To get started, we ask you to consider how children are socialized into different ways of expressing their emotions.

4.1 Learning about emotions

Allow about 20 minutes

A C T I V I T Y 4   Comparing cultures

Box 2 contains summaries of research findings in two contrasting communities, the Inuit Utkuhiksalingmiut (Utku for short) of Northern Canada and a working-class white American community in Southern Baltimore. In each case, what are the processes through which children learn when and how to express their emotions?

Box 2 Utkuhiksalingmiut and South Baltimore

The Utku, Northern Canada

The ideal Utku parent is warm, nurturing and even tempered (photograph by Jean Briggs).

The Utku ideal of a good person is someone who never shows anger or displeasure, but is *naklik*, that is, warm, protective, nurturing and even tempered. The Utku highly disapprove of the expression of anger, resentment or hostility, and of qualities like jealousy, greed, stinginess and bad temper. Briggs (1970, 1998) found that Inuit children are emotionally socialized firstly through adults' behaviour towards them. Adults do not scold or express anger but use much more subtle expressions of displeasure or censure through body language, laughter or other communicative cues to mould children's behaviour. Adults also verbally reinterpret children's feelings for them to move them more towards the Utku ideal, for instance relabelling something a child says is annoying them as *tiphi* (funny or amusing). In addition to experiencing particular kinds of behaviour directed towards themselves and being taught to relabel certain feelings, children are also influenced by hearing adults gossip about the negative 'un-naklik' qualities of other people. Bad-tempered or stingy adults (including Briggs herself) are seen as childish and lacking in *ihuma*, or reason.

South Baltimore, US

In South Baltimore, young white working-class children are actively taught to express aggression

Young girls in South Baltimore are encouraged to stand up for themselves.

and 'stand up for themselves'. The white working-class mothers studied by Miller (Miller and Sperry, 1987) provoked their young daughters into aggression through teasing and pretend fighting, which they saw as helping the girls to learn to defend themselves. Mothers also related accounts involving violent actions (for example wife battering and aggressive and abusive language) in front of their daughters, often adding how they would personally have liked to deal with the aggressor. If the little girls couldn't defend themselves in relation to other children, or stand up for themselves when teased by their mothers, they were told, 'Don't be a cissy.' However, they also had to learn not to direct anger or aggression at their mother, and not to respond angrily or aggressively without reason. If they did either of these, they were labelled as 'spoiled'.

COMMENT

Although these two studies depict communities with very contrasting cultural beliefs about emotion, we can identify similar social processes through which the children are learning when and how to express their feelings:

1   Children are taught when and how to express emotions through their caretakers' reactions to their emotional outbursts and through explicit instructions, for example, 'Don't be a cissy.'

2   Children learn to label events, behaviours and feelings in relation to cultural ideals (for example *naklik, tiphi*, cissy, spoiled).

3   Children learn how the behaviour and feelings of other people are evaluated through listening to the talk and stories of adults around them.

4.2 Language and guided participation

You may have noticed the important role of language in the three processes listed above. Children learn to use language to interact with others, they use it to describe and explain the world and they are surrounded by other people's language. Language is a psychological tool in children's explorations of knowledge and relationships, both externally through dialogue and internally within thought. It is also a cultural tool because it plays such an important role in their socialization into particular cultural settings and culturally valued skills (Vygotsky, 1978). Let's look more closely at the role of language in the adult guidance of a child's activity.

Allow about 15 minutes

ACTIVITY 5   **Analysing dialogue**

Look at the images and examples of dialogue in Box 3 (overleaf). These are taken from a video showing the daily lives of young children in an English town. Four-year-old twins Camilla and Rachel were baking cakes with their mother Elaine and their nine-year-old sister Sophie. Make a note of the ways that Elaine uses language to guide the children's activity, as well as the children's role in the activity.

Box 3 Baking cakes

First Elaine organizes the ingredients, and puts out a bowl for each of the girls. She hands out spoons saying: 'One spoon for you, one for you and one for you.'

After helping the girls weigh out the sugar she says, 'Can you take it off [the scales] and put it in your bowl ... all of it ... good girl.'

Once they also have measured out the margarine she tells them, 'Girls, you can start mixing yours now.' As the girls mix, their older sister Sophie comments, 'Make sure you don't get any sugar over the sides.'

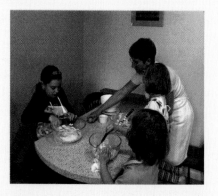

She gives the twins one egg each, and then asks, 'How many eggs do you think Sophie needs?' This leads to a discussion about Sophie needing two eggs because she has doubled the ingredients.

Elaine holds Rachel's hands as she tries to crack her egg, saying, 'Get your thumb ... now open it ... then tip that in there [into the bowl].'

Elaine asks, 'When we made these little buns last time, what did you do Rachel? Did you do vanilla ones?' Rachel replies, 'I did chocolate ones.'

Before they mix in the flour, Rachel echoes her mother's mention of the sieve, saying: 'I need the sieve.' Elaine hands it to her, saying 'Hold the sieve in that hand ... then ... put your [other] hand against there [the side] and tap it.'

COMMENT

Elaine uses language to initiate and organize the activity, and to guide and comment on each stage of cooking. She also uses language to link current and past experience by asking about previous cake-making activities. Much of the time Elaine gives the children very specific instructions about what to do next and about how to carry out specific skills. She also uses the activity to introduce the twins to weighing and measuring, and making simple calculations of quantity. Notice that she transfers responsibility for the easier and safer tasks to the girls (e.g. mixing the ingredients), while she deals with the more demanding aspects of the cooking. And she makes moment-by-moment adjustments according to the twins' skill at each task. So when it comes to egg-cracking, she doesn't just rely on verbal guidance, but also guides their hands directly. Overall, Elaine structures the task and guides the twins in such a way as to increase their participation in the activity and their experience of achieving a successful outcome. Incidentally, while Elaine concentrated on supporting her younger daughters, their older sister Sophie carried out each stage of the cooking without direct help. Elaine adjusted her level of guidance to Sophie accordingly, mostly responding to specific verbal requests (for example about whether to mix in each egg separately). Indeed, Sophie's comment to her sisters about not spilling sugar suggests she was already taking on some aspects of her mother's role.

The American psychologist Barbara Rogoff proposed the concept of 'guided participation' to describe the various ways communities structure and support young children's involvement in everyday activities, as they learn culturally relevant skills and understanding. Guided participation can involve a variety of styles of communication and role taking between adults and children. It can also vary according to expectations about the skills children should be developing and the best ways to teach them. As well as language, children are guided through non-verbal communication and activity, especially in contexts where children are directly involved from an early age in the world of adult work and social life. In these communities, they are expected to learn on their own initiative through observation and imitation, supported by adult carers. In contrast, in communities where children tend to be kept separate from the adult world, care-givers see it as their responsibility to motivate and play with their children and use much more direct verbal instruction (Rogoff *et al.*, 1993).

Despite these variations, Rogoff suggests guided participation generally involves three main features:

1 *Bridging or making connections between the known and the new.* When children encounter a new situation, their care-givers help them to make sense of it in terms of past experience. This bridging by care-givers can involve giving emotional cues about what kind of situation it is, non-verbal cues about how to behave and verbal and non-verbal interpretations of behaviour and events. Remember the linking of past and current experience by Elaine.

2 *Collaborative structuring of the situation.* Care-givers give structure to the children's environment according to their goals for the child's

development. At a broader level there is the overall timetable of the child's day which may be more or less tightly structured with differing amounts of time and weight given to different kinds of activity. On a smaller scale, particular tasks and activities may be broken down and managed in different ways to enable the child to achieve a goal. For the twins, doing a shared activity with their mother is a familiar feature of their daily routine, and their mother divides up the cooking task as we discussed above.

3   *Transferring responsibility.* Children become more competent until they are able to take on complete responsibility for the task, but expectations of when and how this should happen in relation to specific skills and responsibilities vary across different cultural settings. In Box 3, Elaine transfers responsibility for what she considers safe and enjoyable parts of the task that are within each of her daughters' capabilities. You can see this in her encouragement of Sophie to carry out tasks indep-endently while Camilla and Rachel are given much more guidance.

4.3 Community practices and children's activity

In Activity 4 we focused on guided participation in one activity within a family, an interaction between young girls and their mother. We also referred to the influence of broader cultural factors in structuring the children's participation: the overall timetable and routines in their daily life and local expectations about whether they are considered old enough to be competent to, for example, use sharp utensils or cook with gas. Expectations about the kinds of activities children of various ages should be participating in, and their expected levels of competence and independence, reflect local technologies, economic activities and life styles and also beliefs about the nature of childhood. Think, for example, of the different activities and expectations of an eleven-year-old Mundurucú boy, compared with those for an eleven-year-old boy in your own community.

We are now going to step back from an example of guided participation between a mother and her children and look at how children's participation and learning are also structured by the wider organization of their activities within the community. We saw the importance of this wider organization in Reading A about the Mundurucú, and will now look more closely at an example of the structuring of children's specific activities within a rather different cultural context.

In global terms, most children live in rural areas where subsistence and cash farming are the main modes of survival and children help with a combination of household and farming tasks from an early age. In her research in rural Bolivia, Sam Punch found that it was the children's job to collect enough water in the early morning (about twenty-five litres) to last the household until they returned from school in the afternoon and were able to collect more. They also fetched firewood and fed the animals in the afternoon after school. When Punch examined the range of work carried out by different children more closely, she found a distinct age hierarchy in terms of what they said that they could accomplish on their own. Table 2 shows the hierarchy for animal care, agricultural and domestic work. Notice how children's work roles

Table 2 Children's work in a rural community in Bolivia.

Domestic work 3–5 years	6–7 years	8–9 years	10/11+ years
Fetching water, collecting firewood, running errands	Bed-making, cleaning and sweeping, peeling potatoes, washing dishes	Lighting fires, simple food preparation, looking after younger siblings	Washing clothes, making main meals, including bread, shopping for household
Agricultural tasks 4–6 years	**7–9 years**	**10–12 years**	**13–14 years**
Picking vegetables, harvesting peaches, peeling maize stalks	Sowing seeds, watering crops, weeding, harvesting maize	Preparing ground for planting, hoeing, fertilizing, harvesting potatoes	Ploughing, clearing forest land, storing maize
Animal care 3–6 years	**7–9 years**	**10–13 years**	**14+years**
Feeding ducks and chickens, scaring birds from crops	Looking after pigs, milking and feeding goats and cows, plucking a chicken	Harnessing oxen for ploughing, killing a chicken for eating, skinning a pig	Loading up a donkey securely, taking cattle to forest pastures, killing a goat or pig

Six-year-old boy makes afternoon tea for his family.

become more complex and responsible over time, as children themselves become more physically capable, more practically competent and more socially responsible.

Source: adapted from Punch, 2001, pp. 811–2.

The tasks for three to five year olds made an important contribution to the family work, but they were relatively undemanding and could also be combined with play. For instance, Punch saw young children squealing with delight as they chased away birds and hens, applauded by adults for their efforts and proudly enjoying the attention. While children of all ages managed to find opportunities for play in the course of work duties, letting animals out and rounding them up at night was a more responsible job requiring more physical strength, and knowing how to kill an animal or load a donkey needed knowledge and skill which children acquired through helping others and observing and practising until they had enough experience and skill to carry out the tasks on their own. Similarly, in domestic tasks, there was a gradation from simple lightweight jobs to those requiring more physical strength and greater responsibility. Social practices within this community served to give structure to children's activity so that they could progress through different stages of learning appropriate to their own maturity.

Nine-year-old girl washes her two-year-old brother's hair, using water she's fetched from the river.

Eight-year-old girl takes the pigs out to pasture with her five-year-old brother (all photographs by Samantha Punch).

What about guided participation in relation to individual activities? Punch found that many children started to do animal care and domestic tasks at a younger age than is shown in the tables. In these cases they were helping, and helped by, adults or older children. For instance, one mother explained that her eight year old 'knows how to wash but sometimes she doesn't get the stains out very well and when it is adults' clothes she can't wring the soap out, such as if it's a heavy pair of jeans'. Another mother explained:

> Everyone in the country learns how to skin a pig. From ten years upward they begin to help and it depends on the strength they have as to whether they do it alone or not. My son knows how to do it and helps, but he doesn't do it alone.

(Punch, 2001, p. 813)

In both examples the child will be guided by an adult or more competent peer and this will involve collaborative structuring of the task (with, for example, the mother wringing the soap out of the jeans her eight year old has washed), reminders about procedures in previous similar tasks and the gradual transferring of responsibility so that eventually the child can perform the task independently. Since this is a context where children are involved in adult work and social life from an early age, we would expect that children learn more on their own initiative through observation and imitation than through explicit verbal instruction (Rogoff *et al.*, 1993). Part of growing up for these children is becoming able to do more complex and responsible household and agricultural jobs and they feel considerable pride in being able to contribute to the household economy. As children get older they abandon their younger jobs (if sibling composition allows) and for teenagers the work becomes more clearly gender-differentiated, with girls focusing on domestic chores and sibling care and boys on work in the fields. (Punch, 2001, p. 816)

Think back to the quotations in Activity 1 (p. 3) which illustrate children's own awareness of these processes and their ability to locate themselves within the hierarchy of tasks and responsibilities in terms of their past and their future. For example, Bilkis talks about the chores she is expected to do now, as a girl of about eleven, compared with when she was much younger. She is acutely aware of how much direction and guidance she receives, and emphasizes that she has now reached the stage where she takes the initiative in carrying out domestic chores.

Allow about 20 minutes

A C T I V I T Y 6   Experiences of child work

In relation to your own childhood, list the kinds of work you were expected to do at various stages. Was this a source of personal pride, as Punch describes? How did your experience compare with that of children in Punch's study, and with children in your own locality today?

C O M M E N T

Here is the list from one of our childhoods, as the eldest girl in a family with four children growing up in a rural area of the UK during the 1950s and 1960s:

Three to five years: no work

Six to eleven years: help expected with looking after younger siblings, drying dishes, washing clothes (no washing machine at first and I helped to put babies' towelling nappies through the mangle) and fetching the family shopping from the local village shop. I can still vividly remember struggling with heavy bags of potatoes.

Twelve to eighteen years: light housework, e.g. dusting, regular washing up and drying dishes, hanging out the washing, fruit picking in the summer for bottling and jam-making, cooking a wide range of dishes, sewing. There was not much local paid holiday work apart from seasonal potato picking which my parents would not allow me to do. From sixteen to eighteen I took live-in holiday jobs as a mother's help.

Although I helped with household and garden tasks, I did far less work than the children in Punch's study and school was seen as my major activity. My work was not necessary for the family economy but it was an important part of growing up as a girl in my locality. Although I earned very little as a mother's help, my pride in my cooking and child-care skills contributed to my confidence in a particular kind of feminine identity. School is also a major part of my son and daughter's lives and being a particular kind of student an important part of their identities. However, both have regular after-school jobs in the local shopping centre and use their earnings to buy clothes and CDs and to go out drinking and clubbing with friends. Learning household arts is definitely not seen by my daughter as part of her aspiring identity, which is expressed, like my son's, much more through social leisure and consumer interests as well as through their approach to school. Their paid work, which is not gender differentiated, supports their leisure and consumption, and is also an expected activity for young people living in our area. While I learnt to express creativity through sewing, cooking and gardening, they express creativity through particular consumer choices.

When you thought back to your own experience of work as a child, you may also have wondered where school fits in terms of thinking about processes of socialization. After all, school is a major part of daily life for children in many parts of the world, including the rural Bolivian communities studied by Punch. School may be considered much more significant than doing chores because of the cultural value placed on educational achievement. Within schools, children are more formally introduced to skills, knowledge, ways of thinking and behaving than they normally are through participation in community activities. Their learning takes place in a specialized environment, the classroom. They are usually organized in terms of classes or grades, based on age and/or relative competence, and their experiences are strongly structured by a curriculum where expectations for progressive achievement are made explicit across a wide range of skills and subject areas. We shall be looking at children's experiences of school in Chapters 4–5, and in Chapter 6 at how different kinds of curricula for young children are based on different conceptions of the child and how they best learn. In the final section of this chapter we will just briefly touch on a few specific aspects of schooling, and also pick up the theme of identity mentioned in the feedback to the activity above. We also want to emphasize the complexities of children's lives and experiences of socialization, and highlight some of the inconsistencies, discontinuities and contradictions that are part of children's day-to-day experience.

SUMMARY OF SECTION 4

- Children's emotional and intellectual development is culturally shaped according to the societies in which they live.

- Language plays a key role in development and socialization, and in the way in which these are interrelated.

- Some form of guided participation, involving 'bridging', 'collaborative structuring' and 'transfer of responsibility', is found across different cultures in adult interactions with young children.

- Community practices also structure children's activity so that they progress through different stages of activity and learning appropriate to their maturity.

- Children's work may serve a variety of different purposes for themselves and their families, but is always an important part of their developing identity.

5 DISCONTINUITY AND CHANGE

In this chapter, we have treated socialization as an interactive and complex process in which children try to make sense of their environment, including parents and others who shape their lives. They explore, question and resist socialization as well as being shaped by it. In addition to being an interactive process, it is a dynamic one. Children are constantly changing as they grow older and frequently they also have to adapt to and cope with change, inconsistency and conflict in their personal surroundings. At a broader level, few children's lives at the beginning of the twenty-first century have not been touched by global trends of social change, migration and the mixing of cultures. Discontinuities and conflicts are faced by many children, across different contexts and periods of their life.

Moving from home to school is one of the key transition points in children's lives. Many children experience school as an unfamiliar cultural context where they have to learn new ways of acting, talking and thinking. For instance, children may come to school with very different expectations depending on whether they have been expected by their family to learn through observation and imitation or through explicit verbal instruction. Imagine the different expectations about interactions with teachers and other pupils which a young child from the Utku or South Baltimore (see Activity 4, p. 18) might bring to school. Some children are prepared from an early age for the question-and-answer routines that are typical of classrooms in the North and will find similarities between literacy practices at home and at school. Other children find ways of using language and literacy in the classroom much less familiar and this can have quite a significant influence on their approach to learning and their educational success (Heath, 1983). Success in school requires children to take on the school's ways of talking, reading and writing and this depends on, among other things, children's prior socialization.

The ways in which children have learned to talk and think are an important part of their emerging identity. Talking and thinking in new ways at school involves taking on a new kind of identity and, for many pupils, this is not a straightforward process. Children's identities are also shaped by the ways in which their ethnicity, class and gender intersect with their educational experience.

Allow about 10 minutes

ACTIVITY 7 Conflicting discourses

Box 4 describes an incident observed by Ann Ferguson during her ethnographic research in a Californian elementary school in the early 1990s. She wanted to find out why so many African American boys became alienated from education by the beginning of their teens. For her, the incident involving D'Andre and his teacher dramatically illustrated the disjuncture for many African American boys between their racial identification and group membership on the one hand and the school ethos on the other. How does Ferguson characterize the conflict between the discourses of the school and of D'Andre's home community? What dilemma does this raise for D'Andre and how does he resolve it?

COMMENT

Discourse: set of interconnected ideas about people and events which includes particular assumptions, beliefs and values.

Ferguson contrasts the school discourse which characterizes difference as individual and getting into trouble as a matter of personal choice or individual pathology with the African American discourse where race is a fundamental attribute of the self and events in school are interpreted in the context of the racialized relations of power in the wider social world. These two discourses intersect and clash in the moment of the exchange between D'Andre and his white teacher, when she attempts to deflect his blanket condemnation of whites. For D'Andre, accepting this positioning within the school discourse would entail 'acting white' and abandoning his racial identity. He refuses to comply. Ferguson argues that this kind of dilemma is frequently faced by many African American boys, whose developing sense of racial and masculine identity comes into direct conflict with the institutional ethos and values of the school.

Ferguson provides a particularly stark example of the conflict between two very different ways of interpreting a child's behaviour. Often, differences can be more subtle and ambiguous, and are not always consistent. The African American academic Randall Kennedy recalls conflicting instructions from his parents as to the proper way to respond to racial abuse: 'My mother told me to ignore it, my father told me to go to war.' (*Observer*, 20 January 2002, p. 16).

In the same way as we have characterized socialization as a complex interactive process, we see children's developing sense of their own identity as emerging through their engagement in activities and relationships across the different significant sites in their lives. Some of this experience may involve conflict and dislocation. For instance, teachers and parents may have very different views of the same child and, we have seen above, parents themselves may offer conflicting advice. It is also important to remember that

Box 4 (Un)reasonable circumstances

Just after the 1992 Los Angeles riots which followed the acquittal of the white policemen charged with beating a black man, Rodney King, a class of eleven year olds were discussing the riots. A number of children said they wished that Simi Valley, the predominantly white district in Los Angeles where a number of police lived, had gone up in smoke instead of South Central Los Angeles (a mixed-race area). Their white student teacher, Laura, told the children she had an uncle living in Simi Valley, whereupon one of the boys, D'Andre, retorted: 'I'd burn his house down too.' Laura was extremely upset and D'Andre was sent off to the punishing room for his remark. 'You must do something about that boy's attitude,' Laura told the counsellor. 'He's such a hostile kid. He says he doesn't like white people.' (Ferguson, 2000, p. 198).

Ferguson suggests that there are two very different frameworks for interpreting D'Andre's outburst. From the school's perspective, he is disturbingly aggressive and antisocial. Children are taught that conflict should be solved through established channels and verbal negotiation, not violence and lawbreaking. Breaking laws and damaging property is criminal activity. D'Andre is characterized as emotionally disturbed and needing some kind of treatment or help.

However, there is a second possible interpretation of his behaviour. Ferguson writes:

> D'Andre's anger is both predictable and intelligible through a racial lens. He is bringing to school with him, along with schoolbag, textbooks, pencils, and paper, powerful feelings of anger, sadness, and fear after watching conflict and conflagration in Los Angeles on television for three days following the acquittal of the four white policemen who he had watched on TV beating Rodney King, a black man, by an all white jury in Simi Valley. The spectacle of King's savage beating had stirred up strong feelings of outrage in citizens across the nation. In D'Andre's neighborhood, where police harassment and beating of black men was not unusual but had just never been caught on videotape, feelings of anger were tinged by vindication and the unrealized hope of a national spectacle of justice and retribution at the climax of the trial of the police.
>
> (Ferguson, 2000, p. 201)

For D'Andre, Laura's comment about her uncle positions her firmly with the people of Simi Valley, both through the bond of kinship and through the (unstated) bond of race. Laura uses her classroom status as a 'good guy' to suggest that it is individuals like herself who would be attacked, but D'Andre rejects her attempt to shift him into the 'de-raced' school discourse of individual difference and choice. From his community's point of view, D'Andre is remaining true to his roots and expressing justifiable outrage at a miscarriage of justice and at the underlying institutionalized racism in American society.

the notion of identity itself is a culturally biased concept, with its implications of a separate autonomous individual who has a relatively fixed social position and a particular set of attributes. Anthropologists have long pointed out that in many societies a person's relationships with family and community may be seen as far more important than some notion of individual separateness. Beyond the physical sense, the notion of separateness is a myth, as in all but the most extreme circumstances people are constantly in connection with others and affected by them throughout their life. Some contemporary social scientists see important aspects of 'identity' and 'self' as being continually negotiated and reconstructed, as people experience new situations and relationships.

Children and adults often get a sense of their identity through comparison with others and the ways in which they and other people are talked about, signalling to children which qualities are to be admired, and also how their own performance might measure up (remember the gossip about 'un-naklik' people among the Utku in Box 2, p. 18). Folk stories, soap operas and adult talk around them provide children with models of good and bad identities and relationships which they may explore further through talk among themselves.

READING

Read the extract in Reading B from the opening of Edward Said's autobiography *Out of Place*. Edward Said grew up in Palestine, Lebanon and Egypt and later became an academic writer and teacher in the United States.

How is Said's sense of identity as a child expressed both through his feelings about his family background and in the way he acts and interacts, feels, speaks and is spoken about?

Said describes a complex identity, both through his mother's background and use of English and Arabic and through descriptions of himself as intransigent or timid, embarrassed about his name or delighting in hiding at dusk in the Fish Garden. He is referred to by parents and teachers as naughty, a fibber and loiterer and even takes to referring to himself in the third person when arguing with his mother about whether he is lovable. This extract illustrates how a child's identity is woven together from different strands of their social and cultural environment and experience, and how complex a business this can be for children growing up in a context intersected by different cultural forces.

Reading B illustrates how people tell stories which rework their experience and in some senses reconstruct their childhood in particular ways which are linked to their current sense of identity. In our memories we sift through countless hours of living to focus on those moments which seem most telling in relation to who we feel we are. The moment at dusk in the Fish Garden when Said hides and pretends he has not heard his mother calling him symbolizes the ambivalence and the possibilities of the Edward and 'non-Edward' parts of himself as well as the child's simultaneous experience of power and dependency, singularity and attachment.

This evocation of place and relationship brings us back to where the chapter started, with the people, places and activities that are significant in children's everyday experience. The anthropologist Bambi Schieffelin argues that language, place and memory are deeply interwoven in the lives of children, and that the places which are significant for people encode the basic cultural values which shape their lives. When she studied how children became participants in everyday interactions among the Kaluli in Papua New Guinea in the 1970s, Schieffelin noted the importance of place names in family conversations, and how particular sago camps (places where people camped while harvesting sago), streams and gardens provided the key to their local activities and identity. These were talked about in relation to shared activities which involved patterns of social obligation and reciprocity, and as children became more integrated into social life they were expected to talk about as well as experience particular places as 'anchors for memories, feelings of belonging and sense of shared lives'. To express closeness with someone, a Kaluli might address them by the name of a place where they had shared some joint activity. When Schieffelin went back to the Kaluli twenty years later, however, she found radical changes. She writes:

> Among the most profound changes is the shift in the meanings of place and the places of meaning, change initially brought about through Christian missionization. There was a shift in the places where people spent time, as pastors told villagers staying around the village to attend church, in anticipation of the second coming, so less time was spent in the bush. Traditional ceremonies that featured sung place names memorializing past relationships were last performed in 1984. Missionaries encouraged children to attend the mission school where they learned other people's place names in geography classes, places they would most likely never see. These changes were amplified by increased interactions with government and outside business ventures such as mining and logging. Over the last twenty years, for Kaluli who followed this new regime, new places, the local airstrip, school, government and mission station took on some of the meanings that had previously been invested in sago camps and river banks. While place is still important in everyday talk, these new places have become more salient than the old ones, and are indicative of new types of relationships, both within Kaluli society and across its boundaries.

> (Schieffelin, 2001)

As children grow older, the people, places and activities which are significant in their lives will change, and the meanings they ascribe to them will also change, both through their experience of the different stages of childhood and as the result of local and global changes in their environment.

SUMMARY OF SECTION 5

- Children's experiences are more complex than suggested by over-arching models of socialization, especially in contexts marked by cultural diversity and change.

- Discontinuities between home and school are challenges faced by children, for example in relation to uses of written and spoken language.

- Children's race, gender and social class shape their experience and the way they are positioned in terms of available discourses, for example surrounding 'anti-social' behaviour.

- Children's identities and sense of self are negotiated and constructed through their engagement in social practices across different sites in their daily lives.

6 CONCLUSION

In this chapter we have offered a range of perspectives on children's lives, especially ways to think about processes of socialization. We began with children's own accounts, in order to emphasize their role as social actors making sense of their own experiences and to raise the issue of how far children have the ability to shape their lives. In Section 3 we discussed the significance of competing child-rearing models as these inform child-rearing practice and also drew attention to children's own perspectives on the ways they are treated. We also discussed the importance of community practice and children's socialization of each other.

Next we looked in a little more detail at studies of what the processes of socialization involve, introducing the concept of guided participation and emphasizing the significance of language and communication. These themes continued in the final section which looked at the discontinuities faced by many children, especially in relation to competing discourses around ethnicity, gender and social class in the contexts of home and school.

Throughout the chapter, we have offered a variety of resources for studying these themes. We have asked you to consider the individual experiences of children and adults, and some influential concepts for thinking about socialization, as well as some studies of specific processes in different cultural settings. We have emphasized diversity and change in the contexts and processes of socialization. Many of the topics and themes raised in Chapter 1 will be explored in greater detail in the following chapters.

REFERENCES

BRIGGS, J. (1970) *Never in Anger: portrait of an Eskimo family*, London, Oxford University Press.

BRIGGS, J. (1998) *Inuit Morality Play: the emotional education of a three year-old*, New Haven, Yale University Press.

FERGUSON, A. (2000) *Bad Boys: public schools in the making of black masculinity*, Michigan, University of Michigan Press.

HEATH, S. B. (1983) *Ways with Words*, Cambridge, Cambridge University Press.

MILLER, P. J. and SPERRY, L. L. (1987) 'The socialization of anger and aggression', *Merrill Palmer Quarterly*, **33**(1), pp. 1–31.

MONTANDON, C. (2001) 'The negotiation of influence: children's experience of parental education practices in Geneva' in ALANEN, L. and MAYALL, B. (eds) *Conceptualizing Child–Adult Relations*, London, RoutledgeFalmer.

MONTGOMERY, H. K. (2003) 'Childhood in time and place' in WOODHEAD, M. and MONTGOMERY, H. K. (eds) (2003) *Understanding Childhood: an interdisciplinary approach*, Chichester, John Wiley and Sons Ltd/ The Open University (Book 1 of the Open University course U212 *Childhood*).

PUNCH, S. (2001) 'Household division of labour: generation, gender, age, birth order and sibling composition', *Work, Employment and Society*, **15**(4), pp. 803–23.

ROGOFF, B., MOSIER, C., MISTRY, J., and GONCU, A. (1993) 'Toddlers' guided participation with their caregivers in cultural activity' in *Contexts for Learning: socio-cultural dynamics in children's development*, New York, Oxford University Press.

SCHAFFER, H. R. (1996) *Social Development*, Oxford, Blackwell.

SCHIEFFELIN, B. (2001) 'Placing language in children's worlds', unpublished keynote lecture at 'Children in their Places' conference, London, Brunel University.

VYGOTSKY, L. (1978) *Mind in Society: the development of higher psychological processes* (ed. Cole, M. *et al.*), Cambridge (Mass.), Harvard University Press.

READING A

Socialization among the Mundurucú

Yolanda Murphy and Robert F. Murphy

The extended family organization of the Mundurucú household, and particularly the strength of its female linkages, provides the mother with help and support in child rearing. For the first few months after the baby's birth, the mother is responsible for almost all the care of the child. However, as it emerges from early infancy other women of the house increasingly share the burden. If the mother is working at a task in which she will be encumbered by the baby, her own mother may put it in the sling and carry it about. Similarly, her sisters or other household women may tend the child for periods of up to an hour or two, allowing the mother freedom to go to the stream or the fields; if one of them is lactating, she may even feed the child. By the time the baby is six months old, the little girls of the household are pressed into service, and seven-year-old girls are often given the care of their year-old siblings or cousins for hours on end. The ease of the mutual baby-sitting arrangements is such that children are continually being passed back and forth from one woman to another and to the girls between seven and twelve years of age.

Ideally, it would seem that the extended family allows for the development of diffuse emotional attachments, and so it does. And, ideally again, it would seem that the availability of a wide range of mother surrogates acts to provide the child with a sense of security that is impossible to achieve in the American nuclear family, in which all affect becomes focused upon the mother – but this is not true. Mundurucú children are indeed cared for by a number of women and girls, but the baby knows very well which one is its mother and it unmistakably wants the mother. A child passed from the mother to another woman will commonly cry, and it is not unusual for it to continue crying until restored to the mother's baby sling and arms.

[...]

'Toilet training' is relatively simple compared to our own society, in part for the obvious reason that there are no toilets or other narrowly specified places for elimination, nor are there rugs and other finery to be dirtied. At about the age of a year and one-half to two years, [a young child] is brought out of the house when it is apparent to one of the women that he is about to have a bowel movement. If nobody sees the child on time, however, no fuss is made nor is the child reprimanded. Most children are trained by three years of age, though they often eliminate inside the village, and by the age of five the child knows that he is supposed to go beyond the village.

The lack of any strict training regimen is also characteristic of the Mundurucú attitude toward children, which is indulgent and nonauthoritarian. In keeping with this laissez-faire orientation, children are not strongly encouraged to walk and are allowed to proceed at their own pace. When a little one does struggle to his feet and makes his first tentative steps, however, adults and older children guide him and save him from tumbles. But he is not urged, goaded, or pushed to walk, or for that matter, to do anything else. In the same vein, children are almost never given corporal punishment. An irritated parent may swat a child gently to stop it from doing something, but punishment as such or severe thrashings never occurred during our fieldwork.

Fathers have little to do with their children, boys and girls alike, until they are at the walking stage. This disinvolvement from the very young is so pronounced that we cannot remember ever seeing a man holding or carrying an infant in any of the traditional villages, though fathers often pick up toddlers. But after the child starts to walk and venture out into the village, the father often drops into the dwelling to play with the child or simply to watch him. Youngsters also wander out to the men's house, where they lie with their fathers in the hammock. The growing interest of the man in his child often coincides roughly with the arrival of a newborn, given an average spacing of two or three years, and the father serves as a refuge from the mother's rejection, as she turns her attention to the infant.

[...]

Until the age of about four, the lives of little boys and girls are not strongly differentiated. Most of their play is in or near the house and their wanderings through the village are brief. Boys and girls play with each other in small groups of three or so children which generally center on the household. Most, by this time, have younger siblings and they have already learned to seek help and comfort from others in the house aside from the preoccupied mother, though at times when they are hurt or sorely frustrated they still go to her for solace. Grandparents, if still alive, play an important role in the life of the child during this transition which sees them lose the constant attention of the mother. Grandfathers, especially, play with the little ones, dote upon them, give approval for almost anything they do, and, in general, play the benevolent role that we have come to expect of grandparents in most societies.

By the age of five or six, the watershed between boys and girls is reached. The little girls maintain a focus on the household, but the boys begin to range throughout the village and out into the nearby savannahs. This is the start of the classic pattern in primitive societies, which sees the sexes divide into separate play groups, the boys striking out from the home and the girls staying behind. Future sex roles are forged in the activities of the children, and child play is both the template of adult life and the reflection of it.

Boys between about five and seven years form into a loosely defined play group, and those between eight and thirteen another. The younger children wander about the village and its periphery, drifting in and out of houses, playing in unoccupied hammocks in the men's house, hunting cricket with small bows and arrows, stalking mice in the underbrush, bathing in the nearby stream and occasionally touching home base for food. But the attachment of the boys to the household loosens during this period. They go where they please, eat where there is food, and generally confuse visiting anthropologists who are trying to make an accurate house census. Whatever the problem created for the anthropologists, the boys at this age are far less of a problem and concern for their mothers.

This progressive separation from the household and the world of the women is even more pronounced among the boys in the older age group. Their orbit has already shifted from the village itself to the savannahs and forests of the vicinity. Armed with small bows and arrows, they shoot fish in the stream and kill small birds from the seclusion of blinds built near fruit trees. They eat their take in the forests, rounding out the repasts with fruits and whatever they can gather from old gardens. Their evening meals are taken in the village, the very youngest eating in the house and those ten years and over at the men's house, where they wait second turn at the communal meal. By the age of eleven or twelve, they are already sleeping in the men's house, hanging their hammocks in the outermost positions, where they are occasionally drenched by the rains. But these discomforts are more than compensated for by the mark of maturity that comes with leaving the women and the dwelling house.

The older boys maintain a loose sort of attachment to the household. They still depend upon the women for water, for the mending of clothes and for some of their food, but it is a tenuous link at best, held together by sentiment, not by the practical needs of life. In this sense, they are already beginning to approximate adult male status. The proper stance for the prepubescent boy is one of independence. They have little to do with girls, and they take a chary view of the adult world in general. The five or six-year-olds were our constant visitors and companions, but the older boys spent little time in our house. When they did drop in, it was usually to take some tobacco, a luxury for all the boys yet one seldom indulged, not so much because their elders disapproved as because the men kept it for themselves. When our own supplies began to run low, Robert had to limit the boys, much to their outrage. 'You're a passive pederast, white man,' was among the pleasantries they would cast back as they left, which he would respond to with something equally ribald, but in English. In any event, by the time a boy is eight years old or so, it is difficult to speak any more of 'child-rearing', for they have departed from the orbit of the household and operate without substantial adult supervision or interference. Only after they are about fourteen years old and enter into the hunting activities of the men are they reincorporated into the core of the society. In the interim period of boyhood, they have been marginals, albeit very happy ones.

The lot of the girls is wholly different. At five or so, their playmates come to include most of the prepubescent village girls, and their range expands to the entire village. Unlike the boys, however, they do not go beyond the village except when in the company of their mothers or older women. Girls also become economically active at a much earlier age. By the time they are seven, they are helping to care for the babies of the household and they assist in some of the lighter chores of farinha making. Like their mothers, they gravitate around the house and the farinha shed, learning to keep close to other females and learning to take part in cooperative work. As they grow older, and stronger, they are brought more completely into the labour force, and, by the time they are ready for marriage, they are fully productive members of the village. Girls are under adult supervision and in adult company to a far greater extent than boys. Childhood, for the girls, is a period during which ties to the mother and other women of the house are being reinforced and strengthened, but to the boys it is a time of estrangement from their elders. Boys indeed become men, but by the time they do, they may very well be leaving the village for marriage. Girls, on the contrary, are expected to remain and maintain the bonds formed in childhood.

Source

Murphy, Y. and Murphy, R. F. (1974) *Women of the Forest*, New York, Columbia University Press, pp. 169–75.

READING B
Beginnings

Edward W. Said

All families invent their parents and children, give each of them a story, character, fate, and even a language. There was always something wrong with how I was invented and meant to fit in with the world of my parents and four sisters. Whether this was because I constantly misread my part or because of some deep flaw in my being I could not tell for most of my early life. Sometimes I was intransigent, and proud of it. At other times I seemed to myself to be nearly devoid of any character at all, timid, uncertain, without will. Yet the overriding sensation I had was of always being out of place. Thus it took me about fifty years to become accustomed to, or, more exactly, to feel less uncomfortable with, 'Edward,' a foolishly English name yoked forcibly to the unmistakably Arabic family name Said. True my mother told me that I had been named Edward after the Prince of Wales, who cut so fine a figure in 1935, the year of my birth, and Said was the name of various uncles and cousins. But the rationale of my name broke down both when I discovered no grandparents called Said and when I tried to connect my fancy English name with its Arabic partner.

The trials of bearing such a name were compounded by an equally unsettling quandary when it came to language. I have never known what language I spoke first, Arabic or English, or which one was really mine beyond any doubt. What I do know, however, is that the two have always been together in my life, one resonating in the other, sometimes ironically, sometimes nostalgically, most often correcting, and commenting on, the other. Each *can* seem like my absolutely first language, but neither is. I trace this primal instability back to my mother, whom I remember speaking to me in both English and Arabic, although she always wrote to me in English – once a week, all her life, as did I, all of hers. Certain spoken phrases of hers like *tislamli* or *mish ʿarfa shu biddi ʿamal?* or *rouhʿha* – dozens of them – were Arabic, and I was never conscious of having to translate them or, even in cases like *tislamli,* knowing exactly what they meant. They were a part of her infinitely maternal atmosphere, which in moments of great stress I found myself yearning for in the softly uttered phrase *'ya mama'*, an atmosphere dreamily seductive then suddenly snatched away, promising something in the end never given.

But woven into her Arabic speech were English words like 'naughty boy' and of course my name, pronounced 'Edwaad'. I am still haunted by the memory of the sound, at exactly the same time and place, of her voice calling me 'Edwaad', the word wafting through the dusk air at closing time of the Fish Garden (a small Zamalek park with aquarium) and of myself, undecided whether to answer her back or to remain in hiding for just a while longer, enjoying the pleasure of being called, being wanted, the non-Edward part of myself taking luxurious respite by not answering until the silence of my being became unendurable. Her English deployed a rhetoric of statement and norms that has never left me. Once my mother left Arabic and spoke English there was a more objective and serious tone that mostly banished the forgiving and musical intimacy of *her* first language, Arabic. At age five or six I knew I was irremediably 'naughty' and at school was all manner of comparably disapproved-of things like 'fibber' and 'loiterer'. By the time I was fully conscious of speaking English fluently, if not always correctly, I regularly referred to myself not as 'me' but as 'you.' 'Mummy doesn't love you, naughty boy,' she would say and I would respond, in half-plaintive echoing, half-defiant assertion, 'Mummy doesn't love you, but Auntie Melia loves you.' Auntie Melia was her elderly maiden aunt, who doted on me when I was a very young child. 'No she doesn't,' my mother persisted. 'All right. Saleh [Auntie Melia's Sudanese driver] loves you,' I would conclude, rescuing something from the enveloping gloom.

[...]

Much more than my father, whose linguistic ability was primitive compared to hers, my mother had an excellent command of classical Arabic as well as the demotic. Not enough of the latter to disguise her as Egyptian, however, which of course she was not. Born in Nazareth, then sent to boarding school and junior college in Beirut, she was Palestinian, even though her mother, Munira, was Lebanese. I never knew her father, but he, I discovered, was the Baptist minister in Nazareth, although he originally came from Safad, via a sojourn in Texas.

Not only could I not absorb, much less master, all the meanderings and interruptions of these details as they broke up a simple dynastic sequence, but I could not grasp why she was not a straight English mummy. I have retained this unsettled sense of many identities – mostly in conflict with each other – all of my life ...

Source

Said, E. W. (2000) *Out of Place: a memoir*, New York, Vintage Books, pp. 3–5.

Chapter 2

Family, kinship and beyond

Rachel Burr and Heather Montgomery

CONTENTS

LEARNING OUTCOMES

When you have studied this chapter, you should be able to:

1 Explain how the competing claims of blood and social ties are central to understandings of kinship and family.

2 Illustrate how the family is a fluid and very flexible concept which differs across cultures and across time.

3 Recognize that ideas about the family are full of idealizations.

4 Describe how children take an active role in shaping the form and dynamics of the family.

5 Discuss the issues surrounding the provision of care – that parents are not the only possible providers of care and that there exist many informal and formal institutions which provide care for children.

1 INTRODUCTION

Chapter 1 explored children's experiences of socialization, arguing that these are best understood by examining actual examples and social practices in all their diversity and complexity, rather than dealing with abstractions about the influence of families, work and school. This chapter takes the argument a step further, concentrating on the diverse meanings associated with 'family' as the primary site for most children's socialization. Drawing especially on anthropological theories, we will look in particular at questions about the basis for family ties in various contexts, and what the implications are for children.

The subjects of family and parenthood are of course highly emotive concerns, strongly linked to personal issues about one's own family history, and to expectations about the future. It is extremely hard to be objective about families; everybody has personal experiences of being in a family that shape their views of what a family could and should be like. Discussions surrounding family life may be pleasurable or distressing, bringing up happy or painful memories and sometimes unresolved issues. We do not have the scope to do justice to such complex issues in this chapter and neither do we make any attempt to offer right answers or models of how the ideal family should be. This chapter will not attempt to look at family policy or the psychological impact of issues such as divorce on children. Rather it examines the fluidity of family structures in different societies and their diversity within contemporary communities. In doing this it aims to give an analytical framework to the emotive issues that discussions about the family inevitably raise. While acknowledging how sensitive discussions of family can be, this chapter seeks to examine the assumptions that lie behind beliefs of what is a family and what connects children to parents.

Family is central to understanding childhood. Beliefs about childhood are strongly connected to expectations of family, and children's experiences are shaped by family. This chapter will examine the basis of family ties – what makes a family in different contexts, who does the child and their culture recognize as their parents? Who has a claim on the child and who can the child make claims on? In particular it will focus on the conflicting claims of biological ties versus social ties, on nature versus nurture. It will then look at children who do not live with their families and who are cared for by foster carers or in institutions. How far can these children be said to have a family?

2 EXPERIENCES OF FAMILY

2.1 Idealizations

It is important to acknowledge very early on that families come in a variety of forms. They may exist as polygamous families, where a man lives with several wives and all of his children by these various wives; extended families where several generations of the same family live together; families where several husbands share one wife; gay or lesbian families; nuclear families where two parents live with their children; single-parent families where one adult cares primarily for their children; reconstituted or blended

families where a combination of parents, step-parents, siblings and half siblings live together. It is also important to note that not only do general family forms change over time but that within many children's family history, there may be significant changes. Thus a child may be part of a nuclear family, a single-parent family and a step-family during his or her childhood. Some may repeat the process a number of times. In some African societies, a child might be part of a nuclear, extended and polygamous family at various times in their lives and move from one to another. There is no such thing as a universal family, just as there is no such thing as an ideal family.

A 1950s nuclear family – still sometimes seen as the ideal family in the North.

READING

Now read Reading A, 'A virtual bedtime fable for the American century'. This is a tongue-in-cheek and provocative reading, making fun of the ideal American family that is presented, so the author Judith Stacey claims, by the 'family values' lobby in the USA. In the final three paragraphs, her tone changes and she contrasts this ideal with the reality of modern family life with its divorce statistics, different family forms and sense of crisis. Clearly Stacey does not believe that this ideal ever existed and is criticizing what she sees as an over-simplification of the history of the American family. As you read it, think about the vision that she is representing. Is she being too critical? Do you recognize this vision of past family life? Do you think that families are in crisis?

COMMENT

By calling her narrative a fable, Stacey is criticizing the simplistic notion of a past golden age of family life. However, the vision that she presents, while caricatured, does reflect some of the mythology surrounding families. The most important thing about this mythology is that it represents an ideal. Many people do have a tendency to romanticize and idealize the past and you may well feel that family life was easier or less complicated when you were a child. The family is a concept which is both very personal and also an idealized abstract. Most people have an idea of what they would like their own family to be, and even when this does not live up to reality, the idea that there is such a thing as an ideal family, or a golden era of the family, still exists. Indeed for some, the ideal may be more important than the reality and only by clinging to the ideal, can people survive the daily grind of actual family life.

Much of what Stacey says about the US would also be true for other parts of the world including the UK. Some British politicians who claim to stand for family values understand the family institution in a limited and ahistorical way, implying that two married parents with children are the best and, indeed, the only real families. They claim that other families are in some way inadequate (Murray, 2000) or even a 'pretended family' (as Section 28 of the 1988 England and Wales Local Government Act described gay families). However, the ideal of a 'normal' nuclear family where two married parents raise their biological children is questionable, both at the ideological level and at the level of lived experience. It is currently estimated that in the UK, one child in eight will experience life in a step-family by the age of 16 (Ferri and Smith, 1998). Nor is this a peculiarly modern phenomenon. Despite widespread fears about the ill effects of absent fathers, step-families and working mothers, these have long been a feature of family life in the North. In the nineteenth century the average marriage lasted about ten years (Stark, 1985) and although curtailed by death rather than divorce, the situation meant that many children were raised in step-families and many children grew up without one or other of their parents.

2.2 What makes family?

The sociologist Anthony Giddens defines the family as 'a group of persons directly linked by kin connections, the adult members of which assume responsibility for caring for children'. What then is kinship or kin connections? Anthropologists and sociologists use the term kinship to mean the 'connections between individuals, established either through marriage or through the lines of descent that connect blood relatives (mothers, fathers, offspring, grandparents, etc.)' (Giddens, 1998, p. 140). This might seem very complicated. Everyone knows who their family is and why they think of them as family. Although some people might say that a family is based on biological relationships, this is far from straightforward. It is certainly not universal and the terms kinship and family refer to a variety of structures and a variety of cultural beliefs and idealizations. Roger Keesing explains kinship from a Western perspective as follows:

> What *is* kinship? Here we face a recurrent conceptual dilemma in anthropology of trying to make a term from one cultural and linguistic tradition – our own – elastic enough that it fits the range of cultural variations, yet preserve the essential meaning. Kinship, to us, intuitively refers to 'blood relationships.' Our relatives are those connected to us by bonds of 'blood.' Our in-laws, to be sure, are related by marriage and not blood – and so are some of our aunts and uncles. But it is successive links between parents and children that are the essential strands of kinship.
>
> Is this true in other societies? ... [In many societies], there is a gap between presumed physical paternity (or even *maternity*) and socially assigned parentage ... How, then, are we to define 'parentage'? And how can we talk about 'blood' relationship between father and child, or mother and child, in cultures that have quite different theories or metaphors about the connection between parent and child? In some, the mother is thought to contribute no substance to the child, but only to provide a container for its growth. The Lakher of Burma, for example, believe that two children with the same mother and different fathers are not relatives at all ...
>
> Such variations must lead us at the outset to be wary of assuming that kinship is simply a matter of 'blood relationship.' It is safest to broaden our scope considerably to say that relations of kinship are connections modeled on those conceived to exist between a father and child and between a mother and child. In a particular culture these connections may be viewed as the same for father and mother (as with our 'blood' relations) or as different – based on metaphors of seed and soil, of bone and flesh, on substance and container. Moreover, 'modelled on' leaves room for those cases, like ... adoptive parenthood in our society and many others [which are] ... modeled on 'natural' parenthood.
>
> (Keesing, 1981, pp. 216–217)

Keesing's description of kinship points to many of the problems inherent in defining it. It also questions fundamental Western assumptions that kinship is based on biology. In English, phrases such as 'blood is thicker than water', or questions to adopted people such as, 'Do you know your real (i.e. biological) parents?' suggest that biological relationships are fundamental to ideas about family. Yet the existence of step-families, foster families or adoptive families indicates that blood is not the only marker of family. Looking cross-culturally, it is possible to observe that the emphasis on blood or biological ties is not universal and other societies have very different views on what constitutes family. Consider the two cases below.

The first concerns the Nuer, a nomadic group of pastoralists in Sudan. They have a particular idea of kinship which emphasizes the social connections between parents and child rather then the biological ones. The following example outlines their custom of ghost marriage where social ties take precedence over blood ties. Reproductive rights to a woman have been bought by a man's family on marriage and therefore *any* children she bears, no matter who the biological father is, are considered the children of her husband.

Nuer pastoralists.

A Nuer man playing with children.

A Nuer boy tending cattle.

Nuer ghost marriage

In two uncommon but perfectly legitimate forms of marriage among the Nuer, the socially recognized father ... of a child is not the man whose sexual intercourse with the mother is presumed to have led to the pregnancy ... A Nuer woman whose husband has died remains subject to a legal contract through which rights to the children she bears were transferred to her husband's group. By giving cattle to her father's group, the husband's group acquires rights in perpetuity to her reproductive powers. Ideally, if the husband dies, the contract will be sustained by her remarrying, to her deceased husband's brother or some other member of his group. But the children she bears from sexual relations with her second husband are socially defined as the offspring of her dead first husband (hence, 'ghost marriage'). The widow, rather than remarrying, may simply take lovers; but then the children she bears from her sexual relations with them are defined as offspring of her dead husband.

In a more rare form, an old and important woman may (by acquiring cattle) 'marry' a girl. The senior woman finances the marriage transactions as if she were a man. The young woman then bears children by lovers. They are socially defined as the children of the female 'husband,' who in turn is their 'father' ...

(Keesing, 1981, pp. 216–7)

The second example is from an anthropological description of Aboriginal children in Western Australia written in the 1930s. It gives a startling account of how children are conceived and their relationship to their parents. Although they recognize 'kin connections' between parents and children, they give a very different explanation for them.

Aboriginal rock drawing from the Nourlangie area of Kakadu National Park, Northern Territory, Australia. It depicts Namarrgon (lightning man), his wife Barrinj and Namondjolk (a dangerous spirit).

Spirit children

In the Kimberleys, it was held that a special category of 'spirit-children', *djinganara:ny*, were placed in the pools by the Rainbow Serpent in the Time of Long Past before there were any human beings. The spirit-children were not human ancestors, but could be temporarily incarnated in animals, fish or birds as they wandered over the country and played in the pools. Some said they were like little children about the size of a walnut, and others that they were like small red frogs. These beings were said to be found, usually by a man, at specific sites and brought home in a food item such as fish. When a woman was given such food, she would vomit. Her husband would dream of the spirit-child, push it towards his wife, and it would enter her by the foot, making her pregnant ...

Male semen as such was not thought to cause conception, though it was considered to reach the uterus where the embryo might float in it 'like a water lily'. The husband was thought to be shaping the growing child, however, through the provision of food. These doctrines were passed on and absorbed by children at an early age, giving them an answer to the question of 'Who am I?' ... 'Children of eight or nine as a rule ... were interested in the fact that they had once been a fish, bird, reptile or animal prior to the entry of the spirit-child into the mother'. A little girl [related] with pride ...: 'I was a fish at first. Father came up to the water and speared me there. So I was taken to the camp, and to my mother, and I came out as a baby'.

(James, 2000, pp. 171–3)

We draw on these two examples not as exotic cultural myths but as a way of showing that there are very different views on what constitutes parenthood. Although written about fieldwork conducted in the 1930s, many peoples of the world, in Amazonia for example, or Papua New Guinea, continue to hold similar views about the nature of conception and birth. An explanation based on sperm and eggs would make no sense to these people – a father is the parent of a child because he provides food, he looks after the mother and his semen cushions the child in the womb. A child cannot be born without those things and therefore as he is involved in the child's growth, he is the father. A child is created by the ancestral spirits of the mother and the imagination and work of the father. The biological facts are understood very differently.

Some social scientists when studying societies like this concluded that these people were ignorant and primitive. They believed that biological facts about parentage were universal and that people who did not recognize them were simply wrong. They believed that a child is biologically related to each parent and this is the basis of kinship. This, however, misses the point and this sort of ethnocentric thinking makes it impossible to understand other cultures. Communities such as the Nuer or the Kimberley Aborigines acknowledge the links between people that make family relationships, but they emphasize the social links between parent and child, not the biological ones. For this reason social scientists have distinguished between social and biological kinship and looked at why some communities place more emphasis on one than the other. Traditionally European kinship has placed an emphasis on blood ties, privileging them above social ties, hence the continuing ambivalence surrounding adoption (see Section 4). In contrast, in other communities, family ties are based on the social recognition of kinship rather than acknowledged biological ties.

Allow about 30 minutes

A C T I V I T Y I   How would you define fatherhood?

These ideas may seem rather exotic at first but even in British and Western society, ideas about social and biological kinship are deeply embedded. Read the following extract from a newspaper article by Margarette Driscoll, which discusses the case of a man who rejects a child he has raised and nurtured because there is no biological kinship. As you read it, write down the assumptions that 'Keith' makes about fatherhood.

1   How far do you agree with him?
2   Do you see him as Andrew's father or not?
3   If he is not does he have an obligation to support him?
4   Would his obligations be different if a biological relationship existed?

He's no son of mine

The details written on your birth certificate stay there for life. Thus, in future, whenever he needs to produce his birth certificate – to apply for a passport, say, or marry – a little boy growing up in the north of England will see a name in the space marked 'father' that is bound to cause him pain.

The man loved and cared for Andrew until he was seven, believing him to be his son. When he and the boy's mother split up, however, he discovered his 'son' was the result of his former lover's relationship with another man.

He was horrified, hurt, humiliated and, seemingly, determined to wreak revenge. Last week, in a legal first, he was given leave by the High Court to sue his former lover for fraud. The case should be heard in early summer and he is seeking damages of £250,000 to cover the costs of bringing up the child and as compensation for his emotional distress.

It is tempting to assume that Mr X – let's call him Keith – is an unfeeling bastard (none of the parties are allowed to be publicly named to protect the child). What kind of man, you might ask, could demand back every penny he spent on a child he admits he loved? He and the boy played and travelled together, gardened and kept bees and mucked about making things in the shed; in short, built a classic father-and-son relationship of love, trust and mutual reliance.

Yet what kind of woman could stand by and watch such a relationship grow, knowing it was built on a lie? …

The case, Keith insists, is not, and has never been, about money. 'If I make a penny out of it, it will go straight to a children's charity,' he says.

Keith met Pippa, the boy's mother, in 1980 …

Keith was newly divorced (he has two grown-up daughters from his first marriage) and feeling lonely ... [I]n 1987 [Pippa told him] that she was pregnant – and the baby was his – even though he had undergone a vasectomy years before. He was still unsure, so he saw a doctor. 'I was left with the belief that, although I'd had the vasectomy, yes, things could go wrong,' he says.

[...]

The baby was born on Cup Final day in May 1988 ...

At first there were no doubts. But by the time Andrew was four and his personality clearly forming, a nagging feeling set in. 'One of the pleasures of parenthood is seeing yourself, your good and bad points, reflected in your child,' says Keith. 'It's hard to explain. There wasn't the connection with him I'd had with my daughters.'

In 1994, when Andrew was six, Keith secretly had a sperm count. It was negative, but not conclusive. The vasectomy still might not have been failsafe.

Keith accepts that some people can't understand why, at this stage, it mattered. He had a strong relationship with Andrew. People come to accept, and love, stepchildren or adopted children all the time. 'I know that,' he says. 'But if you marry someone with children or adopt a child you make a choice to love that child. I did not have the right to decide. The love I had for him was based on a lie.

'Had she told me it was someone else's child I would have asked her to leave. I wouldn't have thrown her out in the cold, but I would have asked her to make other arrangements and wished her luck. I would not have wanted to form that relationship with Andrew.'

In January 1996 Pippa left, to return to her roots in the northeast and marry a childhood sweetheart. She took Andrew with her. Their informal agreement was that she would support him in term-time and Keith during the holidays, but from the start things were fraught.

Keith did not see or speak to Andrew till Easter, when he came to stay. He was 'delighted' to have him back, but while he was there Keith seized the opportunity to pick a stray hair from one of his jumpers and sent it with one of his own for analysis.

'It's one thing to doubt, but to open the envelope and read "Mr A cannot be the father of child B" was awful. I felt a jumble of emotions; anger, confusion, sadness.'

After that he refused all Pippa's financial demands. She called in the Child Support Agency, continuing to insist he was Andrew's father. Several court hearings later, a blood test established conclusively that the two were not related. The final act was to have Andrew's birth certificate amended. Though Keith's name still appears on it, an official addendum warns readers to ignore it.

He has not seen or spoken to Andrew for nearly five years and has no idea whether he knows about the case. 'It gets easier,' he says, 'but it's almost like the death of a child. I find it hard to think about him, it's too painful.'

[...]

And at the centre of this tangled web is a boy, now 12, who may still believe Keith to be his father and may some day turn up. How will he feel about the legal case?

'I don't know what he will think, but whatever happens he'll be hurt and that could have been avoided,' says Keith. 'He'll want to find his real father and, just like the rest of us, he deserves to know the truth.'

(Driscoll, 2001, p. 4)

COMMENT

Your reactions to this piece will depend on many issues, personal beliefs and experiences. It is a complicated and very emotive case and undoubtedly, if you ask someone else to read this, they will have very different reactions to you. You may feel that Keith has been deceived and should not have to raise a child with which he has no biological connection. You might feel that this is irrelevant and that he once loved the child and should continue to do so. You might feel that both adults in this case have been selfish and put their own concerns above the welfare of a small child. Indeed, it is very obvious how little attention was paid to Andrew's feelings. It was Pippa's decision to deny him knowledge and information about his biological origins. Similarly, it was Keith's decision to abandon the child and Pippa, withdraw support and initiate court proceedings. Andrew's point of view does not count.

Keith claims that biological connection is everything and that parenthood is based on biological relationships and seeing your child as a reflection of yourself. Despite the fact that he claims to have loved Andrew, he also claims that he would not have loved him if he had known that Andrew was not his son. His views may well be seen as extreme, but they do emphasize that even in the contemporary UK, notions of biological versus social ties are still debated, and become issues which involve public discussion and the legal system.

It also raises issues which will be explored later on in this chapter about the effects of technology on the lives of children, and the nature of their families. It is through the issues raised by technological developments that it becomes possible to ask questions about the nature of parenthood and the obligations and ties that it involves. Thirty years ago the technology did not exist to prove paternity in this way and although Keith insists that 'there wasn't the connection with him I'd had with my daughters', he would not have been able to prove it and would have continued to view Andrew as his son.

This case was eventually settled out of court. However, in a preliminary trial, Mr Justice Stanley Burnton found in favour of Keith. He ruled there had been deceit but did not decide the issue of damages. He suggested that the recovery of damages would be difficult because Keith had 'enjoyed for many years the companionship of ... the child' (the case is referred to in legal parlance as *P and B (2001) 1 FLR 1041*). In ruling in favour of Keith, the judge reaffirmed that, in Britain, it is biology, not social ties or love or 'companionship' that lies at the heart of kinship.

In this case, family ties exist as adult constructions. It is Keith, not his son, who is deciding who is family and who is not, who is his child and who is not. However, his case is unusual and in many other circumstances, it is children as much as adults who make sense of their kinship and have strong ideas on who they view as their family.

Allow about 10 minutes

ACTIVITY 2   How do children see their families?

The quotations below are from children we interviewed when researching this book who live in very different circumstances and different locations. We asked them who they thought their family were, and why. Read through the quotations and come up with a list of things that these children see as important in their families.

Sophie is twelve and lives in Oakland, California. She is the child of divorced lesbian parents.

'The people in my family are, I've two mums and I don't have any dads ... I call them Mummy and Mumma. And Mummy is ... my biological mum and she kinda looks like me ... And Mumma, she's kinda, she adopted me. And my parents they divorced even though they weren't really married but they split up and like I was about five going on six. And then I've got my animals.

'Family means like just really close, none of them biological but really close people to you, I mean I even consider my best friend Eve family pretty much. So it's just I think it's just people really close to you, that you are really close to and you really love.'

Moni is about fourteen and lives in Bangladesh with her parents and grandmother and has several uncles and aunts nearby.

'I have so many relatives around me they all live around us and I really like it. I feel very close to them. If they go away I miss them so I really like that they are here ... My grandmother is right by us ... if something happens to the family she is always there. She takes care of us. When my mother can't do it, she always asks us about things and she is always looking after us.'

Shane is about fifteen and works on the streets in Cape Town, South Africa. He is talking about his friend Wilfred to whom he is distantly related.

'I don't know he was family for me and he didn't know I was family for him, then I hear from my parents he's my family and he hear by his parents he's my family, now [when] I saw him have a fight with big boys in Cape Town then I help him – when he saw I have a fight then he help me ... so that's why we together ... We can't go away from each other, we can't forget each other, 'cos ..., three years we are together.'

Sophie with her biological mother.

Shane, Steven and Wilfred.

Moni and her family.

COMMENT

These children are actively thinking about what makes families. All of them, although they claim different people as their family, list the same qualities – families are based on love, on people who look after you and protect you. Some, like Moni, place more emphasis on biology and Shane and Wilfred clearly feel that the blood link between them is important. Sophie, on the other hand, who has obviously thought about biological links because of her situation, sees ties of affection as much more important than biological facts. Sophie's quote is particularly interesting because it is easy to misread. On first reading, many might assume that when she talks about her parents being divorced she is referring to her biological mother and father. In fact she is talking about her two mothers getting divorced. Assumptions about the nature of parenthood run very deep and such a misreading is quite understandable. What is interesting about all three children quoted above is how important nurture and care are to them. They are all concerned not only with what makes family ties but also about what families do, how they act.

This emphasis on ties of affection has other implications for who children view as part of their family. Children often have distinct views of who is in their family. An important example here is pets. Even though some adults might see children's relationships with their pets as irrelevant to family structure, when researchers speak directly to children, their responses indicate that pets are significant family members.

> In a way, [pets are] sort of part of your family, so you like respect 'em, love them. (Jade, 11)
>
> My hamster [is important to me] because he is the only one in the family who I can trust because I can talk to him but he won't speak back. (John, 13)
>
> (Morrow, 1998, pp. 222–3)

It would be interesting to know how universal this view is, or whether it is specific to countries in the North. Certainly pets exist in many societies, but there is little research on whether they are important to children everywhere or seen as part of the family.

SUMMARY OF SECTION 2

- Notions of the family are often idealized and romanticized.
- Family ties are fluid and flexible concepts which differ across cultures.
- There is a tension between social and biological ties which exists when discussing kinship.
- There is no single view or correct understanding of what makes a family but several constructions of family ties exist at any one time.
- These tensions can affect the care of children, when parents consider one view of parenthood more important than another.

3 ASSISTED CONCEPTION

So far, this chapter has examined the different ways that family ties can be understood. In the following two sections, we will look at how these debates about biological and social ties affect two particular ways of family formation – reproductive technologies such as IVF (*in vitro* fertilization or so called 'test-tube' babies) which allow infertile couples to conceive, and the adoption of children. The two issues raise many of the same questions. However, whereas adoption is well accepted in the UK as a means of creating a family, assisted conception is more problematic. Seemingly every day, new moral dilemmas are thrown up as a result of reproductive technology and science is far ahead of public opinion, and understanding, in this field. Assisted conception creates many moral dilemmas and forces us to look at very fundamental questions about childhood, parenthood and indeed life itself.

Reproductive technologies have had a profound effect on family formation. As adoption of infants has become more difficult, it is often medical intervention rather than adoption that people turn to in the UK if they cannot conceive a child. Even in the US, where adoption is much easier, the emphasis is on a child of one's 'own' (Ragoné, 1994). Assisted conception has refocused attention on biological ties and re-emphasized them as the true markers of kinship.

READING

You should now read Reading B, 'Unscrambling parenthood: the Warnock Report' by Peter Rivière, which concerns the dilemmas presented by forms of assisted conception such as IVF, egg donation and surrogacy. In 1986, the British government became very concerned about issues of surrogacy and commissioned a report, led by philosopher Dame Mary Warnock, to look at the implications of assisted conception. This report also shed light on the assumptions that many people in the UK made about parenthood in the 1980s and it raised very interesting issues about the 'naturalness' of these techniques. In his article Rivière argues that although assisted conception raises difficult questions in the UK, an understanding of other cultural situations and other ways of viewing the family may shed useful light on the dilemmas that these technologies reveal. In order to understand the article, it is important to draw a distinction between the social mother or father (i.e. the mother or father who raises the child) and the biological or genetic father or mother – the person who is biologically related to the child (i.e. the person that donates the sperm or the egg). In social science terms this is done by referring to the social mother and father as the *mater* and *pater* and to the biological parents as *genitor* (biological father) and *genetrix* (biological mother).

COMMENT

Technology has broken down the concept of a single biological mother. Birth, conception and family ties are not simply universal facts but have cultural meanings attached to them, which, when disrupted, can cause profound moral disquiet. Other societies view the nature of family ties very differently and social scientists have often studied these as part of looking at the families of people across the world. The Nuer, mentioned previously, for example, find few problems with ideas about non-biological parentage. However, in the North, the new reproductive technologies have made many look again at family ties and have forced people to ask questions about kinship and to examine the question of what it is that makes a parent.

There has been no follow up to the Warnock Commission despite the enormous leaps in medical technology since. IVF is now very widely accepted (since the world's first 'test-tube' baby, Louise Brown, was born in Bradford, UK in 1978, around 100,000 children have been born through similar techniques world-wide). Other issues have now superseded it. Almost every day in the newspaper there is some new advance in medicine or news of a 'miracle' baby. Human cloning has become a possibility, as indeed has the conception of a child from the genetic material of two same-sex partners.

Allow about 30 minutes

A C T I V I T Y 3   Issues of parentage

In the light of Peter Rivière's article, think about the issue of who is a parent in the following scenarios. Ask someone else the same questions and compare notes – on what points do you disagree? Why do you think this might be?

1   A married woman is implanted with eggs donated from her sister which have been fertilized by a sperm donor. When she gives birth, which woman do you believe has the strongest claim to be the child's biological mother?

2   A woman carries a baby as a surrogate for a couple, using the commissioning couple's eggs and sperm. When the baby is born the surrogate does not want to give the baby up. What moral claims could the surrogate make in this situation? How valid do you think these claims are?

3   A child discovers at eighteen that he was born by a sperm donation. He has always wondered why he looked so different from his family. He demands the right to trace the sperm donor, arguing that it is his right to know his real parentage. The courts refuse his request. On what grounds might they do this? What would be the advantages and disadvantages of letting children trace their genetic parents?

C O M M E N T

There can be no right answers here and indeed probably the answers you and the other person gave, and the reasons for doing so, will be very different. It is useful therefore to turn to the law – what does it say in these situations? To whom does it assign parentage? In the first example, there is the problem that the two biological functions of motherhood – providing an egg and carrying a child in the womb have been split. Both women could be said to be the child's true biological mother. There is no correct answer here except that under English law, the carrying mother would be seen as the mother. If a dispute between the sisters arose, the woman who carried the child would be awarded custody and her sister would have no rights over that child. In the second case, also, English law would award custody to the woman who carried the child (the surrogate) even if she used the commissioning couple's sperm and eggs. In contrast, in California, custody would always be awarded to the commissioning couple (even if they had not donated eggs and sperm). They are believed to have conceived the child and brought it into life through commissioning it and, therefore, the child is legally theirs. In neither case does genetics influence the law. You may think this is unfair and unjust, and certainly it has been bitterly contested in the courts. However, both these examples raise unanswerable questions about the nature of biological ties and the cross-cultural differences in understanding them. In the final case, the boy again has different rights depending on where he was born. In Sweden he would be allowed to trace his biological father, in the UK he would not. The Swedish would argue that he needs to know his father for medical purposes and also for social ones – he needs to know his identity and this is bound up with knowing who his biological parents are. Currently, the English courts would disagree. They would see the integrity of the boy's social family, as well as the integrity of the donor's family as paramount. Issues of identity would not be catered for under English law.

A central point that emerges from these scenarios and from Rivière's article is that whose child any of us is is not a straightforward, indisputable 'fact of life' but depends on our belief system informed by the cultural setting in which we grew up. Assisted conception has enabled many people to have children who would otherwise not be parents. In the period 1998–9, 6,450 children were born through IVF in the UK and 1,332 children were born after donor insemination pregnancies (HFEA, 2000). In the US, there are estimated to be 20,000 to 30,000 children born annually from donor insemination (Rubin, 2000). However, these medical developments have raised very important questions about the nature of parentage and childhood in societies in the North. They have outstripped society's existing moral discourses and make ethical reasoning profoundly difficult. For example, resources in the UK are limited; not all health authorities will pay for treatment and many people have to go privately, thus ensuring that in some parts of the country only those with enough money will have the opportunity to try to become parents. This raises further questions about the nature of families and whether potential parents ever have a right to a child.

Similarly, the rights of children born through these technologies need to be examined. Some campaigners, especially those who were born through artificial insemination, have demanded the right to trace their biological parents, arguing that knowing their biological parent is an intrinsic part of their identity. In Sweden, where the law was changed in 1985 to remove the anonymity of sperm donors, donations have fallen by over 90 per cent, leading to a critical shortage of sperm donors and making it harder for potential parents to take advantage of artificial insemination. The other side of this argument, however, is that those men who do donate have fully thought through the implications of their actions and are prepared to enter into some sort of relationship with the child born from their sperm. Similarly at the Berkeley Sperm Bank in California, almost 80 per cent of potential parents ask for an 'identity release donor' so they can tell their children who their biological father is (Rubin, 2000). In the few studies carried out on how children of donor insemination feel about the circumstances of their births, key issues of identity and belonging in families arise, which are very similar to those discussed in the next section on adoption.

> I needed to know whose face I was looking at in the mirror – I needed to know who I was and how I came to be – it was a very primal and unrelenting force which propelled the search and it was inescapable and undeniable.

(Rachel, quoted in Turner and Coyle, 2000, p. 2046)

> I'd like to 'see' the personality traits I've inherited – it'd be fun to recognize them in my donor father. I'd like to know what the donor does for a living, what conflicts he's had, how he's resolved them, what issues he struggles with. My fantasy is that we could learn from each other about how to deal with life. We'd probably have a lot in common, have a closeness that I didn't have with my real parents.

(Rose, quoted in Turner and Coyle, 2000, p. 2046)

SUMMARY OF SECTION 3

- Birth, conception and family ties are not simply universal biological facts but have cultural meanings attached to them.
- Assisted conception focuses attention on issues of who is a parent and the relationship of children to their parents.
- Whose child any of us is is not a straightforward, indisputable 'fact of life' but depends on our belief system informed by the cultural setting in which we grew up.
- The possibilities offered by assisted conception have changed at a faster pace than public opinion and knowledge and have caused ethical dilemmas for societies in the North.

4 ADOPTION

Before the advent of the new reproductive technologies, adoption was one of the few ways that childless couples could create a family. In the same way that medical advances in reproductive intervention have problematized the issue of who or what makes parents, so adoption throws up similar dilemmas. The example of adoption (like that of reproductive technology) is designed to show that issues of kinship are not merely moral or philosophical curiosities but are of central importance to discussions of childhood and parental ties. They are relevant, contemporary issues which are the subject of ongoing debate in society.

Allow about 20 minutes

A C T I V I T Y 4   Views on adoptive and biological parents

Read through the quotations below from adults who were adopted as children. List the different views they have on family relationships. Which person are you most sympathetic to and why?

> Seemingly unlike a lot of people, I have never considered 'family' to be a biological construct. Our biology doesn't make functional families, it only accounts for things like height and 'male pattern baldness.' Parents are not people who conceive children; that can be done in a test-tube. Parents are people who care for and nurture children ...
>
> [Sometimes I] wanted to dance and shout that 'hey, I was chosen to be a son!' I wasn't a fluke of biology. I wasn't the one that my parents drew from chance; I was picked!
>
> (Sample, 1999)
>
> Maybe I am looking for something I never had and which I may never get, but until I meet her [my biological mother] I will never know. I am hoping I can have a relationship with her. She is flesh and blood and there must be a tie ... I've got lots of friends but I want somebody that is like me, that's part of me.
>
> (Adoptee quoted in Triseliotis, 1973, p. 109)
>
> You feel you have no family like everybody else. What you call family is not really yours and the relatives are not your relatives ... there was always a gap between me and my [adopted] parents and I feel such a gap in myself now. Being adopted must make you feel like that.
>
> (Adoptee quoted in Triseliotis, 1973, p. 88)

COMMENT

As ever, there are no right and wrong answers here. Your reactions to this activity will depend very much on your own background in terms of culture, religion, upbringing and also your own personal experiences. The point of this exercise is to emphasize, yet again, that these issues are very complex, they may even be rather personally painful. Discussing these issues goes right to the heart of our closest relationships and most important personal connections. However, in order to widen this debate from purely personal experience, it is important to understand and explore the concepts behind these feelings. Issues of biological versus social kinship and the implications these have for understandings of what families are, and what they should do, become very obvious when discussing adoption and lead to a variety of experiences and viewpoints. At the heart of them, however, lies the question – is it nature or nurture that makes family?

The issue of adoption is a difficult one because it touches directly on the issue of who are 'real' parents. In the UK, it is very controversial because the state intervenes so directly in family life and adoptive parents are subject to a scrutiny and bureaucracy that natural parents are not. Biological parents are assumed to be able to look after their children and only when things go disastrously wrong does the state intervene. Potential adoptive parents have to prove to the state that they are suitable and the process they go through is long and gruelling.

It is worth briefly considering the history of adoption. In England and Wales, these problems are relatively new and are directly related to wider social and cultural issues about the nature of family relationships. Until 1926, blood or marriage were the only markers of family ties. Adoption was not recognized by law because children, by definition, had to be related by blood to their parents. Children were, of course, sometimes brought up by other people but the law did not recognize adoption and always saw them as the children of their biological parents. The Christian church had forbidden adoption for almost 1500 years and acknowledged kin only on the grounds of shared blood (known as consanguinity). In the eyes of the Church, children who were not related to their parents through blood could not be claimed as their children because blood, and only blood, defined the relationship between child and parent. Such reasoning continues today in Islam where adoption is not officially recognized (although many Islamic societies have long traditions of adults fostering and looking after children other than their own). However, formal adoption would confuse the blood lines, the markers of relationship and descent in Islamic society, and is therefore not allowed.

Adoption was allowed legally in England only after 1926 when a thorough-going re-examination of notions of kin by the Church of England and the state allowed for ties other than blood to be recognized as kinship ties. It acknowledged that families can exist successfully based on ties other than blood. The 1926 Adoption Act allowed parents to bring up children who were not born to them and were not biologically related to them and the state would regard these families in exactly the same way as ones in which parentage was based on biology. In order to preserve this unity, contact between natural parents and the children they offered for adoption was strictly forbidden. In the vast majority of cases, names were changed and neither adoptive parent nor child was given information about the birth parents. The new family was protected from any claims from the biological parents.

The early 1970s saw a shift in thinking about adoption in England and Wales. By this point, fewer adoptions were taking place, as a consequence of the availability of contraception, the introduction of legal abortion in 1967, and a greater tolerance of, and support for, single mothers raising their own children. As adoptive children grew up, many began to demand information about the circumstances surrounding their birth and adoption. Many felt, as two of the quotations in Activity 4 implied, that if a child did not know his or her genetic parents, then something very fundamental was missing. Although parents had (controversially) often been recommended to keep the adoption secret, this frequently proved impossible. The more liberal atmosphere of the 1960s and the encouragement of openness within families also meant that this emphasis on secrecy was less ideologically acceptable. Between 1926 and 1976, women who were giving up their children for adoption were told that their records would remain sealed and that the child they were giving birth to would never have any contact with them. The 1976 Adoption Act reversed this and allowed children to trace their biological parents. Suddenly women who had given their children up for adoption could be traced, although an equivalent right for the mothers (to trace their children) was not allowed. Much of the debate surrounding it focused on children's rights to know their biological parents and their need to know their biological identity.

Such a view remains contested. In the US, for example, where many more adoptions take place than England, some states still seal adoption records for 99 years, believing that preserving the integrity of the social family overrides a person's right to know their biological parentage. Others allow limited medical information but deny adopted children contact details, others allow open adoption when the child is free to contact his or her natural parents when they are eighteen. As ever, there are many viewpoints on the good of doing this. Some argue that biology does not matter and that the birth parents should be given privacy, others feel that identity is so tied up with notions of belonging to a biological family that all other considerations are irrelevant.

4.1 Adoption as social engineering

It is also worth noting briefly that adoption raises further issues, not only of biological inheritance, but also of social or cultural inheritance. Again, this is a vast and controversial topic, and we do not have space to do it justice, but it should be mentioned that adoption has also been used as a means of social engineering. One of the notorious cases is of the adoption of

A white Australian woman with her foster children, taken on National Aborigine's Day 1965 in Sydney, Australia.

Aboriginal children in Australia. Between the 1940s and the 1970s, the Australian government removed, sometimes through coercion and trickery, thousands of Aboriginal children from their parents. Many of these children were of mixed race and by placing them in white families it was hoped that they could 'rise' to the level of the whites rather than 'sink' to the levels of their Aboriginal community. However, rather than 'becoming white' as the government hoped, many of the 'stolen generation' (as they now call themselves) felt adrift between two worlds; neither belonging to white Australian society or to their Aboriginal families. Many of these people have recently begun to speak out about their experiences as children:

> They changed our names, they changed our religion, they changed our date of birth, they did all that. That's why today, a lot of them don't know who they are, where they're from.

> (Anonymous Aborigine, New South Wales)

> Most of us girls were thinking white in the head but were feeling black inside. We weren't black or white. We were a very lonely, lost and sad displaced group of people. We were taught to think and act like a white person, but we didn't know how to think and act like an Aboriginal. We didn't know anything about our culture.

> We were completely brainwashed to think only like a white person. When they went to mix in white society, they found they were not accepted [because] they were Aboriginal. When they went and mixed with Aborigines, some found they couldn't identify with them either, because they had too much white ways in them. So that they were neither black nor white. They were simply a lost generation of children. I know. I was one of them.

> (Anonymous Aboriginal woman removed at eight years with her three sisters in the 1940s)

> (Commonwealth of Australia, 1997)

SUMMARY OF SECTION 4

- Adoption is a prime exemplar of the competing claims of biological and social ties.
- Adoption is also closely related to issues of identity and to ideas about belonging and affiliation.
- Adoption has sometimes been used as a means of social engineering.

5 WHO PROVIDES CARE?

The previous sections have dealt with issues of what makes parents: is it biology, social ties or love and care? Having examined these issues in detail, we will now look at who provides love and care for children when their parents cannot or do not. Implicit in the previous discussions about the basis of parentage is the idea that how people understand this term affects the ways in which children are treated. This chapter has also shown us that what is meant by parentage (and family) varies greatly depending on cultural practices and local circumstances. It has also been assumed that it is the family, however that is understood, that should be the primary provider of care for children. Generally speaking, and according to international guidelines, the family unit led by at least one adult member, preferably a parent, is recognized as the ideal setting for raising children. However, not all children live with their parents or immediate families. Here we move away from discussions of biological versus social relationships and look at some of the other social structures outside the immediate family, in which children are cared for, nurtured, and socialized.

5.1 Informal patterns of fostering

In many societies, it is neither parents nor formal institutions that are expected to provide care and socialization of children. Parents are not always viewed as the only people who should provide care for youngsters and others in the child's community often help. Among Xhosa families in South Africa, it is often the maternal grandmother who raises a child. Fatima Dike, a Xhosa playwright, explains this:

> In many cases, when you have your first child, you are considered to be immature, and inexperienced. So [your] mother will bring up the child for you, and you will be there to see how the child is brought up. By the time you have your second child, you actually know what goes into bringing a child up.

(Interview carried out in Cape Town, South Africa, June 2001)

Asanda's Xhosa family includes her sister, cousins, parents, aunt and grandmother.

READING

Now read Reading C, an extract from *All Our Kin* by Carol Stack. This is based on research that Carol Stack carried out in the 1960s in a poor, African-American, urban neighbourhood in Chicago which she calls The Flats. Here she found groups of women raising their children in a variety of family patterns, swapping and sharing children as their social and financial resources permitted. Note down the types of family described.

COMMENT

The extract from Carol Stack's book shows just how adaptive and fluid families can be. In the community she describes, children are shared between their mothers, their friends and their relatives for financial and social necessity. This sort of informal fostering is clearly not regulated by the state and it may seem surprising that it goes on in a modern, affluent country such as the USA with its high degree of regulation and welfare services. However, as a strategy it enables families to survive and confounds expectations of how a parent should act towards a child and who should provide care for that child. It also shows the difficulties of talking about families in the North as a single entity when in fact there are multiple family forms and ways of seeing kinship ties. Carol Stack's article examines the role that fostering plays in many children's lives. This sharing of children is viewed as a positive care system rather than an example of family breakdown.

There are many cases of informal fostering that occur outside state regulations. The example below concerns child-headed households in Rwanda. In Rwanda, after the massacres of 1994, many households became child headed, with siblings taking care of younger children, cousins and even sometimes neighbours because they saw themselves as the only ones able to look after them.

Sibling-headed households in Rwanda

Jean Mureramanzi walks along a dirt road, the sun and his field at his back, the darkening hills ahead ... [He] is making his way toward his home in Butare, in Rwanda's south.

Up ahead in his small mud-brick house, a boy and girl, six and nine years old, roll a ball made from plastic bags back and forth over a dirt floor. Mureramanzi pauses before entering the house, knowing that tonight there is not enough food for the entire family to eat. Normally he can find a day's work, but today his search has proved as fruitless as his field ...

Mureramanzi is 20 years old, and he is not the father of the two young children who stop playing when he opens the door to the fading light. He is their brother. The family of children have lived alone since their parents were killed during Rwanda's genocide of 1994. At that time, Mureramanzi had not been prepared to lead a family. He had dropped out of primary school in 1991, because, he says with a smile, 'I am not intelligent.' Now, on his way to prepare dinner, he walks by his sister, kicks her the ball, thinks of his friends who are finishing their nightly game of football. He thinks of the decision he must make tonight, the decision which no parent should have to make. Is the stomach preferred to the child?

It is a difficult question to answer without first asking, who is the child? Mureramanzi says: 'I am not an adult, and I am not a child. In the middle. I can do the work of men, but I never discuss things with them. The only adult I speak with is my grandmother, but she is worn down. I am not an adult,' he says, 'but I am a father. I provide for my family. I know I have a family because a family is a group of people who are in some way united ...

'I never think about getting married ... because life in the present is much too difficult. I never think about abandoning my brother and sister ... because even if I had to feed only myself, life would not be easier.'

(Cohen and Hendler, 1997, pp. 8–9)

The massacres in Rwanda left millions dead and the social welfare structures of the country in ruins. Many young people like Jean had little option but to look after their siblings, even though they were still children themselves; at the time, Jean was only seventeen. However, Jean clearly feels love for his brother and sister and an obligation to them. In the light of the previous sections, his comment, 'a family is a group of people who are in some way united', suggests that how he thinks of his family is reflected in the way he looks after them. Although he still thinks of himself as a child, he must also take on a parental role. He thinks about what makes a family and consequently what his responsibilities are. Jean, like many children, is showing himself to be both adaptive and resilient, taking on the responsibility for his family without adult support. His story underlines the point that children shape their families, and in some instances, become the only support they have.

5.2 Children and institutional care

The family unit is often seen as the ideal environment in which to raise children and there is a tendency in societies in the North for any other options to be viewed as second rate. However, many children do not live with their family, or with members of their extended families. In some cases, children choose to avoid formal services altogether and instead opt to work and live in other people's houses, or with other children. In other instances, children find themselves in institutional care.

The dominant and most commonly accepted viewpoint is that institutional care should be the last option for children. A great deal of literature exists which documents the problems associated with institutional settings (Bogen, 1992). Historically, many institutions were custodial, designed to keep children off the streets. Frequently, they were unsanitary and the children living in them were barely clothed, not properly fed and had little access to education or any way of improving their lives.

Children with staff at St. Gregory's Home for Babies, Plymouth in the 1940s.

A contemporary independent living scheme for young people in the UK.

Yet orphanages and children's homes continued to care for large numbers of children in the UK for many years. The following extract is taken from the autobiography of a woman named Tina Bareham who was born during the Second World War, and was immediately placed in a children's home run by the Barnardo's charity in London, England. As you can see she places her difficult experiences in a historical context and indicates that provision of care is now approached differently:

> Nobody explained to any of us children living in the Dr Barnardo's home about our families, nor did they ever discuss with us why we were there instead of in an ordinary house with parents, siblings and other kin somewhere around ... I often cried myself to sleep, and dreamt of having a mum and dad of my own, or someone to cuddle me and tell

me they loved me. Although I was adequately looked after in a secure environment, I never received any hugs, not even when I was ill ... Deprived of any contact with my family, I grew up with a profound sense of injustice ... I have found out that I was by no means the only one hurt by the lack of love in our institutionalised upbringing. Many of us still rail against the well-meaning but misguided practices of the past, when little attention was given to the needs of the individual ... Thankfully, these homes are now a thing of the past ...

(Bareham, 2000, pp. 1, 12, 13, 231)

John Bowlby

Tina's recollections reflect many of the concerns that psychologists and educationalists felt about children's homes. Criticism of orphanages was further strengthened in the aftermath of the Second World War on the advice of psychologist John Bowlby. During the war Bowlby had worked with children living in institutional settings and he concluded that maternal attachment is of primary importance during early childhood and that children deprived of it will inevitably suffer. Indeed much of Tina's unhappiness during her childhood focused on the absence of a parental figure from whom she might have received consistent support and comfort.

Partly as a result of Bowlby's work, the aftermath of the Second World War signalled Western preference for care that most closely mirrored family life. Fostering and adoption were seen as more beneficial to children than institutional care. Large orphanages were closed down and where children could not be placed with families, smaller children's homes run by house parents took their place. More recently even small children's homes have begun to fall out of fashion, as Berridge and Brodie showed in a survey of residential child care in twelve European countries. Findings revealed that the declining use of residential care in the United Kingdom is part of a broader trend as a variety of alternative services develop (Berridge and Brodie, 1998). There has been a general move during this period towards providing children with foster care or adoption, which gives children the opportunity to experience family life.

The criticism of institutional care that exists world-wide can make it difficult to ask if there are any benefits to be gained from being in such environments, yet not all children experience orphanages negatively. Children who live in institutional settings do create familial ties among their peers and with staff who care for them. It is not unusual to find older children caring for those who are younger than them and for such close relationships to be formed that children would rather stay put than, for example, go into foster care. Not all children adapt well to being brought up in a new family setting. The following extract is taken from a radio programme in which Peter White talks with Fiona whom he and his wife fostered when she was ten. The experience was fraught with difficulties and Fiona ran away when she was fifteen, but got back in contact three years later and has remained in contact ever since.

My wife and I fostered Fiona when she was 10, and when we already had three children of our own of five and under ... We knew Fiona had lived in a children's home for several years, that she had two natural brothers and that her mother had died when she was still a baby. What we didn't know until much later was that she had had 14 foster homes by the time she was three, and that attempts to establish a relationship between her remarried father and his three children had been messy and unsuccessful ...

Should we have done it in the first place? A heart-stopping moment in the making of this programme, two decades after the event, was when Fiona said to me for the first time: 'I sometimes wonder whether it would have been better if you hadn't fostered me; if I had just stayed in the kids' home. Perhaps I would now have a better relationship with my natural brothers.'

Fiona is entitled to that doubt, and by both agreeing to do the programme we had given each other licence to say what we thought ... Fiona now has her own home, a good job and, in an interview conducted when I wasn't there, she says she loves us. Twenty-four years ago, when she first arrived, I would have settled for that. I hope she can.

(Peter White, 2001)

Some social commentators argue that, while fostering and adoption can be successful, over-reliance on foster and adoptive parents is making life less stable for children who have had disrupted lives. It is sometimes argued that such children may find it difficult to settle and make attachments with new carers. Brindle (2001) reported that in the UK alone two-thirds of children in local authority care are in foster homes. But almost one in five of all those in care has three or more placements in the course of a year. If children are likely to experience short-term foster care would they feel more settled if they were to be placed permanently in children's homes?

McKenzie (1999) argues that institutional care was discredited too quickly and under particular circumstances when institutions were larger in size and a different philosophy towards child rearing existed. His research findings indicate that experiences of children's homes are not always bad. The 1,800 respondents to his questionnaire had lived in children's homes for up to five years. Of these respondents, 86 per cent said that they had never or rarely wanted to be adopted. He also found that respondents had higher high school grades than their age group in the general population. Some of his respondents referred to the orphanage as a secure place in which they were able to identify with people in a similar position to themselves.

It is also often assumed that children who live in institutions have no contact with their birth family and that being an orphan means neither parent is alive. This is often not the case and children may go home for holidays and have quite regular contact with family members. Equally some children may not want to return home and they may have no contact with family.

Institutional settings have been at the centre of intense and emotional debate in countries in the North. However, they evoke different forms of debate in other parts of the world. The terms orphanage and institution are sometimes used interchangeably and alongside each other. There is a tendency among aid agencies, charities and child-focused welfare providers to make a distinction between the term 'orphanage', which is often only used in a historical context, or about countries of the South, and the term 'children's home', which is more likely to be used by professionals and in current literature with reference to child care in the North. The term orphanage can sometimes sound derogatory because it became outmoded in the North when such institutions were restructured to reflect adult-led family life as closely as possible. Reverting to the term orphanage in the context of the South is derogatory because this implies that the care on offer is outdated.

Apart from naming, however, orphanages in the South face a different set of problems to those in the North. According to Susan Hopkins (1996), who researched Vietnamese children's institutions, children in orphanages may be better off economically than other children; however, this may be at the cost of the stability of the wider community. Parents may take advantage of the services on offer at the orphanage and place their children there to give them the best possible opportunities in life. Orphanages, Hopkins claimed, may therefore have the unintended effect of breaking up families and may actually undermine family obligations. Tolfree (1995) further argues that there is sometimes a tendency for social commentators from the North to over-romanticize local cultural practices regarding family life and the duties of extended families and that many families do in fact abdicate responsibility for relatives' children when orphanages are available.

> [O]nce orphanages are established, they may serve to relieve members of the child's extended family of their sense of obligation, providing an 'instant solution' in situations in which other and more appropriate family-based care might be available.
>
> (Tolfree, 1995, p. 38)

This form of harsh criticism glosses over economic, social and cultural reasons for children being unable to continue to live with their families. In some parts of the world, as Hopkins has indicated, children and their parents struggle on a daily basis to cover basic needs. Offering children an education in addition to a reasonable diet and shelter may be an unrealistic possibility. Thus, under some circumstances, living in an institution instead of a family may not have the negative associations that it has in the North, as Tolfree also points out:

> Outside Western countries, however, the term 'institution' is used more widely, though not necessarily with the negative connotations implied elsewhere.
>
> (Tolfree, 1995, p. 6)

Thus when we refer to institutional care the term embraces a wide range of possibilities, and it is clear that children's experiences of growing up in such places vary enormously. McKenzie would have us believe that institutional care is not necessarily detrimental and the experience may even strengthen a person's resolve to do very well in adulthood. But as Tina's reflections indicate the negative experiences of living in a children's home or orphanage can stay with a person for life.

SUMMARY OF SECTION 5

- Parents and close family members are not the only providers of care for children.

- Informal care systems need not be seen negatively as a response to family breakdown but as a positive way of socializing children and sharing resources.

- There is no rigid distinction between institutional care and family life and many children in institutional care retain contact with their birth families.

- Institutional care may provide positive benefits, such as security, education and welfare. However, it may also cause insecurity and distress.

6 CONCLUSION

The relationship between child and parents is a much discussed concept but, as this chapter has aimed to show, it is certainly not straightforward. Who children recognize as their parents differ according to culture and it is impossible to point to any one universal factor. Children live in many sorts of family and recognize a variety of people as their kin. This also changes over time and the nature of parenthood, families and their relationship to children, is constantly in flux, changing through both social transformation and technological advances. This chapter has discussed the various ways of looking at family ties, showing that ideas about the family are contested, controversial and deeply personal.

It has also shown that parents are not the only carers for children. Although in many cases they do provide the main forms of socialization, there are also many formal and informal methods by which children are raised and nurtured. Children themselves take an active part in forming their families, some claim kin, others reject them, and children's experiences of family and non-family life are as variable as the forms of family in which children live.

REFERENCES

BAREHAM, T. (2000) *Search for a Mother,* London, Minerva Press.

BERRIDGE, D. and BRODIE, I. (1998) *Children's Homes Revisited*, London and Philadelphia, Jessica Kingsley Publications.

BOGEN, H. (1992) *The Luckiest Orphans: a history of the Hebrew Orphan Asylum of New York,* Urbana and Chicago, USA, University of Illinois.

BRINDLE, D. (2001) 'Stability the key to good results', Guardian Society, *Guardian*, 2 May.

COHEN, C. and HENDLER N. (1997) *No Home Without Foundation: a portrait of child-headed households in Rwanda,* New York, Women's Commission for Refugee Women and Children.

COMMONWEALTH OF AUSTRALIA (1997) *The Report of the National Inquiry into the Separation of Aboriginal and Torres Strait Islander Children from their Families*, Sydney, Human Rights and Equal Opportunity Commission, http://www.austlii.edu.au/au/special/rsjproject/rsjlibrary/hreoc/stolen/part3.rtf (accessed 8 January 2002).

DRISCOLL, M. (2001) 'He's no son of mine', News Review, *The Sunday Times*, 4 February, p. 4.

FERRI, E. and SMITH, K. (1998) *Step-parenting in the 1990s,* London, Family Policy Study Centre.

GIDDENS, A. (1998) *Sociology*, Cambridge, Polity Press.

HFEA (Human Fertilisation and Embryology Authority) (2000) *Annual Report*, London, HFEA.

HOPKINS, S. (1996) *Situation and Needs of Children in Vietnam*, Hanoi, Save the Children Consortium and PLAN International (internal publication).

JAMES, W. (2000) 'Placing the unborn: on the social recognition of new life', *Anthropology and Medicine,* 7(2), pp. 169–89.

KEESING, R. (1981) *Cultural Anthropology*, Fort Worth, Holt, Rinehart and Winston.

MCKENZIE, R. (1999) *Rethinking Orphanages for the Twenty-first Century,* London, Sage Publications.

MORROW, V. (1998) 'My animals and other family: children's perspectives on their relationships with companion animals', *Anthrozoös,* 11(4), pp. 222–3.

MURRAY, C. (2000) 'Baby beware', News Review, *The Sunday Times*, 13 February, p. 1.

RAGONÉ, H. (1994) *Surrogate Motherhood: conception in the heart,* Boulder, Westview Press.

RIVIÈRE, P. (1985) 'Unscrambling parenthood: the Warnock Report', *Anthropology Today*, 1(4), pp. 2–7.

RUBIN, R. (2000) 'Who's my father?', *USA Today*, 1 November [on-line] http://www.usatoday.com/life/health/general/lhgen111.htm (accessed 9 March 2001).

SAMPLE, N. (1999) 'What I felt like being adopted' [on-line] http://www.stepfamily.net/Adoption.htm (accessed 9 March 2001).

STACEY, J. (1999) 'Virtual social science and the politics of family values in the United States' in JAGGER, G. and WRIGHT, C. (eds) *Changing Family Values*, London, Routledge.

STACK, C. (1974) *All our Kin*, New York, Basic Books.

STARK, R. (1985) *Sociology*, Belmont, California, Wadsworth.

TOLFREE, D. (1995) *Roofs and Roots: the care of separated children in the developing world*, Aldershot, Arena.

TRISELIOTIS, J. (1973) *In Search of Origins: the experiences of adopted people*, Routledge, London.

TURNER, A.J. and COYLE, A. (2000) 'What does it mean to be a donor offspring? The identity experiences of adults conceived by donor insemination and the implication for counselling and therapy', *Human Reproduction,* **15**(9), pp. 2041–51.

WHITE, P. (2001) 'Haven and hell', Guardian Society, *Guardian,* 2 May, p. 6.

READING A

A virtual bedtime fable for the American century

Judith Stacey

> From the wild Irish slums of the 19th century Eastern seaboard to the riot torn suburbs of Los Angeles, there is one unmistakable lesson in American history: a community that allows a large number of young men to grow up in broken families, dominated by women, never acquiring any stable relationship to male authority, never acquiring any set of rational expectations about the future – that community asks for and gets chaos. Crime, violence, unrest, unrestrained lashing out at the whole social structure – that is not only to be expected; it is very near to inevitable.
>
> (Daniel Patrick Moynihan, 1965)

Once upon a fabulised time, half a century ago, there was a lucky land where families with names like Truman and Eisenhower presided over a world of wholesome, middle-class families. Men and women married, made love and (in that proper order), produced gurgling, Gerber [a babyfood manufacturer] babies. It was a land where as God and Nature had ordained, men were men and women were ladies. As epitomised in the mythic 1950s US sitcom characters Ozzie and Harriet, fathers worked outside the home for pay to support their wives and children, and mothers worked inside the home without pay to support their husbands and to cultivate healthy, industrious, above-average children. Streets and neighbourhoods were safe and tidy. This land was the strongest, wealthiest, freest and fairest in the world. Its virtuous leaders, heroic soldiers, and dazzling technology defended all the freedom-loving people on the planet from an evil empire which had no respect for freedom or families. A source of envy, inspiration and protection to people everywhere, the leaders and citizens of this blessed land felt confident and proud.

And then, as so often happens in fairytales, evil came to this magical land. Sometime during the mid-1960s, a toxic serpent wriggled its way close to the pretty picket fences guarding those Edenic gardens. One prescient Jeremiah, named Daniel Patrick Moynihan (1965), detected the canny snake and tried to alert his placid country*men* to the dangers of family decline. Making a pilgrimage from Harvard to the White House, he chanted about the ominous signs and consequences of 'a tangle of pathology' festering in cities that suburban commuters and their ladies-in-waiting had abandoned for the crabgrass frontier. Promiscuity, unwed motherhood and fatherless families, he warned, would undermine domestic tranquillity and wreak social havoc. Keening only to the tune of black keys, however, this Pied Piper's song fell flat, inciting displeasure and rebuke.

It seemed that, overnight, those spoiled Gerber babies had turned into rebellious, disrespectful youth who spurned authority, tradition and conformity, and scorned the national wealth, power and imperial status in which their elders exulted. Rejecting their parents' grey flannel suits and Miss American ideals, as well as their monogamous, nuclear families, they generated a counter-culture and a sexual revolution, and they built unruly social movements demanding student rights, free speech, racial justice, peace, liberation for women and for homosexuals. Long-haired, unisex-clad youth smoked dope and marched in demonstrations shouting slogans like, 'Question Authority', 'Girls Say Yes to Boys Who Say No', 'Smash Monogamy', 'Black is Beautiful', 'Power to the People', 'Make Love, Not War', 'Sisterhood is Powerful', and 'Liberation Now'. Far from heeding Moynihan's warning, many young women drew inspiration from the 'black matriarchs' he had condemned and condemned Moynihan instead for blaming the victims.

... But the thankless arrogance of these privileged youth, their unkempt appearance, provocative antics and amorality also enraged many, inciting a right-wing, wishful, 'moral majority' to form its own backlash social movement to restore family and moral order.

And so it happened that harmony, prosperity, security and confidence disappeared from this once most fortunate land. After disturbing Black communities, the serpent of family decline slithered under the picket fences, where it spewed its venom on white, middle-class families as well. Men no longer knew what it meant to be men, and women had neither time nor inclination to be ladies. Had the Ozzie and Harriet Show still been running, Ozzie would have had trouble finding secure work. He'd have been accused of neglecting, abusing or oppressing his wife and children. Harriet would no longer have stayed home with the children. She too would have worked outside the home for pay, albeit less pay. Ozzie and Harriet would have sued for divorce. Harriet would have decided she could choose to have children with or without a marriage certificate, with or without an Ozzie, or perhaps even with a Rozzie ...

As the last decade of the century dawned, only half the children in the land were living with two married parents who had jointly conceived or adopted them. Twice as many children were living in single-parent as in male breadwinner, female home-maker, families. Little wonder few citizens could agree over what would count as a proper family ...

The era of the modern family system had come to an end, and few felt sanguine about the postmodern family condition which had succeeded it. Unaccustomed to a state of normative instability and definitional crisis, the populace split its behaviour from its beliefs. Many who contributed actively to such postmodern family statistics as divorce, remarriage, blended families, single parenthood, joint custody, abortion, domestic partnership, two-career households, and the like still yearned nostalgically for the 'Father Knows Best' world they had lost. 'Today', in the United States, as historian John Gillis (1994) so aptly puts it, 'the anticipation and memory of family means more to people than its immediate reality. It is through the families we live *by* that we achieve the transcendence that compensates for the tensions and frustrations of the families we live *with*'. Not only have the fabled modern families we live *by* become more compelling than the messy, improvisational, patchwork bonds of postmodern family life, but, as my bedtime story hints, because they function as pivotal elements in a distinctive national imaginary, these symbolic families are also far more stable than any in which future generations ever dwelled.

   Similar evidence of the decline of the modern family system appears throughout the advanced industrialised world, and for similar reasons, but thus far, in no other society has the decline incited responses so volatile, ideological, divisive nor so politically mobilised and influential as in the US. ... Now the popular representational crisis of family order incites acrimonious conflicts in every imaginable arena – from television sitcoms to Congress, from the Boy Scouts of America to the United States Marines, from local school boards to multinational corporations, from art museums to health insurance underwriters, and from political conventions to social science conferences.

References

Gillis, John (1994) 'What's behind the debate on family values?', paper delivered at American Sociological Association Meetings, Los Angeles: 6 August.

Moynihan, Daniel Patrick (1965) *The Negro Family: The Case for National Action,* Washington, DC: US Department of Labor.

Shogren, Elizabeth (1994) 'Traditional family nearly the exception, census finds', *Los Angeles Times*, 30 August: A1, A28.

Source

Stacey, J. (1999) 'Virtual social science and the politics of family values in the United States' in Jagger, G. and Wright, C. (eds) *Changing Family Values*, London, Routledge.

READING B

Unscrambling parenthood

Peter Rivière

The Warnock Report, or to give it its proper title *Report of the Committee of Inquiry into Human Fertilization and Embryology*, appeared in July 1984. The Committee had been set up two years earlier, in July 1982, 'to examine the social, ethical and legal implications of recent, and potential developments in the field of human assisted reproduction' (p. iv)...
   [...]
   I want to discuss the report in detail and add some anthropological commentary ... The point of drawing comparisons is to throw light on our own fundamental assumptions, ideas and practices; those that we take to be 'naturally' right, God-given or whatever. It is to show them to be, like those of others, our own peculiar social and cultural constructs. The theme running through most of my comments will be the relationship of pater to

genitor and of mater to genetrix, or, in other words, of social paternity to biological procreation, for this, in the end, is the problem that the *Report* has so often to confront.

The real meat of the *Report* begins with Chapter 4 which is devoted to artificial insemination (AI) ... The basis of AID is the insemination of the woman by the semen of a donor, usually anonymous. The legal status of the technique is unclear. A Commission set up by the Archbishop of Canterbury recommended in 1948 that it be made a criminal offence. Nothing was done, and in 1960 another Government Commission recommended that it be strongly discouraged. Once again nothing was done. The practice has continued to grow in frequency and almost by default it has become more or less accepted. It would certainly be difficult to ban, given the ease with which AI can be performed. However, while in itself it is not an illegal act, the child born as a result of AID is illegitimate. To quote from the *Report*: 'In theory the husband of the woman who bears an AID child has no parental rights and duties in law with regard to that child; these in principle lie with the donor, who could be made liable to pay maintenance, and who could apply to a court for access or custody' (20). Furthermore, the parents are performing an illegal act if they register the husband as the child's father. In other words, in the eyes of the law the genetic father is *the father*, and no allowance is made for social fatherhood; the role is not even recognized.

The objection to AID centred round the point that the child would be biologically the wife's and donor's, and that the husband would have played no part in the procreation. Another objection was that AID introduces a third party into the marital relationship and thus threatens the stability of the family; indeed, some likened the practice to adultery.

The Committee came down in favour of AID, once again stating that those who found it morally objectionable would be unlikely to practise it, but this should not stop others from doing so. They also recommended that ... the law should be changed so that an AID child should be the full legitimate child of a consenting married couple. However, the wording of the *Report* deserves looking at. 'We ... recommend that the AID child should in law be treated as the legitimate child of its mother and her husband ...' (24) ... We are fully aware that this can be criticized as legislating for a fiction since the husband of a woman who has conceived by AID will not be the genetic father of the child and the register of births has always been envisaged as a true genetic record' (26).

To an anthropological audience it must be abundantly clear that the problem face by the Committee ... is what to do when pater no longer equals genitor. There seems an underlying determination to hang on to this equation. Thus the AID child is only to be 'treated' as legitimate; it is not to be legitimate. The same hesitancy is apparent in the second quotation, and even in this country to envisage the register of births as a true genetic record seems extraordinarily naive. Perhaps one of the earliest lessons in social anthropology is that genealogies are social and cultural constructs, and not biological pedigrees. Of course, in many societies, this pretence is not even aimed at, and marriage is a means of defining social parenthood rather than biological relationship. The obvious ethnographic examples are those from Africa where the legitimacy of a woman's offspring, regardless of who their genitor may be, is defined by marriage, and above all through the passage of bridewealth.

[...]

Next we come to *in vitro* fertilisation (IVF); a technique whose development has triggered off the current debate ... While IVF normally involves the semen and egg of a married couple, the technique opens up a much wider range of possibilities, some less likely than others. For example, there is the counterpart to AID with the semen being donated. Then there is egg donation for cases in which a woman is unable to produce an egg but is otherwise quite capable of bearing a child. An egg is obtained from a third party, is fertilized *in vitro* with the semen of the husband, and the resulting embryo is implanted in the wife. The objections to this practice were similar to those against AID, in that it introduced into the marriage a third party. Arguments in favour included one that saw it have the advantage over AID in so far as both parents contribute more: the father genetically and the mother as carrier. The Committee took the view that, in principle, egg donation does not differ from AID, and therefore recommended the practice subject to various similar safeguards. For example, it is recommended that all rights to the child will pass to the 'carrying mother', and the donating, genetic mother will lose all her rights.

A further variant is embryo donation when both husband and wife are infertile; in other words both semen and egg are donated, fertilized *in vitro* and implanted in the wife. Here, of course, neither parent is genetically related to the resulting child, and this procedure has been described as prenatal adoption, with the advantages over normal adoption in that the practice involves both pregnancy and birth. While the Committee recommended the acceptance of this procedure, it would appear to have done so with some reluctance since in the *Report* it is described as 'probably the least satisfactory form of donation' (40). No explanation is given for this view, and one must assume that it is based on the absence of genetic relationship to either of the social parents. If this is a correct assumption, then the Committee to support this conclusion would have needed to demonstrate that adopted children and the families into which they are adopted suffer some disadvantage from the absence of genetic tie. In fact, the view that adopted children do suffer some undefined disadvantage is probably a popular one, although from a cross-cultural perspective it looks like a self-fulfilling expectation.

Now it is obvious that we do not find in the ethnographic record anything corresponding closely to IVF, a procedure entirely dependent on the development of the requisite technology, which is not replicable by natural means. The result of IVF, as the Committee points out, is that, for the first time in human existence, the roles of genetic mother and carrying mother are separated. While, in the past, the social mother was not necessarily the genetic mother the latter was invariably the carrying mother. Some of the implications of this are best examined after we have considered surrogate motherhood.

Surrogacy is the practice whereby one woman carries an infant for another; the latter, the commissioning mother, takes over the child from the former, the carrying mother, after birth. The logical possibilities here are rather numerous, and depend on how the carrying mother gets impregnated and by whom. Here are some of them:

1   AI by commissioning father;

2   implantation of an embryo formed from semen and seed of commissioning parents;

3   implantation of embryo formed from seed of commissioning mother and semen of a donor;

4   AI by anonymous donor;

5   impregnation by carrying mother's husband (this would not require technological intervention).

And so on...

[...]

Overall, the Committee gained the impression that the weight of public opinion was against the practice of surrogacy. Among the arguments put forward against it, there is first the intrusion of a third party. In this case it was considered worse than AID or embryo/egg donation because 'The contribution of the carrying mother is greater, more intimate and personal, than the contribution of a semen donor' (44–5). Second, it is inconsistent with human dignity that a woman should use her uterus for profit. Third, the relationship between mother and child is distorted by surrogacy, and to become deliberately pregnant with the intention of giving the child away at birth 'is the wrong way to approach pregnancy' (45), although it is not explained what is meant by this. Fourth, 'It [surrogacy] is also potentially damaging to the child, whose bonds with the carrying mother, regardless of genetic connections, are held to be strong, and whose welfare must be considered to be of paramount importance' (45). Finally, 'surrogacy ... is degrading to the child ... since, for all practical purposes, the child will have been bought for money' (45).

[...]

We find in the discussion on surrogacy the following remark: 'We are conscious that surrogacy like egg and embryo donation may raise the question as to whether the genetic or the carrying mother is the true mother' (47). In egg and embryo donation, as in semen donation, the Committee recommended that the donor lose all rights to the donation. In surrogacy the situation is more complex since donation does not formally occur. The commissioning parents may provide the embryo, which is implanted and borne by the carrying mother until birth, when the infant reverts to the commissioning and genetic parents. The quandary the Committee finds itself in over this is that first, it recommends that the legislation that gives the child to the carrying mother in egg or embryo donation be drafted in such a way as to cover surrogacy; in other words, that the carrying mother be the legal mother and not the commissioning and genetic parents. However, the Report continues: 'If experience shows that this gives rise to an injustice for children who live with their genetic mother rather than the mother who bore them then in our view the remedy is to make the adoption laws more flexible so as to enable the genetic mother to adopt' (47). In other words, the woman to whom the child is socially most close is to be regarded as the mother.

Cases of surrogate motherhood in the ethnographic record are rare. The one that comes to mind is that of Abraham who was persuaded by his longtime barren wife Sara to take her Egyptian handmaiden Hagar. Sara said to Abraham 'go in to my maid; it may be that I shall obtain children by her'

(Genesis 16). However, if you remember, things went badly; first, because Hagar when she had conceived started to treat her mistress with contempt; and second because the child was Ishmael, who turned out to be a bad lot. 'He shall be a wild ass of a man, his hand against every man and every man's hand against him; and he shall dwell over against all his kinsmen'. However, it does also say that Sara 'gave her (Hagar) to Abram her husband as a wife'. And 'wife' is the word in the Hebrew text. This puts a rather different complexion on it since it then fits with other ethnographic examples in which a junior wife is expected to bear a child who will then belong to the senior wife. However, in all such cases, the surrogate mother is a wife. I have found no clear cut cases in the ethnography of a woman employed for a short term in order to fulfil a specific function (to bear a child that will not be hers), although some West African examples seem to come close to it. I find this lack rather surprising, given the great variety of ways in which human beings have ordered their sexual and reproductive arrangements; I cannot find any satisfactory explanation for its absence.

Source

Rivière, P. (1985) 'Unscrambling parenthood: the Warnock Report', *Anthropology Today*, **1**(4), pp. 2–7.

READING C
All Our Kin

Carol Stack

Child-keeping: 'Gimme a little sugar'

The black community has long recognized the problems and difficulties that all mothers in poverty share. Shared parental responsibility among kin has been the response. The families I knew in The Flats told me of many circumstances that required co-resident kinsmen to take care of one another's children or situations that required children to stay in a household that did not include their biological parents.

Most of the adults involved in this study had been fostered at one time or another by kinsmen. Some of their own children are currently residing in the homes of kinsmen, or have been kept by kinsmen in the past. These alternatives enable parents to cope with poverty; they are possibilities that every mother understands.

People in The Flats often regard child-keeping as part of the flux and elasticity of residence. The expansion and contraction of households, and the successive recombinations of kinsmen residing together, require adults to care for the children residing in their household. As households shift, rights and responsibilities with regard to children are shared. Those women and men who temporarily assume the kinship obligation to care for a child, fostering the child indefinitely, acquire the major cluster of rights and duties ideally associated with 'parenthood'.

Within a network of cooperating kinsmen, there may be three or more adults with whom, in turn, a child resides. In this cycle of residence changes, the size of the dwelling, employment, and many other factors determine where children sleep. Although patterns of eating, visiting, and child care may bring mothers and their children together for most of the day, the adults immediately responsible for a child change with the child's residence ...

From the point of view of the children, there may be a number of women who act as 'mothers' toward them; some just slightly older than the children themselves. A woman who intermittently raises a sister's or a niece's or a cousin's child regards their offspring as much her grandchildren as children born to her own son and daughter.

The number of people who can assume appropriate behaviors ideally associated with parental and grandparental roles is increased to include close kinsmen and friends. Consequently, the kin terms 'mother,' 'father,' 'grandmother,' and the like are not necessarily appropriate labels for describing the social roles. Children may retain ties with their parents and siblings and at the same time establish comparable relationships with other kinsmen. There is even a larger number of friends and relatives who may request a hug and kiss, 'a little sugar,' from children they watch grow up ...

Natural processes and events in the life cycle create new child-care needs and new household alignments. It is not uncommon for young children residing in the homes of rather aging kin who become too old to care for them to be shifted to another kinsman's home. At these times, the fostering parent often decides who is next in line to raise the child.

Loretta Smart, a forty-year-old Flats resident was raised by her great-grandfather for the first five years of her life. 'When I became five years old,' Loretta told me, ' my daddy just got too old to care for me. My mother was living in The Flats at the time, but my daddy asked my mother's brother and his wife to take me 'cause he really trusted them with me. I stayed with them and their three kids, but my mother came by and took care of us kids lots of times. When I was about nine years old my mother got married and from then on I stayed with her and her husband and he gave me his name.'

Close kin may fully cooperate in child care and domestic activities during times when they do not live together. On the other hand, kin may actively assume a parental right in children, insisting upon joining a household in order to help in child care. Amanda Johnson's mother had a hard time keeping track of her three daughters even when they were pretty young. 'My grandmother decided to move in with us to bring us up right. She was old then, on a small pension, and getting some help from her son. She stayed for about four years, but she and my mother didn't get on. They fought a lot. After my grandmother died, all our kin in The Flats was helping us out and we didn't want for nothing. One of my uncles kept us and fed us every Thursday and Sunday night when my mother worked, and another uncle got us all our clothing. We was really being kept good.'

For many of the families I knew in The Flats, there were circumstances that required mothers and fathers to sleep in households apart from their children. A close look at the housing of children in homes that do not include their biological parents shows how misleading it is to regard child-keeping apart from residence patterns, alliances, and the interpersonal relationships of adults, and from the daily exchanges between kinsmen in the domestic network of the child.

The beginning of a new relationship between a man and woman, or the end of a marriage or consensual union, may cause a family to temporarily separate. Geraldine Penney left her husband because she was told that he had been 'fooling around.' 'After that,' she told me, 'my family was really split in parts for a while. I sent my three oldest children to stay with my husband's aunt (husband's mother's sister), my middle girl stayed downstairs with my husband's mother, and my two youngest stayed here with my mother.'

When a woman enters a new marriage or consensual relationship, occasionally she temporarily disperses her children among kin (Goody 1966; Midgett 1969). Soon after Flats resident Henrietta Davis returned to The Flats to take care of her own children, she told me, 'My old man wanted me to leave town with him and get married. But he didn't want to take my three children. I stayed with him for about two years and my children stayed in town with my mother. Then she told me to come back and get them. I came back and I stayed.'

Occasionally adolescents decide on their own that they want to live with a kinsmen other than the one with whom they are residing, and they have that option open to them. Boys, for example, who have maintained a close relationship with their natural father may choose to go and live with him. Bernard Smith said that his father started buying him clothes when he was half grown. When Bernard was sixteen he decided to go and stay with his father because 'he lived near the center of town.' Bernard is twenty-five now, and even though he visits his mother nearly twice a week, he is still living with his father.

When a young girl becomes pregnant, the closest adult female kin of the girl, or of the unborn child, is expected to assume partial responsibility for the young child. Usually rights in such children are shared between the mother and appropriate female kin. If the mother is extremely young, she may 'give the child' to someone who wants the child – for example, to the child's father's kin, to a childless couple, or to close friends. Lily Proctor ran away from home in Mississippi when she was fourteen. She ran off to Chicago and then went to The Flats. The friends of kin from the South who took her in had two sons. She gave birth to the oldest boy's baby, but, Lily recalls, 'I was in no way ready for a baby. The baby's grandmother (father's mother) wanted the baby, so I gave my baby to her and she adopted her as her own.'

Children are sometimes given to non-kin who express love, concern, and a desire to keep a child. Oliver Lucas, a thirty-year-old Flats resident lives with his mother and his sister and her children. Oliver and his kin have been raising his girl friend's child since she was a baby. 'My girl friend had six children when I started going with her, but her baby daughter was really something else. I got so attached to that baby over about two years that when my girl friend and I quit, I asked if she would give the baby to me. She said fine, and my "daughter" has been living with me, my mother, my grandmother, my sisters and brothers ever since. My daughter is ten years old now. She sees her mother now and then, and her father takes her to church with him sometimes, but our family is really the only family she's ever had.'

Bonds of obligation, alliance, and dependence among kinsmen are created and strengthened in a variety of ways. Goods and services are the main currency exchanged among cooperating kinsmen. Children too may be transferred back and forth, 'borrowed' or 'loaned.' It is not uncommon for individuals to talk about their residence away from their mother as a fact over which she had little or no control. For example, kin may insist upon 'taking' a child to help out ...

A mother may request or require kin to keep one of her children. An offer to keep the child of a kinsman has a variety of implications for child givers and receivers. It may be that the mother has come upon hard times and desperately wants her close kinsmen to temporarily assume responsibility for her children. Kinsmen rarely refuse such requests to keep one another's children. Likewise they recognize the right of kin to request children to raise away from their own parents (Goody 1996). Individuals allow kinsmen to create alliances and obligations toward one another, obligations which may be called upon in the future...

References

GOODY, ESTHER. 1966. 'Fostering of Children in Ghana: A Preliminary Report.' *Ghana Journal of Sociology* 2:26–33.

MIDGETT, DOUGLAS K. 1969. 'Transactions in Parenthood: A West Indian Case.' Unpublished ms., University of Illinois.

Source

Stack, C. (1974) *All Our Kin*, New York, Basic Books.

Chapter 3
Children's changing lives from 1800 to 2000

Hugh Cunningham

CONTENTS

LEARNING OUTCOMES

When you have studied this chapter, you should be able to (particularly in relation to Britain):

1   Outline the development and effectiveness of policies to restrict child labour and to introduce compulsory schooling.

2   Present the arguments used both for and against the restriction of child labour.

3   Describe the role children played in the economy during the process of industrialization.

4   Describe the contribution which children made in the past to the family economy.

5   Describe the attitudes to schooling of both parents and children in the nineteenth and twentieth centuries.

6   Understand changing conceptions of the meaning of childhood during this period of time.

1 INTRODUCTION

A comparison of the experiences of the vast majority of children in European society now with those of their counterparts two hundred years ago suggests:

1   Productive work and a contribution to the family economy are now the exception rather than the norm.

2   Schooling, previously intermittent, brief, or non-existent, has become regular, lengthy (to the age of 16), and compulsory.

Measured against the changes which had taken place in, say, the previous eight hundred years, these amount to something like a revolution. My objective in this chapter is to gain an understanding of how and why these changes have occurred, and their relationship to changing ideas about childhood. Although I will draw on evidence from a number of countries in Europe and North America, I am going to concentrate on Britain. As the first country to embark on the process of industrialization, in the late eighteenth and early nineteenth centuries, Britain was also the first society to come face to face with the issues raised by children working in factories and mines, rather than with their families in the home or in agriculture. In Britain, too, there was prolonged debate about the amount (if any) and type of schooling which should be available to or enforced upon the mass of children.

What you are studying in this chapter, therefore, is the experience of childhood, the policies adopted towards children, and ideas about childhood in a particular society over a particular period of time. The justification for so doing is threefold. First, ideas about and understanding of childhood underwent a transformation in this period. Secondly, because of their economic and imperial power in the nineteenth and first half of the twentieth centuries, societies in the North were able to export ideas and practices to other societies, particularly their colonies. Thirdly, societies in the South have undergone or are undergoing what are, at least superficially, similar economic circumstances to those faced by Britain in the nineteenth century. The British experience, therefore, provides a useful benchmark against which to measure what has happened elsewhere more recently. It would be a mistake, however, to assume that other societies in the North either faced the same problems or responded to them in the same way as Britain did: as you will see in the case of Norway, for example, there could be very different responses to child labour. Nor should one assume that the British experience of childhood in the nineteenth and twentieth centuries, or that of any other society in the North, will be replicated in any straightforward way in other societies: global economic and political circumstances are different, and, equally important, societies bring to the experience of change their own ideas of the proper relationship between family, work and school. It follows that the solutions they arrive at will differ.

The historical study of childhood in any period except the very recent past suffers from the irreversible difficulty that you cannot ask questions of people who are dead – you are dependent on what they may have happened to have left behind. Fortunately, in the two centuries I am concerned with, governments, charities, newspapers and independent investigators carried out numerous enquiries into the state of children, and, although these provide what might be called an official view of childhood, there is sometimes incorporated within them the child's own voice. In addition, childhood was a central theme of imaginative writing, both poetry and fiction, in the nineteenth and twentieth centuries, and this provides us with an unrivalled means of understanding the ideas about childhood which were current.

Young girls cutting hair from hides in East Flanders in about 1900. Children were expected to use large scissors and handle mercury-dipped hides.

2 CHILD LABOUR

It was in Britain that the issue of child labour first came to the forefront of public attention. Child labour in British factories, mills and mines in the early nineteenth century took deep hold on the imagination, and continues to do so in countries in the South today: no country wants to be accused of subjecting its children to what are still called 'Dickensian conditions', a reference to the contribution Charles Dickens's novels, particularly *Hard Times* (1854), made to the outcry against conditions in early industrial society.

2.1 The development of concern

Prior to industrialization it was the norm for children to begin work as soon as they could make a useful contribution to the family's welfare; how early this might be would depend on the local economy. In agriculture there were some jobs, for example crow-scaring, which children could do in their early years, but many agricultural tasks required strength and stamina. As R. H. Greg, a defender of the use of child labour in factories, put it in 1837, 'Boys are of little use, girls of still less, in agricultural countries, before the age of 18' (quoted in Cunningham, 1990). This was overstated, but it accurately identified the difficulty of finding employment for younger children where agriculture was the sole occupation. Simple hand technology in lace-making, straw plaiting and spinning provided much more opportunity, and it was again a commonplace that in these industries in the countryside there was much more scope for child employment – and in the eighteenth century and in many areas into the nineteenth century, middle-class commentators were looking for ways of providing employment for children, fearing otherwise that idleness would lead them into misbehaviour and crime.

In pre-industrial Britain there were no laws specifically governing the work of young children, but once they were of an age to leave home, a corpus of law and custom offered them some protection. Many children left home in their early teens to become farm servants under contracts which bound them to stay at a particular farm for one year. Other children, normally a little older, were bound as apprentices to learn a skill. Parishes took responsibility for binding out children who were in their care because of the poverty or death of the parents. In these apprenticeship arrangements children might be exploited – but one of the reasons we know that might be the case is that court cases were brought against the masters.

It was only when children began to be concentrated in workplaces in the early industrial revolution that there was a more sustained questioning of the appropriateness of certain types of work for children.

Mrs Dobbins's lace school in Stokenchurch, Buckinghamshire, England in 1860.
In European countries lacemaking relied heavily on the labour of young girls.

Young children preparing straw for straw caners in a rural area outside Antwerp in
the early 1900s.

Allow about 20 minutes

ACTIVITY I   Child labour in the 1830s and 1840s

Read the contemporary accounts quoted below, and note down what they can tell us about the nature of the concern about child labour:

> J. H. Green, Esq., FRS [a surgeon at St Thomas's Hospital in London]: ' ... Children were not designed for labour, and although in the artificial state of society in which we live, and considering the imperative demands for sustenance which oblige the poor to employ their children, some labour must be permitted, yet both our conscience and our feelings equally demand that the labour of children should be under such restrictions as will ensure them against their being made the victims of avarice and disease, and as will render it compatible with their physical and moral welfare.'

(evidence to the Factories Inquiry Commission, 1832, in British Parliamentary Papers, 1968a, p. 587)

> Mr Sadler has the misfortune to think that it is not right, nor proper, nor religious, nor Englishmanlike to allow little English children to be kept at work till their limbs are distorted, their health destroyed, their morals corrupted, their minds misinformed, while their able-bodied parents are allowed to witness the unhappy lot of their offspring unemployed and in distress.

(*Leeds Intelligencer*, 13 December 1832, quoted in Cunningham, 1991, p. 86)

> Children employed in factories, as a distinct class, form a very considerable proportion of the infant population. We have found that the numbers so employed are rapidly increasing, not only in proportion to the increase of the population employed in manufacturing industry, but, in consequence of the tendency of improvements in machinery to throw more and more of the work upon children, to the displacement of adult labour.

(Royal Commission on the Employment of Children in Factories, 1833, in British Parliamentary Papers, 1968b, p. 51)

> Sarah Gooder, aged 8 years:– 'I'm a trapper in the Gawber pit. It does not tire me, but I have to trap without a light and I'm scared. I go at four and sometimes half past three in the morning and come out at five and half past. I never go to sleep. Sometimes I sing when I've light, but not in the dark; I dare not sing then. I don't like being in the pit. I am very sleepy when I go sometimes in the morning ... I would like to be at school far better than in the pit.'

(evidence to the Children's Employment Commission, 1842, in British Parliamentary Papers, 1968c, pp. 252–3)

> The young lambs are bleating in the meadows,
>   The young birds are chirping in the nest,
> The young fawns are playing with the shadows
>   The young flowers are blowing toward the west –
> But the young, young children, O my brothers,
>   They are weeping bitterly!
> They are weeping in the playtime of the others,
>   In the country of the free.

(Elizabeth Barrett Browning, 'The Cry of the Children', 1844)

COMMENT

These extracts show that there was medical opinion that nature had not intended that children should be put to work which would impair their physical growth – though it is interesting to note that Green was also concerned about the moral consequences for children of excessive labour. Michael Sadler led the campaign in the House of Commons in the early 1830s against child labour, and the *Leeds Intelligencer* neatly outlines his views. To many people at the time the natural order seemed to be being inverted: parents were unemployed, and children had to work to keep the family alive. Sadler saw this as not only physically and morally harmful to the children, but it was also an affront to his sense of national pride – his Englishness. The same sense of a natural order being overturned and of national outrage ('the country of the free' in the last line refers to Britain) pervades Browning's poem, an example of the close relationship between romanticism and the campaigns to curtail child labour. The poem's impact was immense: 'All honour unto reverence, to Mrs Barrett Browning for her passionate as compassionate lay of the 'Cry of the Children': scalding tears have baptized it with holier chrysm than apostolical hands', wrote George Smith in his *The Cry of the Children from the Brickyards of England*, 1871. The Royal Commission of 1833 carefully avoided any emotional language, but its cool assessment that child labour was on the increase, and that there would be a continuing substitution of child labour for adult, made a powerful case for intervention in the labour market to protect

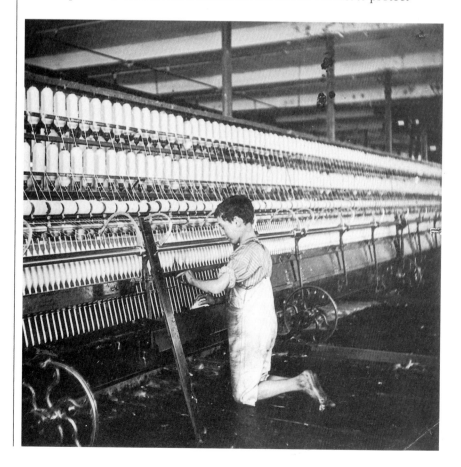

A boy 'piecer' in a spinning mill in Oldham, Lancashire about 1900. Piecing (joining threads during the spinning and winding process) was seen as a children's job.

An illustration from the Royal Commission on the Condition and Treatment of Children Employed in the Mines and Manufactories of the United Kingdom. The Commission's report was published in 1842 and led to the Mines and Collieries Act of the same year, which prohibited boys and girls under ten from working underground.

children: the outcome was the 1833 Factory Act, the first effective piece of legislation. In the fourth extract a child relates her experience of work as a trapper in a mine. Her crucial job, for thirteen and a half hours a day, was to control the flow of air into the pit by opening and closing a trap door. Her sister, aged seventeen, also worked in the pit, and, the Commission was told, their father depended on the work of the two girls to support the family. Although Sarah Gooder's work was not physically demanding except in terms of staying awake (though it would become so as she got older and graduated from trapping to hauling the coal from pit head to shaft), your reaction, like that of most people, is likely to be that it was entirely inappropriate that a child should be working for such long hours in such conditions. But it is worth noting that we do here, in an official enquiry, have a rare opportunity to hear what a child thought of her life and working conditions in a staple industry of the nineteenth century.

2.2 Historians and child labour

Historians have responded in two main ways to the issue of child labour in the industrialization of Britain. One approach has been to use information taken from the ten-yearly censuses to try to build up a picture of the proportion of children who were in employment, and of the types of jobs they did. According to the 1851 census for England and Wales only 2 per cent of boys aged five to nine, and only 1.4 per cent of girls of the same age were in employment. Not surprisingly, a higher percentage of ten to fourteen year olds were shown to be in employment as Activity 2 demonstrates.

Allow about 15 minutes

ACTIVITY 2   Child employment in 1851

Examine Tables 1 and 2 and note down any conclusions you think you can make from them about the amount and kind of work children did. Note also the differences between boys' and girls' occupations.

The information comes from the census taken in 1851. How reliable do you think it may be?

Table 1   Employment of children aged ten to fourteen in England and Wales 1851: boys

Occupation	Number employed	% of 10–14 employed	% of all 10–14
Agricultural labour	73,054	20.7	7.6
Messenger	38,130	10.8	4.0
Farm servant	25,667	7.3	2.7
Cotton	25,613	7.3	2.7
Coalmining	23,038	6.5	2.4
Labourer	13,478	3.8	1.4
Shoemaker	9,700	2.8	1.0
Wool	9,242	2.6	1.0
Building	9,079	2.6	0.9
Worsted	9,061	2.6	0.9
Other occupations	116,537	33.0	12.1
		100.0	36.7

Table 2   Employment of children aged ten to fourteen in England and Wales 1851: girls

Occupation	Number employed	% of 10–14 employed	% of all 10–14
Domestic servant	50,065	26.5	5.3
Cotton	29,038	15.4	3.1
Worsted	10,586	5.6	1.1
Silk	10,533	5.6	1.1
Farm servant	10,085	5.3	1.1
Lace	8,628	4.6	0.9
Wool	7,333	3.9	0.8
Nurse	6,938	3.7	0.7
Milliner (hat making)	6,048	3.2	0.6
Straw plait	5,041	2.7	0.5
Other occupations	44,682	23.7	4.7
		100.0	19.9

COMMENT

The conclusions which most historians draw from these figures are that employment of children was much less widespread than one might have supposed, and that the types of jobs which those children who worked did were predominantly what might be called traditional – agriculture for boys and domestic service for girls. As the final column shows, only 36.7 per cent of all ten to fourteen year old boys were recorded as in employment, and only 19.9 per cent of all girls. The categories of employment listed are those used in the census, and cover over two-thirds of all the boys in employment and over three-quarters of all the girls. In relation to the boys, taking those in agriculture and the farm servants together shows that 28 per cent of all the boys in employment were in that sector of the economy. On the other side, cotton, coal, wool and worsted might count as part of the industrial economy, employing 19 per cent of all the boys in employment. As for the girls, the importance of domestic service is obvious, and some of the 3.7 per cent listed as nurses might be in jobs very similar to domestic service. On the other hand, 38 per cent of all the girls employed were working in textiles (cotton, worsted, silk, lace, wool, straw plaiting). What reliance can be placed on these figures? The information was collected by house-to-house visits by census enumerators who were dependent on what they were told. It seems likely that they may have under-recorded the amount of part-time and occasional work, particularly by girls helping their mothers at home. The census returns, helpful though they are in giving some sense of the map of juvenile employment, leave many questions unanswered.

Historians have taken a second approach to this issue, concentrating on the sectors of the industrializing economy which made intensive use of child labour. They draw attention to manufacturers who claimed that the success of their industries was dependent on the use of child labour, arguing that children's nimble fingers alone could tie broken cotton thread, or that, because of the low tunnels, small children were needed to pull coal to the pit shafts, or that the cheap labour of children alone made their industries competitive in the world market. Children in textiles and mines might be a minority of all children working, but they were nevertheless a significant proportion of the workforce in industries central to the industrializing economy. In the British cotton industry in 1835, 43 per cent of the workers were under eighteen (Nardinelli, 1990, p. 109). In the words of a foreman in a wool mill in 1833, 'factories cannot be carried on without children' (British Parliamentary Papers, 1968c, C1, p. 96). In the British coal industry in the mid-nineteenth century, 13 per cent of the labour force was aged under fifteen; in the Belgian coal and coke industry, 22.4 per cent were under sixteen (Cunningham, 2000, p. 412).

These two positions taken by historians, the one downplaying the significance of the changes in the work that children did during the industrial revolution, the other emphasizing its novelty and importance, often extend to judgements on the morality of what was happening. What this often amounts to is a judgement on the morality of capitalism. The first group of historians points to evidence of exploitation of children in work not associated with the industrial revolution and tends to blame parents for the mistreatment of children, wherever it was happening. The second group, following on from those who campaigned for reform at the time, highlights the evidence of cruelty up chimneys and in factories and mines and lays the blame for it on employers and overseers, or on the competitiveness built into capitalism. This group concludes, in the words of E. P. Thompson, that 'the exploitation of little children, on this scale and with this intensity, was one of the most shameful events in our history' (Thompson, 1963, p. 349). By focusing their attention on different aspects of child labour, and sometimes using evidence selectively, historians draw markedly different conclusions about child labour in industrializing Britain. Historians of child labour may sometimes appear to be engaged in a moral argument as much as in a cool diagnosis of the evidence.

2.3 Reform

The voices calling for control of child labour were powerful ones. By the mid-nineteenth century, legislation was in force to ban child labour in textile mills below the age of nine and in mines below the age of ten, and to control conditions for older children. It was also apparent that such legislation was not, as opponents had feared, going to ruin the industries where it applied. The road was open to legislation in other industries, and a process was set in train whereby child labour laws were passed in industry after industry. Government put its weight behind what became called the 'half-time system' under which children would spend half their time at school and half their time at work, a system which was widely promoted by people of all political persuasions for most of the nineteenth century. It was only towards the end of the nineteenth century that compulsory full-time education was introduced, as you will see in Section 3. Legislative action, however, was by no means a straightforward success story: sometimes an interest group was able to weaken the proposed laws; sometimes the legislation was poorly drafted and its measures avoided by employers and difficult to enforce by inspectors. On top of this, a whole sector of the economy – what came to be called the informal sector (small unregulated backstreet workshops, street trading etc.) – was thought to be beyond the reach of legislation. Nevertheless, no one could doubt that in more and more forms of employment child labour was being brought within the law.

These reforms did not mean that children no longer worked, but rather that they ceased to be of central importance in the key industries of a growing economy. Parents, as you will see in Section 4, still needed the contributions which children could make to the family economy, and children found work in an age-graded labour market on the margin of the industrial economy as messengers, servants, van-boys, street-sellers and such occupations. There was, in the early twentieth century, much concern about this child and youth labour market. The work the young people did seemed to contain no training and thus failed to equip them with the skills necessary for success in the adult labour market. There was worry about the moral consequences of allowing the young, particularly girls, to sell on the streets – many people believed this was the highroad to prostitution. Laws were introduced to try to control this most worrying aspect of the child and youth labour market, but attempts to supplement it with compulsory training and educational sessions came to nothing. A labour market for young people in which they found employment in parts of the service sector became established, and, although the age at which people enter it may have risen, it remains the normal choice for young people seeking work (Lavalette, 1999). For example, best estimates suggest at least 2 million young people in the UK take on part-time work before they reach the official school-leaving age at sixteen (The Open University, 2003).

2.4 Child labour in international perspective

The existence, to this day, of a labour market for children in Britain serves as a useful reminder that those who campaigned against the excesses of child labour did not win all the arguments. By and large, of course, and particularly for children below, say, the age of twelve, the amount of child labour in societies in the North has undergone a major decline since the mid-nineteenth century. It is easy to forget that the process by which decline was achieved was contested, and that the reasons for the decline remain a matter of uncertainty. Nor should anyone imagine that in all European societies, there was a knee-jerk sense that child labour was wrong: Norway provides an interesting case study:

READING

Reading A describes the results of a survey carried out in Kristiania in 1912, comparing it with the results of a previous survey conducted in the 1870s. Note down:

1   What changes does the author, Schrumpf, argue had occurred between the two surveys?
2   In what ways did the experience of work differ for boys and girls?
3   What were the attitudes of teachers to children working?

COMMENT

In 1875 children in Norway worked long hours, often in factories and alongside adults. In 1912 school was the priority in children's lives; they still worked, but now for shorter hours, running errands if they were boys or working in domestic service if they were girls. And whereas in 1875 teachers had worried about the impact of work on schooling, by 1912 they saw work as a beneficial complement to school. We should not, therefore, assume that the decline of child labour was inevitable or necessarily progressive.

By the late nineteenth and early twentieth centuries, the British were celebrating what they saw as the extension around the world of their pioneering approach to child labour, that is the passage of enforceable laws specific to each industry (see Box 1 on p. 112). Other countries did not necessarily see things in the same way as the British did. The British delegate to the first international conference on the issue, at Berlin in 1890, was shocked to find that the British were less advanced in child labour legislation than many other European countries, though he had little success in persuading his compatriots of this fact (Cunningham, 2001, p. 133).

Errand boy at a vegetable market, Oslo, Norway. Painting by Christian Krohg, 1880.

By the 1880s, with the notable exception of the United States, industrializing countries had some sort of child labour laws in operation at national level. Frequently the first attempt at legislation had been difficult to enforce and further legislation was required. Thus in France the 1841 Child Labour Law needed reinforcement by a second law passed in 1874, and in Prussia the law of 1853, which established twelve as a minimum age for work, needed to be supplemented by a further law in 1878.

Reasons for the decline in child labour

The factors which may have led to a decline in child labour can be divided into five categories:

Child labour and technology

It has frequently been argued that advances in technology have progressively reduced the amount of child labour – and that child labour laws are merely supplementary to this process. There is little substance to this comforting argument, comforting because it suggests that extensive use of child labour is merely a transitional phenomenon in any society. It is true that there are cases where a demand for child labour has been reduced by technological innovation, a classic case being the replacement of messenger boys in American department stores by machinery. But against this must be set two kinds of evidence. First, entrepreneurs (as in the British textile industry) have sometimes had machinery designed specifically so that children can operate it. Secondly, the same technology can be in operation in different contexts using very different amounts of child labour: in the American South, for example, there was far higher use of child labour than in the North despite use of the same technology. Technology, then, should be seen as a factor which may influence the level of child labour, but will very rarely determine it.

Child labour and family incomes

Some people have argued (e.g. Nardinelli, 1990) that the amount of child labour used in any society is ultimately a decision of the parents of the children employed. When family incomes are low, then there is a powerful pressure on parents to put their children to work so as to increase family income. As adult wages rise, parents will begin to see some economic advantage in investing in their children by prolonging their education rather than cashing in on their utility by putting them to work at the earliest possible moment. As in the technology analysis, child labour laws are seen as at most supplementary to other more fundamental processes leading to the reduction of child labour as an economy advances.

Child labour and culture

Countries which have passed through similar stages of economic development have made use of different levels of child labour. Belgium, for example, was a heavy user of children's labour from a young age, whereas in Japan the employment of younger children was rare. One explanation for this lies in different attitudes to children in different countries. Western visitors to Japan in the late nineteenth and early twentieth centuries frequently drew attention to the adult love of and tenderness towards children. 'Japan is the paradise for children', enthused an American professor in 1917. It seems likely that this cultural trait had as a consequence an aversion to the employment of children at a young age (Saito, 1996).

School and child labour

Societies which placed a high value on education may also have had relatively low levels of child labour. In some European Protestant countries compulsory schooling was introduced in the sixteenth and seventeenth centuries prompted by the belief that an ability to read the Bible was essential for salvation. There was a further boost to the introduction of compulsory schooling with the eighteenth-century Enlightenment: the 'enlightened despots' who ruled many European countries vied with each other in their plans for education. Furthermore, in contrast to Britain, some other countries or authorities preferred to tackle the issue of child labour by compelling children to attend school rather than forbidding them, industry by industry, from working. The advantage of this approach was that it prevented children simply moving from jobs in those industries where legislation was in force to those in the informal economy where it was not. The effectiveness depended on the extent to which regular attendance at school could be enforced (Weiner, 1991).

International moves to control child labour

One of the arguments used by those opposed to child labour laws was that, applied country by country, they would render those who had outlawed child labour less competitive in a global market. The answer to some seemed to be an approach at international level to lay down standards to which all countries should adhere. The first attempt to do this was at Berlin in 1890, but there was no apparatus to ensure compliance. A factor in this meeting and indeed in all subsequent international meetings on the topic of child labour was a fear that socialists might exploit the child labour issue by arguing that it was an evil intrinsic to capitalism. The International Labour Office (ILO), set up in the aftermath of the First World War and of the Russian Revolution of 1917, had as one of its objectives the elimination of child labour, a programme at least in part motivated by worry about the contagion of Bolshevism. A further factor encouraging a global approach to child labour was the existence of European empires. Countries with empires, such as Britain, sought to extend the laws to their colonies, or were to an extent forced into doing so by ILO conventions, though they normally managed to adjust them to fit the peculiarities of particular labour markets. Faced with a ban on night work in their Indonesian colony, the Dutch authorities imaginatively redefined the meaning of 'night' so that it covered fewer hours (White, 1994, p. 863).

The impact of these various factors which might control the level of child labour varied enormously from country to country. The most obvious disparity was between Europe and the United States where in the first half of the twentieth century there was a prolonged and profound debate about child labour, as we can see in Reading B.

READING

Now read Reading B and consider the following questions.

1   What kinds of arguments were made 'in defence of the useful child'?

2   Who made them?

3   What kind of ideal of childhood was held by those who argued 'in defence of the useless child'?

In the United States, as Zelizer shows, there were powerful ideological forces operating against the imposition of effective child labour laws: not only an adherence to the free market, but also a reluctance to impose federal decisions on individual states; the southern states in the first half of the twentieth century were notorious for their extensive use of child labour. The legacy of slavery could still be seen in local economies based on the labour of poorly paid black children and families. It is a case which shows that any notion of an almost inevitable decline in the amount of child labour as economies develop is misleading and simplistic.

SUMMARY OF SECTION 2

- The industrial revolution disrupted traditional patterns of child labour.
- Historians differ in their interpretation and judgement of child labour in the industrial revolution.
- Labour laws helped to push working children to jobs on the margin of the economy.
- Experts offer differing interpretations of the decline of child labour, and note that attitudes to it varied from country to country.

3 SCHOOLING

That children should receive some schooling was widely though not universally accepted by the beginning of the nineteenth century. As mentioned in Section 2, in some Protestant countries in northern Europe policies to provide schooling for all children had been in place since the sixteenth century. Within Britain, England and Wales, and to a much lesser extent Scotland, were, in European terms, laggards in provision of schooling by the state, but this did not mean that there was no schooling.

3.1 Schooling before compulsion

In England and Wales, by the 1830s working-class children might go to fee-paying private schools (often called dame schools), to Sunday Schools which were initiated in the 1780s and were particularly important where opportunities for child labour were greatest (Snell, 1999), or to one of the

'Old woman's school, Camden Town'.

schools run by Christian charitable organizations which began to receive some state money. Schooling, however, was compulsory only for children in the care of the Poor Law, and, on a half-time basis, for children in textile mills subject to the 1833 Factory Act. There is no evidence of precisely what proportion of children went to school or for how long, or how effective their schooling was. Most children received some schooling, but it was intermittent, fitted around work, and rarely extended beyond the age of ten. We can get some measure of its effectiveness by examining how many brides and grooms were able to sign their names in the register when they got married: in the 1830s it was about two-thirds of grooms and half of brides, proportions which gradually improved to about 95 per cent of both sexes by the end of the nineteenth century – but by then schooling was compulsory.

3.2 The introduction of compulsory schooling

Child labour laws introduced during the nineteenth century imposed increasing restrictions on the work children could do. At the same time there was growing concern about the number of children who were receiving no schooling or what was perceived to be inadequate schooling. Child labour laws, however, proceeded along a different track to schooling laws, and the introduction of compulsory schooling was not, in Britain at any rate, part of a move to halt child labour; rather it was an attempt to bring within the framework of state-recognized schools those children whom the census returned neither as 'scholars' (the name for those who were at school), nor as engaged in productive labour. In short, as the Registrar-General put it in 1871, concern was focused on the 'unemployed children' – themselves often equated with 'street children' who were the focus of much political and social anxiety in the middle years of the nineteenth century. In England and Wales, the state proceeded with caution over a decade and more, only making schooling compulsory at national level in 1880, and then only for those aged five to ten (in Scotland there was less resistance to compulsory school which was introduced in 1873 for those aged five to thirteen).

The enforcement of compulsion was a long-drawn-out process with newly appointed school attendance officers bringing many parents before the courts for the non-attendance of their children: it was until 1916 the most common offence after drunkenness. Associated with it was an attack on the private schools which working-class parents often preferred. These gave parents a measure of control over attendance, punishment and syllabus, aspects of them which the state was determined to change. Over the late nineteenth and early twentieth centuries the private schools submitted, not without protest but generally without avail, to their own demise (Gardner, 1984). The tensions involved in this transition to a society in which compulsory schooling became the norm and state control increased are explored in the extract by Gardner in Reading C.

Early twentieth-century elementary school classroom, England.

READING

Now read Reading C and consider the following questions:

1   Why were politicians and officials worried about the possible consequences of introducing compulsory schooling?

2   In what ways were the attendance officers 'key agents' in establishing compulsory schooling?

3   What light does the extract shed on the acquisition of 'the school habit' in the late nineteenth century?

4   Do working-class parents nowadays think of schools as theirs?

In the early twentieth century children attended in about equal numbers local authority schools and 'voluntary' schools, run by the religious denominations with state aid and state inspection. Contemporaries were well aware that these 'elementary' schools were for the three-quarters of the population who were working-class. In the language of the time, there were 'ladders' which enabled a bright child to sit for a scholarship for admittance to secondary schooling, and the grammar schools had to make 25 per cent of their places available to such children, but for the vast majority of working-class children school was confined to the elementary level with a leaving age of twelve or thirteen. There were many moves to improve the education offered within them: the syllabus was widened, though often in a gendered way, with sewing and domestic science for girls; the design of school buildings was improved with separate

Girls learning to sew at a Church of England elementary school, Liverpool.

classrooms and more light; the close tie between the funding a school received and the performance of children at an inspection, a feature of the system from the 1860s to the 1890s, was broken. Most adults who were interviewed later in life about their experience in the elementary schools of the late nineteenth and early twentieth centuries had positive things to say about it, and seemed to regret leaving (Rose, 1993).

Nevertheless, there is also much evidence of school regimes maintained by harsh corporal punishment, of truanting by children, sometimes with the encouragement of parents who needed help in the home or in increasing family income, of methods of teaching which consisted of little other than rote learning, and of a syllabus designed to instil conformity (Humphries, 1981). Above all, there was a regime of low expectations by most teachers for most children – these were working-class children and most of them would end up in working-class jobs.

SUMMARY OF SECTION 3

- Most children received some elementary schooling before it was made compulsory in 1880.
- The introduction of compulsion in Britain was gradual and hesitant and met with some opposition.
- Children's experience of schooling was highly dependent on their class and gender.

4 CHILDREN AND THE FAMILY ECONOMY

Although children had been moved to the margins of the national economy by the end of the nineteenth century, and although regular attendance at school had become the norm, children in the first half of the twentieth century remained key contributors to the family economy.

Allow about 15 minutes

ACTIVITY 3 Children, work and family

Read the contemporary accounts below and ask yourself:

1 What kind of pressures were there for working-class children to contribute to the family economy in the late nineteenth and early twentieth centuries?

2 What evidence is there in the extracts of the attitude of children to making such contributions?

Election, 1900. Children outside a school in Farnworth, Bolton, with 'half-timers' in the front in their working clothes.

Many of those now in class 'B' [earning 18 shillings to 21 shillings a week, the second lowest earning category] will rise into a higher class as soon as the children begin to earn money, possibly to sink back again, however, when their children marry and leave home. The importance attaching to the earnings of the children in the families of the poor reminds us how great must be the temptation to take children away from school at the earliest possible moment, in order that they may begin to earn.

(Rowntree, 1902, p. 59)

Clifford Hills, born 1904

I went to work at the age of nine for two shillings per week. I went at seven in the morning till ten and then went to school. I come out of school at four o'clock and went as kitchen boy till half past five, mostly it was nearer six. And on Saturday morning I went from seven till one, for two shillings a week ... I probably had to go to the butchers with this two shillings to get the Sunday joint, which lasted us for Sunday dinner time and perhaps Monday dinner time.

(Thompson, 1981, pp. 57–8)

James Brady, born 1898 in Rochdale, Lancashire

... The sheer force of economic necessity drove my astute mother to pre-empt my twelfth birthday by a couple of weeks and find a job for me as an alley-sweeper half-time ... the prospect of 'starting work' pleased me ... with father bringing home less than 30 shillings a week, it gave me satisfaction to know that I would soon become a breadwinner to help the family budget.

(Burnett, 1982, p. 305)

Jane Taverner, recording her experience in the 1920s

I was put in for the scholarship [to proceed to grammar school at the age of fourteen]. I remember the rating I got because I didn't pass. I was fully expected to pass, but I didn't try because I knew that if I passed, I couldn't go. I wanted to pass, but you see it was no use, because although there was help, it wouldn't have been enough for our family ... I would have liked to have been a teacher, but, you see, I knew what I was going to do and it was something I wasn't going to like. I had to go into service, for one thing to make room for the boys to sleep as they got older.

(Humphries, 1981, p. 60)

COMMENT

The first quotation is from Rowntree's influential survey of poverty in York right at the end of the nineteenth century which laid bare the family life cycle, an alternation of periods of poverty and relative prosperity. The poverty was most acute when children were young and not earning, and in old age; but while the children remained at home and were able to contribute something to the family budget, the family was likely to be relatively well-off. Children in working-class families, the eldest in particular, were under considerable pressure to make some contribution to the family budget at an early age. Normally this would begin while they were still at school, early in the morning, after school, or truanting. In rural areas both harvest requirements and family needs meant that schools had to adjust term dates to the agricultural calendar. Children, such as Clifford Hills and James Brady, often felt proud that they were making a contribution to the family, and it was the usual practice for them to hand over any earnings to their mothers who might then give them back a small percentage for their own expenditure. It was when children reached the age at which they could legally leave school that the tensions between individual ambitions and family needs might surface – and the latter nearly always had priority. There are many accounts, like that of Jane Taverner, of children deliberately passing up the opportunity of proceeding to secondary schooling because of the economic or other needs, such as space, of the family. But no one could doubt the importance of children's contributions. The best evidence for it comes from a survey carried out in America and Europe in the late 1880s. The results need to be evaluated against a contemporary assumption that an adult male bread-winner should be able to provide for his entire family. In fact, by the time the adult male was in his fifties, children in the US were contributing about one-third of family income and those in Europe over 40 per cent. Powerful ideological forces and practical reasons explain why families turned to children rather than mothers to supplement adult male wages: the ideology was that nature dictated that women's role should be that of home-maker, and the demands of that role were in fact so considerable that married women tended to avoid full-time regular employment. Children, therefore, became the supplementary wage-earners (Cunningham, 2000, pp. 420–5).

4.1 The decline of contributions by children to the family economy

As they got older and their wages increased, teenagers kept or received back a higher percentage of their earnings, and in the first half of the twentieth century we can begin to see the beginnings of a teenage consumer market which was to receive massive attention from the 1950s. Until then, however, family needs seem to have had precedence over any desire on the part of working-class teenagers to improve their life-chances through further study or to express their individuality through consumption: families needed the children's contributions and children, some doubtless reluctantly, accepted that. Girls, especially, knew from an early age that they would be expected to provide assistance to their mothers in the running of the home.

These expectations collapsed from the 1950s. We know little about the negotiations and doubtless conflicts within families which resulted in a much lower expectation that children could be expected to contribute to the family economy. Factors external to the family undoubtedly affected it: wages were rising, making it more possible for the father to meet the needs of the family; mothers, as their children got older, were beginning to enter the labour market; teenagers themselves were being encouraged by advertising to spend their earnings – and they were enjoying the benefits of a buoyant youth labour market. But overriding these factors was perhaps something more fundamental: working-class families were beginning to place a high value on giving the best to their children; rather than children being expected to make sacrifices for the family, the adults in the family would make sacrifices for the sake of the children. A cameo captures well the nature of the change: in Bethnal Green in the early 1950s a working-class mother recorded how 'When I was a kid Dad always had the best of everything. Now it's the children who get the best of it. If there's one pork chop left, the kiddy gets it' (Young and Wilmott, 1968, p. 28). In Nottingham a decade later another mother explained that 'I think myself you give in to your own where you couldn't have it – you think to yourself, well I didn't get this, and I'll see that he gets it' (Newson and Newson, 1963, p. 239). In Swansea it was found that 'Young and grown children living at home do very little domestic work'; mothers took on the whole burden (Leonard, 1980, p. 58). In brief, social arrangements within households had changed, and the balance of emotional power had switched away from adults towards children, who were now, as Zelizer suggested, 'invested with sentimental or religious meaning' (Zelizer, 1985, p. 11).

Commentators saw the most obvious outcome of this change in the behaviour of teenagers, but the assumption of young wage-earners that when they started working they would keep for themselves the bulk of their earnings, paying perhaps a rather nominal sum to their mothers for maintenance, was itself rooted in behavioural changes in childhood: in lower expectations of any help around the house, in the giving of pocket money to children, in parental encouragement of educational achievement. A consequence of this was that school now became a more central part of children's lives; for one thing it lasted longer, up to sixteen (see Section 5.2). For another parents' hopes that their children's lives might be better than their own were to a considerable degree focused on educational success. Work for children came later in life than it had done up to mid-century and was perceived as a means of adding to pocket money rather than as providing a crucial ingredient of the family budget: in the 1990s only 1 per cent of young people aged thirteen to eighteen gave as a reason for working because it was 'essential for making ends meet for my family' (Cunningham, 2000, pp. 423–4).

SUMMARY OF SECTION 4

- Children in working-class families in the late nineteenth and first half of the twentieth centuries made a key contribution to their family economies.
- In the 1950s the assumption that teenagers should contribute to the family economy began to collapse, reflecting changes in the relationship between parents and children.

5 PROLONGING CHILDHOOD

In the course of the twentieth century common ideas about the age when childhood begins and when it ends changed. There remains much room for disagreement about both the beginning and the ending, but it is very likely that most people now see childhood as a more prolonged stage of life than would have been common at the beginning of the twentieth century. In this section, you will examine the reasons for this and its consequences.

5.1 Nineteenth-century ideas about childhood

On looking back into the nineteenth century, what is most striking is the range of ages which childhood was thought to cover. In 1821 the Society for Superceding the Necessity of Climbing Boys was pleased to be able to report that the master chimney sweeps had agreed not to begin apprenticeships for climbing boys until the age of ten (it had previously been eight), for childhood, it claimed, had by then ended, and a boy could look after his own interests. The Royal Commission of 1833 enquiring into the factories thought childhood ended at fourteen:

> in general at or about the fourteenth year young persons are no longer treated as children; they are not usually chastised by corporal punishment, and at the same time an important change takes place in what may be termed their domestic condition. For the most part they cease to be under the complete control of their parents and guardians. They begin to retain a part of their wages. They frequently pay for their own lodging, board, and clothing. They usually make their own contracts, and are, in the proper sense of the word, free agents ...

(British Parliamentary Papers, 1968b, p. 52).

A boy sweep and his master in the 1860s. Acts of Parliament had banned climbing boys but the public preferred boys to machines and the Acts were not enforced. The first effective act was the Chimney Sweeper Act of 1875.

What this meant was that, in the view of the Royal Commission, they no longer needed any special protection in the employment market. How far the Royal Commission was accurately reporting contemporary opinion is uncertain. Certainly there were those who held a very different view. When in the middle of the nineteenth century the investigative journalist, Henry Mayhew (who himself thought childhood ended at fifteen), interviewed a young watercress seller on the streets of London, he made the mistake of asking her whether she spent her earnings on sweets. 'All my money I earns,' she replied, 'I puts in a club and draws it out to buy clothes with. It's better than spending it in sweet-stuff, for them as has a living to earn. Besides it's like a child to care for sugar-sticks, and not like one who's got a living and vittals to earn. I ain't a child, and I shan't be a woman till I'm twenty, but I'm past eight, I am' (Cunningham, 1991, pp. 108–10). The watercress seller, already in her third job (she had previously helped her mother in the fur trade and looked after an aunt's baby), was giving voice to what was probably a widely held view, that childhood ended when work began If that is so, the later work began, the longer childhood would be.

The nineteenth century also gave rise to a view, not infrequently heard today, that childhood never ends – or perhaps rather that it *should* never end. That view originated in the second generation of Romantic writers in the middle years of the nineteenth century. The first generation of Romantic poets, Wordsworth pre-eminent among them, had helped to give wide circulation to the view that children had qualities and attributes which in many ways made them superior to world-weary adults. It was a logical extension of this that writers like Charles Dickens should present us with compelling portraits of adults who had allowed childhood qualities to dissipate. Scrooge in *A Christmas Carol* is the best known. Equally Dickens could present benevolent child-like adults, like the Cheerybles in *Nicholas Nickleby* who do nothing but good. Keep the spirit and qualities of childhood alive in you was the message, or you will in effect die.

5.2 Raising the school-leaving age

As I suggested above, the raising of the school-leaving age has almost certainly been the key agent in prolonging childhood. It rose gradually from the age of ten, set in England and Wales in 1880, but with exemptions and distinctive local practices; fourteen became the leaving age for all children only with the implementation of the 1918 Education Act. Thereafter it was raised to fifteen with the 1944 Education Act and to sixteen in 1973.

There have been few bigger changes in the experience of childhood than the raising of the school-leaving age. In 1900, as in 1800, all children except those from the upper and upper-middle classes, would have been in the labour market by, at the latest, the age of fourteen. The extension of the school-leaving age was an extension of childhood – for most children saw the day they left school as a transition away from childhood.

Many people believe that raising the school-leaving age has been a progressive change brought about by those with the best interests of children at heart – and to an extent this is correct. But there were also other factors involved which challenge this explanation. Economically, any rise in the school-leaving age removed an age cohort for a further year from the full-time labour market, and might therefore ease fears of unemployment. Socially and culturally, raising the age of leaving could help to resolve the concern that young teenagers were leaving behind, too early, the school's disciplinary, moral and learning framework which might properly prepare them for adulthood. Politically, the rise in the school-leaving age both increased and contained opportunities for working-class children. Under the 1944 Act, all children went to secondary school, but the secondary schools were of three kinds: grammar schools, technical schools and secondary modern schools. The middle tier, the technical schools, were sparse on the ground, and most children underwent a test at the age of eleven which determined whether they would go to the broadly middle-class grammar schools or to the much more numerous and predominantly working-class secondary modern schools. The grammar schools were open to bright working-class children,

Students at a secondary modern in the 1940s.

but their memories of those schools are often of leaving behind friends from their neighbourhood, and entering uneasily into the embrace of a middle-class world (Jackson and Marsden, 1962). In effect, the class structure of education in Britain, rooted deeply in its origins, was preserved. In the 1960s and 1970s the inequalities built into this system of secondary schooling were exposed and attacked, and in most areas of the country comprehensive schools, which had no entry test, came into existence to cater for children of all abilities. Streaming within schools and parental choice, however, have had the effect of counteracting the move towards greater equality of opportunity. In short, raising the school-leaving age has been less obviously beneficial than many of its advocates had hoped.

5.3 The influence of the public schools

If there were inequalities within the state-supported system of schooling in Britain, there was an even greater inequality in the existence of a quite separate private sector. The so-called public schools of Britain (in fact private schools) took children from thirteen to eighteen. Below them was a vast network of preparatory schools, most of them boarding schools, taking children from the age of seven. Throughout this chapter's period the upper and upper-middle classes sent their sons, and increasingly their daughters, to these schools. In the 1830s and 1840s, spearheaded by Thomas Arnold, headmaster of Rugby School, the previously ill-disciplined schools were reformed to put the emphasis on the production of manly Christian gentlemen imbued with a sense of responsibility for the

The Honourable Gerald Lascelles (extreme right), second son of the Princess Royal with a gang of boys at Eton College, January 1938.

future destiny of their country and empire. These schools, catering for an elite minority of society, gained a remarkable hold on the imagination of all sectors of British society. In early twentieth-century working-class Salford, Robert Roberts recalled how he and his friends read in their magazines stories featuring such schools without quite realising that they were entirely beyond their own reach (Roberts, 1973, pp. 160–1). The public schools were the schools to emulate, and their syllabus with its emphasis on two dead languages, Greek and Latin, the ideal.

Many public school boys and girls left school at eighteen, went to university at Oxford or Cambridge, and then emerged to take up positions of influence in the world. They carried with them ideals of how a childhood should be spent. Their experience pointed them in two rather different directions. On the one hand, they had been taught a degree of self-sufficiency and independence from an early age. Their parents tended to be distant figures. In infancy and early childhood they were brought up by nannies and governesses in a part of the house dedicated to children. Separation from parents was reinforced by being sent to boarding school, it being part of the thinking of these classes that boys in particular needed to be toughened up in preparation for the manhood that lay ahead of them. They were therefore likely to be shocked by and disapproving of the much closer relationships between parents and children in working-class families where a formal disciplinary framework was all too often lacking. On the other hand, kept at school till the age of eighteen, they carried with them the idea that childhood should be a lengthy and protracted process. As one headmaster put it in the 1850s, 'How I dread mannikizing [making a boy into a miniature man] a boy. It is just as bad as opening an egg and finding an advanced chicken inside it. What say to a baby with whiskers or mustachios? No, keep boys boys – children children – young men young men' (quoted in Cunningham, 1991, p. 154). Children brought up under public school regimes influenced by such thinking were shocked to find that working-class boys thought they had achieved manhood on the day they left school and started full-time work.

5.4 The invention of adolescence

This public school emphasis on a prolonged childhood was enhanced by the articulation of an ideology about adolescence in the early twentieth century. A key influence was the American psychologist G. Stanley Hall's *Adolescence*, published in 1904. Hall described as adolescent those aged between 14 and 25. It was, he argued, a new birth, one replete with both opportunities and dangers. It was the latter which made most mark. Seeing

The First Bollingdon Girl Guide Company, 1910, England.

life as a process in which an individual experienced as he or she grew older the different stages of humankind's evolution, Hall argued that any arrest or reversion in the years of adolescence spelt disaster for adulthood. It was above all crucial that in these years the young were under proper guidance, and not left to their own devices – for the temptations to go astray were powerful. Such thinking pointed ever more powerfully to the need to extend the period during which a person was dependent, and the most obvious way in which to do that was to prolong schooling. Apprenticeship, to which some analysts looked back with nostalgia, no longer seemed able to achieve what was needed in the twentieth century. Raising the school-leaving age, therefore, was in part a response to a perceived crisis of adolescence. What it in effect did was to prolong childhood.

The same mode of analysis helps to make sense of another phenomenon of the late nineteenth and early twentieth centuries, the spread of youth movements. Starting in Glasgow in the 1880s with the Boys' Brigade, they spread rapidly across Britain, associated to varying degrees with religious denominations (the Church Lads' Brigade, the Catholic Boys' Brigade, the Jewish Lads' Brigade, the Boy Scouts and the Girl Guides). Their success in recruiting members was extraordinary. One out of three adult Britons questioned in the 1960s said they had belonged to the Boy Scouts or the Girl Guides and three out of five men had belonged to a uniformed youth movement (Springhall, 1977, p. 13) – and, like most team sports, they were one of Britain's most important exports to the rest of the world. While most of those who joined the youth movements enjoyed the experience, they were also organizations which provided a controlling framework for the young, and in that sense prevented them from too early an assertion of adulthood.

SUMMARY OF SECTION 5

- In the nineteenth century there were widely divergent views about when childhood ended.
- Raising the school-leaving age has been the key agent in prolonging childhood.
- The public schools, the idea of 'adolescence' and the formation of youth organizations have all contributed to the prolongation of childhood.

6 CONCLUSION

The experience of children in societies in the North at the beginning of the twenty-first century differs in fundamental ways from that of earlier times. Death, which used to remove one-quarter or more of all those up to the age of five, is now an exception. Productive labour for the family, the lot of the vast majority of children in the nineteenth century and for much of the twentieth century, is now equally rare. Schooling, which used to be fitted around other demands and obligations, is now compulsory and prolonged. What has made these changes possible? The first answer is the huge changes in material life which have accompanied the past two centuries. Without industrialization and all that followed from it, in particular a much higher standard of living than enjoyed by previous centuries, the experience of childhood could not have changed in the ways outlined.

What may be most striking about those two centuries as a whole is the novelty of the modern experience of childhood in the North. Although death rates began to decline for young children from the late nineteenth century and for babies from the beginning of the twentieth century, until the middle of the twentieth century death in childhood was not the rarity it has now become. It was equally only in the mid-twentieth century that the sense of obligation felt by children in working-class families to contribute to the family economy in any way they could, and as a matter of priority, began to fade away. Schooling had become compulsory in the nineteenth century, but it took some decades before 'the habit of schooling' became entrenched. In the initial decades of compulsory schooling many parents thought it should take second place to family demands – for girls to help with the laundry once a week for example – and many magistrates were sympathetic to such views: the school attendance officers were not popular figures. Most children seem to have anticipated with some pleasure the moment when they could leave school, and of course they could do so at what now seems a very young age. All this suggests that the ingredients of the contemporary experience of childhood have been in place for about half a century only.

One of the central components of contemporary Western thinking about childhood is a conviction of its importance. That childhood experiences will affect adult lives is a taken-for-granted truth. Not all societies have held such a view. If we look for the origins of the most deeply-held Western assumptions about childhood, we are likely to find them in the experience of childhood over the past two centuries and in reflections on that experience. In reaction to the horrors of child labour in the industrial revolution in Britain, writers drew on ideas about childhood first articulated by the Romantic poets Blake, Wordsworth, Southey and Coleridge in the late eighteenth and early nineteenth centuries. For these writers children were born innocent, not, as in the Puritan tradition, scarred by original sin. Responding directly to the world as they saw it, to nature, children seemed to embody a higher morality than corrupted adults. In many nineteenth-century novels, for example George Eliot's *Silas Marner* (1861), a child is able to reform such a corrupted adult, in this case a miser. With such a high value placed on childhood, it was the more outrageous that children should be subjected to work in mills and mines which ruined their health and morals. Children, it began to be claimed, had rights, and the most fundamental right was a right to childhood itself as a time of happiness and of preparation for the adult world of work (rather than participation in it). It followed from this that adults should not look on children in terms of how useful they might be to adults (nimble fingers and so on), but rather ask what adults could give to children to make their experience better. At one level the answer was good health, no work likely to stunt their growth or development, and the provision of schooling. At another, and perhaps more fundamental, level it meant that within families the perceived needs of children became the key priority.

In one sense this has given children power within families: parents can no longer assume that they can make demands on their children. But the flip-side of this increased power has been a loss of responsibility. Children who recognized the needs of their families and had internalized a sense that they ought as soon as they were able to contribute to those needs, nearly all felt proud when those contributions started – their self-esteem rose. In modern society, where there are few demands on children to contribute to their families' well-being, or expectations that they should do so, it is correspondingly difficult for children's self-esteem not to suffer: they remain dependent for much longer than used to be the case. In the post-Second World War period this dependence on parents was lessened by the buoyancy of the youth labour market, with most teenagers entering the labour market immediately on leaving school at fifteen, and making a rapid transition to marriage: in the 1960s and early 1970s the age of marriage was, in historical terms, exceptionally low, with the most common age being 21 for women and 22 for men. The year 1973 saw not only the raising of the school-leaving age but also, in the aftermath of the oil crisis of that year, the beginning of the problem of juvenile unemployment, and in due course the implementation of policies to provide training or further education for those who had left school. The possibility of early financial independence rapidly receded, and with it came a much more prolonged period of transition from childhood to adulthood. The period of dependence has been further prolonged for many by the spread of mass higher education. And while there remains any sense that childhood is properly a period of happiness without responsibility, the extension of the time during which the young remain dependent on their parents effectively prolongs childhood.

Industrialized countries in the present, it is probably safe to say, are more concerned about childhood than any previous society – the one exception might be seventeenth-century Puritan society which was impelled to try to bring salvation to young children who might otherwise die damned. There are differences in the way this concern manifests itself – in Britain, for example, the impassioned opposition to child labour in industrial conditions has left a legacy of protectiveness towards children, whereas in the Nordic countries, where child labour was more taken-for-granted, children are less dependent – but whatever the particular history , the roots of concern lie in the experience of childhood and the adult response to it over the past two hundred years.

Box 1   Timeline

This timeline includes the most important legislation concerning child employment, schooling and child protection. Geographically it is confined to Great Britain (and in many cases to England and Wales for there was often separate legislation for Scotland). The Acts provide useful benchmarks for assessing how things changed, but it is important to remember that the passage of an Act did not necessarily mean that its provisions were enforced.

1802	Health and Morals of Apprentices Act. Often seen as the first Factory Act. Applies to children who were apprenticed by Poor Law authorities to work in cotton mills and factories.
1819	Factory Act prohibits children under nine from working in cotton mills, but no inspection to enforce it.
1833	Royal Commission on the Employment of Children in Factories.
1833	Factory Act. First Act to be supported by inspection. Applies to textile factories. Employment of children under nine prohibited. Limitations on hours which could be worked by those aged nine to eighteen.
1833	First government grant for education.
1842	Mines Act. Girls and boys under ten prohibited from working underground.
1864	Factory Act extends regulation of child labour beyond textiles and mines to other 'dangerous' industries, including pottery and cartridge-making.
1870	Elementary Education Act allows for the establishment of elected School Boards in areas where existing voluntary supply of schools insufficient.
1874	Factory Act raises minimum working age to nine. Children up to fourteen to work only half a day.
1880	Education Act makes it compulsory for children to go to school between ages of five and ten.
1889	Prevention of Cruelty to Children Act covers wilful ill-treatment in the home and in work, e.g. street-trading, not covered by Factory Acts.
1891	Minimum working age in factories raised to eleven.
1891	Education Act enables elementary schools to cease charging fees.
1894	Prevention of Cruelty to Children Act strengthens and amplifies 1889 Act.
1902	Education Act abolishes elected School Boards, replacing them with local education authorities which have power to provide secondary as well as elementary schooling.
1903	Employment of Children Act. Gives local authorities permissive powers for control of child labour, but few take advantage of it.
1908	Children Act consolidates and strengthens previous legislation on prevention of cruelty, sets up separate children's courts, makes possession of tobacco under the age of sixteen an offence.
1918	Education Act enforces a school-leaving age of fourteen.
1944	Education Act: school-leaving age set at fifteen, and secondary schools (grammar, technical or secondary modern) compulsory for all children.
1973	School-leaving age raised to sixteen.

REFERENCES

BRITISH PARLIAMENTARY PAPERS (1968a) *Industrial Revolution: Children's Employment*, Vol. 2, 'Select Committee on Labour of Children in Factories: Minutes of Evidence', Shannon, Irish University Press.

BRITISH PARLIAMENTARY PAPERS (1968b) *Industrial Revolution: Children's Employment*, Vol. 3, 'Royal Commission on Employment of Children in Factories: Report', Shannon, Irish University Press.

BRITISH PARLIAMENTARY PAPERS (1968c) *Industrial Revolution: Children's Employment*, Vol. 3, 'Royal Commission on Employment of Children in Factories: Minutes of Evidence', Shannon, Irish University Press.

BRITISH PARLIAMENTARY PAPERS (1968d) *Industrial Revolution: Children's Employment*, Vol. 4, 'Royal Commission on Children's Employment: Minutes of Evidence', Shannon, Irish University Press.

BROWNING, E. B. (1844) 'The Cry of the Children' in FORSTER, M. (ed.) (1988) *Selected Poems of Elizabeth Barrett Browning*, London, Chatto and Windus.

BURNETT, J. (1982) *Destiny Obscure: autobiographies of childhood, education and family from the 1820s to the 1920s*, London, Allen Lane.

CUNNINGHAM, H. (1990) 'The employment and unemployment of children in England c.1680–1851', *Past and Present*, no. 126, pp. 115–50.

CUNNINGHAM, H. (1991) *The Children of the Poor: representations of childhood since the seventeenth century*, Oxford, Blackwell.

CUNNINGHAM, H. (2000) 'The decline of child labour: labour markets and family economies in Europe and North America since 1830', *Economic History Review*, **53**, pp. 409–28.

CUNNINGHAM, H. (2001) 'The rights of the child and the wrongs of child labour: An historical perspective' in Lieten, K. and White, B. (eds). *Child Labour: policy options*, Amsterdam, Aksant, pp. 13–26, 132–3.

GARDNER, P. (1984) *The Lost Elementary Schools of Victorian England*, London, Croom Helm.

HALL, G. S. (1904) *Adolescence*, New York, D. Appleton.

HUMPHRIES, S. (1981) *Hooligans or Rebels? An oral history of working-class childhood and youth 1889–1939*, Oxford, Blackwell.

JACKSON, B. and MARSDEN, D. (1962) *Education and the Working Class*, London, Routledge and Kegan Paul.

LAVALETTE, M. (1999) 'The changing form of child labour circa 1880–1918: the growth of "out-of-school work" ' in LAVALETTE, M. (ed.) *A Thing of the Past? Child labour in Britain in the nineteenth and twentieth centuries*, Liverpool, Liverpool University Press.

LEONARD, D. (1980) *Sex and Generation: a study of courtship and weddings*, London, Tavistock.

NARDINELLI, C. (1990) *Child Labor and the Industrial Revolution*, Bloomington, Indiana University Press.

NEWSON, J. and NEWSON, E. (1963) *Patterns of Infant Care in an Urban Community*, London, Penguin Books.

THE OPEN UNIVERSITY (2003) U212 *Childhood*, Audio 3, Band 4, 'Children working in post-industrial societies', Milton Keynes, The Open University.

ROBERTS, R. (1973) *The Classic Slum: Salford life in the first quarter of the century*, Harmondsworth, Penguin Books.

ROSE, J. (1993) 'Willingly to school: the working-class response to elementary education in Britain, 1875–1918', *Journal of British Studies*, **32**, pp. 114–38.

ROWNTREE, B. S. (1902, 4th edn) *Poverty: a study of town life*, London, Macmillan.

SAITO, O. (1996) 'Children's work, industrialism and the family economy in Japan, 1872–1926' in CUNNINGHAM, H. and VIAZZO, P. P. (eds) *Child Labour in Historical Perspective 1800–1985: case studies from Europe, Japan and Colombia*, Florence, UNICEF.

SMITH, G. (1871) *The Cry of the Children from the Brickyards of England: statement and appeal*, London, Simpkin Marshall and Co.

SNELL, K. D. M. (1999) 'The Sunday-School movement in England and Wales: child labour, denominational control and working-class culture', *Past and Present*, no. 164, pp. 122–68.

SPRINGHALL, J. (1977) *Youth, Empire and Society: British youth movements, 1883–1940*, London, Croom Helm.

THOMPSON, E. P. (1963) *The Making of the English Working Class*, London, Victor Gollancz.

THOMPSON, T. (1981) *Edwardian Childhoods*, London, Routledge.

WEINER, M. (1991) *The Child and the State in India: child labor and education policy in comparative perspective*, Princeton, Princeton University Press.

WHITE, B. (1994) 'Children, work, and 'child labour': changing responses to the employment of children', *Development and Change*, **25**, pp. 849–78.

YOUNG, M. and WILMOTT, P. (1968) *Family and Kinship in East London*, Harmondsworth, Penguin Books.

ZELIZER, V. A. (1985) *Pricing the Priceless Child: the changing social value of children*, New York, Basic Books.

READING A

School children in Kristiania, 1912: work and school

E. Schrumpf

... In 1912, a large questionnaire-based inquiry was carried out among Kristiania's schoolchildren, to find out the extent to which they took part in paid work.[1] This initiative was taken by the Kristiania School Board. Class teachers were responsible for collecting the information from their pupils. Therefore, educational authorities and the teachers had a central role in this inquiry. The results showed that children continued to do paid work, with one in five schoolchildren in Kristiania engaged in it: one in three boys and one in ten girls. Although children worked, they also attended school each day. Work was adjusted to their schooling. The majority went to school in the morning and worked in the afternoon. Three out of four working boys were errand boys – one-half of the girls were in service. Only 2 per cent of the children worked in factories. Otherwise, we find children working in cinemas, theatres, cafés and restaurants, in shops, and with veterinarians.[2]

[...]

Even in 1912 some children did paid work at a very young age. Almost 300 children were seven years or younger when they began their working lives. Some of the elementary school pupils said they had been as young as three years of age. But the older the children were the more work they did, adjusting it to their schoolwork. Although school took up much more of a child's day than it had some decades earlier, there is no evidence to suggest any conflict between work and school. Teachers, when asked if they felt that paid work meant that school work was neglected, somewhat surprisingly replied that it did not seem to affect attendance or cause any significant problems. Less attention might be paid to homework and if the combination of schoolwork and paid work was too long, then this reduced the child's time for rest and play. But the teachers stressed that work was good for children. They became accustomed to orderliness, obedience and punctuality. Children learned to use their time to the best advantage, to make the most of it. Work kept children off the streets and helped to keep them in check. In fact, school and work was an ideal combination. Children learned both abstract and practical skills and adjusted to the demands of society with good morals and an effective use of their time. The inquiry had to admit that the children who worked were often the best pupils in the class.

> A short period of work each day must be regarded as a good thing, especially for children aged 11–12 years and above. Children get accustomed to orderliness and obedience and they gain routine in how to use their time. Besides, work keeps them out of mischief on the streets. Many schoolmasters and schoolmistresses say that children who work are often the most diligent and the brightest of their pupils. (...).[3]

[...]

In the 1870s it was the schools that had warned of the unfortunate impact of work on a child's schooling.[4] In 1912 teachers had to acknowledge that children who worked were among the schools' best equipped, both mentally and physically, and that work in no way adversely affected a child's health, at least not the boys. Boys who worked were less likely to be ill than those who did not. However, for girls the reverse was the case. That was not because of work itself but its nature and where it took place, often it was indoors.

[...]

While boys ran about in the fresh air as delivery and messenger boys, the girls' health was weakened in badly ventilated houses and often through heavy physical work. Common to boys and girls, however, was exposure to *moral* dangers at work. Certain moral limits were not to be transgressed. Girls should not work for men living alone. It was also not proper that either girls or boys model for artists, work for hotdog sellers at night, or work in the entertainment business. If these limits were observed, however, work could actually strengthen a child's moral sense.

[...]

The picture is one of *work* as an important feature of childhood. This was the case throughout the period 1875–1912. At the beginning of the period, work itself was the way a child entered adulthood. Children assisted adults. They worked side by side. Often children occupied an essential place in the production process. In addition, they were flexible, with flexibility as their supreme advantage – from a work point of view. Through their place in the labour force they were integrated into society and family, both socially and culturally. Through work they became useful and significant.

Throughout the period children tackled a wide range of jobs. They were everywhere that work was to be found and they were paid for the work they did. As full-time workers they were paid well, especially the boys. At the beginning of the period children could more than support themselves through the wages they contributed to the family economy. Later a reduction in the number of hours they worked meant their pay and contribution to the family fell sharply.

Recruitment was wide-ranging. This appears clearly from the 1912 inquiry. It was not just children from the poorest families who had paid work, but also children from the families of senior public officials and the self-employed. Money was not always the reason why parents wanted their children to work. Rather an important explanation lay in the fact that work was the norm. It accorded with the principles of childrearing.

Changes in children's work had above all to do with changes in hours of work. The length of the working day fell. While it was common in the 1870s for this to last 10 hours, by 1912 merely a small proportion of children's work lasted for such a long day.[5] There was less room for work in a child's life, more for school and organized, or unorganized, leisure time. Yet there continued to be many children in the towns, and probably even more in the countryside, who still had paid work in 1912. Children's work continued to be socially acceptable. But it now took second position in a child's life.

Child labour also changed its character. Whereas Jacob Neumann Mohn had found an enormous number of children in factories in the 1870s, very few remained there in 1912.[6] By that date children working full-time and children working in industry were virtually a thing of the past. Essentially, children were now part-time workers as domestic servants or employed in the service sector generally. The work was child-specific, organized outside the family and cut off from the world of adult labour. It did not provide children with a training for future work. The school was now the most important agent of socialization for the child, at least in the towns. It filled a child's day: 'Since then [1870s] schooling has increased dramatically. So to work 14 hours in 24, as then, would simply not be possible', was how document No. 36 summed up the matter.[7] While in the 1870s it had been the school authorities who had taken the initiative to ensure that child labour was regulated and adjusted to the needs of the school, by 1912 teachers were happily able to say that the school had now taken first priority in a child's life. The working child had become the schoolchild.

Endnotes

1 The answers related to 1 February 1912 and covered 85 per cent of schoolchildren in the city. The Board reckoned that 'the inquiry covered just about all productive employment carried out by schoolchildren in Kristiania'. Document No. 36 1912–1913 p. 9.

2 Document No. 36 1912–1913, p. 29.

3 Document No. 36 1912–1993, pp. 40, 43.

4 Bull, 1984, p. 81.

5 The figures show that in 1871 around one in three boys and one in four girls worked for 10 hours a day or more. By 1912 the percentages had fallen to 0.07 and 0.17 respectively. Document No. 36 1912–1913, p. 52.

6 The figures show that in 1871 some 3.8 per cent of boys and 1.5 per cent of girls in Kristiania's elementary schools, worked in factories. By 1912 the percentages had fallen to 0.42 and 0.08 respectively. Document No. 36 1912–1913 p. 52.

7 Document No. 36 1912–1913, p. 52.

References

Unpublished sources

Forhandlingsprotokoll for Porsgrund Skolestyre 1890–1990. Porsgrunns byarkiv.

Protokoll for Tilsynsutvalget ved Ulefos brugs Skole 1890–1920. Ulefos Brugs arkiv.

Muntlige kilder:

Hans Olsen Solvold, født 1865 på Ulefoss. Arbeiderminnesamlingen Universitetet i Trondheim.

Torleif Albretsen, født 1910 i Porsgrunn. Arbeiderbevegelsens arkiv I Telemark.

Isak Lindalens beretning om sin far, Ole Pedersen Lindalen, født 1859 på Ulefoss. Arbeiderminnesamlingen Universitetet i Trondheim.

Published sources

Dokument nr. 36 (1912–1913). Erhvervsmæssig arbejde blandt skolebarn i Kristiania.

Mohn, Jacob Neuwmann (1875), Angaaende Børns og Unge Menneskers Anvendelse til Arbeide udenfor Hjemmet. I Stortingets forhandlinger 1883, del III, Kristiania.

Literature

Bull, Edvard, (1984) Barn i industriarbeid. In Bjarne Hodne & Sølvi Sogner (ed.) *Barn av sin tid*. Oslo.

Source

SCHRUMPF, E. (1997) 'From full-time to part-time: working children in Norway from the nineteenth to the twentieth century' in DE CONINCK-SMITH, N., SANDIN, B. and SCHRUMPF, E. (eds) *Industrious Children: work and childhood in the Nordic countries 1850–1990*, Odense, Odense University Press, pp. 60–64.

READING B

The child labor controversy

Viviana A. Zelizer

The history of American child labor legislation is a chronicle of obstacles and defeats. At every step of the battle that lasted some fifty years, the sustained efforts of child labor reformers were blocked by an equally determined, vocal, and highly effective opposition. Until 1938, every major attempt to pass national regulation of child labor was defeated. The two groups were divided by conflicting economic interests and also by opposing legal philosophies. Yet, the emotional vigor of their battle revealed an additional, profound cultural schism. Proponents and opponents of child labor legislation became entangled in a moral dispute over the definition of children's economic and sentimental value.
   [...]

In defence of the useful child

In a letter to the editor of the *Chicago News,* a Reverend Dunne of the Guardian Angels' Italian Church bitterly criticized the 1903 Illinois child labor law as a 'curse instead of a blessing to those compelled to earn their bread by the sweat of their brow.' The priest ridiculed a law that transformed the noble assistance of a working child into an illegal act: 'He must not attempt to work; he must not dare to earn his living honestly, because in his case ... that is against the law.'[1] Opponents of child labor legislation defended the pragmatic and moral legitimacy of a useful child. As a controversial article in the *Saturday Evening Post* asserted: 'The work of the world has to be done; and these children have their share ... why should we ... place the emphasis on ... prohibitions ... We don't want to rear up a generation of nonworkers, what we want is workers and more workers.'[2] From this perspective, regulatory legislation introduced an unwelcome and dangerous 'work prohibition': 'The discipline, sense of duty and responsibility, ... which come to a boy and girl, in home, on the farm, in workshop, as the result of even hard work ... is to be ... prohibited.'[3] The consequences would be dire: 'If a child is not trained to useful work before the age of eighteen, we shall have a nation of paupers and thieves.' Child labor, insisted its supporters, was safer than 'child-idleness.'[4]

[...]

For working-class families, the usefulness of their children was supported by need and custom. When parents were questioned as to why their children left school early to get to work, it was often 'perplexing' for the mother to assign a reason for such an 'absolutely natural proceeding – he's of an age to work, why shouldn't he?' As one mother who employed her young children in homework told an investigator: 'Everybody does it. Other people's children help – why not ours?'[5] Studies of immigrant families, in particular, demonstrate that the child was an unquestioned member of the family economic unit. For example, in her study of Canadian workers in the Amoskeag Mills of Manchester, New Hampshire, Tamara Hareven found that the 'entire family economy as well as the family's work ethic was built on the assumption that children would contribute to the family's income from the earliest possible age.'[6] While generally older boys were more likely to become wage-earners, boys under fourteen and girls were still expected to actively assist the family with housework, childcare, and any income obtained from odd jobs.[7]

Government reports occasionally provide glimpses of the legitimacy of child labor: A mother boasting that her baby – a boy of seven – could 'make more money than any of them picking shrimp'; or an older sister apologizing for her seven-year-old brother who was unable to work in a shrimp cannery 'because he couldn't reach the car to shuck.'[8] Work was a socializer; it kept children busy and out of mischief. As the father of two children who worked at home wiring rosary beads explained: 'Keep a kid at home, save shoe leather, make better manners.'[9]

Child labor legislation threatened the economic world of the working class. In 1924, one commentator in the *New Republic* predicted the potential disruption of traditional family relationships: 'The immemorial right of the parent to train his child in useful tasks ... is destroyed ... Parents may still set their children at work; children may still make themselves useful, but it will no longer be by right and obligation, but by default of legislation ...' Many parents resented and resisted this intrusion. A 1909 investigation of cotton textile mills reported that 'fathers and mothers vehemently declare that the State has no right to interfere if they wish to "put their children to work," and that it was only fair for the child to "begin to pay back for its keep." '[10] In New York canneries, Italian immigrants reportedly took a more aggressive stand. One study reports a quasi-riot against a canner who attempted to exclude young children from the sheds: '(He was) besieged by angry Italian women, one of whom bit his finger "right through." '[11] Parents routinely sabotaged regulatory legislation simply by lying about their child's age. It was an easy ploy, since until the 1920s many states required only a parental affidavit as proof of a child worker's age. For a small illegal fee, some notary publics were apparently quite willing to produce a false affidavit.[12]

Middle-class critics also opposed child labor legislation in the name of family autonomy. Prominent spokesmen such as Nicholas Murray Butler, president of Columbia University, warned that 'No American mother would favor the adoption of a constitutional amendment which would empower Congress to invade the rights of parents and to shape family life to its liking'.[13] An assemblyman from Nevada put it more succinctly: 'They have taken our women away from us by constitutional amendments; they have taken our liquor from us; and now they want to take our children.'[14]

In defence of the useless child

For reformers, the economic participation of children was an illegitimate and inexcusable 'commercialization of child life.'[15] As one New York City clergyman admonished his parishioners in 1925: 'A man who defends the child labor that violates the personalities of children is not a Christian ...'[16] The world of childhood had to become entirely removed from the world of the market. Already in 1904, Dr. Felix Adler, first chairman of the National Child Labor Committee, insisted that '...whatever happens in the sacrifice of workers ... children shall not be touched ... childhood shall be sacred ... commercialism shall not be allowed beyond this point.'[17] If the sacred child was 'industrially taboo', child labor was a profanation that reduced 'the child of God (into) the chattel of Mammon.'[18]

The persistence of child labor was attributed in part to a misguided economic system that put 'prosperity above ... the life of sacred childhood.'[19] Employers were denounced as 'greedy and brutal tyrants,' for whom children were little more than a 'wage-earning unit,' or a profitable dividend.[20] Any professed support of child labor was dismissed as convenient rhetoric: 'A prominent businessman who recently remarked that it is good for the children to work in industry is a hypocrite unless he puts his own children there.'[21]

Reformers sympathized with the financial hardships of the working class, yet, they rarely understood and seldom condoned working-class economic strategies. Instead, parents were depicted as suspect collaborators in the exploitation of their own children. 'If fathers and mothers of working children could have their own way, would they be with the child labor reformer or against him?' was a question asked in *The American Child*, a publication of the National Child Labor Committee.[22] Others were more forthright in their indictment: 'Those who are fighting for the rights of the children, almost invariably, find their stoutest foes in the fathers and mothers, who coin shameful dollars from the bodies and souls of their own flesh and blood.' A child's contribution to the family economy was redefined as the mercenary exploitation of parents 'who are determined that their children shall add to the family income, regardless of health, law, or any other consideration.'[23] As early as 1873, Jacob Riis had declared that ' ... it requires a character of more disinterestedness ... than we usually find among the laboring class to be able to forego present profit for the future benefit of the little one.'[24] At the root of this harsh indictment was the profound unease of a segment of the middle class with working class family life. The instrumental orientation toward children was denied all legitimacy: ' ... to permit a parent ... at his or her will to send a child out to work and repay himself for its maintenance from the earnings of its labor, or perhaps ... make money out of it seems ... nothing short of criminal.'[25] Child labor, 'by urging the duty of the child to its parents,' obliterated the 'far more binding and important obligation of the parent to the child.'[26] This 'defective' economic view of children was often attributed to the foreign values of immigrant parents, 'who have no civilization, no decency, no anything but covetousness and who would with pleasure immolate their offspring on the shrine of the golden calf.'[27] For such 'vampire' progenitors, the child became an asset instead of remaining a 'blessed incumbrance.'[28]

Advocates of child labor legislation were determined to regulate not only factory hours but family feeling. They introduced a new cultural equation: if children were useful and produced money, they were not being properly loved. As a social worker visiting the canneries where Italian mothers worked alongside their children concluded: 'Although they love their children, they do not love them in the right way.'[29] A National Child Labor Committee leaflet warned that when family relations are materialistic, 'It is rare to find a family governed by affection.'[30] By excluding children from the 'cash nexus,' reformers promised to restore proper parental love among working-class families. 'It is the new view of the child,' wrote Edward T. Devine, editor of *Charities and the Commons,* a leading reform magazine, 'that the child is worthy of the parent's sacrifice.'[31]

Thus, the conflict over the propriety of child labor between 1870 and 1930 in the U.S. involved a profound cultural disagreement over the economic and sentimental value of young children. While opponents of child labor legislation hailed the economic usefulness of children, advocates of child labor legislation campaigned for their uselessness. For reformers, true parental love could only exist if the child was defined exclusively as an object of sentiment and not as an agent of production.

Endnotes

1 Reprinted in *Charities* 11 (Aug. 8, 1903):130.

2 Elizabeth Fraser, 'Children and Work', *Saturday Evening Post* 197 (Apr. 4, 1925):146.

3 Iredell Meares, 'Should the Nation Control Child Labor?' *Dearborn Independent*, Nov. 8 1924.

4 Letter to the *New York Chamber of Commerce Bulletin* XVI, No. 5 (Dec. 1924):50 cited in Anne Kruesi Brown, *Opposition to the Child Labor Amendment Found in Trade Journals, Industrial Bulletins, And Other Publications for and By Business Men',* M.A. diss. (Chicago, 1937), pp. 35–36.

5   *Report on Condition of Woman and Child Wage-Earners* VII, (Washington DC, 1910):43; Mary Skinner, 'Child Labor in New Jersey', U.S. Department of Labor, Children's Bureau Publication No185 (Washington, D.C., 1928).

6   Tamara K. Hareven, 'Family and Work Patterns of Immigrant Laborers in a Planned Industrial Town, 1900–1930', in Richard L. Ehrlich, ed., *Immigrants in Industrial America* (Charlottesville: University Press of Virginia, 1977), p. 63

7   *Report On Condition of Woman and Child Wage-Earners* VII, p. 158; Claudia Goldin, 'Household and Market Production of Families in a late Nineteenth Century American City', *Explorations in Economic History* 16 (1979): 118–19.

8   Viola I. Paradise, 'Child Labor and the Work of Mothers in Oyster and Shrimp Canning Communities on the Gulf Coast', U.S. Department of Labor, Children's Bureau Publication No. 98 (Washington, D.C., 1922) pp. 11, 17.

9   'Industrial Homework of Children', U.S. Department of Labor, Children's Bureau Publication No. 100 (Washington, D.C., 1924), p. 23.

10 *Report on Condition of Woman and Child Wage Earners* I:p. 353.

11 Virginia Yans-McLaughlin, *Family and Community: Italian Immigrants in Buffalo, 1880–1930* (Ithaca, NY: Cornell University Press, 1971), p. 193.

12 Elizabeth Sands Johnson, 'Child Labor Legislation', in John R. Commons, ed., *History of Labor in The United States, 1896–1932* (New York: Macmillan, 1935), p. 429; Jeremy Felt, *Hostages of Fortune* (New York: Syracuse University Press, 1965), pp. 22–3.

13 *New York Times*, Dec. 7, 1924, p. 19.

14 Cited in *The American Child* (Apr. 1925):6

15 J.W. Crabtree, 'Dr. Pritchett, Dr. Butler and Child Labor', *School and Society* (Nov. 8, 1924):585

16 Quoted in *New York Times*, Feb. 2, 1925, p. 21

17 Quoted in 'The Nation and Child Labor', *New York Times*, Apr. 24, 1904, p. 6

18 Felix Adler, 'Child Labor in the United States and Its Great Attendant Evils', *Annals of the American Academy of Political and Social Science* XXV (May 1905); Charles K. Gilbert, 'The Church and Child Labor', in *The American Child* 9 (Aug. 1927):4.

19 A.J. McKelway, 'The Evil of Child Labor' *Outlook* 85 (Feb. 16, 1907):364.

20 Davidson, *Child Labor Legislation*, pp. 65–6; Elinor H. Stoy, 'Child-Labor', Arena 36 (Dec. 1906):586, 'Education, Psychology, and Manufacturers', *The American Child* 8 (Nov. 1926):2

21 Quoted in *New York Times*, Feb. 2, 1925, p. 21.

22 'Potters' Clay', *The American Child* 8 (Jan. 1926):3.

23 Marion Delcomyn, 'Why Children Work', *Forum* 57 (Mar. 1917):324–25.

24 Jacob Riis, 'The Little Laborers of New York City', *Harper's New Monthly Magazine* XLVII(Aug. 1973):327.

25 Letter to the Editor, *New York Times*, Nov. 4, 1910, p. 8.

26 Alice L. Woodbridge, "Child Labor an Obstacle to Industrial Progress," *Arena* 10 (June 1894):158.

27 Editorial, *New York Times*, Dec. 17, 1902, p. 8.

28 Mrs. A. O. Granger, 'The Work of the General Federation of Women's Clubs Against Child Labor', *Annals of the American Academy* 25(May 1905):104; A.J. McKelway, 'The Leadership of the Child,' ibid. 32(July 1908):21.

29 Quoted in Yans-McLaughlin, *Family and Community*, p. 190.

30 'The Cost of Child Labor', *National Child Labor Committee* 5 (New York:1905):35.

31 Edward T. Devine, 'The New View of the Child', *Annals of the American Academy* 32 (July 1908):9.

Source

Zelizer, V.A. (1985) *Pricing the Priceless Child: the changing social value of children*, New York, Basic Books, pp. 64–72.

READING C

'Our schools'; 'their schools'

Phil Gardner

For most of the nineteenth century, there were two traditions of English elementary education. There were those schools provided for the working class by private philanthropy and State subsidy – 'public' schools; and there were those provided by the working class entirely from their own pockets – 'private' schools.[1] Until the last quarter of the century, the two types of school existed side by side almost everywhere. But following the 1870 Act and Lord Sandon's carefully drafted Act of 1876, working-class private schooling entered a period of terminal decline.[2] By 1888, the Cross Commissioners felt able to conclude that, 'private adventure schools have been largely destroyed by the Education Acts'[3] ... School after school of this kind had been given up in the face of zealous opposition from local school board officials.

[...]

As Harold Silver has reminded us, [the 1870s and 1880s] saw fundamental and unprecedented shifts in the nature of popular thinking about education.[4] Above all, the period saw a broad and enduring popular concession to the State of the right to organize and regulate an interventionist and ultimately compulsory system of national schooling. This was a profoundly important concession of principle, forming the basis of an emerging consensus which was hard won and which in 1870 seemed by no means to be assured. Six years before the Act, for example, HMI Bellairs had expressed 'the impression that an Act subjecting to imprisonment any parent who did not send his child to school, if passed and attempted to be carried out, would produce a national commotion not much less dangerous than that which attended a poll tax ... '; Forster himself considered that, 'in proposing an Education Bill giving a power to compel the attendance of children ... the Government were ... thoroughly conscious of the difficulty and danger of that undertaking ... ', and in the words of a contemporary London magistrate, had too many summonses been granted against parents in the 1870s, 'we should have had an insurrection – we should have had an *emeute*'.[5] Sandon also was aware of, 'the very great difficulty and delicacy of the question of overhauling the poor ... and dragging their children to school. It was, no doubt, a very painful process to drag children from the arms of unwilling parents to school'.[6] Though from different perspectives, policy makers and parents alike would have acknowledged the force of Michael Katz's stark judgement, 'that the first public schools were alien institutions erected in hostile territory'.[7] Yet in a remarkably short time, these were institutions which had become the focal points of deepening popular consensus on the structure of mass education in the future. 'The principle of compulsion', claimed the *Saturday Review* in 1877, 'which was denounced not so long ago as revolutionary in the worst sense, is now placidly accepted on all hands'[8]. In the apt words of Thomas Gautrey of the London School Board, the 'school habit' was being effectively cultured[9] ...

The circumstances in which the new consensus was constructed among the recipients of public elementary schooling, rather than among its designers, have not been much investigated. One area in which some rethinking will be needed is in the assessment of the work of local attendance officers (or 'visitors') in the school board period. These new posts were created as a necessary adjunct to local by-laws requiring compulsory school attendance. Section 36 of the 1870 Act allowed the appointment of 'an officer or officers to enforce any byelaws under this Act with reference to the attendance of children at school'.[10] If the details of the Act itself were a mystery to many working-class parents, then the Act's personification on the streets – the school attendance officer – soon became well known. In Manchester for example, parental awareness of the entire school board apparatus was popularly condensed into the individual person of the attendance officer – known simply as 'The School Board'.[11]

It is certainly true that a large and very familiar part of the work of attendance officers focused on the formal pursuit and prosecution of irregular attenders.[12] This was a high-profile activity, carried out in the public arena of the Police Court and under the gaze of the local press. Our understanding of the attendance officer's role needs, however, to be drawn more carefully. Contact between officers, parents and children took other, more subtle and less often recorded forms. In large urban centres, the attendance officer rapidly became a familiar presence in the streets and a frequent caller at working-class homes. These visits might involve the drawing up of comprehensive schedules of pupils required to attend school, the issuing of informal warnings and more often than not, simply encouraging regularity and extolling the importance of provided schooling. Sandon accepted that, 'it was painful to have to pay these domiciliary visits;

and nothing but the gravest necessity ... would justify the placing of such powers in the hands of the school boards'.[13] Nevertheless, he claimed, it was, 'a necessity acknowledged by the people themselves', though paradoxically he confessed London's population to be, 'so touchy of any interference' in this respect.[14] These words indicate a centrally important ambivalence in the nature of the new consensus, to which we shall return shortly.

Routine domestic visiting was the platform upon which popular support for provided schooling could be built. In Bristol, for example, as soon as the by-laws were in place, an attendance officer – soon reinforced by seven more – set to work.

> promoting regularity of attendance and ... constantly engaged in visiting the homes of the parents ... In the period of two years during which ... the officers have been at work, no less than 51,534 visits have been paid to the homes of the children.[15]

By any standards, this was a massively intensive effort. Few houses escaped visits and, on each occasion, the authority of the newly constituted local board was literally brought home.[16] The primary target for officers was the working-class parent. In the words of John Reeves, one of the very few attendance officers who left any written historical record, the object of the work was, 'to influence and encourage the parents and guardians of children into co-operation with the Educational Authority in the interest of the children ... While the teachers have been educating the children, the visitors have been engaged in the more difficult task of enlightening the parents and bringing into their lives a higher moral tone'.[17] Indeed, according to Reeves, 'the Right Hon. W. E. Forster, MP, speaking at the public opening of a new school a year or so after the (London) Board had commenced operations, referred to the work of the visitor, whose labours he commended very highly, and said "they are entitled to have MP, after their names", as he regarded them as moral Policemen.'[18] Officers – the 'stern officials' celebrated by H. B. Philpott – were appointed with this purpose in mind.[19] Commonly, they were drawn from a military background.[20] In September 1876, the Bristol Board,

> received applications from 96 candidates for the appointment of School Board officer for District No. 3 ... The committee came to the unanimous opinion to recommend Mr. George Pearce, late troop-sergeant-major of the 6th Inniskillin Dragoons, as his testimonials were so excellent, and he seemed so thoroughly fitted for the position.[21]

Attendance officers tended to have another much valued characteristic. They came from working-class backgrounds. They were 'insiders', familiar with working-class habits and behaviour in a way that board members – and HMI – were not.[22]

[...]

With their specialist knowledge, school board officers could expect to influence popular sensibilities in ways which had simply not been possible before 1870. The Cross Commissioners were certainly well aware of their importance;

> We believe a vast amount has been done, in consequence of the existence
> of the compulsory byelaws, to induce parents, by persuasion and warning,
> to send their children regularly to school. Members of school boards,
> managers and attendance officers have, as a rule, shown much tact and
> consideration, and in their house to house visitations have had very great
> influence in persuading and inducing parents to perform their duty to
> their children. We think that the employment of well selected and
> adequately paid attendance officers has been a powerful influence, which
> has often made the appeal to the magistrate unnecessary, and their
> knowledge of the means and conditions of the people makes them useful
> and efficient helpers ... [23]

'Persuasion', 'inducement', and, as Thomas Gautrey put it, 'the growth of
sympathy and co-operation between the school and the home' – these were
the channels, through which, over a relatively short space of time, consensus
was built up.[24] Though John Reeves had 'the highest respect' for school
teachers, he was clear that the key agents in building support for the schools
were the attendance officers. Visitors were 'brought into contact with the
parents – often hostile and offensive – and this had to be met with tact and
patience, and to this is largely due the successful introduction of the
Compulsory System with so little friction ... I believe most sincerely that there
are no public officers whose services have been of more importance than
those of the School Attendance Officer'.[25]

Attendance officers could be resisted, and frequently were, but they did not
go away. Time was on their side and they were tenacious. Their collective
influence was like a steady drip into popular consciousness. In the early years,
they were often frustrated by the 'ill will of the parents who resented the
Board's interference with their "parental rights" over their children ... '[26] And, as
a consequence.

> The life of the visitors proved to be far from a happy one. In the poor
> districts their calls were at first resented, and they were frequently
> subjected to abuse and not infrequently to assault.[27]

But as time and visit upon visit passed – and despite the persistence of
enormous practical problems of irregular attendance – fundamental animosity
to the principle of the State's right to enforce compulsory provided schooling
gave way to acceptance and ultimately to concurrence.[28] 'Perseverance led to
steady improvement. The popularity of the schools grew, as did the 'school
habit' ... the old resentments passed away'.[29] 'Many have thanked me for getting
them to attend school, and have apologised for the trouble they gave in the old
time, and acknowledged the importance of our work'.[30]

It would be wrong to interpret this establishment of the 'school habit' as a
straightforward reversal or incorporation of earlier patterns of cultural
resistance to provided schooling.[31] The picture is much more complex than
this. For many, the new consensus carried an optimistic, even a radical
promise, with horizons extending far beyond the narrow, if genuine,
independence of the old working-class private school. Compulsion by the
State began to bear a promise rather than a threat. In the memorable words of
Thomas Smyth – 'A Representative of the Working Classes' – in evidence
before the Cross Commission, the publicly provided schools had come to be, '
... more our own ... more the people's schools'. 'We feel', he went on, 'that we
have some control over them ... '.[32]

This very powerful notion of 'our schools' articulates, as well as anything can, the changing mood of the final quarter of the nineteenth century. It laid the foundation, and indicated a direction for further State advance in the twentieth century. Yet, a generation before, the idea would have found little currency. Then, if the phrase 'our schools' belonged anywhere, it was with the private school tradition. But for Thomas Smyth and others like him, the time for the private school had passed by. His loyalty was to the new board schools, not because they gave his children a better education, but because he saw them as symbols of an emergent national system which would be unitary, classless and meritocratic.[33]

Endnotes

1   P. Gardner, *The Lost Elementary Schools of Victorian England* (Croom Helm. 1984), Ch. 1.

2   *Ibid.*, esp. Ch. 6.

3   Cross Commission, Final Report. P.P. 1888 xxxv, 164.

4   H. Silver, *Education as History* (Methuen, 1984), 85–6.

5   Bellairs quoted in P. Monroe (ed.) *Cyclopedia of Education* (1912), 287: Forster, Hansard. 3rd Series, vol. ccxxv, 1 July 1875, col. 807; magistrate quoted in D. Rubinstein, 'Socialization and the London School Board 1870–1914; aims, methods and public opinion' in P. McCann (ed.) *Popular Education and Socialization in the Nineteenth Century* (Methuen, 1977), 247.

6   Hansard, 3rd Series, vol. ccxxv, 1 July 1875, col. 810.

7   Michael Katz, rev. of Rubinstein, *Victorian Studies*, vol. xiv, no. 1 (1970), 100.

8   'Education in 1876', *Saturday Review*, 23 June 1877, 764, cited in Silver, *op. cit.*

9   T. Gautrey, *Lux Mihi Laus: School Board Memories* (1937), 36, 81–2.

10 James Murphy, *The Education Act 1870. Text and Commentary* (David & Charles, 1972).

11 F. Coombes and D. Beer, *The Long Walk from the Dark; School Board Man to Education Social Worker* (NASWE, 1984), 7. I am indebted to Dr Peter Cunningham for this reference.

12 This is the principal focus of David Rubinstein's important *School Attendance in London 1870–1914: A Social History* (University of Hull, 1968).

13 Hansard, 3rd Series, 1 July 1875, col. 810.

14 *Ibid.*

15 *Bristol Daily Post*, 12 January 1874.

16 An example of a 'surfeit of visits' resulting in parental abuse of a visitor in Bootle in 1875 is in W. E. Marsden, *Unequal Educational Provision in England and Wales: The Nineteenth Century Roots* (Woburn Press, 1987), 222; also 217.

17 John Reeves, *Recollections of a School Attendance Officer*, (1913), 10; 13.

18 Reeves *op. cit.*, 12–13.

19 H. B. Philpott, *London at School* (1904), 89.

20 Rubinstein, *op. cit.*, 44.

21 *Western Daily Press*, 30 September 1876.

22 'School-Board Work', *Good Words*, 1872, 651.

23 Cross Commission, Final Report. P.P. 1888 xxxv, 337.

24 Gautrey, *op. cit.*, 90.

25 Reeves, *op. cit.*, 13:67.

26 Gautrey, *op. cit.*, 90.

27 Gautrey, *op. cit.*, 35.

28 Rubinstein, *op. cit.*, 51; Reeves, *op. cit.*, 11 'It must be remembered that in the beginning the work was entirely new, and in the popular mind considered 'un-English' and was met with the greatest opposition...'; also 13.

29 Gautrey, *op. cit.*, 36.

30 Reeves, *op .cit.*, 66.

31 For resistance to schooling see particularly Phillip McCann (ed.), *Popular Education and Socialization in the Nineteenth Century* (Methuen, 1977); for the twentieth century, see S. Humphries. *Hooligans or Rebels?* (Blackwell, 1981).

32 Cross Commission, Third Report, P.P. 1887 xxx. 387, qu. 52,498.

33 *Ibid.*, 382, qu. 52,313, qu. 52,321; 387, qu. 52,495.

Source

GARDNER, P. (1991) ' "Our schools", "their schools". The case of Eliza Duckworth and John Stevenson', *History of Education*, **20**(3), pp. 163–9.

Chapter 4

Children and school

Donald Mackinnon

CONTENTS

LEARNING OUTCOMES

When you have studied this chapter, you should be able to:

1   Give a brief account of children's schooling in the world today: its geographical distribution, quantity and quality – and the difficulties in measuring these.

2   Define the terms 'manifest functions', 'latent functions' and 'dysfunctions' as they are used by sociologists, and be able to suggest examples of each type for schooling.

3   Set out the argument that the testing and qualification function of schooling is displacing its teaching and learning function, especially in the South.

4   Analyse the reasons for disaffection with schooling among some children in the North, especially older boys, and give an account of its possible functions.

1   INTRODUCTION

In this chapter and the next, I want to look at two of the most important activities in which children engage – schooling and work. In Chapter 3, Hugh Cunningham introduced you to the history of children's schooling and work in Britain. I now want to look at some aspects of these activities in the world today. And of course I do mean 'some aspects' – it is impossible to do more than scratch the surface of either subject in just one chapter.

I begin the present chapter on schooling by illustrating the immense variety of children's experiences. In Section 2, I present four 'vignettes' of children at school in very different conditions and circumstances, and put them in context by setting out some basic facts and figures about schooling in the world today. I then discuss some of the policies followed by governments and international organizations that have helped to shape it.

How are the facts of schooling and educational policy-making in the world today to be analysed and understood? In Section 3, I set out one way of looking more systematically at them, using a framework taken from sociology and based on the idea of *function*. I go on to consider a range of possible functions of schooling.

In Sections 4 and 5, I will look in more detail at two particularly important functions, by studying two well-known but controversial sociological analyses. Section 4 takes a global view and looks at what one sociologist, Ronald Dore, has called 'the diploma disease'. Alongside teaching and learning, many schools have another important function: to test students and award *qualifications* to those who are successful – certificates or diplomas that 'qualify' them for certain occupations, or increasingly often for still more education or training on the path to these occupations. According to Dore, the testing and qualification function has become ever more important in recent years, to the detriment of the teaching and learning function.

In Section 5, I narrow the focus from the world to the classrooms of England, through another classic sociological study, this one by Paul Willis. In Britain, as in many other countries of the North, where schooling is freely available and even taken for granted, many children seem to be thoroughly alienated from it. Why is this? Is it simply that schooling is imperfect, failing for whatever reasons to fulfil its functions – or does pupils' disaffection have hidden functions of its own?

2 CHILDREN AT SCHOOL

I want to begin by taking a broad look at the significance of school in the lives of the world's children. I will start with four vignettes of children at school, to illustrate the range and variety of their experiences. Naturally, with just four examples, they are *only* illustrative and cannot hope to be either exhaustive or rigorously representative. I will therefore go on to set them in the context of some basic facts and figures. However, all of the vignettes are based on actual children and each one stands for the experience of a large number of children in the world today. Some of the issues raised will be taken up in the rest of this chapter.

2.1 Four vignettes

Hitomi – Japan

Hitomi is fourteen years old, from a professional, middle-class family in Tokyo, where she goes to a junior high school. In a year's time she will sit a competitive entrance examination for senior high school, and preparation for this examination dominates her life. Competition is intense for admission to schools with a high reputation, and Hitomi works very hard. In addition to her daily attendance at school, her parents send her to a *juku* – a private tutorial class – three times a week, and she works at home for several hours every evening after school or *juku*.

Hitomi is used to this way of life. It began for her at the age of two, when she was sent to private infant classes to prepare her for the competitive entrance examination for kindergarten, at four. Further competitive entrance examinations followed – at six for elementary school and at twelve for junior high school, where she is now. When she enters senior high school, she will prepare for university entrance examinations at the age of eighteen.

In all Hitomi's schools, classes have been large and relationships formal, with didactic instruction from teachers and textbooks, and rote-learning and mechanical practice of skills on the part of pupils. Hard work and self-discipline are taken for granted. Both school and *juku* concentrate on the subjects most important for the examinations – mathematics, Japanese and English – at the expense of others. According to many critics within Japan itself, the pressure for examination success leaves little time or incentive for the development of independent critical or creative thinking.

Children at school around the world.

Outdoor school run by
UNITA: Angola.

Primary school library: UK.

Primary school:
Bangladesh.

Urban school: Haiti.

Primary-school classroom: UK.

Portable classroom: Texas, USA.

Secondary-school computer class: India.

Hitomi finds the unending round of study and examinations exhausting and stressful, but she accepts it stoically as inevitable. She knows that a degree from one of the 'best' universities is vital in the competition for a good job. A place at one of the 'best' senior high schools will greatly increase her chances of getting to a good university. And so on, back down the line of schools.

Antonio – USA

Antonio is thirteen and lives with his parents and two older brothers in an apartment in Brooklyn, New York. His parents are unemployed. Antonio goes to a junior high school, but he finds school an unpleasant and unrewarding experience: he attends as little as he needs to in order to keep out of serious trouble with the authorities, and avoids doing any work while he is there. Like more than a fifth of American adults, he has problems with basic literacy and numeracy.

Antonio is Hispanic, a minority ethnic group in the USA as a whole, but the majority ethnic group in his own neighbourhood. Here, there is hostility between Hispanic and other communities, especially among teenage boys and young men, and Antonio has experienced taunts, threats and sometimes assaults. In his turn, he views members of other ethnic groups as potential or actual enemies.

His school, too, is a hostile and dangerous environment, with inter-ethnic tensions, gangs and fights. It looks and feels like a fortress, with security guards patrolling the corridors and searching students at the gates for weapons and drugs.

As yet, Antonio is only peripherally involved with gangs and fighting, and is not involved with drugs or serious crime. His older brothers and many of his friends, however, are more deeply involved, and he expects to get sucked in too as he grows older. He has no aspirations or expectations about his education or future employment.

Mohsin – Bangladesh

Mohsin is ten. He lives with his parents and his six brothers and sisters in a one-room shack in a shanty town near the centre of Chittagong, Bangladesh. His father drives a 'baby taxi' – a small, three-wheeled vehicle – and his mother is a housemaid for a more prosperous family. Mohsin himself works as a mechanic in a baby-taxi garage. He says he is quite naughty at home and his mother sends him to work to keep him out of mischief. His earnings are primarily for his own use – currently he is saving up to buy a bicycle – but his family draw on them sometimes if they need money urgently, such as when his father is ill and cannot work.

Mohsin also goes to school – to one of a number of schools in the cities of Bangladesh established and run by a non-governmental organization (NGO), with international support, to provide part-time education for working children in urban slums. Although Mohsin attends for only two-and-a-half hours a day, he can expect to cover the primary-school curriculum in three to four years instead of the six years taken in government schools. According to the NGO, this is because its schools have smaller classes, shorter holidays and older pupils.

Mohsin's school is bare and austere by the standards of the North, but it is solidly constructed, supplied with running water and sanitation and well resourced by comparison with government schools in the area. Teaching is formal, with pupils sitting in rows of desks facing a blackboard. Pupils attend voluntarily, feel privileged to be able to do so and work hard. They do not wear a uniform, but Mohsin's mother makes sure he is always clean and neatly dressed for school, despite the messy nature of his work.

Mohsin will probably complete his primary schooling, but he is very unlikely to take his education any further. (The NGO that runs his school also runs secondary technical schools, but in Chittagong these have fewer than a twentieth of the places in its primary schools.) He will leave school able to read, write and do elementary arithmetic, but will not sit any public examinations or obtain any formal qualifications.

Mohsin says he enjoys studying. He is happy that his ability to read and write will allow him to help illiterate relations and friends and gain their respect. However, it is his work at the baby-taxi garage and his informal training there as a mechanic that he thinks will help him make a living as an adult – not his schooling.

Anita – India and England

Anita is nine years old and lives in a village in central England, where she goes to the local Church of England school, with about 120 pupils. Her mother is Indian and her father is white British. Anita is bilingual in English and Tamil, her parents' mother tongues. She and her two brothers are the only 'ethnic minority' children in the school.

Anita has been to school in both India and England. She spent her first school year, aged four to five, in Chennai (formerly Madras), at a private English-medium school of the kind favoured by middle-class families. It was run by a Hindu foundation, but on largely secular lines. The school was highly formal. All but its very youngest pupils (aged two-and-a-half) wore a uniform and sat in rows of desks, while their teachers used traditional blackboards, chalk and talk. Children under five attended school only in the mornings, but six days a week. They worked hard, with no play during classroom hours. Homework was given regularly. Classroom control was kindly, but firm, with children expected to keep silent except when answering questions or chanting lessons in chorus. Examinations were set at the end of each term, even for the youngest children, and the results taken very seriously by teachers and parents. Several parents supplemented their children's schooling with private 'tuitions' after hours. Despite what seemed to her parents – especially her British father – a high level of pressure, Anita enjoyed school greatly.

On transferring to her British school a year later, Anita found it very different – 'not like a real school', as she put it. The informality, the relaxed atmosphere, the way children were encouraged to talk to one another in class and expected to find many things out for themselves rather than being told them – these were all disconcerting at first, but soon very welcome.

Since Anita joined this school, however, it has changed dramatically in character. Following national test results that were judged unsatisfactory and an unfavourable report from school inspectors, the entire teaching staff resigned. With its new staff, the school is more formal, pressured and focused on measurable attainment – much more like the school in Chennai. Anita enjoys working hard and rarely gets into trouble, but she is unhappy to see some of her friends regularly 'told off' and sometimes shouted at for unsatisfactory work. She still likes going to school, she says, but not so much as before.

Having read through these vignettes, you should now consider some of the issues they raise.

Allow about 15 minutes

A C T I V I T Y 1   Children's experience of education

What similarities and what differences between the educational experiences of the four children struck you most? How might these be explained?

Please write a brief note of your own in response to these questions before reading mine, which follows in the Comment below. As you know by now, you should not take an author's answers to activities as authoritative, but compare them critically with your own.

C O M M E N T

There are of course many similarities and differences that you might reasonably have identified. I shall look at just two.

The set of similarities and differences that struck me most was the enthusiasm for schooling, although of widely varied kinds, shared by Hitomi, Mohsin and Anita, contrasted with the disaffection and alienation of Antonio.

Obviously, many factors lie behind this difference in attitude. Age probably plays a part, as younger children are often more eager to learn and to please their teachers than older ones. Gender may also be a factor, since boys in many cultures tend to be more rebellious than girls. They do not tell the whole story, however. Teenage boys in Hitomi's school work just as hard as she does.

The difference between a wealthy society, where education can be taken for granted, and poorer societies, where it is scarce and highly valued, is also probably important, but again cannot provide a complete explanation. Japan, for instance, is one of the wealthiest societies in the world, yet education is highly valued there. In other parts of the USA and in different social classes, schooling would be as highly valued as in Chittagong or Tokyo. Antonio is from one of the poorest sections of a rich society, but that might have led him to value schooling for the opportunities it might open up – as Mohsin does. On the other hand, Antonio is at school because the law compels him to attend. Perhaps young men in countries of the South who might be similarly disaffected simply do not go to school.

Another set of similarities and differences that struck me concerned the importance of examinations. This was most obvious with Hitomi in Japan, but examinations and tests were also very important in Anita's Indian school and are becoming more and more important in her British schooling, too.

They were not very significant in Mohsin's schooling and of no significance at all for Antonio. Nevertheless, in other sectors of Bangladeshi and American education, examinations are also very important.

Both of these issues – the importance of assessment in schooling throughout the world and the disaffection with schooling shown by many older children in the North – will be discussed in more detail later in this chapter.

2.2 Facts and figures

I shall now set these vignettes in their context in the world today, beginning with some very basic questions about facts and figures.

- How many children are there in the world today?
- How many of them go to school?
- What kinds of school do they attend?

Unfortunately, none of these questions can be answered with much precision or confidence. To see what can be said about them, I shall make use of a survey of the available research and official statistics, made under the auspices of a major international charity: *The Oxfam Education Report*, by Kevin Watkins (Watkins, 2000).

As this report acknowledges, even the most basic question of all – how many children are there? – is difficult to answer. Richer countries, with highly developed administrative systems, may be able to count their populations accurately; poorer countries cannot. In Bangladesh, for example, an education minister acknowledged in the mid-1990s that official estimates of the number of children of primary-school age in the country varied by about two million. Not surprisingly, then, international agencies, dependent as they are on data from national governments, sometimes reach very different estimates for the world as a whole. For example, UNESCO, UNICEF and the World Bank vary by up to 35 million in their estimates of the number of children of primary-school age world-wide who do not attend school (Watkins, 2000, p. 76).

Nevertheless, the Oxfam report draws a rough and tentative picture from a survey of the available evidence. By its estimate, there are some 625 million children of primary-school age (6–11) in the world today, of whom four-fifths (500 million) attend school and one-fifth (125 million) do not (Watkins, 2000, p. 75).

Of the 125 million who do not attend school, two-thirds are girls, one-third boys. The great majority live in either South Asia (45 per cent) or sub-Saharan Africa (35 per cent). (To put these figures into perspective, South Asia has about 25 per cent and sub-Saharan Africa about 10 per cent of the population of the world.) However, although the numbers of children not attending school are falling in most parts of the world, including South Asia, the numbers in sub-Saharan Africa are rising. If present trends continue, sub-Saharan African children of primary-school age will form 50 per cent of all those in the world not attending school by the year 2005, and 75 per cent by 2015 (Watkins, 2000, Chapter 2).

Not attending school at all is a straightforward matter. Attending school, by contrast, is complicated, as the vignettes and pictures illustrate. There is enormous variation in children's schooling: in the sheer amount of time they spend there, in the kind of education they receive and in its quality – and also in the other experiences, not 'educational' in the strictest sense, that school provides.

It is impossible to offer any world-wide figures on these matters, even figures as approximate and uncertain as those already given. Instead, the Oxfam report offers a qualitative comparison of a 'typical' primary school in rural sub-Saharan Africa or South Asia on the one hand, and in Europe or the United States on the other.

> In much of the developing world, 'school' is often a dilapidated mud building with crumbling walls. More than 80 children, many of them undernourished, might be crammed into a classroom, sitting on the floor with scarcely a book, pencil or notepad to share. Their teachers, most of them untrained, may have second jobs to make ends meet. Rote-learning will be the order of the day. Water and sanitation facilities are likely to be grossly inadequate. Primary schools in industrialised countries face problems of their own – but they are problems of a different order. Teachers are well trained, class sizes are smaller, paper and pencils will be in plentiful supply. The school will have a library and probably computers. The walls will be decorated with the work of the children, maps, and other visual aids. Each child will have access to a set of core textbooks. While the national media and parents' associations may take the view that schools are in a state of perpetual crisis, it is a crisis of a different order than that which prevails in the developing world.

(Watkins, 2000, p. 123)

Of course, portraying 'typical' schools in this way does not tell the whole story, about either the South or the North – as the vignettes in Section 2.1 have shown. For example, the school Anita attended in Chennai was better resourced than most others in its neighbourhood. Antonio's school in New York almost certainly had much greater resources than Mohsin's in Chittagong, but that does not mean he received a better education. In both South and North, there is a great deal of variation among schools and therefore a great deal of inequality in the experiences of the children who attend them. There are schools in the South – a minority, perhaps, but still a very large number – that are soundly constructed and adequately equipped, with well-trained teachers and well-nourished pupils. Conversely, there are schools in the North – a minority, but not a negligible minority – with run-down buildings and shortages of equipment, understaffed or staffed by teachers unqualified in the subjects they teach. Besides, those who do go to school in the South are likely to be eager to work, learn and make use of their opportunities. Those in the North, for whom school is freely available and indeed compulsory at certain ages, are sometimes disaffected and alienated – something you have seen in an extreme form in the vignettes and will look at in more depth later in the chapter. However, to point all this out is not to deny the contrast drawn by the Oxfam report, but to qualify it.

The report identifies three measurable aspects of education that can be used to compare the educational performance of different countries. These are:

- the percentage of children of primary-school age who enrol in school;
- the percentage who complete their primary schooling;
- the ratio of girls to boys who enrol for primary schooling.

Taking enrolment and completion first, at one extreme are countries where almost all children enrol in primary school and complete their primary schooling. These include the developed countries of Europe and North America – but not only these. They also include countries in other parts of the world that differ hugely in size, wealth and political system, including Bahrain, China, Cuba, Indonesia, Mauritius, Singapore, Sri Lanka and Uruguay.

At the other extreme are countries where a much lower proportion of the age group enrols in primary school and a lower proportion still completes primary schooling. They are all from the poorer countries of the world and most, though not all, are in sub-Saharan Africa, where typically between 20 and 40 per cent of children enrol in primary school and 10 to 20 per cent complete their primary schooling (Watkins, 2000, Table A1).

There is also a wide range of variation in gender ratios. There are a number of countries where equal proportions of boys and girls enter primary schooling and there are a few where the proportion of girls exceeds that of boys. But in the great majority of countries the proportion of boys entering primary school is higher, sometimes much higher, than that of girls. Gender disparities in favour of boys are particularly marked in South Asia, sub-Saharan Africa and the Middle East, although exceptions can be found within all those regions: for example, Sri Lanka, Zimbabwe and Egypt all have virtually equal enrolment of boys and girls. World-wide, there are 42 million fewer girls than boys in primary school (Watkins, 2000, Chapter 3 and Table A1).

These are variations *between* countries. There are also important differences *within* countries. Differences between urban and rural areas are often very large, particularly in South Asia. In rural areas, enrolment figures tend to be lower and gender disparities greater. In the Sindh region of Pakistan, for example, very similar proportions of urban boys and girls enrol in primary school (just under 60 per cent of each). In rural areas, however, the proportion of boys enrolling falls to 44 per cent and that of girls to 22 per cent (Watkins, 2000, Figure 3.14).

Secondary schooling has received rather less attention from researchers and activists, as the need to increase access to primary education has been considered more urgent. In summary, though, almost all children of secondary-school age in the developed countries enrol in secondary education and over two-thirds complete their secondary schooling. For South Asia, secondary enrolments are about 50 per cent of the population (just under 60 per cent of boys, just over 40 per cent of girls). In sub-Saharan Africa, about 25 per cent of boys and 20 per cent of girls enrol in secondary education (Watkins, 2000, Figure 3.5).

However, enrolment and completion figures by themselves may sometimes give a misleading impression. Schooling may not always be very effective, regardless of its length. According to a survey of the evidence by UNICEF, more than fifteen per cent of adults in industrialized countries remain 'functionally illiterate'. In some countries, including the USA and the United Kingdom, the figures are over twenty per cent (Bellamy, 1999, p. 19).

2.3 Policies

The statistics outlined above need to be understood in the context of policies at both national and global levels. The United Nations Convention on the Rights of the Child, for example, represents a large body of opinion world-wide in declaring not only that children have a right to education, but that this education should be free and compulsory. Article 28 of the convention states:

> States Parties [those states that have subscribed to the convention] recognize the right of the child to education and with a view to achieving this right progressively and on the basis of equal opportunity, they shall, in particular:
>
> (a) Make primary education compulsory and free to all.
>
> (UN Convention on the Rights of the Child, Article 28)

In this spirit, a number of international conferences were held in the 1990s and ambitious declarations produced. The World Conference on Education for All, for example, was held in Jomtien, Thailand, in 1990, under the auspices of the United Nations and the World Bank, and attended by representatives of 155 governments. It set the world a number of targets (Oxfam, no date), including:

- universal access to basic education by 2000, with 80 per cent of children completing primary education;
- a halving of the 1990 adult illiteracy rates, also by 2000;
- closure of the gender gap in both primary and secondary education by 2005;
- universal primary education by 2015.

As I write in 2002, the targets for 2000 have not been met, and achieving the target for 2005 seems very unlikely. This is not to say that nothing constructive has happened since 1990. There has been much work by international agencies, governments, charities and other non-governmental organizations to encourage the spread and development of education in countries where it is judged inadequate in quantity or quality. A recent survey by UNICEF (Bellamy, 1999) describes a wide range of projects, often originating in the North. It shows how such organizations have become increasingly sophisticated and readier to work in genuine partnership with people in the South, taking into account local conditions, complexities, cultural values and expertise – something not always done in the past.

At the same time, however, some of the policies – especially economic policies – imposed on countries of the South by international organizations under the effective control of countries in the North, arguably have quite opposite effects, undermining both local and international efforts to improve education.

Most importantly, in the 1980s and 1990s, the World Bank and the International Monetary Fund required many countries in the South to engage in 'structural adjustment' of their economies. Structural adjustment is a complex and controversial policy, but some of its features and short-term effects are fairly straightforward and uncontentious.

Central to structural adjustment was the requirement that the countries of the South should substantially reduce expenditure on the public sector of their economies. One direct and immediate effect of this was on education. Carol Bellamy of UNICEF, describes some of the consequences for the teaching profession.

> The profession was hit hard by the financial austerity of the 1980s in the developing world. When governments cut public spending as part of structural adjustment programmes required by the World Bank and the International Monetary Fund (IMF), education budgets (comprised largely of teacher salaries) suffered. Over the 1980s and 1990s, teachers in Africa and in Latin America experienced a general lowering of real income, with rapid and substantial reductions in some cases.
>
> The erosion of salaries in Africa, for instance, has meant that primary-school teachers often receive less than half the amount of the household absolute poverty line. Many teachers have been forced to supplement their meagre incomes by offering private lessons or running their own businesses, to the detriment of their regular attendance and performance in schools – a phenomenon that has spread now to countries in eastern Europe, and in Central and East Asia.
>
> (Bellamy, 1999, p. 39)

It may be that, in the long term, structural adjustment will have the favourable effects on the economies of the South that its advocates predict, and that ultimately more resources will be available for education. But for the moment at least, its consequences for children's schooling have been to reduce the chances of achieving the official goal of improving global access to education.

SUMMARY OF SECTION 2

In this section, I presented four vignettes of children at school in the world today, illustrating the range and variety of schooling – in quantity and kind, in the social functions it fulfils and in the attitudes of children towards it.

I then tried to place the vignettes in their context in the world today.

- Schooling varies widely from country to country and region to region, in the proportions of children who enter and who complete their schooling and in the ratios of boys to girls – though in most places, boys have a distinct advantage. As a general rule, schooling is much greater in quantity and, more arguably, superior in quality in the North compared with the South. However, there are important variations within both the North and the South. These are often associated with differences in social class.

- Various international bodies and governments of the North have encouraged projects to assist and improve education in the South.

- But these efforts have arguably been substantially undermined, at least in the short term, by economic reforms imposed by the North on the South at the same time.

3 FUNCTIONS OF SCHOOLING

3.1 Manifest and latent functions

Having looked at the range of children's experience of school in the world today, with its huge inequalities of provision and access, I now want to turn to questions about what school is for. To do this, I shall begin looking at schooling a little more systematically, through a framework of ideas and theories taken from sociology. I want to look at the *social functions* schooling may be said to perform.

In this framework, schooling has functions of two main kinds, *manifest functions* and *latent functions*. Its manifest, or obvious, functions are what people normally think of as the purposes of education – the effects it has that are intended and recognized by the participants and others in society. The latent, or hidden, functions of schooling are effects that are important for society, but are not intended and perhaps not recognized. Indeed, latent functions may sometimes act against the manifest ones.

These terms were introduced and rigorously defined half a century ago by the American sociologist Robert Merton (1957, p. 51). In this chapter, though, I shall use them much more loosely. Nevertheless, we need to be sure that we understand 'manifest and latent functions' in at least roughly the same way.

Allow about 15 minutes

A C T I V I T Y 2   Manifest and latent functions of schooling

Write down two or three manifest functions and two or three latent functions of schooling.

Do not spend too much time on this and do not try to produce more that a few rough and ready examples to illustrate the two types of function. If you find any problems in doing this, note them down.

C O M M E N T

Here is my own attempt, in the form of two short lists. Inevitably, the first list is rather banal, and the second more speculative and controversial. Do not worry if your lists are different from mine – it would be astonishing if they were the same. All they are intended to do is illustrate the *kinds* of function that may appear under one heading or the other. There are many other possible functions that I might have included and that you may have done.

Manifest functions of schooling

1   Schooling teaches children knowledge, skills and ways of thinking that are valuable in themselves, or of practical use, especially for work in adult life.

2   It introduces children to important elements of their national, religious or community culture. Thus it helps foster their sense of identity as members of a nation, a religion or a community.

3   It helps children, when grown up, to participate as citizens in their society and its political processes.

4   It identifies different kinds and amounts of talent in children, and on that basis selects those children suitable for further and higher education of different kinds, thus helping to channel them into appropriate occupations as adults.

Latent functions of schooling

1   While identifying and selecting a minority of children at each stage for more education, and ultimately for the most desirable positions in society, it also persuades the majority that they do not have the necessary abilities and qualities for these positions, and should be satisfied with less desirable ones.

2   Sending children to school performs several useful economic functions for *adults*. It looks after children for substantial portions of the day, week and year, and frees their parents to work. It gives employment to adults who teach children, or otherwise participate in running educational systems. And by removing children from being possible competitors with adults in the labour market, it enhances the adults' position there.

3   Children's work in school is itself economically productive work.

I shall discuss these functions in the remainder of this chapter and in the next, but first, there is one more sociological concept to be mentioned. What I have said so far may suggest that all the consequences of schooling serve to sustain society as it is. But of course, that is not so. Some consequences – latent or manifest – may be *dysfunctional* (Merton, 1957, p. 51) for society, as you will see.

To avoid possible confusion, though, I must emphasize that to talk of functions is not to express moral approval, any more than talk of dysfunctions expresses disapproval. The point can be clearly illustrated with an extreme example. Educating slaves would probably be dysfunctional for a slave society, in that it might make them discontented with their lot. To say that, however, is neither to disapprove of education nor to approve of slavery.

In the remainder of this section, I want to look in a little more detail at some of the manifest and latent functions of schooling that I identified in my comments on Activity 2.

3.2 Knowledge, skills and thinking

The first manifest function on my list probably covers what most people in most societies would see as the main purposes of education: that it teaches children knowledge and ways of thinking that are valuable in themselves, or knowledge and skills that are of practical use, especially for work in adult life. These purposes are very obvious and not very controversial (though of course disagreements and debates begin as soon as people try to put the general principles into practice). It is for that reason that I shall not spend very much time on them – not because I deny their fundamental importance. (See Chapter 6 for an analysis of such debates in relation to early childhood education.)

What I want to do instead is look briefly at a few items on the lists that are less obvious and sometimes more questionable.

3.3 Culture and identity

Schools may indeed help to assimilate children into cultures and foster identities, as is claimed in the second item on my list of manifest functions, but this can be a more complex and morally ambiguous process than is sometimes acknowledged. First, we need to ask, *which* cultures and identities? Schools are sometimes criticized for alienating children from their community, its culture and sometimes even its language, where that differs from a majority national language favoured in school. I can illustrate this from my own experience.

When my classmates and I started school, on the Scottish island of Lewis in the 1950s, most of us spoke only Gaelic. The first task of the infants teacher was to teach everyone English, which then became the language of instruction for every other subject, and indeed the language for every formal aspect of school. Much more recently I found very similar processes at work in Bangalore, in south India, when I did some research in the 1990s in an English-medium private primary school – the type of school favoured by middle-class families. Children who spoke the local language, Kannada, as their mother tongue had to begin their schooling by learning English, which again became the language used for almost all aspects of schooling.

Neither in 1950s Lewis nor in 1990s Bangalore was the local language forbidden or even discouraged, as has sometimes happened. Indeed, Gaelic and Kannada were taught in the respective schools as subjects in their own right, and of course each continued to be the main language used in the playground and in most homes. From the beginning of primary school, however, children were left in no doubt that English was the language that would be important for their educational and occupational success.

And in both situations, educational success was likely to take children away from their home and community – not just culturally, but geographically. Children in 1950s Lewis who did well at school were likely to move to richer regions of their country, with wider opportunities for employment. In the 1990s, an age of globalization, educationally successful children in Bangalore were quite likely to move to richer countries.

To point all this out is not to criticize schooling, but to recall how complex and morally ambiguous its task is. Children often have a wide range of cultures, identities and possibilities facing them, and schools probably cannot avoid favouring some at the expense of others.

Besides, what is an advantage from one point of view may be a drawback from another. What is from one perspective initiation into a religious culture may from another be indoctrination. What some see as creating a sense of national or community identity, others may regard as chauvinistic, even sometimes racist. In Northern Ireland and southern Scotland, for example, children from Protestant and Roman Catholic families typically attend separate schools. This separation has both supporters and critics: the former arguing that it helps to transmit and preserve the respective faiths; the latter concerned that it helps to create and maintain hostility between the two faith communities. Once again, schooling and its achievements can be morally ambiguous.

And many children in the world today have more than one identity, with the possibility of conflict between them. Anita, in one of the vignettes in Section 2.1, has one parent from a Hindu background and one from a Christian background. She herself has attended a Hindu school in India and now goes to a Church of England school in Britain. At first, she was puzzled as to how the Christianity taught in the latter fitted in with the Hinduism everywhere around her in India. If there have been no serious conflicts of identity for her, this may be because both her schools apply their official religion with a light touch and both her parents regard their religious heritage with a measure of scepticism.

3.4 Education and participation

The claim that education helps children, when grown up, to participate more fully as citizens – the third item on my list of manifest functions – seems plausible enough. Political participation does seem to be enhanced by basic literacy and numeracy, for example, together with some knowledge of the history and geography of one's country and its place in the world.

However, this refers specifically to the future, to a time when the children are children no longer, but grown up. The other side of this coin, it is sometimes argued, is that schooling makes it more difficult for children to participate as citizens *now*, while they are still children. To put the claim in extreme form, schooling can sometimes be said to 'infantilize' children and young people. School pupils in their mid-to-late teens, for example, are often made to live under conditions of close supervision and instruction, forbidden to make their own decisions or take responsibility for their lives. Even their clothing may be chosen for them, in the form of school uniform. At the same age, many of their contemporaries are working to earn their living, raising or supporting families and fighting in wars.

All this suggests that there may be a trade-off for children here. By going to school now, and postponing their participation in society as full citizens, they may be able to participate more effectively when they are older.

3.5 Selection and legitimization

If the final item on the list of manifest functions is correct – that schooling identifies talent and selects children for appropriate further education and employment – then it does appear to be serving a useful function for the wider society. But this may arguably be an oversimplification of what actually happens. Schooling may also have some other functions than teaching, learning and straightforward selection by merit – functions that are not usually openly acknowledged today.

For example, (in the language of sociologists) schooling may serve to differentiate pupils and legitimize the differentiation, as in the first item on the list of latent functions. What this means is that in virtually every society people occupy positions that are unequal in a number of ways. For society to function, so the argument runs, people need to be placed in the different positions and made to accept their place. Taking paid employment as an example, different jobs are extremely unequal in a number of obvious respects: in earnings, working conditions, interest, freedom, power, security, prospects and so on. Why do people accept such inequality, particularly people in the least favoured jobs?

One explanation is that they do so because they accept that, by and large, the allocation of jobs is based on *merit* – some combination of ability and effort. To put it crudely, the people in the best jobs are believed to be, by and large, those with the most merit, and this belief in meritocracy is fostered by schools. In Britain today, and in many other societies too, children are tested and graded almost from the moment they first enter school. By the time they leave they have acquired, or failed to acquire, a clutch of certificates that ranks them fairly precisely among their fellows and opens up or closes off future prospects for education and employment.

How far success or failure at school really is based on merit is arguable. There is a great deal of educational research to support the common-sense view that other factors, such as the social class, education or wealth of parents, have an important influence on a child's success. But according to some writers (such as Bowles and Gintis, 1976), this does not matter. What is important for schools' legitimizing of inequalities is that, rightly or wrongly, success and failure are generally *believed* to be based on merit.

Of course, few people in positions of authority today would describe the function of schools in these terms. Advocates of mass education in Britain and America in the nineteenth and early twentieth centuries were often more frank, stressing the usefulness of enough, but not too much, education in helping to create a productive and docile workforce.

How cogent is this argument? I myself do not have much difficulty in accepting the 'official' view – that schooling identifies and selects children for appropriate further education and employment on the basis of merit – as it applies to more *technical* subjects and occupations. There the knowledge and skills taught in educational institutions are directly related to those required and used in the occupations, and can be objectively identified and readily measured. I do not doubt that, by and large, those who succeed in becoming computer programmers, engineers or surgeons genuinely do so on the basis of merit. I am less sure about the relationship between more *general* educational qualifications and occupations where the skills and knowledge required are harder to pin down. This is an issue to be covered in more depth in Section 4 of this chapter.

3.6 Children's schooling and adults' work

Among the latent functions of children's schooling, I placed some functions schooling might be said to perform for working adults and the economy in general.

- By looking after their children for substantial periods, schooling frees parents to work and contribute to the economy.
- By giving employment to adults – teachers, inspectors, administrators, caretakers and so on – schooling contributes directly to the economy.
- By keeping children out of the labour market, where they might be competitors with adults, schooling reduces adult unemployment and improves adult employees' bargaining power and thence their earnings and conditions.

What makes these surprising and perhaps uncomfortable reading is that they are explicitly about functions of schooling for people other than the children themselves. They are not the sorts of arguments that usually appear in discussions of the purposes of education. Indeed, some might regard them as somewhat cynical, or assume that they were intended satirically. However, all three refer to real and far-reaching consequences of schooling that ought not to be overlooked. Even if they are not what schools are intended and expected to do, they may nevertheless be part of what schooling actually does, with important consequences.

Just how important these functions are varies from place to place and from time to time. The first of them probably applies more to the North than the South. In many parts of the South, as you will see in Chapter 5, children – far from being an economic burden on working parents – are workers and often earners in their own right, making valuable contributions to the income of their families alongside their parents. In this situation, school does not free parents for work by looking after their children. On the contrary, school can impose economic burdens of its own on working children and their families. Sometimes there are formal or informal fees to be paid, books and equipment to be bought and travel to be paid for. Even where that is not so, time spent at school is time not spent on paid work, which may cause severe difficulties for families living in poverty. (See Chapter 5 for further discussion.)

3.7 Schooling as children's economically productive work

The last item on the list of latent functions is probably the most puzzling and controversial.

So far, like most people in the world, I have treated school and work as different things. I shall examine the concept of work in the next chapter, but there are some things I can say about it now. Most people normally assume that children may go to school, or they may work, or they may do both at different times of the day or week, but that these are different activities. Of course, what children do at school is 'work' in some sense, but that is not the same sense as children's work on farms or in factories. It is not economically productive work. Some economically productive work *is* done in schools, but that is done by the teachers and other adult employees, not by the pupils. So, at least, runs the conventional view.

However, this view has been challenged in recent years. The sociologist Jens Qvortrup has argued that, in modern economies in the North, children's 'work' in school not only *is* economically productive work, but is children's most important productive work. By comparison with their school work, he claims, children's paid employment outside the school is relatively trivial – 'residual and anachronistic', in his words (Qvortrup, 2001, p. 93).

If children in school are productive workers, what are they producing? Qvortrup's answer is that they are producing themselves as the future educated labour force. If a modern economy needs an educated labour force, then the production of that labour force is as much part of the economy as any other form of production. For some time, this has been widely accepted as far as teachers are concerned: teaching children in school is widely recognized as economically productive work. For Qvortrup, the same logic applies to children. Their work, as they learn in school, is economically productive too.

This is not just a terminological quibble. If Qvortrup is right, children at school should not be seen as an economic burden on adult society. In the short term, they may be an economic burden on their parents, but for society as a whole, they are producing economic benefits, even if these can only be realized in the future (Qvortrup, 2001; see also James, Jenks and Prout, 1998, p. 117–8).

Qvortrup's argument is intriguing, and often referred to in the literature on school and children's work. However, most writers continue to treat 'child work' as something different from school – and I shall do so here and in the next chapter. It is 'child work' in the sense of farming, domestic service, manufacturing, selling and so on that raises the most acute moral and practical dilemmas. 'Work' in that sense is different from school work, even if that too turns out to have an economically productive aspect.

Having looked briefly at all the functions on my lists, I now want to examine two particularly important functions in more detail. These will occupy Sections 4 and 5 of this chapter.

SUMMARY OF SECTION 3

The sociological concepts of functions (manifest and latent) and dysfunctions provided a framework for analysing schooling in the world today. Some specific functions of schooling were identified.

- Manifest functions were: the teaching of knowledge, skills and ways of thinking; the transmission of culture and the construction of identity; and preparation for participation as adult citizens.

- Latent, and more controversial, functions were: the differentiation of pupils for future employment and the legitimization of the differentiation; the protection by children's school attendance of *adults'* employment; the interpretation of children's schooling as *children's* economically productive work.

4 SCHOOLING AND QUALIFICATIONS

Alongside teaching and learning, I identified another important manifest function of schools at the beginning of the chapter. This was to test students' abilities and attainments, and award *qualifications* to those who were successful – certificates or diplomas that 'qualify' them for certain occupations or increasingly often for further education or training on the path to these occupations. But there may be more to qualifications than that. In this section, I begin to look at some of the latent functions and dysfunctions that may be involved.

I want to approach these issues through a classic text, *The Diploma Disease*, by the sociologist Ronald Dore. Dore first published the book in the mid-1970s and returned to the argument in a second edition some twenty years later (Dore, 1976 and 1997). In a nutshell, Dore argues that the testing and qualification function of schooling is becoming ever more important, to the detriment of the teaching and learning function. This is happening everywhere in the world, he argues, but for various historical reasons, it is particularly marked in Japan and particularly damaging in many of the poorest countries.

To avoid misunderstanding, let me begin by emphasizing some things that Dore is *not* arguing. First, he is not an opponent of education or schooling as such. Indeed, he begins his book by affirming his belief in the civilizing effects of learning, knowledge, understanding and thinking – and of the education that cultivates these, in schools and universities. Nor is he against examinations as such, though he has often been misread in this way. As he wrote in the second edition of *The Diploma Disease*:

> ... the book definitely is not ... a tract on the wickedness of examinations – although I perhaps did not say so explicitly enough in the [first edition] not to be misunderstood. I am all in favour of examinations for vocational courses ... In *general education* in language and literature, maths and science, examinations clearly have their uses, with the exact form of the examination making quite a big difference to the kind of learning activity they encourage and hence to their usefulness. They provide informative feedback to teachers on how effective their teaching has been. For the pupil, the prospect of the sense of achievement at having done well in an examination can supplement the intrinsic pleasures of learning – satisfaction of curiosity, the sense of mastery, of growing and developing – by providing an incentive to stick at the tough slog – of puzzling out the difficult things, of continuous practising and memorising – that a lot of learning entails.

> (Dore, 1997, p. x)

So, what *is* Dore arguing? In his view, much of schooling in the modern world has become the pursuit of ever-higher qualifications that are irrelevant to the occupations for which they 'qualify' their holders. The consequences are at their most extreme and damaging in the South, he believes, but the processes he is describing are occurring in the North, too.

The starting point lies in two straightforward facts: that desirable jobs are offered on the basis of academic qualifications, but that there are not enough jobs available for all those who hold the qualifications. From this, almost everything else follows.

If there are more applicants holding the qualification *formally* required for a particular level of job than there are jobs at that level, employers tend to offer the job to those holding higher qualifications. Such applicants will be available if jobs at the higher levels are similarly oversubscribed by qualified candidates. So, the level of qualifications required *in practice* for a particular level of job tends to rise, and would-be employees, however humble their ambitions, tend to need ever higher qualifications.

As a consequence, Dore argues, the *content* of education becomes less important. As 'qualification escalation' proceeds, the relevance of people's studies to the job they eventually do becomes less and less. And so students tend to be motivated less and less by the content of their studies and more and more by the qualification they will gain from them. Teachers, understandably, concentrate more and more narrowly on the knowledge and skills that will earn their pupils the highest grades, regardless of their educational value in wider terms.

So, education is degraded, becoming, in Dore's words, 'ritualistic, tedious, suffused with anxiety and boredom, destructive of curiosity and imagination; in short, anti-educational' (Dore, 1976, p. ix). And especially in the South, countries spend much of their scarce resources on schooling that is neither fulfilling for the pupils nor productive for the economy.

This process, as Dore has pointed out, is a striking example of how behaviour that is rational at the individual level may be irrational at the level of society. Every individual he refers to seems to be acting entirely rationally in his or her economic interests – the pupils and students who seek higher and higher qualifications, and the parents who push them on; the schools that offer these higher qualifications; even the employers who demand them. But the overall result, he argues, is thoroughly irrational for all the parties involved. Going to school for these purposes, Dore believes, is pointless, wasteful and even damaging. Societies, especially poorer societies, spend a high proportion of their scarce resources on schooling where children and young adults study what is neither of intrinsic interest or value to them nor of practical use in doing their work. In the process, the genuinely educational possibilities of schooling are sometimes pushed aside.

Some of the consequences of the 'diploma disease' at its most extreme are to be seen in Japan – you have already had a glimpse of them in the life of Hitomi. In Japan itself, what has developed is often called 'examination hell', and the phrase was used as the title for Dore's book when it was translated into Japanese. As Angela Little, a research colleague of Dore, explained in a BBC television documentary film:

> Schooling in Japan is based on a single-track, six–three–three–four system: six years in elementary school, three years each in junior and senior high school, and four years at university. For the ambitious, transferring at each stage to the best schools means competitive entry

examinations and often the repetitive learning of facts and knowledge, the very antithesis of what many regard as good education.

(Hill and Little, 1996)

Intense pressure is put on children to do well in examinations at every level, so as to gain admission to the 'best' schools at the next level and, ultimately, to the 'best' universities. Indeed, as with Hitomi, it often starts even before elementary school. (Ironically, the pressure seems to ease during the final stage. Getting into a leading university seems to count for more in the Japanese job market than how well you do when you are there.)

Young children at school: Japan.

As well as their ordinary school, a typical Japanese child will attend a *juku*, a private crammer school, in the evenings and at weekends, and also continue studying at home, often late into the night. Many of the children caught up in this system find it very difficult and stressful, but accept it as a necessary part of life, and even find positive virtues in it. One fourteen-year-old girl at junior high school expressed it like this:

> Well, I think it will be horrible working hard from now on for the examinations, but in order to get into a good high school I think that even though you might call it hell, it is best to study. If there weren't any entrance examinations, I wouldn't take in the lessons very well and I wouldn't do very much revision of what I'd learnt. So I think that after all, because there are examinations, I do my work and I don't lead a lazy life.

(Hill and Little, 1996)

Parents, teachers and academics in Japan often show a similar ambivalence towards the examination system – deploring the stress it places on children and fearing that it stifles creativity and independence of thought, but at the same time seeing it as an effective way of motivating them to study, and as leading to exceptionally high standards of achievement by comparison with most other countries. In any case, few see any way of escaping from it. As the father of two boys at high school put it:

> Entrance examinations are quite unavoidable ... there has to be a balance between the numbers that can be taken in and the excess demand. I think this is something that can only be decided by examinations. It's been like this for some time. It can't be done in any other way.

> (Hill and Little, 1996)

However, the 'examination hell' question has been debated in Japan for some years now, and even as I write, the Japanese government has taken drastic steps intended to reduce the children's workload. The formal academic curriculum has been reduced by between 20 per cent and 30 per cent, pupils are to be given more choice over how they spend their time in school, and compulsory Saturday classes in state schools have been abolished.

However, as Jonathan Watts, a Tokyo-based journalist, reports:

> Many students and teachers welcome the change, but it is far from certain that it will achieve its aims. ... anxious parents are already moving their children to private schools, most of which hold Saturday classes. Others are spending more on evening and weekend cram schools.

> (Watts, 2002)

If Dore's analysis is correct, the pressure on children is caused not by the size of the curriculum, but by the excess of demand over supply for places at prestigious schools and universities, and the rewards available for those who win these places. These reforms will do nothing to change that.

Japan, of course, is one of the most economically advanced and prosperous countries in the world, albeit in the throes of recession at the time of writing. However, similar education and examination systems are developing in many countries of the South – though so far at a less intense level and involving a much smaller proportion of the population. Sri Lanka provides one example, as Angela Little explains, despite the high rates of graduate unemployment there.

> Yet still the education system ... continues to support the expectation that success in academic qualifications will secure a white-collar public-sector job. The numbers sitting public examinations have quadrupled in the last twenty years and, so desperate are the students to succeed that, like in Japan, the private crammer, or 'tutory' as it is called here, is big business. Advertisements for revision courses and private lessons abound as tutories compete in a fierce market. Parents in Sri Lanka spend a large part of their income on extra tuition, proportionately probably far greater than parents in Japan.

> [...]

Private tuition takes many forms. It's organized in large halls, in school buildings after the school day has ended and in private homes by tutors often little older than the students they teach.

(Hill and Little, 1996)

A young tutor takes a class at home: Sri Lanka.

Advertisements for tutories: Sri Lanka.

I myself observed what appeared to be another example of these processes in my research in an English-medium primary school in Karnataka, in south India. (It is illustrated in Reading A.) The children's mother-tongue was Kannada, but all those I observed were fluent in English too, having typically attended school and studied English since the age of two-and-a-half. In Karnataka, the state produces official textbooks for every subject. Although this is a private school, it uses the state textbooks and follows the state curriculum in most subjects, so that its pupils can sit the state examinations at the end of their final year in primary school. The book used in the lesson discussed here was a state textbook.

READING

You should now read 'Boarding a bus' by Donald Mackinnon (Reading A).

In the lesson described in the reading, Mrs Kumaran, with a class of five-to six-year olds, was following a standard pattern that was shared with virtually all text-based lessons in the school. There is some evidence that this basic style of teaching is not peculiar to these teachers or this school, but widespread in India. (For analysis of it and of its roots in indigenous

Indian and British imperial culture, see Jayalakshmi, 1996.) The lesson is dominated by the teacher on the one hand, and the textbook on the other. The teacher reads a passage from the textbook, says something about it or arising out of it, demands some response from the pupils and then moves on to the next passage.

Within this basic style, there is some variation between teachers. Some expand at length on the words of the text; others, like Mrs Kumaran here, confine themselves mostly to repeating, rewording and asking straightforward questions of fact and word-meaning closely tied to the text. And this extract gives only a hint of the repetition involved. The lesson was the second of four devoted to the chapter, in three of which it was read several times in the same manner. And every sentence in the chapter was treated in the same way as this opening one.

I do not fully understand why Mrs Kumaran and many of her colleagues teach in this way. She might seem to be simply getting pupils to repeat words and phrases rather mechanically and pointlessly, over and over again, and asking them undemanding questions with obvious answers. The story is really very straightforward for these children and I doubt if any of them had serious difficulty with reading it, or failed to grasp it the first time round. (The only thing in the sentence that I think might puzzle a reader whose first language was not English is the expression 'was to visit', but Mrs Kumaran did not comment on it.)

However, I do think that Dore's thesis may cast some light on what is happening. I think that at least part of the explanation of the style lies in the Indian examination system and its implications. In the state examination that the children will take at the end of their final year of primary school, most of the marks in English and other text-based subjects are given for recall of the details of the textbooks. This pattern is followed in the school's own examinations and tests at the end of each term. The state examinations are extremely important in determining the pupils' access to different kinds of secondary schooling, where similar examinations will determine access to higher education and thence to different kinds of job. The earlier examinations and tests in primary school need not be treated as of such importance, but many schools, including this one, see them as important stages in the cumulative preparation of pupils for their final examination. And Mrs Kumaran's repetitive drumming-in of the details of the stories is probably very effective as preparation for this kind of examination, whatever might be said for or against it in other respects.

Mrs Kumaran herself had no qualms about the teaching methods used in schools like this one. They may have been necessitated by the requirements of the examination system, but she believed them to be good methods anyway. Like many of her colleagues, she had close relations who had moved to other countries – in her case, brothers and their children in the United States of America. She was well informed about the more relaxed and less didactic way in which teaching is typically conducted there, and was politely unimpressed by its results.

SUMMARY OF SECTION 4

- Ronald Dore has argued that the qualification-awarding function of schooling has to a large extent replaced its educational function.

- This has happened all over the world, but especially in Japan and with most damaging effects in many countries of the South.

5 PUPILS' DISAFFECTION AND ALIENATION

In the last quarter of the twentieth century, a research tradition developed in British sociology of education that came to be known as 'classroom ethnography'. As the name suggests, sociologists were self-consciously trying to emulate their anthropological colleagues, by treating the familiar classrooms of their own country as if they were something alien and barely understood. By making the familiar strange, they hoped to examine and question features of classroom life that had previously been taken for granted.

So, the classroom ethnographer went to live for a sustained period in one of these strange environments, minutely observing and recording what went on and what the participants told them about it, and trying in various ways to explain what they observed.

One of the recurrent themes of this tradition was the way in which many children were alienated from and disaffected with school, particularly after they had passed from primary to secondary stages. They did not always fall obediently, let alone eagerly, into what the school expected of them. On the contrary, getting pupils to meet the school's demands often required hard work on the part of their teachers – work that was not always crowned with success.

The introduction of secondary modern schools was discussed by Hugh Cunningham in Chapter 3.

This is illustrated in extreme form in America in the vignette of Antonio, but the British studies in this section are much less dramatic. An early example of this type of study was conducted in the mid 1970s by Viv Furlong in a secondary modern school in London, a school where he was a teacher as well as a researcher.

Secondary modern schools were part of the state system introduced into England and Wales – and under different names into Scotland and Northern Ireland – after World War II. Under this system there were two main types of secondary school: 'grammar' schools for children judged on the basis of tests of intelligence and attainment to be of high academic ability; and 'secondary modern' schools for those judged less able. Pupils at secondary modern schools were much less likely to obtain formal qualifications from public examinations. This system has now been replaced in Scotland, Wales and most of England by one based on comprehensive schools, though it still remains in Northern Ireland and a few English counties.

Furlong looked particularly at one class of fifteen fourth-year girls, which ranked second from the bottom in the school's streaming system. They were regarded by their teachers as of 'below average ability' and as a 'difficult' class, although not the 'worst' in the school (Furlong, 1977, pp. 162–3).

These girls, Furlong reports, spent a great deal of time 'mucking about':

> ... they were always late arriving for lessons, running round the corridors, cheeking teachers, teasing and playing jokes on each other, talking in class when they should be working, and generally misbehaving. Mucking about was an important feature of classroom life ... Everyone in the class enjoyed mucking about and expected their friends to join in.
>
> (Furlong, 1977, pp. 164–5)

The girls themselves explained this behaviour as their response to the way the teachers treated them.

> Mucking about was always explained away by the girls as being a response to boredom in the classroom ... It was seen as the teachers' responsibility to provide discipline and not for them to control themselves; a repeated lack of control led to boredom. The teachers were also seen as responsible for providing interesting lessons and helping them to learn – even when they were controlled, some lessons could be boring ... There were a number of teachers who were neither able to provide the disciplinary structure that the girls felt they needed, nor able to teach them in a way the girls considered effective. Consequently the girls got bored – instead of working they would arrive late, leave early, talk, shout, even fight – they would do almost anything to get a 'laugh' and reduce the almost unending boredom of an irrelevant school life.
>
> (Furlong, 1977, pp. 166–7)

Strictness in teachers was universally approved of and welcomed by the girls, and its opposite, 'softness', deplored. Furlong asked one girl, Valerie, what she would do if she were a teacher who came into a classroom to find everyone mucking about.

> *Valerie:* Well it would depend on what kind of teacher I was. If I was a strict teacher I'd go 'SIT DOWN', you know once you hit one of them the rest are frightened ... .
>
> (Furlong, 1977, p. 172)

But the pupils' misbehaviour was not all of this character. As well as good-humoured mucking about, there was sometimes serious hostility and open rebellion. The difference between the two was usually much clearer to the pupils than to the teachers, for whom it was all 'misbehaviour'. Hostility and rebellion arose when teachers transgressed the girls' ideas of justice and proper conduct. While they did not object to being scolded or punished for misbehaviour when this was done fairly, they did object strongly when they thought it was unfair. They also distinguished between acceptable and unacceptable types of sanction from the teachers. Hitting as such was acceptable to most of them, though not all, but not hitting on the head. Shouting as such was tolerated, but not everything that a teacher might shout, as Valerie herself illustrated:

> ... one day I came in right, and I was late – I admit I was late, so I kept quiet – I didn't want him to tell me off, and so then I was talking and he shout at me and he went, 'Shut that big mouth of yours Valerie Burnett!' and I said 'No, I don't have to!' and he said, 'Don't talk back' and I said, 'I talk back when I want to, when I feel like it!' and he just went and he started to talk and he was talking about me really, it was about me, right, and I went 'TSSSSSSS' and he heard me and he went, 'Get out of the classroom,' so I went outside and I slammed the door.

(Furlong, 1977, pp. 167–8)

Pupils' responses to what was seen as unacceptable behaviour on the part of teachers could be even more dramatic. On one occasion, Carol recalled, a teacher had pushed her and she had responded by hitting him. This, she explained, was because he had unfairly singled her out.

> *Carol:* (annoyed) ... I wasn't the only one that was running so he just came at me because I was the *last* one and just push me.
>
> *Valerie:* You had no choice.
>
> *Carol:* So I hit him back and I got into trouble then. That was unfair.

(Furlong, 1977, pp. 168)

In his analysis, Furlong takes for granted that there is an inherent conflict between teacher and pupils. He does not attempt to identify the *sources* of this conflict, but confines his attention to the way it is played out in the school and especially the classroom. The questions this conflict raises, however, are intriguing. *Why* is there an apparently inherent conflict in the relationship between pupils and their teachers? *Why* should the girls in Furlong's study demand that their teachers be strict and make them work? *Why* will they muck about if the teachers are soft?

One immediate answer may lie in the character of the school involved and the careers of these pupils within it. It was a secondary modern, widely seen as catering for academic failures. The girls in Furlong's study were particularly likely to think of themselves in this way, since their school was streamed, and they were in a low stream in which they were not prepared for public examinations. If Ronald Dore's analysis is sound, their courses are likely to be regarded as less important than those that lead to qualifications. All in all, it would be understandable if many of these girls saw themselves as rejects of the educational system, which now had little to offer them. Some may have thought they were being made to waste their time in school until they reached the minimum leaving-age – especially, perhaps, as it had only recently (1972) been raised from fifteen to sixteen.

This is an explanation I find plausible, but in its turn it raises further questions. Why did the United Kingdom develop a divided school system of this kind? Which children ended up in which type of school and why? Was it simply a question of intelligence and effort, or were there other factors at work? The second reading for this chapter looks at pupils' disaffection in the light of wider questions such as these. Paul Willis's 'School counter-culture and shop-floor culture' has become a classic study in the sociology of education. Like the Furlong study, Willis's was conducted in the mid-1970s and based on ethnographic methods. He studied a number of schools (and factories) in an industrial conurbation in England, but in this paper he concentrates on 'a friendship group of twelve boys as they proceeded through their last four terms of a single-sex secondary modern school.' He distinguished two basic categories of boys in the school, those who conformed to the demands of the school and those who did not. All the boys Willis studied intensively seem to have belonged to the nonconformists, and he adopted their genial term for themselves ('lads') and their disparaging term for the conformists ('ear-'oles').

Unlike Furlong, Willis also interviewed all the boys' parents and spent some time observing each of the boys after they had started work.

In Britain, the phrase 'shop floor' traditionally refers to manual work in a factory. In this reading, it has nothing to do with shops.

Allow about 2 hours

READING

You should now read 'School counter-culture and shop-floor culture' by Paul Willis (Reading B) and then work through Activity 3.

ACTIVITY 3   School and factory counter-cultures

Please summarize Willis's main arguments and claims and decide how convinced you are by them, before you read my discussion below. You may find the following questions helpful.

*   Why does Willis conclude that what is not supposed to go on in the school may be of more significance than what is supposed to? Do you agree?
*   What similarities does Willis claim there are between the school counter-culture and the culture of the workplace? Do you agree that these similarities exist?
*   What does Willis think the consequences of these similarities are: (a) for the lads; (b) for the ear-'oles? Are you convinced?
*   Willis conducted his research in the mid-1970s. How relevant is it in the changed economic circumstances of today?

COMMENT

My attempt to answer these questions forms the remainder of this section of the chapter. As always, I should like you to compare my answers critically with your own, but certainly not to take mine as definitive.

One immediate answer to the question of why what is not supposed to happen may be more significant than what is supposed to happen is that the former seems to be what actually happens! Willis does not in fact devote much attention to formal teaching and learning in this school, but the information he does provide suggests that, for the lads he studied, there is rather little of it. If Joey's account can be believed, there is no school work, even officially, on Monday, Tuesday or Wednesday afternoons. Thursday and Friday afternoons do have some – 'if you can call it work' – but much 'dossing' and 'wagging' too. Of course, the lads' mornings may be devoted to serious study, but the testimony of Fuzz, who apparently almost succeeded in getting through a term without writing anything, suggests not.

The school, then, does not seem to be very good at fulfilling its manifest function, at least for these lads. However, Willis argues (though not in these words) that it also has a latent function which it fulfils very successfully. This is 'to direct a portion of kids to the unrewarding and basic tasks of industrial production'. This is done in large part through the similarities between the counter-culture of the school and the shop-floor culture.

There are three main similarities, according to Willis.

- There is 'a form of masculine chauvinism' in both.

- In both there is an attempt, often successful, for the workers/pupils to take over control of daily life from the formal holders of authority.

- In both there is a similar atmosphere of rough verbal and physical humour.

How convincing are these claims? Not completely, it seems to me. I can completely accept the third: it seems obviously correct. I can also accept the second, though with one reservation. Both the lads at school and the men at work do seem to take over some control of their daily lives from those formally in authority. But as Willis acknowledges, their purposes in doing so are entirely different. The men organize things so that the work the authorities want done gets done, the lads so that it does not!

However, I am sceptical about the first supposed similarity. Look again at the two quotations on which it is based, the first from a foundryman ('I work in a foundry ... you have to keep going to get enough out.') and the second from his son, Joey ('That's it, we've developed certain ways of talking ... biting his ear and things like this.') Unfortunately, Willis does not analyse or compare these passages in any detail, but simply quotes them and asserts that they show 'a clear continuity of attitudes'. I agree that each passage shows pride in a version of masculine toughness, but thereafter I am much more struck by *dis*continuities between the two versions. (I also do not agree with Willis that the father expresses himself 'in an inarticulate way' – though admittedly this is hard to judge, given how much Willis seems to have edited out of what the father says.)

The toughness of which the father is proud consists in being able to do, and actually doing, physically difficult work well. There is not a hint of this in what his son says; he simply does not mention work here. The toughness the son takes pride in consists of racist, sexist and other chauvinistic ways of talking and acting, above all fighting. I can find no suggestion of chauvinism (let alone racism or sexism) or aggression in anything his father says.

The father's pride also has a strong ethical element – he is proud of doing the best job he can, of 'earning every penny' of the money he is paid. The son's pride involves an explicit rejection of ethics. In his fights, 'There's no chivalry or nothing'; all that is 'cobblers' and 'you might as well go all the way and win it completely by having someone else help ya or by winning the dirtiest methods you can think of ... '.

It also seems telling to contrast the father's attitude to the managers with the son's to his more conformist fellow pupils. The father does take pride in his physical superiority to the managers – they couldn't do the heavy work he does – but he also seems to be on friendly terms with them, and takes pleasure in their seeing him at work and knowing what he can do. The son dismisses conformist boys contemptuously as 'the fucking ear-'oles', for whom he and his friends have developed 'disregards' – a rather more sinister word in its context here than it might otherwise be.

All in all, then, I think Willis exaggerates the similarities and continuities between the counter-culture of the school and the culture of the workplace. I accept, though, that a number of similarities remain that may be important.

Steel works: England, 1970s.

A school rule is broken: England, 1970s.

The consequences of these similarities, according to Willis, are profound.

- It is the lads' counter-culture (rather than any official careers advice) that guides them towards the kinds of jobs where similar values and relationships exist – notably those on the shop floor.

- School counter-culture prepares the lads for factory life: 'there is no shock, only recognition'.

- The division between lads and ear-'oles at school becomes a division between different kinds of worker: the ear-'oles are more likely than the lads to become non-manual workers, or if they do become manual workers, to become skilled manual workers.

- Those ear-'oles who do obtain work on the shop floor are less well prepared for it than the lads. They are more likely to expect job satisfaction, promotion on merit and so on. This makes them more difficult for those in authority to deal with.

- The lads' 'roughness' and readiness to 'stand up for themselves' present less of a threat to management because they are relatively superficial: they are displayed within a fundamental acceptance by the lads of their subordinate position.

- Thus the end result is ironic: the conformists and nonconformists at school have in some ways exchanged places on the factory floor.

These claims are not (at least in this paper) backed up by detailed evidence. They are, however, based generally on Willis's interviews and observations in the factories where the boys worked and they all seem quite credible. There may well be other factors at work, too, of course. For example, the lads' culture at school gives them little chance of obtaining academic qualifications. It is at least possible that their lack of qualifications is a significant factor, alongside the cultural continuity that Willis identifies, in directing them towards unskilled manual work. Other types of work may be difficult for them to obtain.

The picture Willis paints is of vigorous, independent, rebellious boys and young men whose very rebelliousness leads them unwittingly into taking on 'the unrewarding and basic tasks of industrial production', all the while understanding this as natural and inevitable, but somehow also as attractive and freely chosen.

Finally, even if Willis's analysis was valid in the 1970s, how well does it stand up today? Willis himself was confident that the 'complex of chauvinism, toughness and machismo' that he had identified would remain, even if the pattern of industrial work changed.

However, the British economy may have changed more than Willis anticipated. Reporting on a study conducted in secondary schools in the same area some twenty years after his, Mary Jane Kehily and Anoop Nayak summarize what has happened. Willis's argument was persuasive in its time, they believe, but:

> ... a prolonged period of Conservative rule, a decline in the region's industrial base and the erosion of trade union activity, have exacerbated long-term unemployment in the West Midlands area of Britain. Whereas the 'lads' of '77 may have found recognition in the familiar, albeit

constrained enclave of factory life, the young men in our study seemed less optimistic about full-time employment and job security.

(Kehily and Nayak, 1997, pp. 84–5)

And it is only fair to add in 2002 that the five years since Kehily and Nayak's paper was published, years mostly of Labour government, have seen a continuing decline in the numbers employed in manufacturing industry.

Despite these changes to the manufacturing base, Kehily and Nayak discovered, the 'lads' were still to be found in schools, behaving much as in Willis's time. Girls and young women, and subordinate boys and young men, especially if they were identified as gay, were 'seen as targets for comic displays which frequently blur the boundaries between humour and harassment' (Kehily and Nayak, 1997, p. 81). This presents something of a puzzle. 'If they are no longer "learning to labour"?', they ask, 'then what exactly are they doing?' (Kehily and Nayak, 1997, p. 85).

Learning to Labour is the title of the book in which Paul Willis reported on the full research project (Willis, 1977).

It may be, of course, that the culture of the lads has simply persisted thus far through inertia, and that in the changed economic circumstances it will eventually fade away. On the other hand, it may be that the underlying social class conflict is still as real and as strong today as in the 1970s, though different in its outward forms. Kehily and Nayak themselves offer – though only tentatively – a different kind of answer to their own question.

It may be the case that in today's economic climate young men are no longer able to attain a recognizable masculinity through manual labour, so are seeking to authenticate this identity in postures of heterosexuality. [...] It may well be that as long-term manual work declines, in a 'feminised' world of flexible workers and new technologies, male pupils are practising other ways of being 'proper' men that aim to accentuate heterosexuality beyond the emasculating existence of unemployment.

(Kehily and Nayak, 1997, p. 85)

Time – and of course further research – will tell.

SUMMARY OF SECTION 5

- Disaffection and alienation from school – especially on the part of teenage working-class boys in the cities of the North – is a widely recognized problem.
- However, this arguably performs latent functions for societies and their economies, by selecting young men by default for low-paid and intrinsically unrewarding jobs, while persuading them that these are appropriate and fulfilling, particularly in allowing them to express their masculinity.

6 CONCLUSION

This chapter looked at the range and variety of children's schooling in the world today and tried to explain some of its features using a sociological framework based on the idea of social *function*. You will have to decide for yourself how convincing the analysis offered here is, but one of the things it has tried to do is to show that the *manifest functions* of schooling – what it is supposed to do, in the words of Paul Willis – are not always the whole story, or even the main plot. Sometimes schooling can be *dysfunctional* for the society it is meant to serve. And sometimes its *latent functions* – what it is 'not supposed to do', or at least what it does without being fully acknowledged or noticed – may be most important of all.

REFERENCES

BELLAMY, C. (1999) *The State of the World's Children 1999: education*, New York, UNICEF.

BOWLES, S. and GINTIS, H. (1976) *Schooling in Capitalist America*, London, Routledge and Kegan Paul.

DORE, R. (1976) *The Diploma Disease: education, qualification and development*, London, George Allen and Unwin.

DORE, R. (1997) *The Diploma Disease: education, qualification and development*, second edition, London, Institute of Education, University of London.

FURLONG, V. (1977) 'Anancy goes to school: a case study of pupils' knowledge of their teachers' in WOODS, P. and HAMMERSLEY, M. (eds) (1977) *School Experience: explorations in the sociology of education*, London, Croom Helm, pp. 162–85.

HAMMERSLEY, M. and WOODS, P. (eds) (1976) *The Process of Schooling*, London, Routledge and Kegan Paul.

HILL, R. and LITTLE, A. (1996) *The Qualification Chase*, Milton Keynes, BBC OUPC (a television programme for the Open University course EU208 *Exploring Educational Issues*).

JAMES, A., JENKS, C. and PROUT, A. (1998) *Theorizing Childhood*, Cambridge, Polity Press.

JAYALAKSHMI, G. D. (1996) 'One cup of newspaper and one cup of tea' in MERCER, N. and SWANN, J. (eds) (1996) *Learning English: development and diversity*, London, Routledge and Kegan Paul, p. 142–148.

KEHILY, M. J. and NAYAK, A. (1997) 'Lads and laughter: humour and the production of heterosexual hierarchies' in *Gender and Education*, **9** (1), pp. 69–87.

MERTON, R. K. (1957) *Social Theory and Social Structure*, second edition, New York, The Free Press.

OXFAM (no date) 'The Jomtien conference and the right to education', *Education Now,* on-line, http://www.caa.org.au/oxfam/advocacy/education/report/chapter2–1.html [last accessed 20 September 2002].

QVORTRUP, J. (2001) 'School-work, paid work and the changing obligations of childhood' in MIZEN, P., POLE, C. and BOLTON, A. (eds) (2001) *Hidden Hands: international perspectives on children's work and labour*, London, Routledge Falmer, pp. 91–107.

WATKINS, K. (2000) *The Oxfam Education Report*, Oxford, Oxfam GB in association with Oxfam International.

WATTS, J. (2002) 'Japan gives its students a break', *Guardian*, 5 April 2002,
p. 17.

WILLIS, P. (1976) 'The class significance of school counter-culture' in HAMMERSLEY, M. and WOODS, P. (eds) (1976) *The Process of Schooling*, London, Routledge and Kegan Paul, pp. 188–200.

WILLIS, P. (1977) *Learning to Labour: how working-class kids get working-class jobs*, Farnborough, Saxon House.

WOODS, P. and HAMMERSLEY, M. (eds) (1977) *School Experience: explorations in the sociology of education*, London, Croom Helm.

READING A

'Boarding a bus'

Donald Mackinnon

The transcript below is of part of a lesson I recorded in a private, English-medium primary school in a town in south India, in 1998. In it, a teacher I shall call Mrs Kumaran is teaching English to Standard 1, with children aged five to six. This lesson continues from a previous lesson the study of a chapter in their textbook entitled 'Boarding a Bus.' The opening sentence of the chapter is, 'Rakesh was to visit his grandparents in Pune.'

Except where I indicate otherwise, the pupils repeat in chorus what Mrs Kumaran has read. Words read from the book are in italics. A question mark in brackets (?) indicates a rising intonation followed by a pause.

MRS K   Say now, *Rakesh*

PUPILS   *Rakesh*

MRS K   *was to*

PUPILS   *was to*

MRS K   *visit*

PUPILS   *visit*

MRS K   *his grandparents*

PUPILS   *his grandparents*

MRS K   *in Pune.*

PUPILS   *in Pune.*

MRS K   Where were his grandparents living?

PUPILS   Pune

MRS K   So he wanted to go and visit there his (?) grandparents. He was going to (?)

PUPILS   Pune.

MRS K   Say it again. *Rakesh*

PUPILS   *Rakesh*

MRS K   *was to*

PUPILS   *was to*

MRS K   *visit*

PUPILS   *visit*

MRS K   *his*

PUPILS   *his*

MRS K   *grandparents*

PUPILS   *grandparents*

MRS K   Who are the grandparents?

[Two seconds' pause.]

Who are your grandparents?

PUPILS   *[shouting, words inaudible]*

MRS K   Your mother and grandfather [sic]. Your mother's mother, your father's mother, isn't it like that? They are your (?) grandparents. Yes. You know, you have learnt it in Social [Social Science lessons].

[To a pupil.] No, not now.

[To the class again.] Rakesh

PUPILS   *Rakesh*

MRS K   *was to*

PUPILS   *was to*

MRS K   *visit*

PUPILS   *visit*

MRS K   *his grandparents*

PUPILS   *his grandparents*

MRS K   *in Pune.*

PUPILS   *in Pune.*

MRS K   So who's going to meet him, the grandparents?

PUPILS   Rakesh

MRS K   Rakesh. Yes. Where were they living?

PUPILS   *[shouting]* Pune/In Pune

MRS K   In Pune. Yes. *He was...*

Source

MACKINNON, D. (1997) unpublished field notes.

READING B

School counter-culture and shop-floor culture

Paul Willis

[Note: *Groups of three dots in square brackets […] indicate my omissions from Willis's original text. Groups of dots in round brackets (…) or not in brackets are reproduced from Willis's own text.*]

The really central point about the working-class culture of the shop floor is that, despite harsh conditions and external direction, people do look for meaning and impose frameworks. […] This is the same fundamental taking hold of an alienating situation as one finds in [school counter-culture].

[…]

More specifically, the central, locating theme of shop-floor culture – a form of masculine chauvinism arising from the raw experience of production – is reflected in the independence and toughness found in school counter-cultures. Here is a foundry-man talking at home about his work. In an inarticulate way, but for that perhaps all the more convincingly, he attests that elemental, essentially masculine, self-esteem in the doing of a hard job well – and to be known for it.

> I work in a foundry … you know drop forging … do you know anything about it … no … well you have the factory know the factory down in Bethnall Street with the noise … you can hear it in the street … I work there on the big hammer … it's a six-tonner. I've worked there 24 years now. It's bloody noisy, but I've got used to it now … and it's hot … I don't get bored … there's always new lines coming and you have to work out the best way of doing it … You have to keep going … And it's heavy work, the managers couldn't do it, there's not many strong enough to keep lifting the metal … I earn 80, 90 pounds a week, and that's not bad is it? … it ain't easy like … you can definitely say that I earn every penny of it … you have to keep it up you know. And the managing director, I'd say 'hello' to him you know, and the progress manager … they'll come around and I'll go … 'all right' (thumbs up) … and they know you, you know … a group standing there watching you … working … I like that … there's something there … watching *you* like … working … like that … you have to keep going to get enough out.

Here is Joey, this man's son, in his last year at school and right at the heart of the counter-culture:

> That's it, we've developed certain ways of talking, certain ways of acting and we developed disregards for Pakis, Jamaicans and all different …, for all the scrubs and the fucking ear-'oles and all that (…) There's no chivalry or nothing, none of this cobblers you know, it's just … if you'm gonna fight, it's savage fighting anyway, so you might as well go all the way and win it completely by having someone else help ya or by winning the dirtiest methods you can think of like poking his eyes out or biting his ear and things like this.

There's a clear continuity of attitudes here, and we must not think that this distinctive complex of chauvinism, toughness and machismo is anachronistic or bound to die away as the pattern of industrial work changes. Rough, unpleasant, demanding jobs *do* still exist in considerable numbers. A whole range of jobs – from building work, to furnace work to deep-sea fishing – still involve a primitive confrontation with exacting physical tasks. The basic attitudes and values developed in such jobs are still very important in general working-class culture, and particularly the culture of the shop floor; this importance is vastly out of proportion to the number of people involved in such heavy work. Even in so-called light industries, or in highly mechanized factories where the awkwardness of the physical task has long since been reduced, the metaphoric figures of strength, masculinity and reputation still move beneath the more varied and richer, visible forms of work-place culture. Despite, even, the increasing numbers of women employed, the most fundamental ethos of the factory is profoundly masculine.

The other main [...] theme of shop-floor culture – at least in the manufacturing industries of the Midlands – is the massive attempt to gain a form of control of the work process. [...] It does happen, now, sometimes, that the men themselves actually run production. Again this is effectively mirrored for us by working-class kids' attempts, with the resources of their counter-culture, to take control of classes, insert their own unofficial timetables, and control their own routines and life spaces.

> *Joey: (...)* of a Monday afternoon, we'd have nothing right? Nothing hardly relating to school work, Tuesday afternoon we have swimming and they stick you in a classroom for the rest of the afternoon, Wednesday afternoon you have games and there's only Thursday and Friday afternoon that you work, if you call that work. The last lesson Friday afternoon we used to go and doss, half of us wagged out o' lessons and the other half go into the classroom, sit down and just go to sleep, and the rest of us could join a class where all our mates are.

> *Will: (...)* What we been doing, playing cards in this room 'cos we can lock the door .

> [...]

> *PW:* What's the last time you've done some writing?

> *Will:* When we done some writing?

> *Fuzz:* Oh ah, last time was in careers, 'cos I writ 'yes' on a piece of paper, that broke me heart.

> *PW:* Why did it break your heart?

> *Fuzz:* I mean to write, 'cos I was going to try and go through the term without writing anything. 'Cos since we've cum back, I ain't dun nothing. *(It was half-way through term.)*

Put this against the following account from the father of a boy who was in the same friendship group as the boys talking above. He is a factory hand on a track producing car engines, talking at his home.

Actually the foreman, the gaffer, don't run the place, the men run the place. See, I mean you get one of the chaps says, 'Allright, you'm on so and so today.' You can't argue with him. The gaffer don't give you the job, the men on the track give you the job, they swop each other about, tek it in turns. Ah, but I mean the job's done.

[...]

Of course there is the obvious difference that the school informal organization is devoted to doing nothing, while in the factory culture, at least, 'the job's done'. But the degree of opposition to official authority *in each case* should not be minimized, and production managers in such shops were quite as worried as deputy heads about 'what things were coming to'. Furthermore, both these attempts at control rest on the basic and distinctive unit of the informal group. This is the fundamental unit of resistance in both cultures, which locates and makes possible all its other elements. [...] It is the massive presence of this informal organization which most decisively marks off shop-floor culture from middle-class cultures of work, and the 'lads'' school culture from that of the 'ear-'oles' (the name used by the 'lads' of my research to designate those who conformed to the school's official culture).

The solidarity, and sense of being 'in the group', [are] the basis for the final major characteristic of shop-floor culture that I want to describe here. This is the distinctive form of language, and the highly developed humour of the shop floor. Up to half the verbal exchanges are not serious or about work activities. They are jokes, or 'piss-takes', or 'kiddings' or 'wind-ups'. There is a real skill in being able to use this language with fluency: to identify the points where you are being 'kidded' and to have appropriate response in order to avoid further baiting.

[...]

Associated with this concrete and expressive verbal humour is a developed physical humour; essentially the practical joke. These jokes are vigorous, sharp, sometimes cruel, and often hinge on prime tenets of the culture such as disruption of production or subversion of the bosses' authority and status.

[...]

This atmosphere of rough humour and horseplay is instantly recognizable among the 'lads' in working-class schools, and obviously missing from the more hesitant 'polite' exchanges amongst the 'ear-'oles'. The ethnography of school cultures is full of similar – virtually interchangeable – incidents. There is the same felt desire to brighten grey prospects with a 'larf'. Certainly for the group of 'lads' who were the focus of my 'main' case study, reliance on the group, verbal humour and physical trickery, was the continuous stuff of their informal relations.

> *Joey:* You know you have to come to school today, if you're feeling bad, your mate'll soon cheer yer up like, 'cos you couldn't go without ten minutes in this school, without having a laugh at something or other.

[...]

There is no space to pursue the point any further, but in more detailed ways, from theft, vandalism and sabotage to girlie books under the tool-bench or desk, it is apparent that shop-floor culture and school oppositional culture have a great deal in common.

The parallelism of these cultures suggests, of course, that they should both be thought of as aspects of the larger working-class culture, [...]. The fundamental point here is to stress that anti-school culture should be seen in the context of this larger pattern, rather than in simple institutional terms.

[...]

I do not wish, here, to go into the complex questions concerning what makes working-class culture [...] what it is. Nor – having, I hope, established the similarity between shop-floor and anti-school culture – do I want to claim any simple causation between them. My aims are more limited; my immediate text is that of job choice among working-class lads.

[...]

In terms of actual 'job choice', it is the 'lads'' culture and not the official careers material which provides the most located and deeply influential guides for the future. [...] The located 'lads'' culture supplies a set of 'unofficial' criteria by which to judge not individual jobs or the intrinsic joys of particular kinds of work – indeed it is already assumed that all work is more or less hard and unrewarding – but generally *what kind* of working situation is going to be most relevant to the individual. It will have to be work where he can be open about his desires, his sexual feelings, his liking for 'booze' and his aim to 'skive off' as much as is reasonably possible. It will have to be a place where people can be trusted and will not 'creep off' to tell the boss about 'foreigners' or 'nicking stuff' – precisely where there were the fewest 'ear-'oles'. Indeed it would have to be work where there was a boss, a 'them and us' which always carried with it the danger of treacherous intermediaries. The experience of the division 'ear-'ole'/'lads' in school is one of the most basic preparations for the still ubiquitous feeling in the working class proper that there is a 'them' and an 'us'. [...] Generally, the future work situation would have to be one where people were not 'cissies' and could handle themselves, where 'pen-pushing' is looked down on in favour of really 'doing things'. It would have to be a situation where you could speak up for yourself, and where you would not be expected to be subservient. The particular job would have to pay good money fairly quickly and offer the possibility of 'fiddles' and 'perks' to support already acquired smoking and drinking habits.

[...]

The typical division in school between the 'lads' and the 'ear-'oles' also has a profound influence on thoughts about work. [...] The 'ear-'oles'/'lads' division becomes the skilled/unskilled and white-collar/blue-collar division. The 'lads' themselves could transpose the divisions of the internal cultural landscape of the school on to the future, and on to the world of work outside, with considerable clarity.

Talking about 'ear-'oles':

> *Joey:* I think they're *(the 'ear-'oles')* the ones that have got the proper view of life, they're the ones that abide by the rules. They're the civil servant types, they'll have 'ouses and everything before us (...) They'll be the toffs, I'll say they'll be the civil servants, toffs, and we'll be the brickies and things like that.

Spanksey: I think that we ..., more or less, we're the ones that do the hard grafting but not them, they'll be the office workers. (...) I ain't got no ambitions, I don't wanna have ... I just want to have a nice wage, that 'ud just see me through.

[...]

The young adult, therefore, impelled towards the shop floor, shares much more than he knows with his own future. When the lad reaches the factory there is no shock, only recognition. He is likely to have had experience anyway of work through part-time jobs, and he is immediately familiar with many of the shop-floor practices: defeating boredom, time-wasting, heavy and physical humour, petty theft, 'fiddling', 'handling yourself'.

[...]

Now, curiously enough, those conformist lads who enter the factory unaided by cultural supports, diversions and typical, habituated patterns of interpretation can be identified by those in authority as more threatening and less willing to accept the established *status quo.* For these lads still believe, as it were, the rubric of equality, advance through merit and individualism which the school, in its anodyne way, has more or less unproblematically passed on to them. Thus, although there is no surface opposition, no insolent style to enrage the conventional onlooker, there is also no secret pact, made in the reflex moment of an oppositional style, to accept a timeless authority structure: a timeless 'us' and 'them'. Consequently, these kids are more likely to *expect real* satisfaction from their work; to expect the possibility of advance through hard work; to expect authority relations, in the end, to reflect only differences in competence. All these expectations [...] make the conformist lad very irksome and 'hard to deal with'. In manual and semi-skilled jobs, then, those in authority often actively prefer the 'lads' type to the 'ear-'ole' type. Underneath the 'roughness' of the 'lads' is a realistic assessment of their position, an ability to get on with others to make the day *and production* pass, and a lack of 'pushiness' about their job and their future in it. Finally, the 'lads' are more likeable because they have 'something to say for themselves' and will 'stand up for themselves', but only in a restricted mode which falls short of one of the 'us' wanting to join the 'them'.

[...]

What is surprising in this general process of induction into the factory is the voluntary – almost celebratory – nature of the 'lads'' choice. The recognition of themselves in a future of industrial work is not a question of defeat, coercion or resignation. Nor is it simply the result of a managed, machiavellian process of social control. It is a question, at any rate in part and at least at this age, of an affiliation which is seen as joyous, creative and attractive. This fact is of enormous importance to us in understanding the true complexity of the reproduction of our social order: there is an element of 'self-damnation' in the acceptance of subordinate roles.

It is the partly autonomous functioning of the processes we have been considering which surprisingly accomplishes the most difficult task of state schooling: to 'direct' a proportion of kids to the unrewarding and basic tasks of industrial production.

[...]

We have looked at aspects of the process whereby some typical working-class kids come to regard their future in the factory as natural, inevitable, and even freely chosen. We have seen the pivotal importance of the 'lads' [school counter-culture] in this process.

[...]

What is *not supposed* to go on in school may have more significance for us than what is *supposed* to go on in school.

Source

WILLIS, P. (1976) 'The class significance of school counter-culture' in HAMMERSLEY, M. and WOODS, P. (eds) (1976) *The Process of Schooling: a sociological reader*, London and Henley, Routledge and Kegan Paul, pp. 188–200.

Chapter 5
Children and work

Donald Mackinnon

CONTENTS

When you have studied this chapter, you should be able to:

1 Explain the contemporary meanings of children's 'work'.

2 Describe the nature of children's work in the world today (its different kinds, quantity and geographical distribution) and some of the difficulties in measuring it.

3 Set out and evaluate arguments about the value of work for children, with particular emphasis on those challenging the conventional wisdom, in Britain and some other countries, that any work is bad for young children, and that more than a small amount is bad for older children.

4 Summarize and discuss recent research into the views of working children about work and school.

1 INTRODUCTION

As I explained in Chapter 4, that chapter and this one have been written as a pair. *School* and *work* (along with *play*, which is considered in another book in this series (Kehily and Swann, 2003)) dominate the lives of children throughout the world. Of course, they do so in very different ways and proportions. In the North, school plays a central part in the lives of most children and work is usually much more peripheral, especially when the children are young. In the South, the picture is more varied. For some children there too, as you have seen, school dominates their lives, with work playing little or no part. But for a great many more, it is work that dominates, and school has to be fitted in alongside it – if indeed they go to school at all.

Besides, at the beginning of the twenty-first century, school is believed almost everywhere in the world to be a good thing for children, whereas children's work is often viewed in the North with unease, if not hostility. As you will recall from Chapter 3, this has not always been so. In Chapter 4, I suggested from time to time that the contrast may not be quite so straightforward, and that schooling may have its drawbacks as well as its benefits. In the present chapter, I want to look squarely at the advantages and the disadvantages of child work. I want to examine and sometimes challenge various beliefs, assumptions and value judgements about children's work in the world today. Let me briefly explain the structure of the chapter.

As a framework for the rest of the discussion, I try, in Section 2, to get a sense of the scale of children's work in the world today, and of the central issues it raises.

In Section 3, I move on to two case studies of children at work, in urban Bangladesh and rural Zimbabwe. These have been chosen as examples of two of the most important categories of work that were identified in the initial survey of the world.

These case studies raise, sometimes very dramatically, a number of deep and difficult moral questions about children's work, and I go on to address these directly in Sections 4, 5 and 6.

Finally, in in the Conclusion, I sum up Chapters 4 and 5 by looking at a research study that sought out the views of working children in the South on both work and school.

2 THE SCALE OF THE ISSUE

I tried in Chapter 4 to give some idea of the scale of children's schooling in the world today; now let me try to do the same with children's work. As before, the starting point will be a survey conducted under the auspices of organizations dedicated to improving the lot of children – this time, *What Works for Working Children*, by Jo Boyden, Birgitta Ling and William Myers, published jointly in 1998 by Rädda Barnen (Save the Children Sweden) and UNICEF.

Once more, the obvious place to begin is with some very basic questions about facts and figures.

- How many children are there in the world today?
- How many of them work?
- What kinds of work do they do?

You will remember from the discussion in Chapter 4 that even the most basic question of all – how many children there are – is difficult to answer, and all estimates involve a large element of guesswork. Most of these estimates place the total number of 'children' in the world (in the sense of all those under eighteen) at somewhere around 1.8 billion. The author of *The Oxfam Education Report*, you may recall, was also prepared to estimate that about four-fifths of the world's children of primary school age attend school and one-fifth do not (Watkins, 2000). The authors of *What Works for Working Children* are not prepared to give even as rough an estimate as that of the number of children who work, for reasons I will look at in a moment.

Before I do so, however, there are some terminological issues to be sorted out. The first is which word to use. Probably most discussions of this issue have referred to child *labour*, but many authorities, including Boyden and her colleagues, now prefer to say child *work*. This is because they believe 'child labour' to be confusing, with too many different meanings to be useful. In particular, 'child labour' is used sometimes for children's work generally and sometimes only for those types of children's work that are harmful to them. The latter usage is particularly tricky since there is no universal agreement about what is beneficial and what is harmful to children. (See also James, Jenks and Prout, 1998, pp. 108–115.)

I find these arguments convincing, and I will myself normally use the term 'work' rather than 'labour'. However, as one of these authors points out in a later piece (Myers, 2000), many other people will neither stop using the term 'child labour' nor standardize its meaning – and these include some of the writers to be discussed in this chapter. In quoting or summarizing them, I shall follow their usage, trying only to ensure that this does not cause any confusion.

Choosing the word 'work', however, is only a beginning. What exactly does children's *work* mean?

Allow about 10 minutes

A C T I V I T Y 1   Children's work

What do you understand by children's 'work'? What activities would you include and what would you exclude?

Please spend ten minutes or so thinking about this and write down at least a note of your answer before reading mine.

C O M M E N T

My suggestions here are based closely on the arguments of Boyden *et al.*, (1998) who claim that many of the most common definitions in academic and official use are unsatisfactory. I shall look at a few.

At one extreme are narrow definitions, such as *paid employment*. This one is just too narrow, however. It would exclude some of the most widespread and important of children's activities popularly referred to as 'work', namely those within a family. Children who are active and important in the running of a farm, a shop or even a household are normally said to be 'working', even if no money is paid.

At the other extreme, some definitions – such as, *any activity to do with shaping one's life and environment* – are simply too broad to be useful. There seems to be very little that this definition would actually exclude.

A widely used economic definition of work, broader than 'paid employment', is that of *economic activity*, which Boyden *et al.* define as any activity that contributes to the gross domestic product of a country as measured by internationally agreed accounting methods. Though broader, this definition is still too narrow to cover everything that most people would want to call work, as Boyden *et al.* illustrate by imagining a young rural African girl who helps her family in a number of different tasks throughout the day.

> When she gets up an hour before sunrise to help clean the house, fetch water, and make breakfast, she is not working, according to official definitions. That is because these activities are not considered to contribute to the national economy. But when she goes outside to help her mother tend the garden from which they sell products in the local market, she now begins to work, as indeed she still does when they go together to the market to sell some produce. However, when she takes vegetables from the same garden inside and prepares the midday meal from them, she is no longer working. Later she goes out to fetch firewood, which is heavy to carry and must be brought from over a mile away, but she is not working. Then she goes back out to gather fodder to feed the farm animals which are used for traction, and is now working again. She is also officially working when she helps her family in the fields. When she goes back inside to clean up in the kitchen and to help

bed down her younger brother and sister, singing them to sleep long after sundown, she is not working. And, of course, she was not working during the three hours she spent in school. According to the way governments usually define work for purposes of statistics about work and workers, she worked only a minor part of the day. In common parlance, however, most of us would agree she was a very busy little girl who in fact worked a long day with little or no time for rest and play. To confuse the matter even further, she would in many places not be counted as working at all. The reason is that she goes to school. Official statistical systems often will not record children as working if they are enrolled in school, even if they have a paid job for more hours than they study [...] which of course would make it appear in the statistics that work and school are mutually exclusive.

(Boyden *et al.*, 1998, pp. 20–21)

Rather than a formal definition, Boyden *et al.* end up with a somewhat rough and ready characterization of children's work – one I shall adopt here, in an even rougher form. I take 'working children' to be *those in paid employment, or active in money-making tasks inside or outside the home, or involved in unpaid home maintenance, for at least ten hours per week.* Boyden *et al.* describe this as work 'in its popular sense', though they acknowledge that it does not correspond to everything children themselves call work, which sometimes includes 'any assigned task they dislike doing' (Boyden *et al.*, 1998, p. 22). It also makes work something separate from schooling and therefore does not follow the proposal of Jens Qvortrup discussed in Chapter 4.

Using 'work' in that sense, Boyden *et al.* provide a brief summary of children's work in the world today. As I mentioned above, they do not even try to estimate the number of working children in the world. They quote the International Labour Organization's 'guesstimate' of 250 million, but are sceptical about it. National and international statistics are so unreliable, they believe, that nobody knows how many children in the world work. All Boyden *et al.* themselves offer, and offer tentatively, are 'some vague orders of magnitude and a very general child worker distribution profile' (Boyden *et al.*, 1998, p. 22), contrasting the reality of children's work with popular perceptions of it that are sometimes distorted.

According to Boyden *et al.*, then, the vast majority of child workers are in developing countries – the South, in the terminology of this series. In absolute numbers, most child workers are in Asia (which has most of the population of the world), but perhaps a higher proportion of the children's population works in sub-Saharan Africa. Boyden *et al.* (1998, p. 24–5) divide child workers in the South into four main categories.

- Child workers in rural areas, mostly giving unpaid help to their families, mostly in agriculture: they form the 'vast majority of children who work'.
- Domestic child workers and baby-minders, working either in their own homes, or as employees in other people's homes; they are overwhelmingly girls and their numbers are 'perhaps equal in size to that of children working in agriculture'.

- Child workers in the 'informal sector' – small shops and stores, small-scale building work and back-alley workshops. This category is also very large, but the most visible and highly publicized members of it, the street-trading children, 'are almost always a small minority of working children, and may not be among the worst off'.

- Child workers in the 'formal sector' – 'comparatively modern, larger, and more established industrial and commercial establishments'. By contrast with the categories above, this one employs only a small minority of child workers, and only a minority of these produce goods for export, despite the concentration of attention on this sector by many people and organizations in the developed world.

These categories are not always mutually exclusive: for example, there is probably a great deal of overlap between the first two above, as one of our case studies in Section 3 illustrates.

Agricultural work:
Chad, Africa.

Domestic work:
Vietnam.

The informal sector:
Bangladesh.

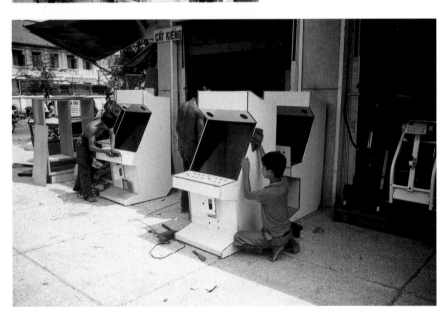

The formal sector:
Vietnam.

Children's work in Britain.

In countries of the North, the picture is very different. In Britain, for example, almost all working children work part-time and most of them combine work with schooling. (Virtually all of them do so if under the minimum legal school-leaving age of sixteen.) Estimates of the numbers of working children vary between researchers, as do estimates of the amounts of time for which they work, but figures such as the following are typical. About a million children aged thirteen to fifteen work – roughly 40 per cent of the age group. Of these about half work up to five hours per week, a third work from six to twelve hours and a sixth over twelve hours per week. The average is about seven or eight hours per week. By way of comparison, the average child in this age-group spends some 28 hours per week at school (McKechnie, Stack and Hobbs, 2001).

The kind of work done by these children is bluntly summarized by the authors of a recent study as 'low quality work', by which they mean it is generally 'unskilled work around the edges of the formal labour market' (Mizen *et al.*, 2001, p. 39). It is poorly paid, often repetitive and carried out in unpleasant conditions.

> The most vivid examples of this were jobs performing simple and repetitive manual tasks at high volume: packing clothes, chocolates or confectionery in small workshops and factory units; picking fruit and vegetables on farms and market gardens; and working from home packing greetings cards or undertaking light assembly work 'put out' from local suppliers.
>
> (Mizen *et al.*, 2001, p. 39)

However, most children's work is in the service sector: for example, in retail and distribution and, especially, catering, where the fast-food industry has become the biggest single source of employment for school leavers.

Children under school-leaving age are less likely to be employed by the larger chains of shops, supermarkets, franchised restaurants and fast-food outlets than by small employers.

The restaurants, cafés, sandwich shops, fish and chip shops, mobile burger bars and hot dog stands, coffee and tea shops that make up this independent sector compete directly with the large national and multinational catering organisations, frequently selling similar products to the same customers.

[...]

Some of the children had been employed in the stock rooms of corner shops and off-licences, on the checkouts of small supermarkets or grocery stores, or serving customers in hardware, electrical, clothes and shoe shops. Others still had found work stacking shelves, pricing goods or cleaning the corner shops, newsagents and convenience stores that populated their communities ... Many of the children had at some time or another held a newspaper round before or after school.

[...]

For these types of organisations children can offer a ready source of cheap and flexible labour, one that is available at short notice, tolerates irregular hours and has low expectations of work.

(Mizen *et al.*, 2001, pp. 40–41)

The bigger chains prefer to employ older children and young people, especially since the expansion of further and higher education in the 1990s, combined with the introduction of tuition fees and the disappearance of maintenance grants, has created a large pool of students looking for part-time work.

SUMMARY OF SECTION 2

- 'Working children' are defined as those in paid employment, or active in money-making tasks inside or outside the home, or involved in unpaid home maintenance, for at least ten hours per week.

- Different categories of child work are distinguished. The vast majority of child workers in the world are agricultural or domestic workers in the South. They may not be the worst treated, but they are so many that they ought to be the focus of more concern than they currently receive.

- By contrast, the child workers who are the focus of most international concern – those in the formal sector producing goods for export to the North – are a small minority of working children.

- Child work in the North is typically in the service sector – part-time, unskilled and poorly paid.

3 WORKING CHILDREN: TWO CASE STUDIES

Now I want to turn from the more general discussion above to the everyday reality of life for some particular working children. The two case studies between them illustrate the most important of Boyden *et al.*'s categories. The first is an example of child workers in the informal sector – specifically, in back-alley workshops in Dhaka, the capital of Bangladesh. Child workers in this sector, though a minority of working children, are still very large in number and, as you will see, the conditions of work are among the worst that children experience anywhere. In the second case study, I turn to Boyden *et al.*'s 'vast majority of children who work' – those engaged in domestic or agricultural work, or both, in rural areas of developing countries: in this case, in the Zambezi Valley, Zimbabwe.

But I do not want you to just read through these case studies; I want you to think as you read of the advantages and disadvantages of children's work. Activity 2 below suggests some questions that you might like to think about. I suggest that you look at these questions twice. First, before you read, please write down brief notes of your initial thoughts in answer to these questions. Then, after you have worked through the case studies, return to your notes and reconsider them in the light of what you have read.

I myself will follow a similar procedure. Immediately after Activity 2, I will give my own brief answers to its questions. Then after the case studies, I will go back over these in more detail.

Allow about 20 minutes

A C T I V I T Y   2   Advantages and disadvantages of children's work

In answering the questions below, you may find it helpful to recall the rough and ready definition given in Section 2, in which working children are 'those in paid employment, or active in money-making tasks inside or outside the home, or involved in unpaid home maintenance, for at least ten hours per week'. (By this definition, you will remember, work is treated as something separate from schooling.)

1   List any important *disadvantages*, as you see them, of children working. These may include disadvantages for the children themselves and disadvantages for others. How do these differ for different types of work?

2   List any important *advantages* you see in children working, which again may be advantages for the children or for others. Again, how do these differ for different kinds of work?

C O M M E N T

My own initial lists are as follows.

1   Disadvantages of children's work.

    (a) It is inherently wrong, even unnatural: childhood should be for learning and for play.

    (b) Work interferes with children's physical and mental development.

    (c) Work can be dangerous or damaging for children.

(d) Work interferes with children's schooling.

(e) Children's work is unfair, in that it has a differential impact on children: for example, on poor children as compared with rich; or on girls as compared with boys.

(f) Working children harm adults who work or want to work.

2 Advantages of children's work.

(a) Paid work gives the child worker an income.

(b) Unpaid work enables children to contribute to the economic life of their family.

(c) Work can give dignity and a sense of purpose to life. It can even give a sense of identity.

(d) Work can enable children to develop their skills, their knowledge and their personal qualities.

(e) Work can be enjoyable.

Now please read the following case studies, keeping the possible advantages and disadvantages in mind as you do so.

3.1 Case study: urban Bangladesh

In 1999, Tareque Shahriar made a film, *Kalighar* (*The Black House*) for the organization Steps Towards Development. It was a study of child labour (as he called it) in the Lalbag and Kamrangirchar districts of Dhaka, and shows children as young as twelve (or so the film reported – some look even younger) working in small factories or workshops in the 'informal sector' of the economy. According to Boyden *et al.*, as you have seen, this type of work accounts for a minority, but still a very large number, of working children in the world.

The work shown and the conditions in which it was done, were obviously unpleasant, unhealthy and often dangerous. It includes the following:

- breaking up batteries for recycling, separating the components by hand;
- polishing steel utensils on an electrically powered grindstone;
- moulding glass bangles on an open flame;
- welding with a blowtorch;
- melting down metal goods on an open forge for recasting;
- picking through rubbish to sort out what could be recycled and burning the rest.

There was little sign of concern for safety or health. Grindstones, power saws, flames, forges and vats of molten metal were unguarded. With the single exception of two boys who wore sunglasses as they welded, there was no protective clothing: no overalls, no gloves, no masks for the mouth or nose, no goggles for the eyes. Ventilation was obviously poor and the air was often thick with smoke, fumes and metallic and chemical dusts that formed a visible coating on the children's skin. Hours were long – 7 am to 6 pm, six days a week, two children reported – and wages very low. The children were routinely tired, weak and ill. When they missed work through illness, they earned nothing.

Back-alley workshops in urban Bangladesh.

Tareque Shahriar, the film maker, was himself a resident of Dhaka, living not far away from these areas. But until he began work on the film, he tells us, he had been unaware of what went on there. He discovered that the children, parents and factory owners have what he called 'a specific outlook about child labour which differs with our conventional ideas about it'. His interviews with the parents suggested that children were sent out to this kind of work only after disaster struck a family, often the loss of the husband and father from death or desertion, or his becoming ill and unable to work. The mothers all had jobs, sometimes in the same factories as their children, but one income was not enough for their families to survive. Some families had moved to Dhaka out of desperation, following floods or famine in their home villages. In the city, they could at least make a living, however wretched. No parent wanted to send their children to work like this, and no child wanted to go. They all knew only too well how harmful it was, but none could see any alternative.

For example, Jashim, whose age is not given (my guess is that he was twelve at the most) was well aware of the circumstances that had led to his working in a metal-casting factory. The family's land in their home village had been divided among five brothers, following a quarrel, and split into portions too small to be workable. His parents, with his two brothers, his sister and himself, had come to Dhaka, where his father had obtained a job as a rickshaw puller and his mother worked as a domestic servant. But his father had become too ill and weak to work, and his mother's earnings were not enough for the family to live on. With Jashim's wage, small as it was, they could just survive. His mother described her feelings like this.

All the speech in the film was in Bengali; all the quotations here are the English translations used in the film's subtitles.

When I see him at work in the factory, I feel like stabbed in my heart. For what did I send him to this work? To earn bread? What pain he takes sitting by the fire. He feels pain in his body, headache. Does not seem good. Doesn't want to have food, only stay laid after work. [...] Yes, even does not take a shower, only stays laid down.

Jashim's father, apparently close to tears, added that despite the alarming effects of the work on his son's health, 'I am compelled to send him. I have a problem: I can't manage.'

Rekha and her mother both worked in the battery recycling factory. In sending Rekha to work, her mother had possible future as well as present troubles in mind.

> After marriage, if the husband leaves her away or if we die then she will be able to survive with this work. What else to do?

Jashim's employer admitted and explained some of the health problems.

> ... our main problem is the smoke. No other problems. Here a lot of water and fire-related works are done. There is a big factory of Singer at Tajgaon with same type of fire. I bring this coal from there. Boys like here also work there. But they are more older. I have seen myself. There is a proper system of blowing out the smoke there. We don't have that system. It is local. [...] Our economic condition is bad. We are businessmen of small capital.

However, he offered hope for the children's future.

> As they grow, they develop the skill and become good technicians. Say, Jashim, by his age of twenty will completely learn the work and become a technician. Then he will get a salary of 3000 taka.

But this did not seem to be borne out by Shahajalal, a young man in the same factory who had worked there from a 'very tender age', after his father's death. He had started off with a wage of 20 taka per week; now he received 450 taka. (Note, a wage of 450 taka per week in 1999 would have been equivalent to about £5.70 sterling.)

Rekha's employer was breathtakingly frank about his motives for employing children to break up batteries for recycling.

> Think, the work the child labourer does is a help, we can pay less wages. If the same work is done by a grown-up labourer, higher wages are payable. The output of a child labourer equals that of a grown up one, but it brings more profit, it is advantageous for us.

But he insisted that the work did the children no harm.

> There is no harm here, because four of our six brothers, born here, grew here in this black dust, did not contract any disease.

The children themselves were aware, not only of why they were going to work, but also of what they were missing by doing so. Shahajalal, now grown up, said sadly, 'I didn't get any chance to play in my childhood'. Rekha wanted to learn to read, but her mother had told her this was not possible as they were poor. Ayesha, a friend of Rekha, who worked in the same factory, had briefly been to school, but had had to leave because her family needed her earnings.

In the course of making the film, Tareque Shahriar experienced the dilemma faced by the parents in an unexpectedly personal way. The employment of such young children in factories is illegal in Bangladesh, and at one stage, the owner of the casting factory became alarmed by the filming and dismissed Jashim. Unemployment would mean disaster for the boy and his family, so Shahriar, a committed opponent of child labour, found himself pleading for a child to be reinstated in one of the worst examples of child employment he had ever seen. His pleas were successful.

3.2 Case study: rural Zimbabwe

In the second case study, I turn to those identified by Boyden *et al.* as the vast majority of child workers in the world: the children engaged in domestic or agricultural work in rural areas of the South.

In 1984–85, Pamela Reynolds conducted a study in Zimbabwe of 'children's work in the context of subsistence agriculture' (Reynolds, 1991, p. xix). The

Agricultural work in Africa.

study was located in the Zambezi Valley, in the village of Chitenge. It had a population of some 700, living in just over 100 households – a household being defined locally as those who eat food prepared at one fireplace. Reynolds studied twelve of these households in detail. Although her main interest was in children (aged over nine), she studied adults, too: she wanted to see children's work in the context of the distribution of work among all the members of a household.

The present case study consists of edited extracts from Reynolds's report, with brief comments from me to link them and place them in context. She used a variety of research methods, of which I shall make particular use of two: her own systematic observation of the children's work, and the diaries that she asked the children to keep.

Observation

The main advantage of systematic observation, according to Reynolds, was that it picked up children's work that even the children themselves did not seem to notice. Children's work, she argued, is often not acknowledged as being work. For example, one fourteen-year-old girl, when asked what work she had done that morning, replied, 'Nothing'. Yet, as Reynolds had observed, she had collected water twice from a source over two kilometres away, she had prepared porridge for her own and her young brother's breakfast and she had washed the plates from the previous evening's meal.

From her observations, Reynolds was particularly struck by the division of labour by age and gender. First, girls under sixteen spent almost all of their time, 98 per cent, on 'work-related activities' – more than adult women (who spent 92 per cent) and much more than boys (who spent 59 per cent, if aged over ten, and only three per cent if under ten). Reynolds did not observe adult men sufficiently to be able to give comparable figures for them.

Her second observation referred specifically to child care.

> Women were noted as occupied with the care of infants or little children for 20 per cent of their observed time, girls for 33 per cent and boys for 4 per cent [...] Girls under ten spent 56 per cent of their time caring for infants or children younger than themselves. [...] That girls under ten spent over half of their time on child care confirms my observation that child care is the prime responsibility of women and girls between the ages of four and ten.

> (Reynolds, 1991, pp. 80–81)

Reynolds also noted that girls' greater responsibility for child care did not mean less responsibility for farm work. On the contrary, girls over ten spent 21 per cent of their time on farm work, as compared with two per cent of their time for boys.

> This confirms another observation, that boys' labour on farms is most often called upon during peak labour times, whereas girls' labour is called on more often for routine tasks. Women say that this is because they can control girls: boys ignore their call for labour contribution. A number of incidents that I observed confirm this.

At 4 p.m. on 11 June 1985, Dansu, a twelve-year old boy, had just spent 35 minutes caring for his three younger siblings one of whom was an infant. His mother left the spot where she had been grinding and returned to the group and Dansu said, 'I am going now to play with Gora.' She replied, 'Wait, stay with the children as I want to go and collect water from the stream.' Dansu faded quietly away and went toward his friend's house. His mother half-heartedly called for him to return. He did not. His mother continued for the next hour to grind, to attend a pot of rice cooking on the fire, to care for the little ones and to order older ones to perform certain tasks. She was awaiting the return of the eldest daughter, aged eight, from school so that she could leave to collect water. Meanwhile Dansu had gone with his friend into the bush to trap birds. I asked if she were not angry with him. She said, 'Yes. But I can do nothing. If he does it again, I shall beat him.' I then asked her what she would have done had a girl responded thus. She replied, 'I would have beaten her at once. A girl's duty is in the home.' She has three boys older than her first daughter but the girl is her mainstay.

(Reynolds, 1991, p. 81)

However, although boys do much less work overall than girls, they do have some specific responsibilities.

From the age of ten a boy ... is expected to be able to build a house. As a mark of his growing into manhood he builds his own. ... In Chitenge I knew of eighteen houses that boys built in 1984 and 1985. ... Five were built by a group of boys from another area who lived alone in order to attend school.

[...]

The possession of one's own house is an assertion of independence. Girls must wait until they marry and their husbands build them houses.

(Reynolds, 1991, pp. 120–21)

The observations above obviously present the adult observer's view of children's work. By contrast, the interviews Reynolds conducted with children, and even more the diaries she asked them to keep, present more of the children's own viewpoints. Reynolds introduces the diaries as follows:

Girls' diaries

In [Chitenge] the people have an ideal of the sort of woman a girl ought to aspire to. The ingredients of the ideal have an international flavour: a woman should be shy and demure, hard-working and efficient, clean, patient, attentive to others' needs, well-mannered, respectful, uncomplaining and pleasant. The girls' diaries reflect on the ideal, sometimes seeming to parody it.

[...]

I saw ... little aggression either from adult to child or between children. This makes the girls' entries on being beaten for refusing to work of particular interest.

[...]

Entries that refer to discipline over work follow.

> I saw Emeria being beaten by her mother because she refused to go to the field.
> Nyangu (13), 11 September 1984

> Mother beat me for not working and I was very angry. I didn't eat anything, I just ate *sadza* in the evening. Myself, I didn't beat her because she is older than me. It is not possible to beat a mother.
> Changu [11], 14 September 1984

> Yesterday I saw Fungai being beaten by her mother because she refused to go to the field.
> Karungu (13), 13 November 1984

> It was on Sunday when mother beat me because I refused to wash plates. After beating me she told me to go and wash them. After that mother did not beat me at all.
> Zvaipa (13), 28 November 1984

(Reynolds, 1991, pp. 105–6)

Not all the diary entries refer to the realities of everyday life, however. Intertwined with these were 'fantasies of travel and good food and fine clothes and even of hunting'. One girl 'dreams of sleeping between sheets', another describes a fantasy trip to Harare to visit her relations there. 'Fantasies of food – onions, tomatoes, meat, oil and fish – appear as often as entries recording the girls' hunger' (Reynolds, 1991, p. 107).

Boys' diaries

Boys cover a greater range of emotion, they touch on a broader canvas of topics and they reflect on a wider sphere of exploration in their diaries than do girls. They talk about work but much more as episodes in the day rather than as markers of the day's passing. For example, Taitos (aged fourteen) writes:

> I woke up today at 5:05 a.m. I got out from the house and went to the field. Before going to the field I cleaned my teeth and washed my face.

> In the field we were six of us [five boys and their mother].

> We worked in the field about one hour then mother went to cook our breakfast. The breakfast was porridge.

> We ate the porridge after that we went back to the field again.

> We weeded and weeded until the rain came. When the rain came we didn't run away but we continued weeding until the rain came worse and worse. After that we went home and mother cooked *sadza*.

> 18 December 1984 (written in English)

(Reynolds, 1991, p. 115)

The boys' diaries, too, contained a 'mix of comment on village life and fantasy' (Reynolds, 1991, p. 116), much of the latter about winning girls' love. But there was another significant difference.

> School appears in the diaries of boys more often than in those of girls and seems to dominate their days more. A number of entries describe beatings at school – an issue that is often raised among adults in the village who find beatings on the scale given both unnecessary and distasteful. The authorities listen neither to the children's nor the adults' complaints.
>
> [...]
>
> In contrast with the above, many entries express the boys' pleasure in fishing and gathering wild fruit and in nature.
>
> [...]
>
> Taitos expresses his pleasure at the coming of the rains: 'When I went to bed there were many clouds in the sky. In a little while I went to sleep. Suddenly I heard rain falling and I was very happy that the rain has come and we will plant our seed if it continues to fall'.
>
> 6 November 1984
>
> (Reynolds, 1991, p. 117)

Having worked through these case studies, please return to your notes (and mine) in answer to Activity 2 at the beginning of this section, and see if you would like to develop or reconsider any of them in the light of what you have just read. My own more detailed comments form the next two sections of this chapter, but please think through your answers and write down at least a brief note on them before reading mine. Do not be surprised or worried if your answers do not correspond closely to mine, when you come to them. It would be astonishing if they did, given what a huge and complicated subject this is, and what different values people bring to bear on it. You should certainly not treat my answers as in any way definitive or necessarily better than your own. Please subject both your answers and mine to critical scrutiny.

SUMMARY OF SECTION 3

- Children's work can be close to its worst in the informal sector in cities of the South. It may be recognized as dangerous and damaging by all those involved, and entered into only through dire necessity, but with all its faults, it may be preferable to the only available alternative – destitution.
- Children's work in rural areas of the South can be all-consuming, especially for girls, who are often expected to do as much agricultural work as boys and also a substantial amount of domestic work. Nevertheless, children can often find enjoyment and fulfilment in and alongside their work.

4 DISADVANTAGES OF CHILDREN'S WORK

Collecting fuel in Nepal.

For Activity 2 in Section 3, you were asked to draw up two lists. The first list was of supposed disadvantages of children's work and now I shall go through the items on my initial list in turn.

4.1 Children's work is unnatural

I begin with this argument, not because I think it is particularly strong or persuasive, at least in so naïve a form, but because I think it is widespread, at least in Britain. Indeed, I have to admit that when I myself see young children working, my own immediate, unreflective reaction is often along these lines. Such reactions, however, must be treated with some suspicion. Like most people in Britain, I am accustomed to seeing children, especially young children, at school or at play, not at work, and my reaction may be no more than unease at what is unfamiliar.

Or it may be a little more. To look more personally at the issue for a moment, I myself have young children, who go to school and play in various ways, but do not work in Boyden *et al.*'s sense. And I would not be happy for them to do substantial work instead of all or some of their schooling, or play. What does this mean? Is it that, like many parents, I want my own children to live better lives than I know are lived and, perhaps, can be lived by most children in the world? Or am I mistaken in assuming that a life without work really is better for a child? (See Chapter 3 for an historical perspective on this.)

Although the claim that children's work is unnatural does not stand up to serious examination, it is possible to construct a more defensible argument along similar lines. Take, for example, the kind and amount of work the girls of Chitenge had to do: according to Reynolds, it occupied no less than 98 per cent of their waking hours – as close to all their time as makes no serious difference. Besides, although the *kind* of work the girls had to do was different for different ages, with girls under ten concentrating on caring for still younger children, the *amount* did not seem to change. It is difficult to avoid feeling that the girls were being made to live very restricted lives and deprived of the opportunity to do many other things.

Certainly the girls themselves did not always want to do the work they were expected to. On some occasions, their mothers had to resort to beatings to make their daughters work.

4.2 Work interferes with children's development

This argument, if correct, would give a firmer basis to the previous one – but is it correct? Developmental psychologists have sometimes argued along these lines, but their arguments have recently come in for criticism. The subject is somewhat technical and I cannot go into it in depth here. However, I shall look at the basic criticism in outline.

Martin Woodhead's critique of developmental psychology in general is given in Chapter 3 of the first book in this series (Woodhead, 2003).

One prominent critic, Martin Woodhead, has argued that developmental psychologists in America and Europe have constructed a model of an 'idealized child', based on what is usual in their own countries. In this model, childhood is 'a period of life spent mainly in the contexts of family and school, where the emphasis is on care, play, learning and teaching, at least until adolescence' (Woodhead, 1999a, p. 12). This, Woodhead argues, is an incomplete picture. It does not take account of the diversity of developmental pathways in the world as a whole – in particular those associated with children's work – and sometimes leads psychologists to regard any divergence from the Euro-American pattern as pathological. Woodhead believes, though, that this model is now beginning to be replaced by attempts to study development in its diverse contexts, including those where children work, without building in any assumptions that this is inherently harmful.

The extent of Woodhead's critique should not be exaggerated. What he is denying is a connection between children's work *as such* and interference with child development. He does not deny that there is a core of universal biological and psychological processes in child development underlying all the variation from culture to culture. Some particular types of children's work can therefore interfere with a child's development if they cross:

> ... the boundaries of adequacy beyond which children's work is likely to have pathological consequences, by any standards, in terms of stunted growth, emotional disturbance, social isolation, learning disability etc.

> (Woodhead, 1999a, p. 37)

4.3 Work can be dangerous or damaging for children

Certain sorts of work undoubtedly are dangerous, or damaging, or both. The work many children do in the back-alley workshops of Dhaka falls squarely into this category. This is children's work, if not at its worst, at any rate of a sort that few people in any country would find defensible, let alone desirable. Even the children's employers did not seem to defend it with much conviction.

In that case study, the dangers were obvious, but there may also be danger and harm in work that many outsiders would assume to be safe – including agricultural and domestic work, which, as you saw above, are by far the commonest types of children's work in the world today:

> ... contrary to the romanticized suppositions of people not familiar with rural life, much agricultural work is unsafe or unhealthy for children, and therefore its huge scope and significant risks would seem to make it the most logical focus of concern by 'child labour' activists. But life is not always logical, and the rural child workers who should be at the very centre of world concern about 'child labour' are largely ignored.
>
> [...]
>
> Such studies as exist on child domestics suggest that they are massively exploited and subject to serious physical, mental, and sexual abuse. It is very dangerous work for children, especially when they must live in the homes of their employers, cut off from family and friends.
>
> (Boyden *et al.*, 1998, pp. 24–5)

It does not follow, of course, that all children's work is dangerous or damaging, or that none is actually beneficial.

4.4 Work interferes with children's schooling

Obviously, time that children spend working (by my definition) is time that they do not spend at school. Obviously, too, where children's work is very tiring, they may not have sufficient energy to cope with school studies even in what free time they have. So children's work undoubtedly can and often does interfere with their schooling.

That is not the whole story, of course. Where children work part-time, it is possible for them to have some schooling too. Indeed, combining work and schooling in some way may be the experience of most children in the world today. If this is to be successful, though, it is necessary for schools to take account of their pupils' working lives and make arrangements to suit them. Frequently this does not happen – sometimes, indeed, schools seem to make life even more difficult than it need be for children trying to combine attendance with work. One example among many comes from a rural Muslim community in Kerala, in South India, where the problem is particularly acute for girls. They report frequent beatings from the teacher in the Koranic school because they are often late. This is because they have to do housework before they come to school, unlike boys in the community (Nieuwenhuys, 1994, p. 70).

School arrangements can also interfere with children's ability to combine schooling with work in more subtle and unexpected ways. For example, the sociologist Sarah Oloko argued in a BBC interview that a change in methods of assessment in Nigerian schools, from end-of-year examinations to continuous assessment, made it very difficult for working children to continue their education. When school assessment consisted of a single examination at the end of the school year, clever and ambitious working children could attend school irregularly and infrequently, but still pass the examination by studying hard in whatever free time they could find. But continuous assessment, introduced with the best intentions, did not allow this. The change meant that children who could not attend school regularly could no longer obtain educational qualifications (Oloko, 2000).

4.5 Working children may be treated harshly or unfairly

One of the most striking aspects of the Zimbabwe case study is surely the ways in which girls are treated with respect to work, compared with both adult women and boys of their own age. At one point, Reynolds invites her readers to compare the diary entries of a sister and brother, Zvaipa and Taitos, for a single day (12 December 1984). Here they are together, Zvaipa first and then Taitos.

> I rose from my bed and I look some plates to be washed. When I came back I had to return to the stream to wash clothes for my mother and father and other family members. On returning from washing clothes, I went to the field. In the evening I cooked *sadza*. When we finished eating our *sadza* we all went to bed.
>
> (Reynolds, 1991, p. 107)

> I started the day with preparation of going to re-plant the seeds. Today we were re-planting *maila* and *nzembwe*. I worked in the field for about three hours then I came back home from the field.
>
> When we arrived home I saw my sister Zvaipa busy working. She was preparing our lunch. Before lunch we drank tea with bread. When I finished eating my lunch I went to the store. To the store I saw my friends and we talked about weeding and re-planting of seeds in our fields.
>
> After that I went to Chiweshe to see Chipo or Kanense!!!
>
> (Reynolds, 1991, p. 115)

Allow about 5 minutes

ACTIVITY 3   A girl's day and a boy's day

What differences between Zvaipa's and Taitos's day strike you as most significant?

COMMENT

Two main differences strike me. First, although both children have to work, Zvaida's work lasts from when she gets up in the morning until she goes to bed again at night, whereas Taitos's lasts three hours, after which he is free to go to the store with his friends (admittedly to talk about work, as he tells the story) then to town. I do not know what he did there, but his multiple exclamation marks suggest that he enjoyed himself. Secondly, their days fit in with Reynolds's observation that boys are called on to work at peak times, girls as a matter of routine. Taitos is planting seeds, a task for a particular time in the year; Zvaida is washing plates and clothes and cooking meals, routine tasks for every day (though she too has to work in the fields in between the cooking and washing).

As you may also recall, failure or refusal by boys to do work assigned to them usually seems to be tolerated. Any refusal by girls seems to be punished by a beating. This needs to be interpreted with caution, however. The word 'beating' in modern English may well suggest harsher treatment than the children actually received. Perhaps milder English words, such as 'smack' or 'slap', would be more appropriate.

It remains true, even so, that children in Chitenge were often reluctant to work and made to do so, especially the girls, by the threat or reality of punishment by their mothers. This is not universal, however. A vivid contrast is provided by Hoa, a Vietnamese woman who recalled her childhood at a conference on child participation held in Hanoi in 1998 under the auspices of Save the Children.

> When I was growing up I went to school and worked. I worked from home in the evenings on our family loom and it made me feel special because I was contributing to the family income. My mum would watch over me and make me stop if I was tired or had too much homework to do. I enjoyed working as a child and my experiences have shown me the importance of making a distinction between different types of child work. Like me not all children are exploited and like me some children feel that their position in the family is more equal and better valued because of the work they do.
>
> (Quoted in fieldnotes for Burr, 2001)

Such inequalities as those found in Chitenge are not inherent in the nature of children's work, and not universal. For example, Samantha Punch found that, in a rural community in the south of Bolivia, work for children under ten years old was 'gender neutral' – boys and girls did the same kind and amount of work, even though there was a marked division of labour by gender between adult men and women. In this and other respects, children's work is not always a reflection of adults' (Punch, 2000; see also Chapter 1, pp. 22–26).

Admittedly, however, inequalities between boys' work and girls' work seem to be prevalent in most societies that have been investigated. And inequality is also not confined to gender differences. Similar inequalities in children's work could be found with respect to wealth and poverty, social class, caste or ethnicity.

4.6 Working children harm adults

There are two common arguments here. The first is that child workers *directly* harm adults who want to work, by taking jobs the adults could do. The second is that child workers *indirectly* harm even adults with jobs, by being more docile, less well organized, and prepared to work for lower wages, thus forcing down wages and undermining the adults' bargaining power.

However, the contribution of children's work to the economy as a whole is a complex and uncertain matter. It is often claimed that its effect is harmful, but some scholars do not believe the processes involved are well enough understood to justify such claims. I shall not attempt to analyse these issues, but simply try to illustrate some of the difficulties involved.

Thus, even if a child worker takes a job that would otherwise have gone to an adult, that is not the whole of the child's contribution to the economy – any more than it would be the whole contribution of an adult taking a job from another adult. For example, by earning an income, a child worker can also become a consumer, or an investor, thus contributing like any other worker to the employment of others.

On the other hand, if a child is paid less than an adult would be for the same work, then he or she has less to contribute as a consumer or investor. But then, as a low-cost worker, the child might have more to contribute than an adult to the profits of their employers – as you may recall from the Bangladesh case study. This need not be a matter of sheer greed on the employer's part: such considerations might mean the difference between failure and survival for struggling firms on the margins of economic viability.

Myers sums up the position like this:

> ... strange as it may seem after so many years, we still do not have a decently fleshed-out theory of why children's economic participation would produce a negative macroeconomic impact. Only now are economists trying to develop one... and even if a well-developed theory did exist, we do not have adequate data by which to test it.

(Myers, 2000)

It is uncertain, then, how far there really is a conflict of economic interests between children and adults over children's contribution to the economy.

Indeed, I am not sure that it makes sense to talk of *any* long-term conflict of interests between adults and children. If one takes only a single snapshot at one point in time, then some people are children and others are adults – and those who are children at that point may well have different interests from those who are adults. And it may seem reasonable or even obvious that the interests of the children should outweigh those of the adults.

But if one recalls that children and adults are members of the same species at different stages of their life cycle, all that seems much less obvious. Those who are adults now were once children. Those who are children now will one day, barring misfortune, become adults. In the longer view, children and adults are the same people, and it makes less sense to oppose their interests. If there is a recurring conflict of interest between people in the first quarter or so of their life-span and *the same people* in the last three-quarters, it is not self-evident that the interests of the earlier period should be privileged.

> ### SUMMARY OF SECTION 4
>
> - Children's work can have many disadvantages, but these are not universal or inherent in children's work as such.
> - Some of these disadvantages are for children themselves, such as being dangerous, damaging to their health or development, interfering with their schooling and often involving unfair treatment of girls compared with boys.
> - Other possible disadvantages are for adults, who may be deprived of work, or whose bargaining position at work may be weakened, because employers find children cheaper and more malleable.

5 ADVANTAGES OF CHILDREN'S WORK

My second list was of supposed advantages of children's work. Again, I shall look at these in turn.

5.1 Paid work gives an income

The fact that this is such an obvious benefit should not lead to its being taken for granted and overlooked. In the case of child workers, the income is usually small. Nevertheless, it can be of great importance, not just to the child worker but to their family. As *The Black House* film illustrated, it can sometimes be what enables the family to survive. And in conditions of less extreme poverty, a child's income from work can be what enables him or her to go to school: this is discussed below.

In more affluent societies, such as Britain, the income earned by children from such part-time jobs as delivering newspapers and serving in shops or burger bars is not usually a significant contribution to family incomes. But it can still be important for the child workers themselves (Mizen *et al.*, 2001). For most of them, money is the main reason for working, outweighing other reasons such as the sociability of the workplace or any intrinsic interest in the work. Most child workers spend their earnings on clothes, entertainment and 'the "things" that have become the staple of children's social worlds: the odd piece of cheap jewellery, make-up, toiletries, magazines, games, CDs, videos, confectionery and fast food' (Mizen *et al.*, 2001, p. 47). In this way, they gain some control over important parts of their lives and aspects of their identity. Indeed, children who do not work are in danger of being excluded from many of the places and activities enjoyed by their working peers, simply because of the costs.

All this is especially important where parents are not affluent, and by working, children can avoid feeling too much of a burden on them. In a minority of cases, even in the more affluent countries of the world, working children do give financial support to their parents – sometimes in tactfully indirect ways, such as casually buying food on their way home. But even where parents are better off, working children's incomes give them a sense of independence and self-respect.

5.2 Unpaid work contributes to the family economy

This most obviously happens when a child makes a direct contribution to the running of a family's economic enterprise, such as a farm or a shop. Indeed, children's contributions are sometimes essential for the enterprise to survive. But children can also contribute indirectly by performing household or family tasks that free parents for other work. An obvious example of this is the child-care responsibilities of girls in the Zimbabwe case study. Overall, girls spent a third of their time on caring for younger family members. Most strikingly, girls under ten spent over half their time looking after even younger children. Thus they made an extremely important contribution to the economy of their families and the village as a whole, by releasing adult women (on whom the care of children would otherwise have fallen) for more immediately productive work.

5.3 Work gives meaning to life

In the countries of the North, it is generally acknowledged that work gives meaning to life for many adults. From their work, they acquire dignity, purpose, independence and even a sense of identity. (Asked who or what they are, people often reply in terms of their occupation.) This is one reason why unemployment for adults is regarded as a serious social problem. Not only are the unemployed deprived of an income, but they are also thought to incur psychological risks. The economic dependency on others that unemployment often brings is thought to be damaging to people's dignity and self-respect. Not having a job may mean lacking any obvious purpose in life, any motivation to take proper care of oneself, even any reason to get up in the morning. If people's unemployment is by choice, they are often criticised as lazy and irresponsible. If it is not, they may be regarded with some measure of pity.

In the North, such arguments are less often applied to children. For them, dependency is generally accepted as natural and proper. They have other purposes in life, such as preparation for adulthood, mainly through education. To a large extent, their identity is created for them by their parents or other adults in their lives.

The contrast between North and South should not be exaggerated, however. For working children in Britain, a greater independence is one of the reasons for taking a job. Part of this comes from having independently earned money to spend, but there are other aspects too. Child workers also report that they have greater freedom of movement than before, with less direct supervision from employers than from parents or teachers, and more control over decision making (Mizen *et al.*, 2001, p. 44).

Nevertheless, it remains true that children in the South are generally regarded as more like adults than those in the North. This is illustrated in the Zimbabwe case study by the pride that boys like twelve-year-old Chimbu take in their prowess as house-builders.

> It was on a Saturday that I returned from building my house. I had been cutting the poles into sizes so that my house would be an admirable one. I felt happy as I did this for I was confident my house will be one of the most beautiful in the area.
>
> (Reynolds, 1991, pp. 120–21)

Building and owning one's own house is an assertion of independence, Reynolds explains. It is startling for readers in the North to realize that this is possible for boys as young as twelve in Chitenge. It should be remembered, however, that all this applies to boys only. 'Girls must wait until they marry and their husbands build them houses' (Reynolds, 1991, p.121).

5.4 Work can be enjoyable

House building in Chitenge is an obvious example of work that the children find intrinsically enjoyable and there are many others. Besides, work can often be made enjoyable by what happens alongside it. Reynolds mentions in passing that, in Chitenge, children's work in general is accompanied by 'play, songs, laughter and quarrels' (Reynolds, 1991, p. 76). Work can also provide the opportunity for children, out of the sight of adults, to enjoy illicit activities, such as hunting and trapping animals and what Reynolds calls lovers' trysts (Reynolds, 1991, p. 85).

Of course, children's work is often very far from being fun – the Dhaka case study in Section 3.1 is a disquieting reminder of this.

One method of buffalo herding, Vietnam.

5.5 Work enables children to learn

A young South American street vendor.

It is often recognized in the North that work enables *adults* to learn – to develop skills, knowledge and personal qualities. Even though children are acknowledged to have both more need and more capacity to learn, it is generally held that school, not work, is the place for this to happen.

In some circumstances, however, work *can* help children to learn, sometimes more effectively than school.

Over a period of some ten years, researchers in Brazil studied what they called 'street mathematics' – the mathematical methods developed, learnt and used by children and adults in the course of their work as farmers, fishermen, carpenters and street vendors. This they compare and contrast with 'school mathematics', as taught and learnt formally in the local schools. The account below is an example of street mathematics in action.

In this example, a researcher conducts what the authors of the study call an 'informal test' of the mathematical competence of a twelve-year-old coconut vendor, by acting as a customer. The boy's method is then analysed.

(It is not clear whether the boy attends school as well as working. He is described as a 'third grader', but I do not know whether that indicates the class he would be in if he were at school, or a class he actually belongs to.)

CUSTOMER: How much is one coconut?

M.: Thirty-five.

CUSTOMER: I'd like ten. How much is that?

M.: [Pause] Three will be one hundred and five; with three more, that will be two hundred and ten. [Pause] I need four more. That is ... [Pause] three hundred and fifteen ... I think it is three hundred and fifty.

This problem can be mathematically represented in several ways: 35 × 10 is a good representation of the question posed by the interviewer. The subject's [i.e. the boy's] answer is better represented by 105 + 105 + 105 + 35, which implies that 35 × 10 was solved by the subject as (3 × 35) + (3 × 35) + (3 × 35) + 35. The subject can be said to have solved the following subitems:

(*a*) 35 × 10;

(*b*) 35 × 3 (which may already have been known);

(*c*) 105 + 105;

(*d*) 210 + 105:

(*e*) 315 + 35;

(*f*) 3 + 3 + 3 + 1.

When one represents in formal mathematical fashion the problems solved by the subject, one is in fact attempting to represent the subject's mathematical competence. M. proved to be competent at finding out how much 35 × 10 is, even though he used a routine not taught in third grade, since in Brazil third graders learn to multiply any number by 10 simply by placing a zero to the right of that number. Thus, we considered that the subject solved the test item (35 × 10) and a whole series of sub-items (*b* to *f*) successfully in this process.

(Nunes *et al.*, 1993, pp. 18–19)

<table>
<tr><td>Allow about 10 minutes</td><td>

A C T I V I T Y 4   **Street mathematics and school mathematics**

How would you (provisionally!) assess the advantages and disadvantages of street mathematics as against school mathematics, using just this one example? Please write a note of your reactions before reading mine.

C O M M E N T

My reaction is ambivalent. On the one hand, I am impressed by the sophistication and skill of M.'s mental arithmetic, above all his ability to hold in his memory all the different stages of the calculation until he puts them together at the end to obtain the correct answer. On the other hand, I am struck by the unnecessary effort his method involves, compared with the simplicity of the school mathematics recipe for multiplying by ten.

But I also find the researchers' report a little frustrating. I wonder if using multiplication by ten as the only example may be unfairly favouring school mathematics. I should like to know how M. would have fared if asked to multiply by, say, seven or thirteen. His method looks as if it would work just as well with these numbers as with ten. On the other hand, using school mathematics to multiply by these numbers is more difficult than multiplying by ten – and in the case of thirteen, much more difficult.

</td></tr>
</table>

But of course, one cannot make sensible judgements on the basis of a single example taken from ten years of research. From their analysis of the entire programme, Nunes and her colleagues draw a number of conclusions. Most involve technical issues in the psychology of teaching and learning mathematics, and will not be discussed here. Others conclusions, however, are of more general interest.

- Many of the children (and adults) engaging competently in street mathematics have been unsuccessful in the formal study of mathematics at school. The process of using mathematics in work has often proved a more effective teacher.

- Street mathematicians vary a lot in the methods they use to solve the same problem, unlike school mathematicians, who use standard methods. This suggests that to some extent individual street mathematicians develop their own methods, rather than having them all handed down by older practitioners.

- Street mathematics genuinely is *mathematics*, it 'is not the learning of particular procedures repeated in an automatic, unthinking way, but involves the development of mathematical concepts and processes' (Nunes *et al.*, 1993, p. 153).

- Compared with school mathematics, street mathematics has both advantages and disadvantages in tackling similar problems. School mathematicians typically have a more abstract and more easily generalized knowledge of mathematical procedures, but street mathematicians often have a better understanding of the meaning of the procedures they are following.

Nunes and her colleagues, then, do not make extravagant claims for street mathematics, and certainly do not say that it is unequivocally superior to the school variety. Their work does provide evidence, though, that school is not the only place where serious learning happens and sometimes it is not the best or the most effective place. On the other hand, they acknowledge that street mathematics has developed in the context of deficiencies in the Brazilian school system, where 'not only are there not enough places for all children of school age, but also the quality of the system ... produces markedly poor results' (Nunes *et al.*, 1993, p. 8). One of the ways in which they believe that the school system could be improved is by learning from street mathematics and building on it – something that they report is beginning to happen.

More broadly, the young street traders are learning much more than mathematics – they are also learning all the social and economic skills involved in successfully plying their trade. Coconut vendors, for example, have to learn where to obtain their coconuts, how much to pay for them, and perhaps how to bargain with suppliers over the price. Then they must know how to set their own prices, how to interact with customers and potential customers and how to relate to fellow traders and potential rivals. These are skills it is hard to imagine being taught successfully in classrooms. Their workplace – the street itself – where the skills are to be practised, seems the only likely place to learn them.

Not all children's work teaches such skills, however, or even allows the workers to exercise such skills and talents as they already have. In Britain today, children's work involving any element of skill or creativity is rare.

> Only occasionally would a job allow, for example, the chance to acquire some specific skills: basic book-keeping or accounting, knowledge of

administrative practices, specific techniques in animal husbandry or other specialist farming practices. Opportunities for creativity were similarly absent and largely limited to those few children who had managed to harness a particular musical or artistic talent to a commercial opportunity: performing a song and dance routine for a parent's cabaret act or painting murals for family or local businesses.

[...]

These types of jobs were the exception, however, and employment was far more likely to mean unskilled work around the edges of the formal labour market.

(Mizen *et al.*, 2001, p. 39)

SUMMARY OF SECTION 5

- Children's work can have many advantages, though they are not universal.
- Advantages include giving an income, contributing to the family economy and giving meaning and purpose to life. Children's work can also be a means of learning and a source of enjoyment.
- Apart from being a source of income, child work in the North arguably brings fewer of these advantages than in the South.

6 BALANCING ADVANTAGES AND DISADVANTAGES

I believe the advantages of children's work discussed above are genuine and important, but I cannot end without a word of caution. Not all work is of the kind that gives obvious dignity or purpose to life, or makes it easy for the workers to believe they are contributing anything of value to society. Not all work contributes to the development of the worker. Much work is long, tedious and exhausting, leaving the workers with the predominant feeling that they are letting their lives slip by, serving or making profits for someone else. Some work is positively harmful, to the workers and to others. But those reservations can apply to adults and children alike.

So far, the chapter has looked separately at various advantages and disadvantages of child work. Now I want to consider briefly whether the balance of advantages and disadvantages favours children's working or not.

Most people agree that some of the work children do in the world today is too dangerous and damaging to be tolerable, from almost any moral standpoint. But there is fundamental disagreement between those who argue that children's work is intrinsically intolerable and should be outlawed, and those who believe it can have positive advantages; for the latter, children's work needs to be accepted, but regulated and controlled.

In real life, of course, people find themselves making compromises. Every moral choice is a choice among options, and everyone has to try to find the best (or the 'least worst') option among those available. This applies equally to children and their families seeking schooling or work or both, and to thinkers and activists trying to decide what is best for working children. In the case study in Section 3.1 based on the film *The Black House*, where the work chosen seems to be almost as bad as it could be, the parents and the children alike were clear-eyed about the options available to them. None of the children wanted to go to work of this kind and none of the parents wanted to send them. All of them, however, accepted it as necessary because, presumably, it was better than the only alternative they could see, destitution.

In the course of making the film, its director – a committed opponent of child labour – had to make his own moral compromise, when he pleaded successfully for the reinstatement of Jashim in a casting factory. This was because he judged the alternative – destitution for Jashim and his entire family – to be even worse.

For similar reasons, it is hard to argue that governments or international bodies should intervene to stop even harmful work, unless they can offer more decent alternatives for the children (and adults) involved, and can be sure they are not going to make matters even worse for the children and their dependants. This does not mean they should not attempt to regulate children's work and improve working conditions as much as they can.

Finally, I have been looking at these questions in the abstract, but in real life they are asked and answered by real people, in very different social positions and with very different ideas and interests. Who among these has the competence, and who has the right, to make judgements about children's work?

Rather obviously, some people are *not* in a good position to do so. In *The Black House* example, it is easy to see how the employers' judgements of right and wrong may have been clouded by their economic interests. But who *is* in a good position?

One obvious answer is the children themselves. Since it is they above all who will suffer any disadvantages of work, should they not be the ones who weigh up these disadvantages against any advantages, especially advantages for other people? In the Dhaka film, they seemed to do that in a responsible, if gloomy and fatalistic manner. There was no evidence there of any conflict of opinion between the children and their parents. Both thought the work appalling, but both believed it had to be done.

In the Zimbabwe case study, by contrast, there was conflict between parents and children. The children sometimes tried to avoid doing the work their parents had given them. The parents sometimes tolerated this for boys, but at other times they enforced their instructions with the threat or reality of punishment. Girls' attempts to avoid work were never tolerated. Who was right – the parents or the children? I cannot deny (and what I have written earlier probably did not conceal) that I find myself unreflectively taking the side of the children, especially the girls – required to work from dawn to dusk every day, beaten if they refuse and all the time seeing their brothers lead much easier, freer lives. Maybe the work has to be done and children have to be involved, but could the parents not share it out more equally between the sexes, so that both also had a share of leisure time? I do accept that these judgements of mine may be clouded by prejudice and simple ignorance, but I cannot see that they are *necessarily* disqualified because I live in the relative prosperity of the North.

SUMMARY OF SECTION 6

- Child work can have advantages and disadvantages for the children and others.
- The balance of advantages and disadvantages of child work is often complicated and hard to draw. There is a tendency in the North to overlook the advantages and exaggerate the disadvantages.
- Child work customs and practices in the South that differ from those in the North are not automatically wrong, but nothing in either the South or the North is exempt from critical judgement.

7 CONCLUSION: CHILDREN'S PERSPECTIVES ON WORK AND SCHOOL

So far in Chapters 4 and 5, school and work have been considered separately. Now I want to conclude with some research that takes them together. In the mid-1990s, a major international research project placed children's perspectives on work and school at the centre of attention and studied them systematically. It was carried out under the auspices of Rädda Barnen (Save the Children, Sweden), and involved working children in four regions of the South. The main report of the study, by Martin Woodhead, was published in 1998 (Woodhead, 1998) and the following year, he published a paper summarizing some of its conclusions and discussing its implications (Woodhead, 1999b). An edited version of this paper is a reading for the present chapter.

These percentages refer to the working children in the research sample, and do not necessarily reflect overall school attendance in the countries concerned.

As well as working, about 60 per cent of the children studied were also attending school (full or part time) at the time of the study, a further 20 per cent had gone to school at some time in the past and the remaining 20 per cent had never been to school. These overall figures, however, mask wide variation among the different regions and countries. At one extreme, all the children studied in Guatemala, in Central America, were currently going to school; at the other, only eight per cent of those in Bangladesh were doing so (Woodhead, 1999b).

The research ranged widely across the children's lives, relationships, ideas, beliefs and values, but in this summary paper, Woodhead concentrates on just three of these:

- children's preferences among different types of work;

- children's judgements about the 'good things' and the 'bad things' about work and school;
- children's views about how school and work might be combined.

Discussing work and school: shoeshine boys, Ethiopia.

READING

Now please turn to the Reading.

As you read, you may find it helpful to make brief notes, jotting down what seem to be the main findings and also commenting on anything that seems particularly significant, unexpected, puzzling or perhaps questionable.

COMMENT

The paper is very clearly and straightforwardly written and I do not think a summary from me is necessary. Instead, I shall pick out a few major points that struck me as I read – points that seem to be significant and sometimes, to me at least, unexpected.

The children's approach to these activities was impressively rational, demonstrating 'their ability to weigh up multiple considerations, about income, independence and autonomy, security, safety, health, openness to abuse, gender appropriateness, etc' (p. 32). This does not mean (and Woodhead does not claim) that the children's views are always the last word on these subjects. For example, there was a strong tendency overall for the children to favour their own occupation, and to have a gloomier view of the drawbacks and dangers of other occupations than was held by those working in them. This may be for a number of reasons – children may simply be ignorant of jobs other than their own; their loyalty to an occupation, especially if it is one traditional in their family, may outweigh consideration of what it is actually like; or they may be trying to comfort themselves in difficult circumstances. But their views cannot be dismissed or ignored: they deserve to be taken seriously by anyone trying to understand – let alone intervene in – child work. As the example of international action against the Bangladesh garment industry shows, well-meaning but ill-informed outsiders can do more harm than good to working children.

Child work has many 'good things' about it for working children and school many 'bad things'. What particularly surprised me was the emphasis placed by so many children on 'humiliation/punishment' and 'beatings/abuse' as bad things about school. I do not really understand the distinction between these two categories, but taken together they appear to be the source of most unhappiness with school. (I have to say that cautiously, because it is not clear how much overlap there may be between the 50 per cent of groups who mentioned humiliation/punishment and the 42 per cent who mentioned beatings/abuse.) Beatings and abuse are far from unknown at work too, but they seem to loom larger in children's perceptions of school.

For the great majority of working children studied in every region (in round figures, between 70 and 80 per cent), the preferred way of life was one that combined school and work, rather than school alone or work alone. This was not an abstract, idealized choice, but one geared closely and realistically to their present circumstances. Besides, school and work were not seen as alternatives, let alone rivals for their time. On the contrary, it was often the income from children's work that made their schooling possible.

Of course, listening to children does not provide a definitive answer to any questions, any more than listening to adults. Like adults, children sometimes form their beliefs and wishes on the basis of limited or even distorted information. Like adults, too, children often disagree with one another. When they have been heard, children's views must also be weighed alongside those of adults, such as their parents, politicians in their own countries and experts and activists from the wider world. But hearing children's voices is an essential part of any attempt to understand or change their lives.

REFERENCES

BOYDEN, J., LING, B. and MYERS, W. (1998) *What Works for Working Children*, Stockholm, Rädda Barnen/UNICEF.

BURR, R. (2001) *Living in Difficult Circumstances? A study of children's lives in Vietnam*, London, Brunel University (unpublished PhD thesis).

JAMES, A., JENKS, C. and PROUT, A. (1998) *Theorizing Childhood*, Cambridge, Polity Press.

KEHILY, M. J. and SWANN, J. (eds) (2003) *Children's Cultural Worlds*, Chichester, John Wiley and Sons Ltd/The Open University (Book 3 of the Open University course U212 *Childhood*).

MCKECHNIE, J., STACK, M. and HOBBS, S. (2001) 'Work by secondary school students in Scotland', *International Journal of Educational Policy, Research and Practice*, **2**(3), pp. 287–305.

MIZEN, P., POLE, C. and BOLTON, A. (eds) (2001) *Hidden Hands: international perspectives on children's work and labour*, London, Routledge Falmer.

MIZEN, P., POLE, C. and BOLTON, A. (2001) 'Why be a school age worker?' in MIZEN, P., POLE, C. and BOLTON, A. (ed) (2001), p. 37–54.

MYERS, W. E. (2000) 'Appreciating diverse approaches to child labour', on-line article, http://www.childrightseducation.org/english/myersarticle.html [last accessed September 2002].

NIEUWENHUYS, O. (1994) *Children's Lifeworlds: gender, welfare and labour in the developing world*, London, Routledge.

NUNES, T., CARRAHER, D. W. and SCHLIEMANN, A. D. (1993) *Street Mathematics and School Mathematics*, Cambridge, Cambridge University Press.

OLOKO, S. (2000) unpublished interview with Martin Woodhead, Milton Keynes, BBC/Open University Production Centre.

PUNCH, S. (2000) 'Children's strategies for creating playspaces: negotiating independence in rural Bolivia' in HOLLOWAY, S. L. and VALENTINE, G. (eds) (2000) *Children's Geographies: playing, living, learning*, London, Routledge, pp. 48–62.

REYNOLDS, P. (1991) *Dance Civet Cat: child labour in the Zambezi Valley*, London, Zed Books Ltd.

WATKINS, K. (2000) *The Oxfam Education Report*, Oxford, Oxfam GB in association with Oxfam International.

WOODHEAD, M. (1998) *Children's Perspectives on Their Working Lives; a participatory study in Bangladesh, Ethiopia, The Philippines, Guatemala, El Salvador and Nicaragua*, Stockholm, Rädda Barnen.

WOODHEAD, M. (1999a) *Is There a Place for Work in Child Development?* Stockholm, Rädda Barnen.

WOODHEAD, M. (1999b) 'Combatting child labour: listen to what the children say' in *Childhood: a global journal of child research*, **6**(1), pp 27–49.

WOODHEAD, M. (2003) 'The child in development' in WOODHEAD, M. and MONTGOMERY, H. K. (eds) (2003) *Understanding Childhood: an interdisciplinary approach*, Chichester, John Wiley and Sons Ltd/The Open University (Book 1 of the Open University course U212 *Childhood*).

READING

Listen to what the children say

Martin Woodhead

In much of the debate about the detrimental effects of work, attending school is assumed to be the solution. [...] The implicit assumption is that schooling will be both a positive experience and will benefit children's long-term prospects. By asking children about their perceptions of school in relation to work, we were able to gain a perspective on these issues, from the consumers' point of view.

[...]

The study was carried out by local fieldworkers in four regions: Bangladesh, Ethiopia, the Philippines and the Central American countries: El Salvador, Guatemala and Nicaragua. More than 300 girls and boys participated in groups during 1996/7, most aged 10–14 years. The choice of occupations was intended to reflect a wide range of rural as well as urban working situations including: farming, plantation work, fishing, mining, market work, porters, shoeshine and sex work. Only a selection of these occupations are represented in the brief account that follows.

[...]

[The research method used is based on] group work with participants of similar age, occupation and gender. It requires a minimum of two fieldworkers, one to facilitate the group and the other to record the information ... . The groups are conducted informally, ideally spread over several days. [This] yields a combination of quantitative and qualitative information, supported by verbatim quotations from children. Fieldworkers are encouraged to adapt the objectives to local circumstances, in order that children can represent their feelings and beliefs in whatever ways are most meaningful to them, including drawings, mappings, role play as well as group discussion. At the heart of the [research] are a series of semi-structured activities and games focusing on key themes in children's lives. Many are based around locally produced picture cards which children can compare, sort and rank, yielding a combination of individual and group responses.

[...]

Children talk about work and school

[...]

Children were asked about the good things about being a working child, the things that made them feel happy, pleased, proud, confident. They were then asked about the bad things about their work, the things that make them sad, frightened, angry, bored. Once the children's ideas had been fully explored ... the procedure [was] repeated [for school], asking first about good things, and then about bad things. The second part of the activity asked children to compare school with work and judge what was best for them in their present circumstances, and why.

Tables 1 and 2 summarize children's comments about both the 'bad things' and the 'good things' about work. Major themes are listed, along with the percentage of groups in which each of these themes was mentioned. Note that in presenting group data of this kind, it is not possible to know how many children within the group expressed these views, nor the relative importance of each theme to them personally.

Table 1 'Bad things' about work: major themes in girls' and boys' groups

Major themes	All groups (Total = 49) % groups*	Girls' groups (Total = 24) % groups*	Boys' groups (Total = 25) % groups*
Hazardous conditions	76	83	68
Health/injury risk	51	58	44
Humiliation/abuse	45	42	48
Economic exploitation	43	46	40
Effects on schooling	27	25	28
General insecurity	49	54	44

*Percentage of groups mentioning this theme.

'Bad things' about work

Hazardous working conditions was the most consistently mentioned theme, for example among these boys mining for lead in Guatemala:

> We get tired because we have to crawl when we work ... we have to come out bent over carrying the load. We can't stand up because then we hit our heads on the rock ... we have to use a light, a lamp that we strap to our foreheads.

Some occupations also talked about fatigue, monotony and the constant demands for more work to be done, illustrated by participants who make fireworks in Guatemala:

> I get bored and tired of always sitting down or standing up, we hardly move from the same place.

In the Philippines, young girls (7–10 years old) working in the sugar plantations listed some of the problems they face:

> We work barefoot and the ground is hot. ... The tools are sharp. ...The soil is hard to break ... I get scratches ... I get itchy.

Some participants were so familiar with these hazards, that they took them for granted:

> I hurt myself with a scythe ... but I think this is a natural part of growing up.

A girl brick-chipper in Bangladesh described the risk of eye injuries, as well as the effects of the heat:

> It is very painful when a splinter from the brick gets into your eyes. One can go blind. ... I don't like sitting under the sun without any

shade and brick-chipping. My head spins. I often get fever at night. Many people die working under the sun.

A recurring theme in the children's comments is not so much about the work itself, but about the way they are treated. Children feel vulnerable to those with greater power and authority. They talk about people who bully, extort money, make unreasonable demands, mislead them, ridicule them, humiliate them, beat them or abuse them in other ways. Sources of abuse include employers, customers, police, members of the public and other children. Domestic workers (girls) were among the most vulnerable to ill-treatment by employers. Comments from girls in the Philippines and Bangladesh included:

> They shout at me and I am always reprimanded. ... I work until midnight. I cannot rest or go out. ... The dog's food is better than mine. ... My employer controls my life.

> Whenever my employer is going out, she locks me in from the outside, as if I'm going to steal everything in their house.

Street work is another context where children can feel vulnerable. Boys and girls working as vendors, porters or shoeshine all described incidents of humiliation, intimidation and abuse, as in this example:

> When at times a customer is kind and gives us a fruit while [she is] buying some, we feel good. But as soon as the customer is out of sight, the fruit seller will snatch it away from our hands and accuse us of stealing.

Just under half the groups also spoke about their experiences of economic exploitation. Young people complain about being deprived of earnings, not being paid on time or that they are cheated out of what they feel they deserve. Whether young people saw their work as interfering with school depended on their local situation. The pressures of reconciling work with school attendance and performance were most keenly felt by young people in the Philippines. For example:

> We are always late for school ... our teachers don't bother about us because we are always absent.

> I should be concentrating on school, not work ... even when I am tired I must go to school.

'Good things' about work

The interrelationship between school and work also shows in comments about 'good things'. Not surprisingly, the economic benefits of work were uppermost in children's minds. Three girls (in Bangladesh, Nicaragua and the Philippines) sum up this theme:

> In our life, money is the most important thing.

> I can support myself from my work without needing anybody else's help.

> You give money to your mum, to buy rice, beans and sugar.

A common theme referred to earning money in order to pay for the costs of schooling:

> We buy shoes and clothes that our parents can't give us, we also buy notebooks, books and pencils for our studies.

Table 2 'Good things' about work: major themes in girls' and boys' groups

Major themes	All groups (Total = 48) % groups*	Girls' groups (Total = 23) % groups*	Boys' groups (Total = 25) % groups*
Earning money	76	71	80
Supporting family	63	62	64
Skills and training	37	46	28
Pride and respect	29	25	32
Friendship/having fun	22	33	12
Others	29	29	28

*Percentage of groups mentioning this theme.

In most groups earning money was closely linked to supporting their family:

> My mother is happy when I am able to pay for my family's daily expenses.

> We help our parents with household expenses.

While participants were most aware of the economic benefits of working, work was also seen as offering skills and training. As a girl working in fishing in the Philippines said:

> I learn to be industrious and helpful ... I am being trained for the future when others will employ me.

Several other young people were even more reflective about working hard now in order to ensure their future:

> I learn how to work young so that when I get married I can already feed my family.

A gender difference was found in the importance attached to work as a source of friendships and social support (eight girls' groups vs three boys' groups). For a brick-chipper, working was a social experience:

> It gives me the chance to sit alongside my friends and work as well as chat. It keeps me happy and I can break a lot of bricks.

Friends were also important in times of crisis, as a girl snack seller in Ethiopia described:

> I feel happy ... if I do not have any money to buy Kollo for selling ... my friend lends me money.

Despite the difficulties of their circumstances, young people also talked about having fun. The same snack vendors in Ethiopia talked about when they visit the bars:

> I feel happy when I get the chance to watch TV in bars and also sell. ... When I see a person with his money being drunk and losing himself I laugh. ... We feel happy when a customer comes along smiling.

'Good things' about school

Table 3 summarizes children's comments on the 'good things' about school. As before, major themes are listed, along with the percentage of groups in which each of these themes was mentioned. Literacy and numeracy was the most consistent theme, mentioned even more frequently among girls' than boys' groups, for example as by a girl farm worker in Guatemala:

> We learn to read and write in order to defend ourselves in life.

Only half the groups in this study referred to the theme of improved job prospects as one of the benefits of school, as from this participant in the Philippines:

> I want to learn more. I want to raise our standard of living. I can escape from the work on the farm.

Table 3 'Good things' about school: major themes in girls' and boys' groups

Major themes	All groups (Total = 48) % groups*	Girls' groups (Total = 23) % groups*	Boys' groups (Total = 25) % groups*
Literacy/numeracy, etc.	69	78	60
Improved work prospects	56	57	56
School achievements, etc.	33	30	36
Learning skills and discipline	31	30	32
Peer relationships	60	61	60
Being able to play	46	30	60
Relationship with teacher	25	30	20
Gaining respect/feeling good	25	17	32

*Percentage of groups mentioning this theme.

A boy in fireworks manufacture in Guatemala was reflective about the best way to improve prospects, not just for himself but for his own children:

> Study helps us to improve ourselves and obtain a better job in which we make more money, because then our children will not suffer or have to go to work.

The second most commonly mentioned category of good things about school was about making friends:

> I like September because it is the time I meet my friends.

> [School is good because] schoolmates help you and lend you things.

School was also a rare opportunity to play with friends, especially for boys' groups:

> I have time to play ball with my friends, because I don't have time to play during my working hours.

Establishing positive relationships with teachers was also important to some groups:

> They guide us, love us, support us and take care of us, they teach us new things.

Good experiences in school were closely linked in many participants' minds to their self-respect in the community:

> When I get good results, everyone in the family and neighbourhood praises me.

For some children, exchanging their work clothes for school uniforms was the attraction:

> I want to become a schoolchild because they look so clean in their uniforms.

'Bad things' about school

While children recognize the potential for school achievement as a 'good thing' about school, for many the reality is much less positive (Table 4).

Table 4 'Bad things' about school: major themes in girls' and boys' groups

Major themes	All groups (Total = 48) % groups*	Girls' groups (Total = 23) % groups*	Boys' groups (Total = 25) % groups*
Humiliation/punishments	53	57	50
Beatings/abuse	45	48	42
Peer relationships	55	61	50
Low achievement	51	57	46
Teacher absence	15	17	13
Tiredness/boredom	23	30	17
Costs of schooling	19	22	17
Competing pressures	19	22	17
Others	40	35	46

*Percentage of groups mentioning this theme.

A shoeshine boy in Ethiopia explained the many reasons why he was disillusioned with school:

> I feel ashamed when I fail in examinations, when I am not able to answer when a teacher asks me something, when I repeat the same grade, when I miss classes, when I am not able to do my homework.

Working children cannot be expected to make much progress in school if their teachers do not show up. Absentee teachers were a particular concern for participants from one Guatemalan village, where both groups reported the problem:

> Teachers often lie to us. They say, we are going to come such-and-such a day and then they don't come after all.

A very common theme was about school being a harsh and humiliating experience, as expressed by these young people in the Philippines:

> [They] pinch us ... throw erasers at us ... pull our hair ... hit us with big sticks ... make us kneel, hands raised and put books on our hands.

Another comment came from a group of farm workers in Bangladesh:

> They beat us with a cane or a bamboo stick on our palms or back. ... At times they also push our head under a table and hit us on the buttocks.

A snack vendor in Ethiopia described what happened to her:

> When my parents did not buy exercise books, the teacher beat me.

Other children can also be a source of humiliation at school, as recounted by young people in Nicaragua, Ethiopia and the Philippines:

> Children from richer families tease and insult us by mentioning our work.

> Boys bully us in the school compound and outside.

> They laughed at me because I have no shoes and I have dirty clothes.

Once again, school issues were closely linked to work issues in many children's minds. Participants referred to the costs of schooling, compounded by the loss of earnings while in school:

> I cannot earn money ... I have not enough money for my school expenses.

Even if working children manage to cover the costs of schooling, they still face major practical pressures of combining the demands of school with the necessity of work, as in these comments from Bangladesh and Guatemala:

> Before going to school, my mother asks me to do some work. By the time I complete the work I'm late for school.

> When I used to be late for school because I had to complete my household chores before leaving for school, the teacher used to beat me. She did not listen to what I said.

Children talk about combining work with school

So far, I have briefly summarized some of the themes expressed by children when asked to talk about their work and school. Participants in this study were also asked their views on the place of work and school in their lives.

[...]

'In your present family circumstances, which is best for you?

- only going to work
- only going to school
- going to work and attending school.'

For this part of the [research], individual responses were collected for 300 working children. It is important to emphasize that children were asked to comment on their present situation. They were not asked to speculate about idealized futures, and this no doubt affected their judgement.

Combining work and school was the overwhelming preference, by 77 percent of children in this study. These children recognized the potential benefits of attending school, but they were also aware of the difficulties, both the direct costs (fees, etc.) and indirect costs (loss of income), as well as the other negative aspects of schooling revealed by the earlier part of the activity. Comparing boys with girls, the pattern is broadly similar, although more girls favour 'only school' and more boys 'only work'.

However, these results conceal the wide range of situations faced by children in this study, which shapes their judgement. A comparison between child workers in Central America, the Philippines, Ethiopia and Bangladesh illustrates the point (Table 5).

Table 5 Which is best for you in your present circumstances?
Comparing four contexts

	Groups in Bangladesh (72 children) (%)	Groups in Ethiopia (42 children) (%)	Groups in the Philippines (81 children) (%)	Groups in Cent. America (106 children) (%)
Work only	24	29	4	1
Work and school	76	69	79	78
School only	0	2	17	21

A feature of children's judgements is the consistency with which combining school with work is favoured as the core option (between 69 percent and 79 percent in each region). Many of these participants did not see them as alternatives. Schooling is desirable, but work is a necessity. Work provides the income to support basic necessities, for self and family, and in many cases makes it possible to afford the additional costs of going to school, as illustrated by the following examples.

It will not do us any good if we just work. We will have to go to school. Learn to write our names. First we have to complete our work and then go to school.

We have to help our parents, if we are very poor, we have to help them with the costs of studying and other things that are lacking in the home.

Isn't it natural for children to work and study at the same time? ... All study makes your body weak, and all work makes your mind poor.

Even a king's food finishes one day, so it is important to continue working a little.

In summary, 'work and school' is the majority choice across all local studies. In drawing this conclusion, it is important to emphasize that this study is not based on systematic sampling of working children, and children's views may not be representative of the wider population in each region.

The minority choices in Table 5 are also instructive. 'Work only' was chosen by 24 percent of participants in Bangladesh and by 29 percent in Ethiopia; very few chose 'school only'. By contrast, 'school only' was the favoured alternative for 17 percent of participants in the Philippines and 21 percent in Central America, and very few chose 'work only'. These contrasts appear related to the availability and economic significance of schooling in these countries. School attendance among participants varied: 8 percent in Bangladesh, 57 percent in Ethiopia (part-time), 79 percent in the Philippines, 58 percent in Nicaragua and 100 percent in Guatemala. But other factors also come into play, associated with children's specific, occupational situation. In Central America, more than half the children who chose 'school only' as the best option were from the three farm worker groups in Guatemala. One girl said:

It's the best way to become somebody in life, work should be left for after when one is more responsible.

In Bangladesh, where few participants had the opportunity to attend school, none saw 'school only' as a realistic choice, while 24 percent favoured 'work only'. Twelve out of these 17 participants were boys working in the embroidery and sari weaving workshops in the informal sector. These boys and their families were committed to long working hours that would make schooling impractical:

Considering our present family situation we have no choice but to work now ... [The boss] will not allow us to take a few hours off for studies ... After working the whole day, I don't feel like coming home and starting to study. I would not be able to concentrate.

The situation of sex workers offers the strongest example of the way an occupational situation constrains working children's options. These young people feel their occupation stigmatizes them and makes attending school impossible. All favoured 'only work':

School and work will not go together because if we go to school as well as work, at school students and teachers will insult us and abuse us and so we cannot attend.

In summary, young people in these groups reflect on their circumstances, and consider the options available to them. The great majority value the opportunity of schooling, but they do not see this as an alternative to working – in their present circumstances.

[...]

Conclusion

In this article I have presented some evidence from a study into how children perceive the place of work in their lives. ... studying children's perspectives is not a substitute for conventional evaluation research. Medical, social and psychological research is urgently required to identify the way multiple dimensions of 'work' relate to specific indicators of health, psychosocial adjustment and educational achievement. Children's perspectives offer an essential, additional perspective on these processes, from the children's point of view.

Source

WOODHEAD, M. (1999) 'Combatting child labour: listen to what the children say' in *Childhood: a global journal of child research*, **6**(1), pp. 27–49.

Chapter 6
Shaping early childhood education

Linda Miller, Janet Soler and Martin Woodhead

CONTENTS

When you have studied this chapter, you should be able to:

1 Trace the origins of early education in relation to school systems.

2 Understand how early childhood education is shaped by and in turn shapes beliefs about and expectations of young children's needs, learning and development.

3 Critically discuss the way in which professional beliefs and wider political agendas affect children's experiences of curriculum in early childhood.

4 Analyse these debates about education in respect of three curriculum models: the English foundation stage curriculum, Te Whāriki in New Zealand and Reggio Emilia in Italy.

I INTRODUCTION

1.1 Different experiences

Earlier chapters of this book have examined some major debates about the middle years of childhood, especially around the place of work and school in children's lives. In this chapter and the next we will be concentrating on issues at the boundaries of compulsory school. Chapter 7 is about major transitions of later childhood, around the time of leaving school. This chapter is about the years before children start school – which are frequently referred to as the pre-school years. The use of this term 'pre-school' is itself interesting. In affluent, industrialized countries, school has become such a powerful reference point for thinking about children, that even very young children who have not yet reached school age are defined in relation to it.

'Pre-schooler' can mean very different things according to where a child is growing up, because the age for starting compulsory school varies from country to country. Within Europe, Britain has a comparatively early statutory starting age (five years old), while children in several Nordic countries (Denmark, Sweden and Finland) are not required to start school until seven years old. Most countries in Europe set six as the age for compulsory schooling (e.g. France, Belgium and Italy), and six is also the starting age in the USA, Australia and New Zealand (OECD, 2001).

These compulsory school starting ages are in some ways misleading, because they do not relate at all directly to the ages at which children *actually* start attending school, or start going to a nursery, kindergarten, playgroup or crèche, where they are looked after, play and learn – usually alongside other young children. For example, in Sweden full-day *Förskola* is attended by 34 per cent of one to two year olds and 64 per cent of three year olds, even though these children will not begin compulsory school until seven years old (OECD, 2001, p. 47). It is for this reason we use the phrase 'early childhood' in this chapter in preference to 'pre-school'. By 'early childhood' we mean children of approximately nought to six years old. The chapter concentrates on how contrasting visions of early childhood are expressed in a range of approaches to the curriculum. We are especially interested in exploring debates about the kinds of learning and teaching considered important for this age group, and about who should decide these questions. Sections 2, 3 and 4 of the chapter ask you to look in detail at three very different contexts for these debates, in England, in New Zealand and in Italy. In the space of one chapter we are not able to examine several other major issues, notably surrounding day care for young children. We are concentrating on children's experiences in the context of organized educational services for young children – typically where groups of young children play and learn together under the supervision of trained staff. These trends towards planned systems of early education are a feature of modern childhoods in affluent countries. They need to be understood in the context of informal learning and teaching provided in families and communities, as explored, for example, in the first chapter of this book.

For the rest of Section 1 we sketch in some of the background to early education debates. We begin by asking you to reflect about your own personal experiences as a young child.

Allow about 30 minutes

A C T I V I T Y 1 Experiences of early childhood

Think about your own experiences of early childhood or talk to someone you know about the experiences they may have had. This may have been as a child or parent. Make short notes about the following:

1 What were your early experiences of school? Did you attend a nursery or some other kind of early childhood provision, such as a day-care centre, childminder or playgroup?

2 What do you remember about play and how you were taught?

3 How structured was your learning? Were you encouraged to choose activities or did you practice reading and writing? Did you move freely about or did you sit at tables or desks?

4   What do you remember about when you started learning the three Rs (reading, writing and arithmetic)? Did you learn at home, at nursery or at school, and at what age? From your experience, what age do you think these skills should be introduced?

5   How do you think your experiences as a child differ from those of children in today's early childhood provision, for example in nurseries and playgroups?

COMMENT

Here are two responses to this activity, from adults who grew up in very different cultural contexts. You might like to compare your experiences to these.

Example 1: Lorraine – England

I grew up in the North of England, not far from Manchester. I didn't attend a nursery although some were available at that time. I spent my pre-school years at home with my mother – this was a typical situation at that time, the 1950s. My first memories are of starting in what was called the 'reception class' in my local primary school. This was soon after my fifth birthday. There was a clear distinction between formal learning and play. Apart from brief periods of freedom at official 'playtimes', when we all hurtled around the concrete outdoor playground, we spent long hours sitting at low tables, engaged with activities such as colouring in pictures, drawing around shapes, tracing over letters and learning to read the alphabet. I can remember rote-learning maths tables by chanting and writing them down. An early memory of learning to read involved a group of children standing round the teacher's table, each taking turns to 'read' out loud a page from the same reading book. Everyone dreaded not being able to read the words. On one occasion the child at the end of the table nearest the teacher was hit on the side of the head for failing to read a word. This caused a chain reaction as each subsequent child fell against the next one and on to the floor. Friday afternoon was when we could play – with sand and water, washing the dolls' clothes and shopping in the shop that had been set up in a corner of the classroom.

In England today, far more children go to a nursery before they start school, and I think that they seem much happier. Everything seems far more informal yet the children seem to learn the same things but in a more playful way and corporal punishment is banned in English schools by law. I still think, though, that children should be prepared for when they go to school by learning more about the three Rs in pre-school.

Example 2: Bharat – Nepal

I grew up in the village of Gumdi near Kathmandu in Nepal in the 1960s. I never attended any kind of nursery or school because there wasn't any pre-school education available in my country at that time. I was born into a high-caste family and my parents managed my teaching by hiring a priest/teacher in our own home. This was not for me alone as I was in an extended family and we were taught by the priest together in a temporary cottage in a field near our home.

When it rained (and we got wet), or if the priest did not want to teach us, we were allowed to go home or do what we wanted.

The focus was completely on the rote learning of religious books and Sanskrit by sitting and keeping our feet crossed. If you did anything else other than chanting with the priest and sitting in this position we were punished. Once he gave me a mathematical problem which I could not solve, he put his palm so forcefully against my cheek that it left an imprint. He would also pull the small hairs near my ear. What I learnt was totally managed by the priest. Priority was given to good handwriting and the memorization of the learned religious and cultural texts. The priest would go to sleep at times and we would be able to run away from the cottage and play.

Now the situation has changed and we have early childhood classes in Nepal, but they are not accessible for everyone. The government and local community and other national and international organizations are trying to extend early childhood education. There is still overall an emphasis upon traditional, formal education for children in Nepal.

These examples offer very contrasting experiences of starting school, in terms of organization of learning, styles of teaching and discipline, as well as goals for education. Lorraine recalls the tension between play and formal learning, the beginnings of three Rs teaching, while Bharat's memories are of the religious texts he was expected to learn by heart, and the painful consequences of making mistakes. One thing Lorraine and Bharat agree is that more young children now attend some kind of early education provision than when they were children. To conclude this introductory section, we want briefly to trace the origins and growth of early education, and then explore some of the main issues about children's early learning that will be discussed in the rest of the chapter.

1.2 Origins of early childhood education

The idea that early childhood is an important time for children's learning and development goes back a very long way. The Greek philosopher Plato took the fact for granted: 'The first step, as you know, is always what matters most, particularly when we are dealing with those who are young and tender. That is the time when they are taking shape and when any impression we choose to make leaves a permanent mark' (Plato as quoted in Clarke and Clarke, 1976, p. 4). The importance of early childhood may not be disputed, but how and what children should learn during these tender years has been fiercely debated. Many pioneers of early childhood education have offered distinctive visions of early childhood and some are still present in the names of nurseries and kindergartens today. Comenius is usually attributed with being one of the first to set out a systematic treatise on early education in *The School of Infancy* (1630). During the late eighteenth century, Oberlin set up one of the first schools for young children in Alsace, France, while in Switzerland, Heinrich Pestalozzi was setting up experimental schools, influenced by Rousseau's theories about respecting children's natural development. These ideas were taken further during the nineteenth century by Friedrich Froebel, in *The Education of Man* (1826), and it was Froebel who established the first kindergarten ('children's garden') in Germany in 1837. Later in the nineteenth century, Rachel and Margaret McMillan began working with slum children in Bradford and, later, London. They were so alarmed by the incidence of malnutrition and inadequate physical care amongst school-age children that they turned their attention increasingly to preventive work, including setting up the Open-Air Nursery School in Peckham, London in 1914. At this time in Italy, Maria Montessori developed a distinctive approach to sensory training from her work with slum children in Naples, which is still widely practised in Montessori nurseries today.

While these early pioneers differed in the details of their ideas, they shared a conviction that early education should be constructed around the needs, interests and developmental stages of young children.

In 1911, Margaret and Rachel McMillan set up a pioneering early childhood project at Evelyn House, Deptford, London. Margaret announced 'We must open our doors to the toddlers … we must plan the right kind of environment for them and give them sunshine, fresh air and good food before they become rickety and diseased' (Bradburn, 1976, pp. 33–4).

1.3 Early childhood and the school system

One central debate in early education was – and still is – about how far it should anticipate what children were expected to do when they started formal school. For example, in Britain, Robert Owen, the socialist factory owner, had set up an infant school at New Lanark in 1816. He encouraged the very youngest children in the village to attend, but he was adamant that this was not for formal instruction:

> The children were not to be annoyed with books but were to be taught uses and nature or qualities of the common things around them, by familiar conversation when the child's curiosity was excited so as to induce them to ask questions respecting them ... with these infants everything was to be amusement.
>
> (Owen, 1858, p. 140, quoted in Blackstone, 1971, p. 17)

Owen's views went largely unheeded. Towards the end of the nineteenth century very large numbers of very young children attended school, often sitting alongside much older children. The Education Acts of 1870 and 1880 had set five as the age when compulsory schooling should start, but they did not prevent younger children attending school. Official statistics record the proportion of three to four year olds in school in England and Wales as 24 per cent in 1870, rising to 43 per cent in 1900 before dropping to 15 per cent by 1920. The sudden decline in young children in school in part resulted from a report written in 1905 by inspectors from the Ministry of Education. They considered the regime in elementary school classes as totally unsuited to the educational needs of the youngest children, aged three and four years. One of the most outspoken of these inspectors was Katherine Bathurst, and she went on to write about her impressions of the elementary schools she visited in Manchester, England.

> Let us now follow the baby of three years through part of one day of school life. He is placed on a hard wooden seat (sometimes it is only the step of a gallery), with a desk in front of him and a window behind him, which is too high up to be instrumental in providing such amusement as watching the passers-by. He often cannot reach the floor with his feet, and in many cases he has no back to lean against. He is told to fold his arms and sit quiet. He is surrounded by a large number of other babies all under similar alarming and incomprehensible conditions, and the effort to fold his arms is by no means conducive to comfort or well being
>
> [...]
>
> What possible good is there in forcing a little child to master the names of letters and numbers at this age? The strain on the teachers is terrific. Even when modern methods are in vogue and each child is provided with coloured counters, shells, beads or a ball frame, the intellectual effort of combining three plus one to make four, or two plus two for the same total, has no value at such an age. The nervous strain must reduce the child's physical capacity, and this, again, reacts unfortunately on the condition of the teeth, eyes and digestion.
>
> (Katherine Bathurst, 1905, reprinted in van der Eyken, 1973, pp. 120, 122).

The babies' bench, from The Graphic, a national weekly magazine, 1891.

Learning through play in a modern nursery.

Bathurst went on to propose a system of national nurseries, designed specifically for young children, where the emphasis would be on learning through play and practical activities, appropriate to their developmental stage.

1.4 Early childhood as an investment?

Understanding of young children's learning greatly increased during the twentieth century, at the same time as the numbers of young children attending kindergarten, nursery schools and other forms of early education grew. But it would be a mistake to view early childhood as being of interest only to parents, teachers, psychologists and social reformers. From time to time, early childhood has become a central theme of government policy. One of the earliest examples of political interest in early childhood came in 1964 with the launch of the American Head Start programme by President

Johnson, as part of his 'war on poverty'. By 2000, Head Start was offering comprehensive services for 800,000 disadvantaged children and their families, and costing the federal government $4.7 billion. But early childhood services were not just seen as a cost. They were also seen as an investment.

Dozens of studies have been carried out to evaluate the cost effectiveness of Head Start. One of the most influential studies followed the fortunes of 123 children, approximately half of whom attended an experimental pre-school program in Michigan in the early 1960s. This was a very carefully planned and well-resourced program, but sufficiently similar to Head Start for generalizations to be made about the power of Head Start to change children's lives (Woodhead, 1988). This research team was also one of the first to translate their evidence into a cost-benefit analysis. In 1982, they prepared a background paper for a conference of state governors in which they argued that the initial costs of providing early education were more than paid for in terms of the reduced need for remedial and special education, reduced levels of juvenile crime, teenage pregnancies and early school drop-out:

> For every $1000 that was invested in the pre-school programme, at least $4130 (after inflation) has been or will be returned to society – better than the average rate of return to private investors.

(Breedlove and Schweinhart, 1982)

A more recent, comprehensive economic analysis drew the more modest, but still positive conclusion that the benefits of a large-scale public programme like Head Start could offset 40 to 60 per cent of the costs (Currie, 2001).

These economic analyses of early childhood education have influenced governments in other countries too. For example, in 1999 the UK government launched Sure Start as an anti-poverty strategy targeted at the very youngest children and their families. The aim of Sure Start was: 'to promote the physical, intellectual and social development of babies and young children – particularly those who are disadvantaged – so that they can flourish at home and when they get to school, and thereby break the cycle of disadvantage for the current generation of young children' (www.surestart.gov.uk, accessed August 2002).

Investment in early childhood education has also become a priority for international agencies such as Unicef. Introducing early childhood programmes is even one of the strategies adopted by the World Bank for the world's poorest countries. Intervening in young children's lives is seen as a way to increase the efficiency of primary and secondary school, reduce the long term cost of health care and public services and ultimately increase labour productivity and income (Young 1998; for a discussion see Penn, 2002).

These debates may seem far removed from young children's daily lives. They serve as a reminder of the wider political significance of questions about what children should learn and who should decide.

1.5 What should children learn and who should decide?

In the rest of this chapter, we offer three examples of early childhood curricula. We have chosen these examples because, taken together, they demonstrate how struggles over the curriculum can result in different outcomes in terms of who controls curriculum content, the ways in which it can be taught, which cultural and theoretical views of the child dominate and what early childhood education is preparing the child for. The examples are:

1   The English foundation stage curriculum. This is a centralized curriculum framework that provides guidance to early childhood practitioners and teachers to enable them to prepare children for the next stage of schooling.

2   Te Whāriki in New Zealand. This is also centralized, but it is a learner-centred, bicultural curriculum, catering especially for issues of cultural difference.

3   Reggio Emilia in Italy. This is not a national curriculum framework with a formal curriculum policy. It is a localized, learner-centred approach often described as an 'emergent curriculum'.

Even within England and New Zealand, these examples are not comprehensive curriculum models. Early education in England is shaped by many influences other than the national curriculum, not least by the rich legacy of educational principles and psychological theories mentioned earlier. But the English government's intervention in early childhood curricula offers a very powerful illustration of the tension over who should control what and how children learn. Te Whāriki, also a centrally defined curriculum, is distinctive because of the attempt to address cultural and language issues, European and Maori. Finally, in Italy, central government has traditionally been much less prescriptive about what children should learn at any stage of education. The Reggio approach is one among many influential curricula for early education. Besides being an interesting case of a decentralized system, Reggio Emilia offers a distinctive vision for early childhood which has been extremely influential on professional thinking in countries throughout the world.

The term 'early childhood curriculum' refers to planned activities that are designed to achieve particular developmental and educational aims

In this chapter we use the term 'early childhood curriculum' in a very broad way to refer to planned activities that are designed to achieve particular developmental and educational aims. Developing early childhood and school-based curricula involves making decisions and choices about what children should learn. Making these choices involves different groups such as early childhood practitioners, teachers, educational experts and policy makers. Tensions arise when different groups disagree over what is appropriate content and what are appropriate ways of teaching.

The early childhood curricula discussed in the remainder of this chapter are either based on official guidance issued by government and ministers, or curricula generated more locally for different early childhood settings. We have chosen these particular examples in order to identify and compare the different views of childhood and the resulting debates and struggles over appropriate approaches to early childhood curricula. In our discussion of these examples, we will explore the struggles between different visions of childhood and how particular views about childhood became embedded in these curricula.

SUMMARY OF SECTION 1

- We have outlined the background to the debates about the nature of early childhood education, both in international and English contexts.
- We have briefly indicated how ideas about what and how children should learn have changed over time and how they are also dependent on culture and context.
- We have noted that there are different and often conflicting views about the nature of education for young children which can result in very different experiences of early schooling.

2 THE FOUNDATION STAGE CURRICULUM IN ENGLAND

In England since 1988 there has been a national curriculum framework for primary and secondary schooling (DfEE, 1999). For the first time English schools were bound by a centrally defined national curriculum based on subjects. The introduction of the national curriculum broke the tradition of local control within which schools and teachers had a great deal of autonomy to decide what children learned and how they were taught. The national curriculum applied to children from five to sixteen. The early childhood curriculum in England remained outside central government control until 1996. Even so, the centralization of the primary school curriculum gradually affected English early childhood education. The demands of the primary school curriculum on young children entering school at the age of five, put pressure upon early childhood educators to provide a more formal curriculum in the pre-school period.

Many practitioners and experts did not agree with early childhood education becoming a preparation for future schooling. The Early Years Curriculum Group stated that early childhood is a valid stage in its own right, not a preparation for work or for the next stage of education (Early Years Curriculum Group, 1989). This opposition to the pressure to use pre-school as preparation for schooling resulted in a struggle between the Government and early childhood experts over the structure and content of the curriculum.

The disagreements were not just between policy makers and experts but also among early childhood educators. Edwards and Knight (1994) argued that in the recent past the early childhood curriculum in many settings had been neither explicit nor coherent and had not always been planned. They believed that young children were entitled to a curriculum that would offer a sound basis from which they could develop into literate and numerate adults. The first central government initiative to standardize the early childhood curriculum came in 1996. It was the first of a series of government initiatives culminating in the introduction of the *Curriculum Guidance for the Foundation Stage* in 2000. We will briefly trace the debate around this short history.

In 1996 a document entitled *Desirable Outcomes for Children's Learning on Entering Compulsory Education* (SCAA, 1996) was introduced by government to all early childhood settings with four year olds. Although the document claimed that the contents did not specify a curriculum, it described learning outcomes to be achieved by the age of five in six areas of learning linked to the subjects of the national curriculum. These learning areas were:

- personal and social development
- language and literacy
- mathematics
- knowledge and understanding of the world
- physical development
- creative development

For each learning area, specific goals were listed, for example among the 21 goals for language and literacy were:

- listen attentively
- enjoy books
- recognize their own names
- write their names with appropriate use of upper and lower-case letters

Many early childhood practitioners and experts saw this development as an attempt by government to introduce a standard early childhood curriculum across the wide range of settings. The Government also introduced a centralized system of inspection and assessment (QCA, 1998). The early childhood community criticized the prescriptive nature of the learning outcomes and the links made to the national curriculum in primary schools (Anning and Edwards, 1999; David and Nurse, 1999). The changes conflicted with the view of many practitioners and experts that children should learn through play rather than through structured teaching towards specific goals. They saw the changes as influencing the early childhood curriculum from the outside rather than from within and as placing top-down pressure on those working with young children to introduce more formal approaches. However, Margaret Hodge, then Minister for Education, argued for the right of all children to have a curriculum which prepared them well for primary school. She felt that in early childhood settings young children's time is most valuably spent learning about numbers and the letters of the alphabet, rather than learning informally through play, a view shared by some parents. Chris Woodhead, chief inspector of schools at that time, suggested that the debate had become too polarized, that there was no conflict between making learning enjoyable and purposeful and that inspection evidence

Group story-time in a nursery class in England.

Outdoor play in a nursery class in England.

showed both extremes could be damaging. He argued that four year olds enjoyed structured learning, but also needed ample opportunities for play and a choice of activities (Carvel, 1999). Drummond (2001, p. 90) noted that 'At stake here are different constructions of childhood, different conceptualizations of what it is that young children should do and feel, know and understand, represent and express'.

In 1999 the Government took the process a stage further by introducing a foundation stage of education for children aged three to six which set out what children should be learning up to the end of their first year in primary school. The 'desirable outcomes for children's learning' were replaced by 'early learning goals' (QCA, 1999). The learning goals were set within six areas of learning which were linked to the subjects of the national curriculum in primary schools; literacy and numeracy were seen as particularly important because of the Government's drive to raise standards in these areas. The goals were reported in one newspaper as 'targets for toddlers'.

Targets for toddlers

Naming and sounding all the letters of the alphabet;

Reading a range of common words and simple sentences independently;

Showing comprehension of stories;

Holding a pencil effectively and forming recognizable letters;

Using phonetic knowledge to make plausible attempts at complex words;

Writing their own names and forming sentences, sometimes using punctuation;

Counting reliably up to 10 everyday objects;

Recognizing numerals 1 to 9;

Understanding the vocabulary of adding and subtracting;

Asking about why things happen and how things work.

(Carvel, 1999)

Although the document mentioned the role of play in learning, many practitioners and experts felt that it prescribed *what* rather than *how* young children should learn. Subsequently the early childhood community protested. Their views are reflected in a cartoon which appeared in *Private Eye*. You may like to pause to think about what message the cartoon is intending to convey about these changes to the early childhood curriculum.

The cartoon comments upon these changes and reflects the criticisms from early childhood practitioners and experts at that time. It implies that the pressure to prepare children for the first stage of the national curriculum (i.e. key stage 1) is denying children the right to learn through play.

NURSERY RHYME
Boys and girls come in from play,
The sun doth shine so bright today.
Leave your skipping and hide-&-seek
And revise for Key Stage 1 next week.

Issue No. 797, *Private Eye*, 25 June 1999

Following these protests, the Qualifications and Curriculum Authority introduced new curriculum guidance, *Curriculum Guidance for the Foundation Stage* (QCA, 2000), after consulting widely with experts and practitioners within the early childhood community. Although the goals for learning were retained, the emphasis was on appropriate ways to help children work towards the goals, rather than on achieving them. This made the foundation stage curriculum more acceptable to the early childhood community, but they still had reservations about how the guidance would be interpreted by practitioners with different skills, knowledge and levels of training.

The English foundation stage curriculum was implemented in early childhood settings in September 2000. As you can see from Figure 1, it represents a view of child development as a series of linear steps. Each learning area has designated goals to be achieved. Steps towards these goals are clearly described and represented as three colour bands broadly linked to age. As these goals are to be achieved by the age of five, by the end of reception year, the steps follow a suggested order. There is therefore, an expectation of what children should be doing at certain ages and stages. This is why many commentators see this curriculum as incorporating a prescribed, linear notion of progression in learning and development (The Open University, 2003).

The guidelines suggested that children's development and learning take place in a sequence which can be assessed and itemized at predetermined levels. In structuring the curriculum and its assessment in this manner, the policy makers have made assumptions about where the levels begin and end for most children. They have also determined what skills and specific knowledge can be learnt, although practitioners were free to interpret *how* they would work towards the early learning goals. Policy makers viewed this centralized model of curriculum as helpful to practitioners because it provided clear guidance on the consistent implementation of the early learning goals across all settings. Some practitioners also saw the guidance as helpful, particularly those working with four and five year olds in reception classes, as the foundation stage guidance meant that they did not have to adhere to the national curriculum for primary age children. Supporters of the foundation stage curriculum argued that the early learning goals laid secure foundations for future achievement and therefore gave children the best possible start as lifelong learners (Staggs, 2000). These goals were, therefore, based upon the need for schools to provide a curriculum that would equip pupils with the knowledge, skills and understandings that they would need for adult life and employment. However, critics said that the guidance was framed mainly by people who stood outside of young children's experiences and who did not understand how they learn and develop. They supported Kelly's (1994) view that those responsible for such models are concerned more about what education is for, rather than what the experience of education might entail, and that the approach is driven by economic needs and commercial competitiveness.

Although it claims to be an inclusive curriculum that encompasses all children (Staggs, 2000), the emphasis on competitiveness and achievement suggests that the main goal is to support those who can succeed and reach attainment targets. The requirement that children achieve school-based knowledge and skills at an increasingly younger age is in conflict with the curricula for young children promoted by the pioneers discussed earlier in this chapter. Other curricula, as we show in our other examples, do not give priority to centralized, subject-based organization of the curriculum which links to later schooling.

Although they were writing before the introduction of the foundation stage curriculum guidance in 2000, Anning and Edwards express concerns which relate to those we discussed earlier in this section. Reading A argues that the outcome of such struggles can lead to very different and sometimes harmful experiences for young children in early childhood settings if they experience formal learning too soon. The reading is critical of the impact on early education of the national curriculum for older pupils and the 'male' discourse of policy makers about accountability and value for money in education, which has prevailed over what might be perceived as the more 'female' concerns about physical and emotional well-being. Policy makers' preoccupation with literacy standards in schools has pushed its way into practices in early childhood settings and even into the home. Anning and Edwards also note the erosion of play in the curriculum as a consequence of emphasis on narrower aspects of learning. This, they argue, is more appropriate to the needs of the nineteenth century to train a docile and unthinking workforce in basic skills. They raise questions about how 'success' is measured as an outcome of the early childhood curriculum.

Stepping stones	Examples of what children do
Engage in activities requiring hand–eye coordination Use one-handed tools and equipment	Connor spent a long time pouring water from a jug into containers of different sizes, sometimes accurately and sometimes spilling it over the sides.
Draw lines and circles using gross motor movement Manipulate objects with increasing control	Kyle enjoys using paint. He covers the paper using large brush strokes. Darren helps to feed the goldfish, using a pincer movement with his finger and thumb as he sprinkles the food in the tank. Angela arranges the furniture carefully in the doll's house. She picks up the tiny crockery and places it carefully on the dresser.
Begin to use anticlockwise movement and retrace vertical lines Begin to form recognisable letters	Angus uses a bucket of water and large brush to paint the wall with water. His arm goes up and down over the same spot to make sure he has covered it. Callum and Stella were making a drawing of the minibeasts they had found outdoors. 'There were lots of caterpillars,' Stella told the practitioner, 'and they looked like this,' pointing to the Cs she had drawn. 'Like my name,' said Callum.
Use a pencil and hold it effectively to form recognisable letters, most of which are correctly formed	Osman was writing a caption to put next to the felt-tip pens he had just tidied. He found the packet and wrote 'felt tip pens' on the piece of card he had chosen.

Figure 1 Pages from the foundation stage guidance showing the developmental model as stepping stones and footsteps (QCA, 2000, pp. 66–7).

What does the practitioner need to do?

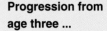

- Provide activities that give children the opportunity and motivation to practise manipulative skills, for example cooking and playing instruments

- Teach children the skills they need, for example cutting with scissors, and plan opportunities for them to practise those skills

Progression from age three ...

- Provide opportunities for children to explore shapes and direction using the whole body, for example by playing games involving moving in circles, forwards and backwards

- Provide opportunities for large shoulder movements, for example helping children to fix ribbons to the end of sticks to swirl in the air, throwing, batting balls suspended on rope, dancing, making patterns in soapy sand and painting

- Provide opportunities for children to develop fine motor control by, for example, pouring water into tiny cups, finger games and setting out cutlery

- Model large anticlockwise and up-and-down letter movements, for example using sky writing, drawing in sand and painting

- Give opportunities to practise repeating the same movement

- Encourage children to practise letter shapes as they paint, draw and record, for example the sun or caterpillars, and as they write, for example, their names, the names of their friends and family or captions

- Encourage children to hold pencils and small tools efficiently

- Provide a variety of writing tools and paper, indoors and outdoors

- Provide opportunities to write purposefully by, for example, placing notepads by phones or making a reservation list in the café

- Give children extensive practice in writing letters, for example labelling their work, making cards, writing notices

- Continue writing practice in imaginative contexts, joining some letters if appropriate, for example 'at', 'it', 'on'

Early learning goals for handwriting

- Intervene to help children hold a pencil effectively
  Use opportunities to help children form letters correctly, for example when they label their paintings

... to the end of the foundation stage

READING

Now read Anning and Edwards' discussion in Reading A. Note what they perceive to be the negative impact of the national curriculum on the early childhood curriculum and subsequently on children's experiences in early childhood settings. The questions below may help you in your note taking:

1   What are the key criticisms made by Anning and Edwards about the impact of the national curriculum on the early childhood curriculum?

2   What are their concerns about play as a feature of the early childhood curriculum?

3   What are their views on a subject-based curriculum in early childhood, in particular in relation to school-based literacy?

4   What are their concerns about the future of early childhood education in England?

COMMENT

Anning and Edwards argue that the view of children's development and learning embodied within the national curriculum is primarily concerned with academic achievement and does not take into account 'outcome measures' such as children's well-being, which is about young children feeling happy and secure and 'feeling good about learning'. The area of social and emotional development should be accorded the same importance as 'school subjects' within the early childhood curriculum. They also believe that play is seen by many policy makers as a time-wasting feature of early childhood, despite research evidence to the contrary.

Anning and Edwards describe the influence of a 'back to basics' approach to the curriculum with a strong emphasis on literacy, which they say is 'colonizing' pre-school settings and even spreading its influence into some children's bedrooms and playrooms, as parents seek to improve their children's literacy skills.

In the conclusion to the chapter the authors contend that policy initiatives in primary schools, such as the national curriculum and the national literacy and numeracy strategies which are part of the Government's drive to raise standards, are ultimately damaging young children. They cite research that supports the view that a 'too formal, too soon' approach is likely to have a negative, rather than a positive effect, on young children's development and learning.

In an interview for the Open University course U212, *Childhood*, in 2001, Angela Anning, who is professor of early childhood at the University of Leeds, was asked what was distinctive about the foundation stage curriculum guidance in England and what vision of the child was contained within the curriculum. She described the curriculum as a 'leading into school' type of curriculum model, which views the child as 'becoming a pupil' (The Open University, 2003).

Is this view of the child embodied in the English foundation stage curriculum guidance the only possible view of childhood and the purpose of schooling? In the following examples of curricula we want to investigate different views of early childhood and of schooling. We also want to ask what, if any, impact these differing visions have on children's individual experiences of schooling and adult constructions of childhood. The notes you made from the reading and activities above will have prompted you to think about the impact such views of the curriculum have on young children's experiences in early childhood settings. From reading Anning and Edwards' chapter you will be aware that these may not always be positive. Nor may they achieve the intended aims and objectives.

SUMMARY OF SECTION 2

- We have briefly traced the history of the first centralized guidance for the early childhood curriculum in England. We have said that this curriculum is designed as a series of steps or stairs progressively leading to primary education.

- We have described the struggle over the implementation of this guidance, which stems from conflicting beliefs held by politicians, practitioners, parents and experts about what and how children should learn in the earliest years of schooling.

- We have also said there are concerns that the outcomes of a goal-led curriculum for young children may not be positive.

3 TE WHĀRIKI IN NEW ZEALAND

Our second example highlights the way in which differing cultural perspectives and ideas form part of the debate over what and how young children should be taught. In this section we will be looking at the Te Whāriki early childhood curriculum in New Zealand. Childhood academics, practitioners and the Maori community have attempted to incorporate Maori cultural values and traditional knowledge into the Te Whāriki curriculum. This resulted from a growing recognition that Maori children may not share the dominant culture's ways of seeing the world. How a Maori child's perspective on the New Zealand school curriculum might differ from a teacher's view is shown in Patricia Grace's story 'Butterflies'. This story was written by a Maori author about the experience of earlier generations of Maori children and is reproduced in Box 1. The story shows how the values of teachers and educationalists who usually had a European-based or 'pakeha' background often acted to exclude and alienate Maori children in educational settings.

Arriving at a Maori early childhood centre.

Box 1   Butterflies

The grandmother plaited her granddaughter's hair and then she said, 'Get your lunch. Put it in your bag. Get your apple. You come here. Listen to the teacher,' she said. 'Do what she say'.

Her grandfather was out on the step. He walked down the path with her and out on the footpath. He said to a neighbour, 'Our granddaughter goes to school. She lives with us now.'

'She's fine,' the neighbour said, 'She's terrific with her two plaits in her hair.'

'And clever,' the grandfather said, 'Writes every day in her book.'

'She's fine,' the neighbour said.

The grandfather waited with his granddaughter by the crossing and then he said, 'Go to school. Listen to the teacher. Do what she say.'

When the granddaughter came home from school her grandfather was hoeing round the cabbages. Her grandmother was picking beans. They stopped their work.

'You bring your book home?' the grandmother asked.

'Yes.'

'You write your story?'

'Yes.'

'What's your story.'?

'About the butterflies.'

'Get your book, then. Read your story.'

The granddaughter took her book from her schoolbag and opened it.

'I killed all the butterflies,' she read. 'This is me and this is all the butterflies.'

'And your teacher like your story, did she?'

'I don't know.'

'What your teacher say?'

'She said butterflies are beautiful creatures. They hatch out and fly, in the sun. The butterflies visit all the pretty flowers, she said. They lay their eggs and then they die. You don't kill butterflies, that's what she said.'

The grandmother and grandfather were quiet for a long time, and their granddaughter, holding the book, stood quite still in the warm garden.

'Because you see,' the grandfather said, 'your teacher, she buy all her cabbages from the supermarket and that's why.'

(Grace, 1987, in Cazden, 1992, pp. 171–2)

This story offers one example of the need to recognize different cultural understandings and how they impact on young children. These are issues which the New Zealand early childhood curriculum seeks to recognize and address within a centralized national curriculum. The New Zealand early childhood curriculum is usually referred to by its shortened title of Te Whāriki (New Zealand Ministry of Education, 1993b, 1996). Te Whāriki attempts to incorporate cultural diversity and to move away from a reliance on European cultural viewpoints. The full title of the current version of the curriculum is *Te Whāriki: He Whāriki Mātauranga mō ngā Mokopuna o Aotearoa: Early Childhood Curriculum* which includes the Maori and English language, meanings and ways of representing the world. Te Whāriki, as is often the case within Maori language, conveys multiple metaphoric meanings. It draws upon terms used in flax weaving, a central area of learning within traditional Maori culture.

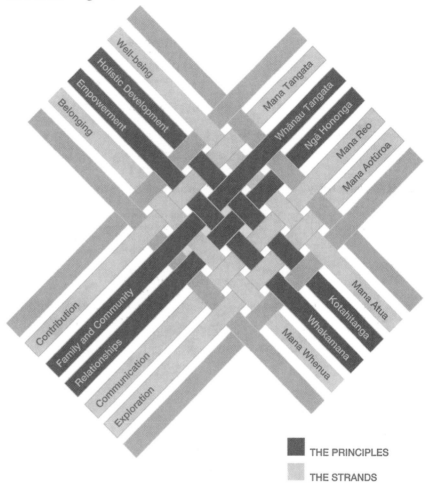

THE PRINCIPLES

THE STRANDS

Te Whāriki is represented as a woven mat, integrating different culttural view points.

READING

Now read Reading B, Margaret Carr and Helen May's account of the differing groups' visions and resulting tensions that they encountered while developing the Te Whāriki early childhood curriculum. During your reading make notes summarizing the views of the following groups and note the possible tensions between them.

1   New Zealand government and policy makers.
2   New Zealand early childhood practitioners.
3   National and international groups of childhood experts and their publications.
4   Maori and other ethnic and cultural groups.

How were the tensions and different visions resolved by Carr and May within the Te Whāriki framework?

COMMENT

Carr and May, as developers of the New Zealand early childhood curriculum, were working in a context similar to that which shaped the early childhood curriculum in England. They had to link the New Zealand early childhood curriculum to the New Zealand National Curriculum Framework, which, like the English National Curriculum, stressed education and skill development for competitive economic development and future employment. The New Zealand government of the time was pressing for national curricular frameworks which organized learning and content into packages and emphasized a form of assessment designed to measure the acquisition of facts and skills during each stage.

Working under this pressure, Carr and May developed a curriculum framework which also attempted to integrate Maori cultural values. As those responsible for co-ordinating the development of the New Zealand early childhood curriculum, they also had to take into account the views of early childhood practitioners who expressed a local and often personal view of the early childhood curriculum. This view did not necessarily fit with the government objective of establishing a national curriculum framework. Many local early childhood practitioners also objected to applying the word 'curriculum' to early childhood practice.

Within New Zealand there are other cultural groups including a large group of recent Pacific Island immigrants, as well as the indigenous Maori population. The incorporation of these groups was yet another tension to be confronted in the development of a 'bicultural' curriculum. Carr and May argue that New Zealand educators have responded to this by incorporating Pacific Island cultural views and extending the development of Maori immersion early education programmes to include the Pacific Island population.

As well as the ideas of the political, professional and cultural groups, Carr and May also wanted to draw on national and international academic literature expressing a sociocultural view of curriculum and childhood. These views of curriculum also advocated 'equitable educational opportunities and quality early childhood policies and practices' (Carr and May, 2000, p. 53).

As Carr and May point out, Te Whāriki refers to a woven mat on which everyone can stand, yet which interweaves central principles and goals into different patterns or programmes which individual early childhood centres can develop to address their own particular learning situations.

Another metaphoric meaning which the curriculum developers intended to be conveyed in the title is the notion of a 'spider-web' model of curriculum. Carr and May saw the notion of a web as a key feature of the conceptualization of the curriculum. Thus, Te Whāriki in name and content implies a move away from the 'step' model of curriculum development which envisages a series of linear, independent steps to a final exit point, with each step capable of being assessed by measurable outcomes. The Te Whāriki model envisages the curriculum as a web or woven mat and so differs from the foundation stage curriculum in England which conceptualizes the curriculum as a set of steps.

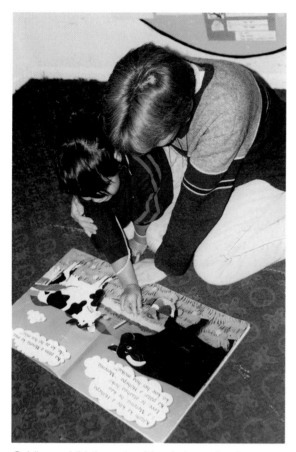

Books for young children are published in Maori.

Guiding a child through a Maori picture book.

Maori legends and motifs are displayed around the classroom.

Aotearoa-New Zealand includes the Maori and European names for New Zealand.

Te Whāriki views the curriculum as a complex and rich experiential process arising out of the child's interactions with the physical and social environment. While the curriculum developers recognized and integrated dominant global principles inherent in early childhood curricula, they argue that the guiding principles, aims and goals of this curriculum have been developed in consultation with Maori elders. The curriculum guidelines related to Maori world views are expressed in the Maori language. The guidelines therefore, express bicultural and community values that are specific to Aotearoa-New Zealand.

Allow about 30 minutes

A C T I V I T Y 2   **Making decisions about what and how young children should learn**

Now that you have been introduced to the issues and tensions associated with the development of the English foundation stage curriculum and Te Whāriki, we will conclude this section by taking a few moments to think about how you feel about the following statements. You may want to keep in mind how these statements apply to your own views about early childhood education and the sort of provision that should be made for your own young children or children you personally know.

1 A curriculum should prepare children for employment by teaching them relevant skills and knowledge for the workforce.

2 A curriculum should be learner-centred to cater for diversity, disabled children, and children of different socio-economic and cultural backgrounds.

3 A curriculum should set out clearly the knowledge and skills and stages for learning so that teachers have more precise guidelines about what and how to teach and can monitor children's progress through testing.

4 A curriculum should be organized in a step-by-step framework so that there is consistency throughout the country.

5 A curriculum should focus upon the way children learn through experience rather than imparting particular knowledge and facts.

6 Parents, teachers and schools working together should develop their own individual curricula to meet the diverse needs of their own pupils and the community those pupils come from.

7 It is important to teach all children in any one country in the dominant language as it disadvantages minority groups of children to teach the curriculum in their own language.

COMMENT

The examples featured so far in this chapter reflect tensions and debates over who decides the early childhood curriculum. Curriculum developers have made conscious decisions over issues such as:

1 prescribing content or allowing more flexibility;

2 whether to follow sequential stages;

3 organizing according to subject content or allowing a more integrated thematic approach;

4 acknowledging cultural differences in beliefs about early childhood.

For example, the English foundation stage curriculum emphasizes key areas of learning through which children are meant to progress in a sequence of identifiable developmental stages. Te Whāriki modifies this concept of child development and knowledge acquisition to allow for greater diversity and learner-centred approaches. There are, however, tensions that arise from this compromise between catering for children's individual needs and diversity, while adhering to a national framework designed for a country with mass education and large groupings of pupils. Even though Te Whāriki sees the learner's needs as central, there is still a prescribed developmental sequence, although this sequence is seen as relatively flexible. In this situation the individual learner cannot be the sole source of curriculum development as stated in the Te Whāriki document. There is, therefore, an inherent tension within the compromise struck by adapting a curriculum framework to learner-centred experiences.

Our final example, Reggio Emilia, like Te Whāriki, is based upon sociocultural principles and emphasizes a learner-centred curriculum. However, unlike Te Whāriki, Reggio Emilia is not a compromise between the demands of a national curriculum framework and a learner-centred curriculum framework. This is because Reggio Emilia does not follow any predetermined curriculum framework.

SUMMARY OF SECTION 3

- We have briefly examined the vision which underpins the New Zealand Te Whāriki early childhood curriculum.

- This curriculum has attempted to integrate differing cultural perspectives and divergent views, particularly those related to Maori cultural values and knowledge.

- In attempting to do this, the curriculum developers have integrated the views of early childhood practitioners, Maori viewpoints and the developers' sociocultural view of curriculum and childhood into a vision which represents this early childhood curriculum as a web or woven mat.

- This integration of cultural viewpoints has not eliminated the tensions arising from differing agendas and emphases that are reflected in this early childhood curriculum.

4 REGGIO EMILIA IN ITALY

So far in this chapter we have tried to draw your attention some of the links between different early childhood curricula such as the foundation stage curriculum in England and the Te Whāriki early childhood curriculum in New Zealand, and also to the approaches and philosophies which underpin these contrasting examples. What is distinctive about the Reggio Emilia approach to early childhood education is that it is a learner-centred and community-supported approach which stems from the inspiration of one man, Loris Malaguzzi. The political contexts that Malaguzzi encountered during the Second World War and post-war Italy inspired him to engage in a struggle to implement his vision of a learner-centred curriculum that would not be part of national guidelines.

Reggio Emilia is a community-supported child care and schooling system situated in a wealthy region of northern Italy. It exists alongside a national system of pre-schools for three to six year olds as well as pre-schools provided by the Church. The network of early childhood educational services is operated by the Municipality of Reggio Emilia; it consists of nineteen pre-schools for children aged three to six and thirteen infant-toddler centres for children aged three months to three years. The pre-schools serve a total of 12,999 children and the infant-toddler centres serve 820 children. There are also three infant-toddler centres managed by co-operatives which have a special agreement with the local administration, and one infant-toddler centre managed by parents which has a similar agreement with the city. These cater for another 144 children (Municipality of Reggio Emilia, 1996). While the numbers of children directly influenced by the Reggio Emilia approach are relatively small compared with those covered by the centralized curriculum models in Sections 2 and 3, the influence of Reggio on early childhood practitioners throughout the world has been immense.

The 'piazza', Diana School, Reggio Emilia.

4.1 Loris Malaguzzi's vision of the early childhood curriculum

The Reggio Emilia system of early childhood education arose from Loris Malaguzzi's experiences of a fascist regime during the Second World War. After the war, Malaguzzi, along with others, dreamed of building a decent society in which to live. The fascist regime had taught them that people who blindly conformed and obeyed were dangerous. He believed that a new society should nurture children who could act and think for themselves (Malaguzzi, 1995).

Malaguzzi therefore gave priority to children's views and designed an early childhood education system founded on the perspective of the child. Carlina Rinaldi, who worked alongside Malaguzzi for many years, said that Reggio Emilia was based on the image of children as rich, strong and powerful. Children were seen as unique subjects with rights rather than simply needs. (Rinaldi, 1995). In order to achieve his vision, Malaguzzi left his state-school teaching post to become involved in community initiatives to build and run schools created by parents in the town of Reggio Emilia. This was an expression of his belief in a pluralistic approach which involved the commitment of children, parents, teachers, administrators and politicians. The first municipal preschool was set up in 1963. By 1967, 12 per cent of the town council budget was allocated to funding the early childhood programme.

In developing the Reggio Emilia system, Malaguzzi drew on Vygotsky's theory that a child learns by socially constructing knowledge with a more able 'other'. Within this sociocultural approach knowledge is not 'transmitted' by the adult, but is co-constructed by the child and adult as they search for and find meanings together. The nature of the relationship between the child and adult is central to the work in Reggio Emilia. Peter

Moss, a British-based professor of early childhood provision and an advocate of Reggio Emilia, said that Reggio Emilia describe this as a 'pedagogy of relationships' and a 'pedagogy of listening' (Moss in The Open University, 2003).

Also central to the development of Malaguzzi's vision was continual discussion within Reggio Emilia centres which questions and challenges existing scientific, philosophical and educational viewpoints and accepted teaching practices and approaches. This questioning was shared with the children, parents, teachers, administrators and politicians and educators from other countries. The adults working within Reggio Emilia have challenged the dominating discourse and accepted practices of early childhood pedagogy by 'deconstructing' (i.e. taking apart existing ideas and theories) to look at how these dominant ideas and theories have shaped our conceptions and images of children and childhood (Dahlberg, 2000). This contrasts with the development of other approaches to curricula discussed earlier.

No way. The hundred is there.

The child
Is made of one hundred.
The child has
a hundred languages
a hundred hands
a hundred thoughts
a hundred ways of thinking
of playing, of speaking
A hundred always a hundred
ways of listening
of marvelling of loving
A hundred joys
for singing and understanding
a hundred worlds
to discover
a hundred worlds
to invent
a hundred worlds
to dream.
The child has
a hundred languages
(and a hundred hundred hundred
more)
but they steal ninety-nine.
The school and the culture
separate the head from the body.

(Malaguzzi (translated by Leila Gandini), 1996, frontispiece)

Within the early childhood centres in Reggio Emilia, the distinctive vision of the child was seen as a starting point for what has been described by others as an 'emergent curriculum'. This approach to teaching and learning has evolved because the schools of Reggio Emilia have not been bound by external factors such as meeting government objectives, the pressures of an externally imposed assessment system or the need to implement prescribed curriculum content. This is in contrast to the English foundation stage curriculum guidance, and even to the Te Whāriki curriculum framework, where May and Carr worked within government constraints to develop a child centred curriculum drawing upon similar social constructionist and progressive views of childhood.

In the extract to the left from his poem 'No way. The hundred is there', Loris Malaguzzi is expressing his vision of the child, which is embodied within the Reggio Emilia approach. The extract illustrates the 'hundred ways' in which he believes children learn.

Because they saw the emergent curriculum as a socially constructed process, the pedagogues (teachers) in Reggio Emilia were against prescribed rules, goals and methods. They therefore do not have a written curriculum that can be readily transferred and applied to another cultural context (Dahlberg, 2000); it is a localized approach to curricula. The approach has been criticized for not having a written curriculum and not being accountable to the wider society. Advocates of the approach argue the curriculum process is recorded in detail, so opening practice to criticism and scrutiny.

The children's work has been documented through photographs, slides and film and in the form of publications and a travelling exhibition. This approach has been described within Reggio Emilia as a 'pedagogy of documentation', a very different form of accountability from inspection by an external agency which accompanies other curriculum approaches. Malaguzzi's philosophy was to make the teaching of Reggio Emilia visible to others in order to share, extend and enrich his vision.

Rinaldi has described how the emergent curriculum approach works in practice. Each year, each school in Reggio Emilia outlines a series of related projects, either long or short term. An example of the origins and development of a project within an early childhood centre is summarized in Box 2.

Box 2   The crowd project

The project began just before the summer vacation. The teachers discussed with the children the idea of collecting memories or fragments of their holiday experiences. The teachers discussed some ideas with the children and with the parents. Each family agreed to take on vacation a box with small compartments in which the child could save treasures such as a shell from the beach, a rock from the mountains or piece of grass. In the autumn when they returned to school, the teachers were ready to explore and revive the children's memories by asking them what they had seen or heard. The teachers' expectations were that they would hear stories about days spent on the beach, about seeing waves or travelling on boats. Instead these four and five year olds brought a very different perspective. A little boy, Gabrielle, recalled his vivid experience of crowds. He said:

> 'Sometimes we went to the pier. We walked through a narrow long, street called the "gut", where one store is next to another, and where in the evening it is full of people. There are people who go up, and people who walk down. You cannot see anything, you can only see a crowd of legs, arms, and heads.'

(Rinaldi, 1995, p. 109)

The word 'crowd' was noted by the teacher who asked the other children what this word meant to them. Subsequently a project was launched. The children drew their thoughts and words about the crowd. The teachers noted that the children's level of representation did not match their verbal descriptions. The children were then encouraged to develop their work through revisiting their earlier taped descriptions. Consequently, their drawings became more elaborate and detailed. The children and teachers went to the centre of the town where they mingled with and observed and photographed the people in the busy streets. Back in the classroom the slides were projected and the children were encouraged to represent their ideas in many ways through drawing, painting, collage. For example they sculpted figures in clay and used cut-out figures for puppet plays and dramatization as illustrated in the photographs below. Malaguzzi refers to these different means of representation in his poem in Box 2, where he refers to the 'hundred ways' in which he believes children learn.

Clay figures from the crowd project.

READING

Now read Reading C by Rebecca New. This is an outsider's account of Reggio Emilia by a visiting educator from the United States; as you will see, Rebecca New is an enthusiast of this system of early childhood education. We hope that you will see how a particular vision of childhood has shaped the early childhood curriculum in the Reggio Emilia centres and the experiences of the children and adults who teach and learn in these contexts.

As you read the article make notes on what you consider to be the main features of the approach. The following questions are intended to help you with these notes:

1   What is the role of the wider community in relation to the Reggio Emilia centres?

2   What role do parents play in the curriculum?

3   What role do children play in the curriculum?

4   What is the role of the adults in the curriculum?

COMMENT

We noted the following features and linked them to the vision of childhood embodied within Reggio Emilia. You may like to compare our points with the ones you noted.

1   There is a high level of community support for and participation in the Reggio Emilia centres. This demonstrates a shared community-based vision of childhood education rather than a centralized, uniform, government-initiated system.

2   Parents are seen as central to the programme and are closely involved from an early stage. The information they offer about their child is fed back into the children's activities and experiences. This is a way of keeping the child as a learner at the centre of the curriculum.

3   The children contribute to class projects. These projects arise from the children's responses to their natural environment, the local community and their particular interests. They serve as the main framework for the emergent curriculum. The children's experiences and responses determine the course of the project. This is yet another way of ensuring that the curriculum takes account of individual children's needs and interests.

4   Adults working within Reggio Emilia view group work as an important form of social learning. Groups of children stay with the same teachers over a three-year period in order to create a stable and secure environment and to provide for continuity of learning experiences for the children. This shows that educators see the curriculum as being as much to do with developing social relationships as with imparting knowledge. The role of the adults is as a facilitator of children's learning; adults help children to explore ideas and to identify problems that arouse their interest. This again shows a learner-focused view of learning.

Adults have the responsibility for organizing educational settings and learning environments but have differing views of the nature of the child and about the nature of knowledge. These views and beliefs influence the relationship between teachers and children and place varying emphasis upon the role of the child in the curriculum. Some curricula, like Reggio Emilia, see the child as the centre of the curriculum, while others tend to place an emphasis upon curriculum content and future outcomes.

You may have also noted that there were differences in how far the interaction between the child and the curriculum was seen to be a dynamic process. Malaguzzi emphasized the dynamic nature of this interaction, while others advocated a more static, taken-for-granted structure. Malaguzzi's vision focused upon catering for the nature and role of the child, whilst other curricula were more concerned with the knowledge and skills to be imparted to the child. The vision of the child which is adopted by early childhood educators has the potential to shape and influence the initial experiences children have in educational settings.

SUMMARY OF SECTION 4

- This section described a curricular approach, Reggio Emilia, where one man's distinctive vision of the child resulted in a unique and localized approach to the curriculum.

- Within this approach, the child is seen to be at the centre of a curriculum within which knowledge is socially constructed between the child and the adult.

- The approach has been shared with the international community through a travelling exhibition and publications and is having a worldwide influence.

5 CONCLUSION

Activity 3 invites you to think about and summarize some of the main points made in this chapter. We would like you to link these to the different curriculum approaches and frameworks that you have been introduced to, in order to contrast and compare the different visions of childhood underpinning the three approaches. It may be helpful to draw upon the discussions in this chapter and the reflections and notes that you have made for the activities.

Allow about I hour

ACTIVITY 3   Comparing three early childhood curricula

In this final activity we would like you to look back at all three early childhood curricula examples. Use the text, readings and photographs. As you revisit each example, make brief notes about what you consider to be the most significant aspects of each approach.

You may want to organize your notes for each curriculum example under the key questions for the chapter below.

Who decides what children should learn?

1   To what extent does the curriculum revolve around the child's interests and experiences?
2   To what extent is the curriculum negotiated between adults and children?
3   To what extent is the curriculum constructed primarily by adults?
4   To what extent is the curriculum content driven by government policy?

What and how should children learn?

1   To what extent is the curriculum emphasizing formal skills-based learning and/or informal play-based learning activities?
2   To what extent does the curriculum actively try to take account of the child's culture and local environment?
3   How would you say the curriculum affects the classroom environment and organization?
4   To what extent is formal assessment and testing of children's learning emphasized?
5   To what extent does the curriculum view children's development as a step-by-step process?

We began this chapter by suggesting that experiences of schooling in early childhood can be very different depending on their place in time, on context and culture, on the starting age for compulsory schooling, and on expectations of what young children should have achieved by the time they start compulsory education. In the chapter we have offered you three very different and contrasting visions of early childhood education and have used these examples to illustrate the debate about, and struggle over, what and how young children should learn, and who should decide what they learn. We have tried to show how this debate stems from particular social constructions of or views about children contained within these different curricula examples.

As we have seen in this chapter, a major debate within early childhood has stemmed from different views about the content of what young children should learn and how they should be taught. This debate has tended to be polarized around views about formal versus informal learning and the role of play in learning. At the centre of the English foundation stage curriculum is a view of the child as a future pupil. This has led to curriculum content which emphasizes 'subject' related learning goals and has resulted in practitioners feeling the need to prepare children for entry to school through more formal teaching approaches. Play is seen to be marginalized. In contrast, in Reggio Emilia the child is viewed as a powerful partner who 'actively co-constructs' the content of the curriculum with a more able 'other'. Within the Te Whāriki curriculum, although content is broadly mapped, the bicultural nature of early childhood is celebrated through a curriculum which allows for the individual mapping of 'strands and threads' to reflect the needs and interests of local groups.

Within the debate about 'who decides' what young children should learn, there could be said to be two main contrasting viewpoints. One viewpoint argues for curriculum guidance largely decided by ministries or governments in order to meet national needs and targets. The English Foundation Stage curriculum is an example of this centralized, competency-oriented curricula, as it establishes and specifies national educational goals and content in advance. An alternative viewpoint argues for more localized and individualized models, generated to meet local needs in order to support collaborative community visions for young children. The Reggio Emilia emergent curriculum offers this alternative view, as it regards a centralized, prescriptive approach as stunting the potential of children by formulating their learning in advance. Reggio Emilia educators advocate an approach in which adults outline flexible, general educational objectives, but do not formulate pre-specified goals. These two examples could be said to be at opposite ends of a continuum. Somewhere in between these two approaches is a 'framework consultative' approach to curricula, such as Te Whāriki, which provides the main values, orientations and goals for the curriculum but does not define how these goals should be achieved. Interpretation and implementation are left to local decisions (Bennett, 2001). These three examples could be said to fit along a continuum ranging from localized, individualized models through to centralized goal-oriented frameworks. We hope that you can see that where a particular curriculum is located on this continuum influences the answer to the question of who decides what children should learn. This in turn influences the answer to the question of what and how young children should learn.

REFERENCES

ANNING, A. and EDWARDS, A. (1999) *Promoting Children's Learning from Birth to Five: developing the new early years professional,* Buckingham, Open University Press.

BATHURST, K. (1905) 'The need for national nurseries' in Eyken, W. van der (1973) *Education, the Child and Society,* Harmondsworth, Penguin Books.

BENNETT, J. (2001) 'Goals and curricula in early childhood' in KAMERMAN, S. (ed.) *Early Childhood Education and Care: international perspectives*, New York, Columbia University Institute for Child and Family Policy.

BLACKSTONE, T. (1971) *A Fair Start: the provision of pre-school education*, London, Allen Lane.

BRADBURN, E. (1976) *Margaret McMillan: framework and expansion of nursery education,* Redhill, Denholm House Press.

BREEDLOVE, C. AND SCHWEINHART, L. J. (1982) 'The cost effectiveness of high quality early childhood programs', Report for 1982 Southern Governors Conference, Michigan, High/Scope Press.

CARR, M., and MAY, H. (2000) 'Te Whāriki: curriculum voices' in PENN, H. (ed.) *Early Childhood Services: theory, policy and practice,* Buckingham, Open University Press.

CARVEL, J. (1999) 'Play is out, early learning is in', *The Guardian,* 23 June

CAZDEN, C. B. (1992) *Whole Language Plus: essays on literacy in the United States and New Zealand*, New York, Teachers College Press..

CLARKE, A. M. AND CLARKE, A. D. B. (1976) *Early Experience: myth and evidence,* London, Open Books.

CURRIE, J. (2001) 'Early childhood education programs', *Journal of Economic Perspectives,* **15**(2), pp. 213–38.

DAHLBERG, G. (2000) 'Everything is a beginning and everything is dangerous: some reflections of the Reggio Emilia experience' in PENN, H. (ed.) *Early Childhood Services: theory, policy and practice,* Buckingham, Open University Press.

DAVID, T. and NURSE, A. (1999) 'Inspection of children under five and constructions of early childhood' in David, T. (ed.) *Teaching Young Children*, London, Paul Chapman.

DEPARTMENT FOR EDUCATION AND EMPLOYMENT (DfEE) (1999) *The National Curriculum: handbook for primary teachers in England,* London, HMSO.

DRUMMOND, M. J. (2001) 'Children, yesterday, today and tomorrow' in COLLINS, J. and COOK, D. (eds) *Understanding Learning: influences and outcomes,* London, Paul Chapman.

EARLY YEARS CURRICULUM GROUP (1989) *Early Childhood Education: the early years curriculum and the national curriculum,* Stoke on Trent, Trentham Books.

EDWARDS, A. and KNIGHT, P. (1994) *Effective Early Years Education: teaching young children*, Buckingham, Open University Press.

EYKEN, W. VAN DER (ed.) (1973) *Education, the Child and Society: a documentary history 1900–1973*, Harmondsworth, Penguin Books.

KELLY, A. V. (1994) 'A high quality curriculum for the early years', *Early Years*, **15**(1), pp. 6–12.

MALAGUZZI, L. , trans. GANDINI, L. (1996) 'No way. The hundred is there' in MUNICIPALITY OF REGGIO EMILIA (1996).

MALAGUZZI, L. (1995) 'History, ideas and basic philosophy: an interview with Lella Gandini' in EDWARDS, C., GANDINI, L. and FORMAN, G. (eds) *The Hundred Languages of Children: the Reggio Emilia approach to early childhood education*, Norwood (NJ), Ablex Publishing Corporation.

MAY, H. and CARR, M. (1997) 'Making a difference for the under fives? The early implementation of Te Whāriki, the New Zealand national early childhood curriculum', *International Journal of Early Years Education*, **5**(3), pp. 225–36.

MAY, H. (1997) *The Discovery of Early Childhood: the development of services for the care and education of very young children, mid eighteenth century Europe to mid twentieth century New Zealand*, Auckland, Auckland University Press.

MUNICIPALITY OF REGGIO EMILIA, INFANT-TODDLER CENTRES AND PRESCHOOLS (1996) *The Hundred Languages of Children: catalogue of the exhibition*, Reggio Emilia, Reggio Children S.r.l.

NEW, R. (1990) 'Excellent early education: a city in Italy has it', *Young Children* (September), pp. 4–12.

NEW ZEALAND MINISTRY OF EDUCATION (1993a). *The New Zealand Curriculum Framework*, Wellington, Ministry of Education Learning Media.

NEW ZEALAND MINISTRY OF EDUCATION (1993b) *Te Whāriki: draft guidelines for developmentally appropriate programmes in early childhood services*, Wellington, Ministry of Education Learning Media.

NEW ZEALAND MINISTRY OF EDUCATION (1996) *Te Whāriki. He Whāriki Matauranga mo nga Mokopuna o Aotearoa: early childhood curriculum*, Wellington, Ministry of Education Learning Media.

ORGANIZATION FOR ECONOMIC COOPERATION AND DEVELOPMENT (OECD) (2001) *Starting Strong: early childhood education and care*, Paris, OECD.

THE OPEN UNIVERSITY (2003) U212 *Childhood*, Audio 4, Band 5, 'Early childhood curricula', Milton Keynes, The Open University.

PENN, H. (2002) 'The World Bank's view of early childhood', *Childhood*, **9**, pp.119-133

QUALIFICATIONS AND CURRICULUM AUTHORITY (1998) *The Baseline Assessment Information Pack: preparation for statutory baseline assessment*, London, Qualifications and Curriculum Authority.

QUALIFICATIONS AND CURRICULUM AUTHORITY (1999) *Early Learning Goals*, London, Qualifications and Curriculum Authority.

QUALIFICATIONS AND CURRICULUM AUTHORITY (2000) *Curriculum Guidance for the Foundation Stage*, London, Qualifications and Curriculum Authority.

RINALDI, C. (1995) 'The emergent curriculum and social constructivism: an interview with Lella Gandini' in EDWARDS, C., GANDINI, L. and FORMAN, G. (eds) *The Hundred Languages of Children: the Reggio Emilia approach to early childhood education,* Norwood (NJ), Ablex Publishing Corporation.

SCHOOL CURRICULUM AND ASSESSMENT AUTHORITY (SCAA) (1996) *Desirable Outcomes for Children's Learning on Entering Compulsory Education,* London, Department for Education and Employment/ School Curriculum and Assessment Authority.

STAGGS, L. (2000) 'Curriculum guidance for the early years', *Early Years Educator,* **2**(6), pp. 21–3.

WOODHEAD, M. (1988) 'When psychology informs public policy: the case of early intervention', *American Psychologist,* **43**, pp. 443–54.

YOUNG, M. E. (1998) 'Policy implications of early childhood development programmes', *Nutrition, Health and Child Development,* Washington DC, Pan American Health Organization/World Bank, pp. 209–24.

READING A

Language and literacy learning

Angela Anning and Anne Edwards

... Curriculum models are socially constructed. They are designed by adults with particular beliefs about what constitute appropriate activities for children at a particular moment in history. The beliefs of these adults emanate from the dominant values of the culture and society ... within which they live and work. But most significant in shaping their beliefs about what children should do and learn before school are the culture and ideologies of their training, professional backgrounds and daily work experiences at the micro-level of their early childhood workplace settings.

It was the distinctive belief systems of 'education' that were exemplified in the 1996 *Desirable Outcomes for Learning* definition of what young children should learn:

> The desirable outcomes are goals for learning for children by the time they enter compulsory education. They emphasize early literacy, numeracy and the development of personal and social skills and contribute to children's knowledge, understanding and skills in other areas. Presented as six areas of learning, they provide a foundation for later achievement.
>
> (DfEE/SCAA 1996:1)

It is not surprising that those whose backgrounds were outside education felt threatened by the tone of *Desirable Outcomes for Learning*. The words were hard-edged – goals, compulsory education, literacy, numeracy, knowledge, understanding, skills, achievement. The definition was couched in terms of a 'high status' framework of preparation for academic achievements. Its focus was on the mind.

[...]

In the *Desirable Outcomes for Learning* (DfEE/SCAA 1996) document 'play' was scarcely mentioned. The language used is an indication of the construction of childhood that dominates our policy in early years services in the UK. 'Happiness' and 'play' are derided by a male dominated society which emphasizes the logical, scientific aspects of learning and the power of rational thought (see Anning 1994 for further discussion of play and the legislated curriculum). Play is dismissed as trivial or time wasting. Yet ... for early years practitioners play is perceived as the natural vehicle by which young children learn. Fromberg (1990) reviewed significant research evidence of the contribution of play to children's development. Yet, he points out, 'at the same time that the research literature on the value of play appears to expand geometrically the presence of play in early childhood classrooms has been dwindling' (p. 237).

It is significant that education has been assigned the lead role in the government's policy on integration of services for children. Current government policies on early childhood education prioritize children's academic achievements, not their emotional and social development, nor their physical well-being. Practitioners with educational backgrounds feel secure. So during the project, we never heard those with backgrounds in educational services apologize about their lack of knowledge and understanding of children's physical and emotional needs. We think these should be priorities. Even at a pragmatic level of measuring 'success', if children are not happy and comfortable, they are unlikely to feel good about learning and to make good progress in academic achievements. Equally, from a moral and ethical point of view, young children's emotional and physical well-being should be of paramount importance. It may be that those with educational backgrounds could learn from their colleagues in the care sector about catering for aspects of children's needs which are emotional and physical.

However, it is the discourse of 'school' subjects, not of children's general well-being, which has dominated curriculum reform for young children since the Education Reform Act of 1987. Of all the 'subjects' of the school curriculum, English is the one with which early childhood workers in all kinds of pre-school settings are most comfortable. However, depending on their backgrounds and belief systems, they will approach the 'subject' in rather different ways. For example, local authority funded day care settings have a tradition of prioritizing language development in the activities they plan for their children. This emphasis is the result of the 'compensatory' framework of the care sector because, ... historically their population has been skewed to 'disadvantaged' families and children 'at risk'. However, day care workers' approach to language development is very different from that in, for example, nursery classes in the maintained sector, where a particular 'school' view of language and literacy prevails. Their focus is on the development of spoken language.

The foundations of the school concept of literacy are the nineteenth-century elementary school traditions of 'reading and writing'. Children are required to learn to write in 'a fair hand', often by laboriously copying poems from the established canons of English literature or morally uplifting tracts. They had to learn the discipline of parsing sentences in order to access the syntax of the English language. They had exercises in the comprehension and paraphrasing of high-status texts. Finally they learned to read from 'primers' of the Janet and John, Dick and Dora or Peter and Jane variety! All these activities were geared to the needs of training a docile working population reading to operate in working contexts where a particular, narrow version of literacy prevailed. Much of the nostalgic call for a 'back to basics' curriculum during the 18 years of Tory government in England and Wales up until 1996 was a hankering for a return to this simplistic notion of training a docile workforce. It could be argued that New Labour policy has simply added the word 'adaptable' to the requirement.

However, even if we were to accept the questionable view that the *raison d'être* of a curriculum is to prepare children for work, such a backward looking model takes no account of the rapidly changing nature of literacy as we move into the twenty-first century. The computer, word processor, Internet and microfiche have entirely altered the notion of what it means to be literate ...

Yet our education system is still geared to promoting literacy with a strong emphasis on 'conventional' reading and writing and this model is increasingly 'colonizing' pre-school settings. The sign systems of school literacy – alphabet charts, words blu-tacked onto door, chairs and tables, workbooks and worksheets – which set the boundaries of literacy in the formal settings of many early years classrooms are infiltrating the informal settings of day care centres, childminders and even some young children's bedrooms or playrooms at home. Parents are pressurized into joining this version of 'the literacy club' by a burgeoning industry in 'out-of-school'/ homework educational materials. In supermarkets parents are urged to invest in an array of workbooks, videos and educational games, all designed to improve children's basic skills in reading and writing. In 1998 all children in primary schools of compulsory school age were required to be taught a 'literacy hour' every day. From September 1998 they were tested by baseline assessment systems on recognition of initial sounds in words, letters by both shape and sounds, and ability to write their names and words independently. Young children learn to position themselves within this dominant model of literacy. For example, reading is perceived to be about decoding text in books. So Scollon and Scollon (1981) report a young child explaining 'when my baby brother's hands are big enough to hold a book, he'll be able to read'.

We have to question both the appropriateness and effectiveness of this kind of curriculum model for language and literacy learning for young children ...

[...]

The fact is that despite the current policy of promoting an early introduction to 'school' versions of literacy, British children, particularly boys, are scoring less well on measures of achievements in language and mathematics than children from systems in other European countries (for example, Hungary, Switzerland and Belgium) where pre-school experiences place an emphasis on talk and structured, active play which enable children to move freely between enactive, iconic and symbolic modes or representation. In these countries children do not start their formal schooling with its emphasis on symbolic representation until they are 6.

Researchers for a Channel 4 programme, *Britain's Early Years Disaster,* argued that:

> The evidence suggests that Britain's early years education, far from helping young children, actually damages many of them. Unlike successful pre-school systems abroad – which move slowly from the concrete to the representational and avoid the abstract – British early years provision rushes children into abstract letters, words and numbers. While elsewhere primacy is given to developing confidence and precision in spoken language, here teaching is dominated by reading, writing and recorded arithmetic.

> While brighter children and those from privileged backgrounds can cope with the demands this makes less fortunate children suffer, lose confidence and probably never recover. It seems likely that this helps explain Britain's long tail of under-achievement.

> (Mills and Mills 1998:17)

It is not only the curriculum content that appears to be inappropriate for our young children, but also the danger that the pedagogy of early childhood will become one of curriculum delivery. The current government emphasis on 'direct instruction' and 'whole class teaching' in primary education, exemplified in the arguments for the National Literacy and Numeracy Strategies, is impacting on Reception and even some nursery classes in England and Wales. Yet we have research evidence that young children who are exposed to too formal a schooling regime too soon may suffer long-term disadvantages. Much of this evidence was summarized by three women researchers in the early 1990s when pressure was building up from central government policy to introduce more formal styles of pedagogy into primary schools (see David *et al.* 1993). For example, results of the research in the USA (Schweinhart and Weikart 1993) ... indicated that three groups of children, one of which had experienced a formal pre-school curriculum and the other two play-based programmes (one a curriculum called High Scope and another less structured programme similarly based on active learning) showed increased IQs at school entry. However, in a follow-up study of the three groups at the age of 15, those that had attended the formal programme engaged more in antisocial behaviour and had lower commitment to school than those from the play-based programmes. In a more recent paper Sylva (1997) again used research-based evidence to argue that 'a curriculum in pre-school settings that is too formal will lead to poorer performance, disincentives to learn and low self-esteem' (p. 4).

References

Anning, A. (1994) Play and the legislated curriculum: back to basics, an alternative view, in J. Moyles (ed.) (1994) *The Excellence of Play*. Buckingham, Open University Press.

David, T. (ed.) (1993) *Educational Provision for our Youngest Children*. London, Paul Chapman.

Department for Education and Employment/School Curriculum and Assessment Authority (1996) *Desirable Outcomes for Children's Learning on Entering Compulsory Education*. London, DfEE/SCAA.

Fromberg, D.P. (1990) An agenda for research on play in early childhood education, in E. Klugman and S. Smilansky (eds) *Children's Play and Learning: Policy Implications*. New York, Columbia University Teacher's College Press.

Mills, C. and Mills, D. (1998) *Britain's Early Years Disaster* (survey of research evidence for Channel 4 television documentary *Too Much, Too Soon*). London, Channel 4 Television.

Schweinhart, L. and Weikart, D. (1993) *A Summary of Significant Benefits: The High Scope Perry Pre-School Study Through Age 27*. Ypsilanti. MI, The High Scope Press.

Scollon, R. and Scollon, B.K. (1981) *Narrative, Literacy and Face in Inter Ethnic Communication*. New York, Ablex.

Sylva, L. (1997) The early years curriculum: evidence based proposals. Paper presented at the SCAA conference 'Developing the Primary Curriculum, The Next Steps'. London, SCAA.

Source

Anning, A., and Edwards, A. (1999) *Promoting Children's Learning from Birth to Five: developing the new early years professional*, Buckingham, Open University Press, pp. 78–92.

READING B

Te Whāriki: curriculum voices

Margaret Carr and Helen May

Introduction

In 1996 the Prime Minister of New Zealand launched the final version of Te Whāriki Matauranga mo ngā Mokopuna o Aotearoa: Early Childhood Curriculum (Ministry of Education, 1996a). From August 1998, early childhood services receiving funding from the Ministry are required to demonstrate that their programmes are operating according to the four principles, five strands and eighteen goals outlined in *Te Whāriki* (Ministry of Education 1996b).

The writing of the curriculum began in 1991 when we were contacted by the Ministry of Education to coordinate the development of a national early childhood curriculum that would: make connections with the new national curriculum for schools; embrace a diverse range of early childhood services and cultural perspectives; and articulate a philosophy of quality early childhood practice. The story of the development of *Te Whāriki* illustrates debate and negotiation between three voices: the voice of government interests at a time of political and curriculum change (a voice that by 1991 had become focused on the role of national curriculum and assessment policies in creating an efficient and competitive economy); the voice of early childhood practitioners and families from a diversity of services and cultural perspectives (a voice that took a local, situated and often *personal* view of early childhood curriculum – and sometimes rejected the term 'curriculum'); the national and international early childhood voices advocating for equitable educational opportunities and quality early childhood policies and practices (voices that have taken an increasingly sociocultural view of curriculum and childhood, but frequently rejected a totally relativist view of curriculum).

The political voices

[...]

By 1991 the new Conservative Government had ... introduced a discussion document: *The National Curriculum of New Zealand* (Ministry of Education 1991). It emphasized the need to 'define a range of understandings, skills and knowledge that will enable students to take their full place in society and to succeed in the modern competitive economy' (1991: 1). It set out seven principles, three of which were explicitly to do with education needed for work, or for the needs of the economy. After scant public consultation (McGee 1997: 61), the final 1993 *New Zealand Curriculum Framework* (Ministry of Education 1993) emerged very little changed from the 1991 document. It defined nine principles, three of which mention the economy or preparation for the 'world of work', seven traditionally subject-based learning areas (health and physical well-being, the arts, social sciences, technology, science, mathematics, language and languages) and eight groupings of essential skills (one grouping is described as 'self-management and competitive' skills, although the list of sub-skills for this grouping does not mention the word 'competitive'). This curriculum covered both primary and secondary schooling, and included policy proposals for national assessment at key transition points: school entry (age 5); at the start of year 7; and at the start of year 9 (the first year of secondary school). Finally, the new curriculum framework included the principle 'the New Zealand Curriculum recognizes the significance of the Treaty of Waitangi' (Ministry of Education 1993a: 7): a landmark treaty that in 1840 set out rights and responsibilities for the relationship between the Maori (the indigenous people of New Zealand) and the British Crown. In response to the perceived responsibility to Māori curriculum, Māori versions of the subject based curriculum statements were subsequently developed: these came after the English text was developed and tended to be translations rather than cultural alternatives (McKinley and Waiti 1995). It was against this backdrop that in 1990 the government decided there would also be a national early childhood curriculum.

[...]

The local and national early childhood voices: the writing of *Te Whāriki*

Early childhood organizations and practitioners, including ourselves (with backgrounds including experience as kindergarten and childcare practitioners), were originally wary of the idea of a national early childhood curriculum; were concerned that it might constrain the sector's independence and diversity. But the alternative strategy of *not* defining the early childhood curriculum, was now becoming a potentially dangerous one for the early childhood organizations, since the developing national curriculum for schools might start a 'trickle down' effect, particularly as the government was also proposing more systematic national assessment during the early school years. Our curriculum project at the University of Waikato won the early childhood curriculum contract with the Ministry of Education; the project began in 1991 and a draft curriculum was delivered to the Ministry at the end of 1992 (Carr and May 1992).

By 1991 and 1992 the national government curriculum themes so far had included: curriculum decisions at the national level: educational continuity leading to a competitive and efficient workplace (education as a branch of economic policy); an interest in national assessment and levels of achievement; a subject based school curriculum, and curriculum documents that would be later translated for Māori. We wondered, given this text, what an early childhood curriculum might look like. A brief summary outlines the main features of what eventuated; the detail is in Ministry of Education (1993, 1996a) and earlier overviews of the philosophy and an early implementation are in Carr and May (1993b, 1994, 1996, 1997).

Firstly, a set of four principles underpins the aims and goals for children. These principles are as follows, with the English text elaborated:

Whakamana *Empowerment:* the early childhood curriculum empowers the child to learn and grow;

Kotahitanga *Holistic development:* the early childhood curriculum reflects the holistic way children learn and grow;

Whanau tangata *Family and community:* the wider world of family and community is an integral part of the early childhood curriculum;

Nga hononga *Relationships:* children learn through responsive and reciprocal relationships with people, places and things.

The principles and aims of the curriculum are expressed in both Māori and English languages, but neither is an exact translation of the other. They were negotiated early in the curriculum development process as equivalent. Secondly, a set of five aims (later to be renamed 'strands', fit in with the language of the school curriculum documents) provided the framework for goals (and later, learning outcomes) for children:

Mana atua	Well-being
Mana whenua	Belonging
Mana tangata	Contribution
Mana reo	Communication
Mana aotūroa	Exploration

Once again, neither is a translation of the other: an acceptable cross-cultural structure and the equivalence were discussed, debated and transacted early in the curriculum development process. The conceptualization of early childhood curriculum therefore took a very different approach to either the subject based framework of the school curriculum, or the more traditional developmental curriculum map of physical, intellectual, emotional and social skills. Instead, the strands defined an interpretation of the major interests of infants, toddlers and young children: emotional and physical *well-being;* a feeling that they *belong* here; opportunities to make a *contribution;* skills and understandings for *communicating* through language and symbols; and an interest in *exploring* and making sense of the environment ...

In other words, in conceptualizing the early childhood curriculum in this way, the Early Childhood Development Team motored upstream to resist the philosophical principles of the early 1990s. In our opinion, a major reason for this was the capacity by 1991 for local and national early childhood interests to speak strongly and loudly, and when necessary, with one voice. The articulation of this voice in the new curriculum domain was certainly facilitated by setting up a Curriculum Development Team with a broad representative base, and insisting on wide consultation throughout the process.

[...]

New Zealand is a small country of 3.7 million people. The early childhood network, although fiercely parochial in some matters, could speak together when they saw a united purpose and the structures gave them the platform and the power to do so ...

By 1991, the curriculum development process could build on this increasing integration and strength. In particular, before any curriculum framework was decided upon, four decisions were made. The first was to establish a broadly based Curriculum Development Team with links into the diverse early childhood networks. Six specialist working groups of four practitioners with a coordinator were established: infant and toddler; young child; te Kāhanga reo; tagata pasefika (representing Pacific Island language groups; home based services; and children with special needs.

Each group consulted with their own networks, and argued their case in the smaller Curriculum Development Team of coordinators. The second was to write a series of 'position papers' and use these as a focus for consulting widely with the early childhood community. During the fourteen months of curriculum development the authors travelled to seminars of practitioners throughout the country. The third decision was to negotiate a bicultural framework from the beginning. The fourth decision was to use a weaving metaphor to define the curriculum: Te Whāriki refers to a traditional floor mat woven from harakeke (flax).

The weaving metaphor

The title of the curriculum, Te Whāriki, is a central metaphor. Firstly, the early childhood curriculum is envisaged as a Whāriki, a woven mat 'for all to stand on' (Carr and May 1992: 6). The principles, strands and goals defined in the document provide the framework that allows for different programme perspectives to be woven into the 'fabric'. There are many possible 'patterns' for this, as individuals and centres develop their own curriculum pattern through a process of talk, reflection, planning, evaluation and assessment (Carr and May 1994). Secondly, the metaphor describes a 'spider web' model of curriculum for children, in contrast to a 'step' model (Eisner 1985: 143). The 'step' model conjures up the image of a series of independent steps that lead to a platform from which the child exits and at which point measurable outcomes can be identified. The Te Whāriki model views the curriculum for each child as more like a spider web or weaving than a series of steps, and emphasizes the notion that developing knowledge and understanding in young children is like a tapestry of increasing complexity and richness. This is in tune with the idea that:

> The developmental potential of a setting enhanced to the extent that the physical and social environment found in the setting enables and motivates the developing person to engage in progressively more complex molar activities, patterns of reciprocal interaction, and primary dyadic relationships with others in that setting.
>
> (Bronfenbrenner 1979: 163)

Te Whāriki defines three age groups – infants, toddlers and the young child – but, consistent with the idea of the curriculum for each child as being more like a tapestry than a flight of stairs, these age groups were not defined as self-contained stages. The document included a 'developmental continuum' of learning and growing during the early childhood years, linked to age but recognizing that development will vary for individual children in unpredictable ways. In tune with the principle that children learn through responsive and reciprocal relationships with people, places and things, where they are, who they are with, and what the children perceive as the agenda, will all make a difference. Te Whāriki emphasizes that curriculum for the early childhood years must be able to embrace the everyday realities of rapid change, leaps and regressions, uneven development and individual differences, and recognize that learning is distributed across people, places and things (Salomon 1993).

[...]

References

Bronfenbrenner, U. (1979) *The Ecology of Human Development.* Cambridge, MA, Harvard University Press.

Carr, M. and May, H. (1992) *Te Whāriki* Early Childhood Curriculum Development Project Final Report to the Ministry of Education. Hamilton, University of Waikato.

Carr, M. and May, H. (1993) 'Choosing a model: reflecting on the developmental process of *Te Whāriki,* National Early Childhood Curriculum Guidelines in New Zealand', *International Journal of Early Years Education,* **1**(3): 7–22.

Carr, M. and May, H. (1994) *Weaving patterns: developing national early childhood curriculum guidelines in Aotearoa-New Zealand.* Australian Journal of Early Childhood Education, 19(1): 25–33.

Carr, M. and May, H. (1996) 'Te Whāriki, making a difference for the under-fives? The new national early childhood curriculum', *Delta,* **48**(1): 101–12.

Carr, M. and May, H. (1997) 'Making a difference for the under-fives? The early implementation of Te Whāriki, the New Zealand national early childhood curriculum', *International Journal of Early Years Education,* **5**(3): 225–36.

Eisner, E. (1985) *The Educational Imagination: On the Design and Evaluation of School Programmes.* New York, MacMillan.

McGee, C. (1997) *Teachers and Curriculum Decision-Making.* Palmerston North, The Dunmore Press.

McKinley, E. and Waiti, P. (1995) *Te Tauāk? Marautanga Pātaiao: He tauira – the writing of a science curriculum in Māori,* in A. Jones (ed) SAME Papers 1995. Hamilton, CSMTER, University of Waikato.

Ministry of Education (1991) *The National Curriculum of New Zealand: A Discussion Document.* Wellington, Learning Media.

Ministry of Education (1993) *The New Zealand Curriculum Framework.* Wellington, Learning Media.

Ministry of Education (1996a) *Te Whāriki. He Whāriki Matauranga mo nga Mokopuna o Aotearoa: Early Childhood Curriculum.* Wellington, Learning Media.

Ministry of Education (1996b) *Revised Statement of Desirable Objectives and Practices (DOPs) for Chartered Early Childhood Services in New Zealand.* The New Zealand Gazette, 3 October.

Salomon, G. (ed.) (1993) *Distributed Cognitions: Psychological and Educational Considerations.* Cambridge, Cambridge University Press.

Source

Carr, M. and May, H. (2000) 'Te Whāriki: curriculum voices' in Penn, H. (ed.) *Early Childhood Services: theory, policy and practice,* Buckingham, Open University Press, pp. 53–73.

Excellent early education: a city in Italy has it

Rebecca New

[...]

School is a community of exchange

The Reggio Emilia program reflects a long-standing commitment to co-operative and supportive home school relationships, advocating a partnership among parents, teachers, and community members. A blending of beliefs about what is best for young children and their families facilitates this partnership in a number of ways ... From the outset, teachers acknowledge the critical role of both parents, emphasizing that the child is also capable, at a very young age, of developing other quality relationships. Because teachers and parents consider isolation from one another a hindrance to professional *and* child development, they have designed formal and informal strategies to establish a rich community of exchange.

Groups are long-lasting, like families

Schools begin the process of collaboration by keeping the same group of children and teachers together for a three-year period, so that children who begin as infants remain together at the *asilo nido* ('nest' or day care) until the third birthday, at which time they move into preschool classrooms where they remain with a new preschool teacher for another three years ... Besides creating a stable and secure environment for children, the three-year grouping provides a degree of continuity and familiarity that enables more effective relationships among parents and teachers, and results in a large community of adults around a group of children.

Parents actively collaborate

Parents are initiated into the program as soon as a child is enrolled ... Albums are created for each child upon entry into a class, for family members and school personnel to fill with observations, photographs, and anecdotal records ... Another advantage for parents is the opportunity to develop among themselves a stable network of families of young children. The strength of this network is apparent in the subsequent level of parent co-operation and participation in school projects ...

Parental involvement extends beyond individual classrooms to include decision making at the school and community levels. Each school has a Parent–Teacher Board made up of elected representatives of staff, parents, and citizens; parents consider this board important enough that 85 per cent of eligible families participated in recent elections. ...

This community of adults shares the understanding that no one has a monopoly on deciding what is best for the children ...

Perhaps no topic has provoked more thought and discussion among these adults than what pedagogical approach to take in the Reggio Emilia classrooms. The resulting curriculum is a testimony to the virtues of ongoing staff development, parent involvement, and respect for children's interests and capabilities ...

Problems, projects, and the symbolic languages: a natural combination

Reggio Emilia teachers believe that children's learning is facilitated by actively exploring problems that children *and* teachers help determine. They also believe that art is inseparable from the rest of the curriculum, and in fact, is central to the educational process as a form of both exploration and expression (Gandini & Edwards, 1988). Reflecting this centrality, children's efforts with various media are referred to as 'symbolic representations' rather than 'art'.

Each school has an art teacher who is available to work with the children and their teachers throughout the day ...

Project-based teaching

One strategy that provides numerous reasons for symbolic representation and maximizes opportunities for shared problem solving is the use of short and long-term projects. The 'art' work that results from such projects astounds and delights most viewers ...

Though some projects last only several days, others may continue for months, reflecting a belief in the need for long periods of time for both children and teachers to stay with an idea ... Projects, which may involve the entire class or only a small group of children, are of three broadly defined types; those resulting from a child's natural encounter with the environment, those reflecting mutual interests on the part of the teacher and children, and those based on teacher concerns ... (Gandini & Edwards, 1988; Edwards, Forman & Gandini, in preparation).

... Another type of project that involves more advance planning is based on the teachers' understanding of the keen interest young children display in themselves – their bodies, their feelings, their sense of being alive. Such a project also corresponds to a curriculum goal of helping children learn to appreciate themselves as unique individuals ... Discussions of children's images often lead to other related problems, such as discovering how we communicate through body language, how our voices convey emotion, and exploring the variations in the human form associated with movement.

The third type of project is one that is initiated by the teacher(s) in response to an observed need on the part of some or all of the children ...

In these and other Reggio Emilia projects, children are given problems to solve, opportunities to explore and interact with each other, and materials and objects related to the quest. They are encouraged to reflect on and reconsider their perceptions and understandings, and to share their ideas and experiences with parents and other children through one or more means of symbolic representation. Throughout, teachers serve as the "memory" of the group, making photographs and tape recordings of children's activities and discussions ...

The use of space supports the curriculum

Visitors to Reggio Emilia are often astonished by the visual appeal of the preschool and infant/toddler classrooms. One Reggio Emilia parent, reflecting on her first impressions, remembers an ambience that was ... luminous, serene, and stimulating at the same time (Department of Education, 1986) ...

The environment informs and stimulates

What one sees upon entering any one of the community preschools includes the work of children (drawings, paintings, sculptures) and their teachers (photographs and displays of projects in process), often with the dramatic use of graphics. Such displays convey ongoing curriculum and research projects in a manner that keeps families informed about and interested in children's school activities and captures the interest of other children in the projects.
[...]

The environment fosters sustained working and a sense of community

When discussing the issue of space, teachers make reference to more than the physical plant, alluding to the social environment as well. Each classroom includes a large central area where all children and teachers can meet, in addition to smaller work spaces, and a '*mini atelier*' (small art room) where children can work on long-term projects ... Each school also has a large central *atelier* (workroom) where the art teacher works with children as well as teachers.

Classrooms typically open to a large area that connects each individual classroom to the entire school ... Gardens and courtyards also extend the classroom, and each school has rooms in which parents can meet and families can gather ...

References

Department of Education (1986) *Dieci anni di nido*. Reggio Emilia, Italy, Center for Educational Research.

Gandini, L. & Edwards, C.P. (1988) Early childhood integration of the visual arts, *Gifted International, 5(2)*, 14–18.

Edwards, C. Forman,G. & Gandini, L. (in preparation) *Education for all the children: The multi-symbolic approach to early education in Reggio Emilia, Italy*.

Source

New, R. (1990) 'Excellent early education: a city in Italy has it' *Young Children* (September), pp. 4–12.

Chapter 7

Moving out of childhood

Virginia Morrow

CONTENTS

This chapter concludes the book by focusing on the social changes that take place at the juncture between childhood and adulthood. When you have studied this chapter, you should be able to:

1 Recognize that the later stages of childhood and towards adulthood are not natural or given, but differ widely between and within societies.

2 Understand that children's roles within families change as they get older, are expected to undertake more responsibilities, and move towards independence.

3 Recognize that the transition to adulthood in many societies is not so much a sharp distinction but rather a process that takes place gradually, over a period of time.

4 Understand that how the transition to adulthood takes place, and what it means, and the experiences it gives rise to, are influenced by a range of factors such as gender, class, disability, religious practice and traditional customs.

1   INTRODUCTION

Allow about 10 minutes

ACTIVITY 1   **Transition points**

Jot down some of your own experiences as you moved from childhood to adulthood. Were there any key moments? For instance, did you undergo a religious initiation ceremony that confirmed you as a member of your faith? Did you celebrate your twenty-first or eighteenth birthday in a distinctive way? When did you feel 'adult'? When you first had sex? When you left your parents' house? When you started your first job? At the birth of your first child? When you passed your driving test? When you left school? When you were able to vote in an election?

COMMENTS

This activity is designed to get you thinking about how there is no single, clear, distinct moment at which one 'becomes adult'. Most people experience the transition to adulthood as being quite gradual. Also, there is a difference between 'being adult' and 'feeling adult'. Have you experienced this disjunction in your own life?

This chapter focuses on the end of childhood and the transition into adulthood in different cultures. If the word 'transition' is taken to mean 'a change from one condition or state to a different condition or state', then it can be seen that children undergo all kinds of transitions as they pass through childhood, such as starting school, moving school, transitions from one friendship group to another, undergoing religious initiation, moving house in the case of parental separation, physical changes involved with

Does becoming a parent mean the end of childhood?

puberty, becoming sexually active, leaving school early to enter the labour market or to work on family farms, becoming parents, moving to further or higher education, changes in the kinds of responsibilities they undertake and so on. Indeed, people (whether children or adults) make transitions throughout the course of their lives – transition is not something that happens abruptly at the 'end of childhood'.

Psychological theories of child development traditionally describe stages of children's mental development as if the final stage is reached towards the end of childhood, when children become capable of abstract reasoning. In Piaget's theory, this is known as the stage of 'formal operations'. Increasingly, psychologists have adopted a 'lifespan perspective' which recognizes that development is a process that continues from birth to death (Woodhead, 2003). What you have probably gathered by now is that the end of childhood, as well as the beginning and the middle, is not fixed by chronological age. There is a mass of different entitlements and expectations that make the boundary between childhood and adulthood very blurred. One could say that there is a global marker, that set by the United Nations Convention on the Rights of the Child, which stipulates a cut-off point at eighteen years. However, this is only a marker and, as earlier chapters make clear, young people's and children's roles and activities differ very widely according to time and place. In other words, childhood as a category is largely socially constructed.

The same applies to the concept of adulthood. According to *The Chambers Dictionary*, an adult is simply 'a grown up person': but what does this really imply? As Jenny Hockey and Allison James, two British social anthropologists suggest, the Western idea of adulthood involves some sense of complete and whole 'personhood' and full membership of society. However, they also note that notions of 'personhood' are defined with respect to a particular set of cultural ideas about what it means to be fully human. So, for instance, in some cultures, if a man or woman doesn't produce any offspring, they never become a full 'person' (Hockey and James, 1993). The transition is best thought of as a set of dynamic, constantly changing processes, as children move from childhoods shaped and constrained by race, class, gender, religious tradition and disability, to adulthood statuses that are similarly structured.

Rites of passage are rituals marking a person's transition from one status or life stage to another.

This chapter explores the move towards adulthood, and how it is different in different historical periods and cultures; how, in many 'traditional' societies, there used to be (and sometimes still is) a sharp, clear transition from the status of child to the status of adult, often marked by symbolic rites of passage; how, in industrial societies, the transition is often much messier and fragmented; and how the transitions in pre-industrial societies, have also changed and continue to change. I will be exploring a range of different examples of transition in this chapter:

- biological changes – growth and puberty as experienced by boys and girls;

- cultural and community practices marking the transition, including rites of passage;

- formal entitlements and responsibilities encoded in national and international laws;

- subjective feelings about personal responsibility, autonomy and independence which may be very fluid and variable according to situation and mood.

The chapter is divided into four main sections. Section 2 begins by looking at rites of passage and exploring the transition to adulthood in sub-Saharan African countries, focusing on South Africa and Tanzania, and considering some effects of social change. It then moves on to look at transitions to adulthood in Britain and how these have also been changing. Section 3 explores some psychological and sociological theories that attempt to explain the transition to adulthood in Western cultures, and discusses some limitations of these theories by exploring in more depth ideas about independence and autonomy. Section 4 looks at how transitions from school to work are experienced by different groups of young people. Finally, Section 5 explores the ways in which biological processes of maturation have a social meaning, focusing particularly on menstruation and sexuality.

2 MARKING TRANSITION: CROSS-CULTURAL PERSPECTIVES

One of the clearest indicators of a transition is when this is associated with a ritual. Your activity at the beginning of this chapter will have started you thinking about rituals that might have been associated with school, or church, or mosque. In some societies these rituals are very significant.

2.1 Rites of passage in sub-Saharan Africa

Allow about 30 minutes.

READING

Read Reading A, an extract from Nelson Mandela's autobiography *Long Walk to Freedom* that describes his Xhosa initiation. As you read, note the important ideas about manhood for Nelson Mandela at the time of his initiation. What rights and responsibilities are conferred on a Xhosa youth when he enters adulthood? In what ways is his transition to adulthood gendered?

COMMENT

Mandela's account describes how the definition of 'manhood' is socially constructed by the Xhosa. Once their initiation is completed, boys are expected to take on new kinds of behaviour, rights and responsibilities. These include the right to inherit wealth, own land, set up a home, get married and have children. As men, they can be admitted to the community council and have a voice in community decisions. However, there was also another powerful image of manhood for Xhosa boys: that of the men recruited to work in the mines. Although Mandela technically became a man after his initiation, he suggests that, because of the oppression of his people, he only truly became a man many years later.

The ritual Mandela describes is typical of what anthropologists call rites of passage. Rites of passage mark a person's transition from one status to another within his or her society, and hence their changing social relationships. Rites of passage are often related to significant changes in the life cycle, whether birth, maturity, or death; they are, or were historically,

apparently more or less universal. The classic study of rites of passage was by the French anthropologist and folklorist, Arnold van Gennep (1909). Van Gennep noted that initiates are first ritually separated from the rest of the community (as Xhosa youths are in their grass huts) and, after a set period, reincorporated back into everyday life, symbolically reborn in an altered state. At the end of this chapter, I will return to rites of passage and ask how far the treatment of girls when they begin to menstruate may constitute a less dramatic kind of rite of passage.

An eighteen-year-old South African Xhosa youth during his initiation ritual in 2001.

In industrialized countries, rites of passage have become less common as societies have become more secular, though minority ethnic groups and different religious groups continue to celebrate them. There are also initiations into particular interest groups – such as the Scouts, Freemasons, Hells Angels, or the complex initiation rites involved in fraternity and sorority societies of elite US academic institutions.

Changing transitions

As socio-economic and political situations of societies change, so too do rites of passage. For instance, in contrast to Nelson Mandela's experience in 1934, a recent law passed in South Africa stipulates that boys have to be at least eighteen years old before undergoing circumcision, and the seclusion period in the bush is often timed to start at the beginning of a school holiday. While many *ingcibis* still use traditional methods, a few are drawing on Western medicine and offering a more comfortable (and more expensive) initiation experience.

Not only are the organization and techniques in initiation rites changing, but also the nature of the transition to adulthood itself. A study that was carried out by Tanzanian researchers on the situation of children in Tanzania sheds light on some of these changes (Ahmed *et al.*, 1999). The study used participatory research methods and official data sources to build up a contemporary picture of what the category 'child' means, and explored the implications of these meanings for the transition to adulthood. In Tanzania, chronological age is not the key marker of identity and, particularly in rural areas, most people don't know their exact age. In fact, some Tanzanian legislation refers to 'apparent age' rather than precise chronological age. Rather, passage through these stages 'is defined by the gradual assumption of responsibilities'. There are different terms for 'child' in Swahili, depending on their gender and age group (see Table 1). Interestingly, none corresponds to the English term 'adolescent' or 'teenager'.

The Tanzanian study showed that initiation is the most important differentiation point in childhood; though when this takes place does vary between regions, as well as by gender. Initiation is also clearly being affected by modernization, as are other aspects of transition into adulthood. In rural areas:

> In the past a suitor would have proposed to a girl's parents when the girl was as young as 14 years. After betrothal, a boy would stay in his in-laws' compound with the girl, until she became pregnant. Once pregnant, the girl would remain indoors until she gave birth, after which she could accompany her husband to his parents' homestead ... [By the late 1990s] respondents told researchers, girls and boys start relationships on their own and quite early in life (although no specific ages were mentioned). This may lead to sexual activity. If she becomes pregnant a girl may be abandoned by her sexual partner and left to the care of her parents. In a few families, girls are chased from home when they become pregnant. Whereas it was formerly prohibited for women to become pregnant before initiation and circumcision, it is not uncommon now for a girl to become pregnant before both, which can contribute to her outcast status.

(Ahmed *et al.*, 1999, p. 106)

Table 1 Kiswahili life stages, English equivalent terms and chronological age

Kiswahili stage	English translation	Chronological age
Mtoto mchanga	Very young child, baby: literally in the early stage of growth	From birth to between 3 and 6 months
Mtoto anaenyonya	Suckling child	7 months to 2 years
Mtoto mdogo	Small child	3 to 6 years
Mtoto	Child	7–9 years (girls); 7–14 years (boys)
Kigori	Pre-pubertal girl	10–12 years for girls
Mwali	Pubertal girl	13–15 years (boys and girls)
Balehe	Pubertal boy	
Msichana	Post-pubertal girl	16–24 years
Mvulana	Post-pubertal boy	
Vijana	Youth (male/female)	
Mtu mzima	Whole/mature person	25–35 years
Mtu wa makamo	Mature person	36–50 years
Mzee	Old	51–65 years
Mkongwe	Very old	More than 65 years

Source: Ahmed *et al.*, 1999, p. 103.

In common with other parts of Africa, respondents seemed to associate changes in the practice of initiation and the behaviour of young people with the pressure of schooling and the breakdown of traditional family practices. 'The biggest issue in the initiation ceremony is respect and training to assist mothers and fathers in the household chores. But nowadays some people do not see the importance of that, everyone does what he wants without consultation'. (Ahmed *et al.*, 1999, p. 107). The initiation ceremony is now performed much earlier so as not to interfere with school routine, and people reported that this contributes to children's early exposure to sex and ultimately to early pregnancy. As soon as the children come out of the initiation training, they start to practise what they were taught and thus 'make each other pregnant'. This example from Tanzania shows how traditional rites of passage and stages in the life cycle are changing. Other factors are also driving social change, particularly in sub-Saharan Africa – for example, the devastating impact of HIV/AIDS in the region is likely to impact upon the work roles and responsibilities of older children, as they are assuming greater responsibilities for younger siblings in child-headed households.

2.2 Transitions to adulthood in Britain

I will now move on to look at some examples from Britain, where the transitions into adulthood are often more fragmented.

In Britain (along with other industrialized societies) the transition to adulthood is usually thought of as comprising the following interconnected elements that may be accomplished in stages, with much ambiguity. Notice how these elements compare with the attributes of adulthood associated with the initiation rites described by Nelson Mandela. Some elements are the same and some indicative of the differences between the societies. Compare also your own responses to Activity 1 with the list below:

- leaving school and entering work or further/higher education;
- leaving one's family of origin to set up a new home;
- becoming involved in sexual relationships;
- cohabiting or marrying;
- becoming a parent;
- becoming a full adult consumer, able to purchase commodities that signify adult status;
- becoming a full adult citizen, with voting rights (in parliamentary democracies).

The transition to adulthood in Britain is also affected by a range of different social structural factors. Bearing in mind that the pattern is somewhat similar in most industrialized or post-industrial countries, young people are able to leave school at the age of sixteen and go into full-time work, where they may receive adults' pay levels (though they are not, at the time of writing, entitled to receive the full minimum wage until twenty one). However, young people are now much more likely to stay on in further education, higher education or training, or to become unemployed, than they are to go into full-time work. Further, young people are not eligible to claim full social security benefits until they are twenty-five years old. These factors mean that young people are frequently economically dependent upon their families until well into their mid-twenties, and this may restrict their ability to participate in consumer markets. Socially and sexually, however, they expect to be able to develop separate, independent identities and lifestyles. Evidence from the National Sexual Attitudes survey (Johnson *et al.*, 1994) suggests that there has been a steady decline in the reported age of first heterosexual intercourse from an average age of twenty years for men born between 1931 and 1935 to seventeen years for those born in 1966–1975. The survey reports that, by 1994, about 28 per cent of young men and 19 per cent of young women were having sexual intercourse before the minimum lawful age of sixteen. On the other hand, young people are tending to delay becoming parents for longer, frequently until their late twenties or early thirties. All this suggests that the different aspects of 'adulthood' have become disconnected from each other and that there is now a disjunction between the acquisition of various 'adult' attributes. Young people are becoming adult in terms of sexuality much earlier, while remaining economically dependent much longer. Table 2 summarizes ages of legal entitlement in Britain alongside four other European countries.

Table 2 Ages of legal entitlement in five European countries

	Britain	Czech Republic	Germany	Netherlands	Norway
Vote in elections	18	18	18	18	18
Get married	16	18	16	18	18
Work part-time	13	18	13	16	13
Purchase beer and wine	18	18	16	16	18
Join army	16	18	18	18	19

Source: Council of Europe, 1996, pp. 11–12, 21–22, 46–49, 69–71.

Social changes have had a profound impact on the situation of young people in industrialized and post-industrialized countries. In the longer term, these include the following trends, which were also discussed in Chapter 3, Section 5:

- Changes in the social institution of childhood: childhood has become increasingly segregated from the adult world as the school leaving age has risen (in the UK, to fifteen in 1944 and to sixteen in 1972). This in turn causes problems when a young person at the end of their childhood needs to be integrated into adult society, as the gap between the child's world of school and the adult world of work has widened. (In practice, in nearly all industrialized countries, significant proportions of children do undertake part-time paid work, but this is used largely to finance their personal consumption rather than to help support the household.)

- Greater affluence, particularly since the 1950s, has had a marked effect on young people's transitions to adulthood, with the identification of young people as an important consumer group and the subsequent rise of youth subcultures and teenage consumerism. This has probably contributed to a growing expectation of separate, independent living among young people and their developing a distinct identity from their parents. The expectation was largely fulfilled during the 1960s and 1970s as increased affluence made it possible for young people in their early twenties to find jobs, leave home (whether to cohabit, marry, live singly or in shared households), and have children.

During the 1980s and early 1990s, however, a combination of a series of economic recessions, a shortage of housing and increased poverty of young people made the transition to adulthood more difficult and protracted, with important differences according to social class and ethnicity. However, the *anticipation* of independent adulthood has probably not changed. Pat Allatt and Sue Yeandle found, in a study carried out in the mid 1980s with forty families in Newcastle, both the parents and young people themselves fully expected young people to become independent and set up their own households (Allatt and Yeandle, 1986). However, there may now be a time lag between changing social and economic circumstances and young people's (and indeed their parents') expectations of what they might expect to attain in terms of the material accoutrements of adulthood. Western individualism, with the (ideal) definition of 'adult' as 'independent' (discussed in the next section) is contradicted by policies and social changes that have the effect of prolonging dependency and delaying the transition to independent adulthood for young people who, after all, attain citizenship, at least in the form of voting rights, at the age of eighteen (Morrow and Richards, 1996).

SUMMARY OF SECTION 2

- The definition of maturity differs across cultures.
- Ceremonies or rites of passage are often used to mark the transition in status from child to adult.
- Both of the above are subject to change in accordance with changing socio-economic circumstances.
- In industrialized countries, while there are parallels with the patterns described in other parts of the world, the transition to adulthood isn't fixed or static, nor marked by a clear, sharp change in status.
- Elements in this more fragmental transition in industrialized countries have also been affected by a range of structural factors, such as changes in social policy and economic changes.

3 WESTERN THEORIES AND EXPLANATIONS

Theories put forward by Western developmental psychologists, social theorists and sociologists to explain the processes involved in the transition to adulthood have tended to assume that to be adult is essentially to be a competent, mature, independent, autonomous individual. For instance, the psychologist Erik Erikson (1968) highlighted the importance of physiological changes at puberty, in combination with identity formation, as the two key tasks of adolescence, with the outcome of a person in the form of a 'unitary, individual subject'. The first social scientist to comment on adolescence, the American, G. Stanley Hall, referred to it both as 'a marvellous new birth' (meaning for society) and also as a period of storm and stress and the age 'when most vicious careers are begun' (Hall, 1904, cited in, Jones and Wallace, 1992, p. 7). This conception of the adolescent as difficult and incomplete, who becomes a coherent autonomous individual at adulthood, is still influential in Western societies.

As you saw in the last section, however, transitions into adulthood in many parts of the world have been affected by social change. One of the key sociological theorists, Ulrick Beck, has developed a theory of individualization to explain the impact of modern social life on young people (Beck, 1992). He argues that as the old certainties of industrial society, such as stable employment and stable families, give way to modern risks, people have become increasingly emancipated from social ties. People no longer feel the need to conform to set ways of behaving and organizing their social lives, but rather, are exposed to all kinds of risks which have to be negotiated throughout the life course. This is thought by Beck to lead to individualized lifestyles, with people seeking to achieve their own aims in a highly competitive world and actively constructing their own biographies, which may involve them detaching themselves from established family or class patterns. In other words, people are the agents of their own destiny and this is particularly true for young people.

Other sociologists, like Furlong and Cartmel (1997), have argued that Beck has somewhat overstated the case. While it is certainly true that social change has had a considerable impact on patterns of education and employment opportunities, young people's leisure activities and their relationships with family and friends, they argue that there are clearly continuing effects of social class, gender and ethnicity in structuring young people's life chances and reproducing inequality. Let's look more closely now at some examples of young people's own feelings about this point in the life cycle.

3.1 Independence versus dependence: or inter-dependence?

The psychological and sociological theories briefly mentioned above seem to imply that there is a final end point of 'independence' that young people aspire to and generally achieve. However, family relationships are in fact very important for transitions to adulthood in Western cultures, more so than might be assumed from the theories outlined above.

Allow about 20 minutes

A C T I V I T Y 2   **Moving towards independence?**

Read the extract in Box 1, taken from a study by Val Gillies and colleagues based on qualitative interviews with young people and parents of young people in England. It illustrates very clearly the importance of emotional support from family members for young people as they approach adulthood. However, this research also found that independence was a key feature of interviewees' discussions of their relationships and their lives together: 'Both young people and their parents explained how over the years they had gained greater independence from each other, while retaining significant personal, emotional and practical bonds' (Gillies *et al.*, 2001, p. 14) In what contexts does the question of independence arise for the young people quoted in Box 1? What evidence is there of individualization?

Box 1

Independence as agency

Teenagers saw acquiring a level of independence and self determination as indicative of their accountability as young adults. While they generally welcomed their increasing autonomy as a new freedom, the process of becoming independent was understood in terms of responsibility as an individual. The majority of the young people we interviewed saw independence as signifying a new liberty to act as an individual, but also as obligating them to account for the consequences of these individual actions.

Teenagers appeared to construct independence as a personal resource that they themselves had built and developed over the years. For many young people, becoming more independent was a gradual process associated with adaptation and negotiation. They described how they actively manipulated opportunities and altered the status of their relationships in order to become more self determining. Again, accepting responsibility was presented as the key to gaining greater respect and independence from parents. Young women in particular emphasized the role of trust in gaining greater independence ... For example, Leonie explained how her mother now felt able to allow her greater autonomy, while Julia described how she now makes her own decisions:

> ... she knows that I need my freedom now. And that I'm, like I'm always out anyway working and everything so she knows that I'm responsible and sensible enough now.
>
> (Leonie, African-Caribbean, middle-class young woman)
>
> I always like to get back on time to tell them and because only recently, enough of my friends have passed their driving test, so that they wouldn't be coming out to get me anyway. But, I mean, I normally don't say a time. I

For teenagers in Britain, increasing independence brings a mixture of new freedoms and new responsibilities.

normally say when I expect to be back and they'll be in bed anyway, so I just go and wake them up when I get back, just to let them know that I'm in really.

(Julia, White, middle-class young woman)

Independence as responsibility

Teenagers' notions of independence were not confined to discussions of freedom and restriction. Notably, some young people's interpretations of independence contained a strong conception of an emerging responsibility to other family members ...

Although Imran did describe how he had obtained greater personal autonomy and freedom, his family relationships clearly limited the extent to which he felt able to act purely in his own interest. He explained how, when his family returned from Bangladesh, he considered moving away from home to ease the overcrowding:

I don't know, it's like, my mum came back and I told her that I'm thinking of moving out and she didn't take it really too well, she like ... she burst out with laughter, 'no, shut up, what you talking about, you're only a kid, only 16', she just said it like that, then she saw that I was talking seriously, and ... she looked very worried, like, oh, 'when you going to go?', so I thought 'forget it, don't want the hassle'... I think when I'm older it will be easier. Maybe not, because then, my brother moves out, and there'll be space in the house for me. And then they'll expect me to stay there.

(Imran, Bengali, working-class young man)

For Imran, independence was not just associated with self-sufficiency, but with a responsibility to consider other family members ...

Source: Gillies, Ribbens McCarthy and Holland, 2001, pp. 14–15.

COMMENT

This extract shows that while young people may talk about independence, their close relationships with family members and particularly parents remained very significant. They described not only increasing individual responsibility, but also an increasing sense of responsibility for other family members. So while there is some evidence of individualization in Beck's sense of the word, there is also evidence of a strong sense of the continuing importance of relationships with family members.

In addition to financial help, it appears that families still provide support for young people at this point both in terms of socialization, in that some young people internalize their parents' aspirations and expectations for the future, and in terms of practical use of family social networks for information and influence about local job opportunities and higher education opportunities. While some psychological studies have focused on the 'storm and stress' of adolescence and risky behaviour, children and young people themselves talk more about family relationships being reciprocal, with implications for them about gaining responsibility and choice, but retaining inter-dependence in family relations. And it is not clear that Beck's individualization theory can be sustained by empirical evidence. Seeing independence and dependence as binary opposites is not always relevant to everyday life and, perhaps, a concept of interdependence might be more helpful. Older children may provide reciprocal care and services within their families, both in the form of domestic labour and labour input to family businesses, but because the tendency in sociology has been to classify the relationship between children and parents as one in which the former are dependent on the latter, people ignore what may well be elements of exchange or reciprocity. For example, there are many young carers (an estimated 50,000) in the UK who take on a good deal of responsibility for helping to look after ill or disabled parents (Aldridge and Becker, 2002). This is Lucie, age fifteen, who lives with her mother who has had a bad back and has battled against cancer on three separate occasions. Her father often has to work away from home.

> 'When my dad is away I have to look after my mum and younger brother. I have to cook, clean the house and help my mum. I have to fetch my mum's pills and help her to get out of bed. It's hard work and sometimes I feel really tired ... When my dad is away I become responsible for everybody and the house. I don't get on with social workers because they keep trying to take me and my brother away from my mum when my dad is working'

(Becker, 2000)

Children also help with caring for brothers and sisters. This is a description from a fifteen-year-old English girl, describing her everyday life outside school (Morrow, 1996):

> 'At home I help out to a degree; by running errands to family and friends ... I also do some shopping depending on the times of school; this is normally for things such as shampoo, toothpaste and other small items. However, occasionally I do the week's grocery shopping for our family of seven. Other things which I do at home include babysitting the other 5 children, two of which are [adopted] babies, and one of 16 who has a mental age of 7. I do this when my Mum goes out (my dad died when I was 4). I also help with the cleaning and cooking as well as stimulating my two adopted baby brothers who are both Downs. When my Mum is ill I take care of the whole family until she has recovered.'

(Morrow, 1996, p. 70)

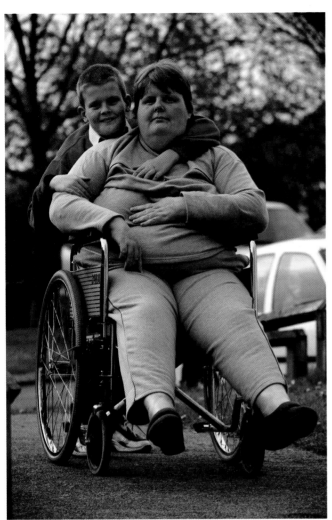

The girl in Morrow's quotation was obviously making a significant contribution and it seems from her point of view that her mother may rely on her for a lot of help. One could say they were interdependent. In other words, her mother is not independent and neither is she. It is too simplistic to see dependence and independence as polar opposites, for the relationship is more complex. Children who have heavy caring duties may well have dependants to look after, but they still also lack independence. Furthermore, adults are also frequently interdependent, but the cultural emphasis on individualism and independence in adulthood often masks this interdependence. The fact that childhood is constructed as a period of dependency prevents us from 'knowing' about those cases of children undertaking domestic work, because such work, particularly caring, is socially defined as an adult role and is a marker of adult status.

Ten-year-old Shaun contributes to the household by sharing the shopping, cooking and washing with his older brother.

SUMMARY OF SECTION 3

- The idea of Western individualism is problematic. Not everyone achieves the 'unitary individual subject' of Erikson's theory. Indeed, it isn't clear that anyone ever does achieve this and it is in fact an 'ideal type'.

- People move between states of dependency, independence and inter-dependence throughout their lives. Some children provide a significant amount of care and services within their families, but this work is hidden by a cultural construction of childhood as dependent. This presents a challenge to individualization theories and ideas that adulthood is in fact a state of 'independence'.

4   TRANSITIONS FROM SCHOOL TO WORK

One of the key markers of adulthood is often the move into more or less full time work. In Chapter 3 Hugh Cunningham discussed how shifting patterns of work and schooling over the last two centuries were related to changing Western conceptions of childhood. Chapters 4 and 5 raised further issues and complexities about what counts as work and as education for children in different parts of the world, and examined how in some places work may be an integral part of a child's life from an early age. In this section I will begin by looking at the factors affecting how different groups of young people in Britain currently experience the transition from school to work and then broaden out the discussion using an example from another part of the world.

In Britain, increasing proportions of young people from some social groups remain in education or training, and this has the effect of delaying the entry into work or unemployment. Further, social class differences are persistent, in that unqualified young people are likely to have parents with manual occupations and are more likely to be unemployed, particularly if they live in an area with a depressed labour market. Gender, ethnicity, disability and geographical location all interact to constrain and influence the opportunities available to young people when they leave school.

4.1 Work, class and masculinity

One classic text, and the basis for much research since, is Paul Willis' (1977) study *Learning to Labour: how working class kids get working class jobs* which examines how school acts as a key site for the reproduction of different kinds of working class labour. You may remember the discussion of Willis' work in Chapter 4, Section 5. Willis spent time in secondary modern schools in Wolverhampton (central England), interviewing low achieving boys and observing their education, behaviour, attitudes and language. He found that the boys left school with few qualifications, but were effectively 'ready to labour', and got unskilled or semi-skilled jobs in the manufacturing industries around Wolverhampton. He suggested that young working-class men were disadvantaged in the labour market in many ways, not least by their low aspirations, a culture of masculinity that valued disruptive or disaffected behaviour in school, and the limited opportunities available to them. He argued:

> The wage packet is the provider of freedom, and independence: the particular prize of masculinity in work ... A trade is judged not for itself, nor even for its general financial return, but for its ability to provide the central, domestic masculine role for its incumbent ... The male wage packet is held to be central, not simply for its size, but because it is won in a masculine mode in confrontation with the 'real' world which is too tough for the woman.

(Willis, 1977, p. 150)

Many young working-class men in Britain are now moving into service industries rather than manual labour.

Changing social conditions have altered the experiences of young men, however. Recently, Linda McDowell conducted a study with young fifteen- to sixteen-year-old working-class men in Sheffield and Cambridgeshire, in the context of the decline in manufacturing industry and the growth of the service sector of the economy. She found that instead of 'learning to labour', these young men are 'learning to serve', in part-time, low-paid jobs in shops and restaurants (McDowell, 2000, p. 412).

This age group of young men has generated concern in Britain, because of a perceived 'crisis of masculinity' – particularly among working-class young men, with increased likelihood of truancy, increased suicide rates, increased levels of violence, and a widening gender gap in educational performance and outcomes. The educational sociologist, Sara Delamont (2000), suggests that this 'crisis' is directly related to changes in the economy – problems with the availability of the kind of jobs and apprenticeships in manufacturing, construction and heavy industry that existed in the past and enabled young working-class boys with limited or no educational qualifications to become financially independent. Consequently, some young working-class men now find it more difficult to make the transition from full time education into the labour market than young women do, at comparable stages in their careers. Because of this greater difficulty, they may have very little to offer these young women, economically, in the marriage market.

Similar patterns can be found in other industrialized societies, for instance, McDowell cites Australia and Canada. Educational researchers have called this a reversal of the gender politics of the 1970s, when there were widespread concerns in Britain about underachievement among girls and young women. However, it seems to be a particular group of young men who are currently most at risk: those who thirty years ago would have been 'learning to labour'. The 'crisis of masculinity' is therefore not simply a gender issue but also to do with class. The British 'crisis of masculinity' is the result of the combination of the effects of economic and social change on young men in a particular working-class position.

4.2 Young working-class women's transitions to work

In spite of achieving the same or higher qualifications as boys, working-class young women in Britain appear to be channelled into different, and often less well-paid, occupations from the young men who do find work. Small-scale studies that have focused on young women's transition to work, like that of Christine Griffin, have shown how young women's work identities have to be integrated with their identities as young *women*, and suggest that femininity plays a crucial role (Griffin, 1985). This is an important point because it highlights how structural factors also shape transitions. Despite the intended widening of equal opportunities for young people through government training schemes in the 1980s, particularly at the lower end of the labour market, Inge Bates (1993) asked 'Why do working-class girls continue to enter working-class, gender-stereotyped jobs?' Bates studied a group of sixteen- to eighteen-year-old girls who were training for jobs in the field of institutional care, such as working in old people's homes. She found that a number of factors helped to answer her question, including: the occupational culture of institutional care; aspects of gender socialization in working-class families; vocational training; and the wider context of youth unemployment and job scarcity. Some of the girls in her study described undertaking considerable amounts of domestic work at home. This extended to looking after younger brothers and sisters, as well as undertaking housework. For example, Jane described how she regularly looked after her five-year-old brother at night. Jane explained:

> ... there's a spare bed in my room so if like he's not very well or he wakes up in the night, he usually comes in that bed ... he chokes a lot, you know, when he's laid on his back, he's sick most nights. So like rather than me mum taking him into her bed, and disturbing me dad, he comes into my bedroom and he sleeps in the spare bed.

(Bates, 1993, p. 27)

Working-class girls' experience of domestic work and serving others makes it easier for them to take on caring work and responsibilities in their adult lives.

Bates makes the point that Jane has acquired a set of 'cultural resources', skills and experience, from her family context, that are then useful to her in the process of training to become a care assistant. Bates gives another example, of Kay, who described undertaking a good deal of housework, including cooking Sunday lunch (traditionally an important British family ritual) while her mother was at work, while her brother 'doesn't do a damned thing and he's not been to school since he were 13 and he doesn't even wash a pot' (Bates, 1993, p. 26). Bates suggests the experience of domestic work, serving others, denying their own needs (for example, for regular sleep at night, for time off on Sunday) were demands to which these working-class girls were well accustomed by the age of sixteen. Thus these girls' transitions to adulthood are bound up in their childhood experiences, which make it easier for them to accept domestic and caring responsibilities in their adult lives.

4.3 Minority ethnic status and religious background

Other factors, such as belonging to a minority ethnic group or specific religion, may intersect with gender to influence young women's position in the labour market. Heidi Mirza's research in Britain on young black (African–Caribbean) women's transitions from school, found that while at school the young women had high aspirations for the jobs they wanted when they left school, regardless of their social class background. However, they were also aware that the labour market could be racist. When Mirza followed her sample up four years later, many of the young women had entered occupations characterized by a distinct lack of variety and scope. For these women, the overwhelming concentration of employment opportunities in low-grade office work regardless of their aspirations, together with unfulfilled aspirations towards careers in caring professions, was a clear pattern. A major constraint was the existence of a racially and sexually segregated labour market that had limited the occupational opportunities for these young black women (Mirza, 1992).

Different religious and cultural traditions intersect for young people whose families have migrated to Western countries, and a range of pressures are felt by young people themselves. Haleh Afshar (1995) highlights some of the dilemmas described by Muslim women in West Yorkshire in the north of England.

> Young Muslim men dress and generally behave in ways which are not easily distinguishable from their Western counterparts. Many assert their birthright to do so. Although their parents frown at drinking and smoking, the best amongst them may refrain from taking these habits home, but many feel quite free to mix and play with their contemporaries of all races, beliefs and colours. Yet the same young men all too often expect their sisters, future wives and daughters to behave in a distinctly different way; to dress in the way that their mothers and grandmothers had done, to remain separate from the host society and to retain the identity that is so dear to the heart of the immigrant society ....

This same identity, which has gone through changes and has evolved and developed through time in all the home towns of the migrants, has been held static in its embodiment in the West. The immigrants in Bradford, like immigrants everywhere, have ossified some of the values of their past and have demanded rigid adherence to these unchanging roles. In the context of a changing world, a changing Europe and evolving Islamic concepts of self and identity, the immigrants have retained an idolized idea of the past and have imposed the duty on their women to guard and maintain this identity and to nurture it and transmit it to the next generation ...

As ... Mrs B reported:

> We have to teach our children two separate sorts of things; one is about cooking and cleaning and things like that. The other is about *sharme* and manners. We also have to teach them about religion and their own history and background, about the family.

> I do my best to pass on things that I was taught by my elders so they can pass them on to their children. Maybe not everything, but most of what we were taught was right and we should pass it on.

(Afshar, 1995, p. 134–5)

The expectations of parents, religious identity and cultural practices, combine to structure the transition to adulthood for young people as they juggle these sets of expectations with those from the wider societies in which they are located. These various expectations affect the work opportunities and choices of these young people.

Young Muslim women in Western countries are often expected to guard and maintain a traditional Islamic identity.

4.4 Disability

How do disabled young people experience the transition to adulthood? In research in Scotland with young people with disabilities, Sheila Riddell emphasizes how 'the dynamic of transition for young disabled people is influenced both by the nature of their impairment and by wider social and political factors which impinge upon their lives and have a profound impact on the way in which impairment is understood by themselves and others' (Riddell, 1998, pp. 193–4). She shows that not only are young people with physical disabilities, learning difficulties and mental illnesses denied some of the legal markers of adulthood (such as the right to consent to medical treatment), they are also excluded from 'financial independence, paid employment, independent living and adult social relationships, including parenthood' (p. 194). Non-disabled adults often treated these young people in a patronizing and infantilizing manner. For instance, eighteen-year-old Linda, who has a form of ataxia (inability to co-ordinate voluntary movements) which severely affects her mobility, was irritated by the assumption that people with physical impairments also have learning difficulties. Linda was a strong advocate of integration and wider acceptance by the community:

> 'the public really annoys me because first of all they're ignorant of anybody with any disability. Somebody with sticks – they stare at you when you go past because they see there's something different … One incident that sticks in my mind – she was an old lady and I must have been about 15 or 16 and I was sitting in a shop in my wheelchair. She comes up to be and says: "What are you getting from Santa Claus?" Now that is really so degrading!'

> (Riddell, 1998, p. 201)

Linda had always enjoyed physical activities, was an excellent swimmer and wanted to be a PE teacher. She said:

> 'I think if I'd given in to her [the careers adviser] then I would either be doing a YTS or an office job – not doing what I wanted to do but what she wanted me to do … Then I was offered the [Physical Education and Community Studies] place at college and I think she was even more surprised than me because she'd been so negative all the way through.'

> (Riddell, 1998, p. 202)

After completing the college course, Linda found that regulations prevented her from entering a teacher-training course. When Riddell interviewed her, she had applied unsuccessfully for more than forty clerical posts, but later succeeded in getting work with a travel agency, which she felt would be more fun than a traditional nine-to-five office job. Although still partially dependent on her parents, Linda had taken independent decisions about her future and was keen to move into her own home. Above all, she resisted being seen as having a 'disabled identity'. Of course, for young people who are more severely disabled, work opportunities are even more limited.

4.5 Transitions to work in rural Bolivia

So far in this section, I've concentrated on transitions from school to work in the British context. As you have seen, how these transitions are experienced is strongly shaped by a range of factors, in a specific advanced industrialized nation. I shall now introduce a very different situation, that of rural Bolivia, and consider how young people make decisions about whether to stay at school or start working.

Allow about 15 minutes

ACTIVITY 3 From school to work

Read the quotation in Box 2, from Samantha Punch, a social geographer who carried out research on youth transitions in Churquiales, a village in rural Bolivia. (You may remember the discussion of Punch's research on rural Bolivian children's work in Chapter 1.) Note down your answers to the following two questions:

1   What are the important factors influencing Santiago's decision to leave school?

2   How do these compare with factors influencing young people in your experience?

COMMENT

The example of Santiago shows how complex the decision-making processes can be for young people in their different school-to-work transitions. A range of factors influenced Santiago's decision, especially the interdependence of relationships in his family. In this case, rural young people in Bolivia may achieve economic independence sooner than they do in many affluent parts of the world, but interdependent family relationships are maintained throughout the life course. Punch suggests the concept of 'negotiated interdependence'…'is a more appropriate way to understand relations between young people and adults in rural areas of the majority world' (Punch, 2002, p. 132).

SUMMARY OF SECTION 4

- A wide range of factors – social class, dis/ability, gender, ethnic background and religious beliefs – interact to structure and influence young people's transitions to adulthood; this section has focused in particular on the transition from school to work.

- The example of Santiago, from Bolivia, shows how complex decisions have to be made about whether to stay at school or whether to start work. However, Santiago is not necessarily 'independent' and retains important links and relationships with his family.

Box 2

In Bolivia, where a state welfare system does not exist, there are strong expectations that children should be responsible for their parents in old age, whether that be physical care or financial support. In Churquiales, most young people have a strong sense of responsibility towards their family, and negotiate ways to fulfil their individual needs whilst also contributing to the household. They balance family demands and personal ambitions, and also integrate the different contexts of their lives at school, home and work. The decisions which they make in one arena, within the limited range of opportunities they have, can only be understood if one knows what is happening in the other contexts of their lives. The constraints which face young people at home affect what they do at work or at school, and vice versa.

Santiago (13)'s choice of school-to-work transition is an example of how interdependence is worked out in practice. He left school and began to work as an agricultural day labourer in the community even though his parents were prepared to make the financial sacrifice to send him to secondary school: 'If I wanted to study, I would have just gone.' However, in the end, he decided: 'It's not worth it, what happens if I fail? If I don't fail, I'd just have to keep on going, but I almost don't like studying now. I want to work. Studying is easier, but I want to work.'

By working as a day labourer, he provided for his own clothing and social needs. Other times, when his labour was needed, he worked on his household's land, thereby fulfilling his family responsibilities. When his parents offered him a small piece of land for his own crops, he declined because he was aware that the land was needed for family consumption rather than for the market: 'In my house there's always food for me and I know that if I need something then it'll be bought for me.'

Santiago's decision not to continue his education might be considered irrational if it is only seen within the school context rather than within the interconnecting arenas of home, school and work. He was aware that continuing school would cause financial sacrifices for his family. He was also uncertain about the long-term value of schooling which was exacerbated by his lack of an educational role model to follow. His two older brothers had migrated to work in Argentina and their material success led him to aspire to similar economic gain. His relatively sheltered social world within Churquiales meant he was not keen to migrate to study on his own and would prefer to migrate to work with his brothers. Therefore, he opted for working and acquiring greater autonomy which enabled him to contribute to his household rather than studying and remaining financially dependent on his parents. In 2000 it was heard that he was working in Argentina with one of his brothers. Santiago's decision shows that young people make rational choices within a range of constraints and opportunities which intersect the different arenas of their lives. Such decisions need to be understood not only within the interconnecting arenas, but also within the wider social, cultural and economic context in which they are made.

(Punch, 2002, pp. 130–131)

5 PUBERTY, SEXUALITY AND CHANGING IDENTITY

Allow about 15 minutes

ACTIVITY 4   Teenagers

Think about the following questions and make a note of your responses:

1   What does the word teenager conjure up for you in terms of appearance and behaviour?

2   Would you say a teenager who had passed puberty was sexually mature?

3   What sexual behaviour would you see as appropriate for a fifteen year old?

4   Do you feel most people you know would agree with you?

COMMENT

In many affluent societies, the teens are seen as a time of rebellion, expressed through personal appearance, clothing and behaviour. 'Between childhood and adulthood, obedience and responsibility, innocence and maturity, it is an interstitial, sometimes awkward category with a quite different set of connotations to those of childhood; connotations that are much more in keeping, and which resonate, with an anxious, suspicious and sometimes punitive public response to troubled and troublesome "youths" at home' (Hall and Montgomery, 2000, p. 15). One area adults often find troublesome is teenagers' sexual activity. Depending on their generation, gender, ethnic and social group and religious beliefs, people often have different expectations about what is appropriate. I shall discuss young people's sexual activity in more detail below, but first I shall examine how physical changes at puberty may be viewed and dealt with in quite different ways.

5.1 Menstruation

The response to girls' menstruation in different societies is a good example of the ways in which physiological processes associated with the transition to adulthood become socially meaningful. Section 2 looked at rites of passage associated with the transition to manhood for young men in South Africa. It also looked at how some of these rituals are changing. In the Reading below, you are asked to contrast two very different accounts of girls' experiences of the onset of menstruation.

READING

Please read the two extracts in Readings B and C. What differences strike you about the experience of girls in these two very different contexts? Reading B is taken from an ethnographic account of the rituals surrounding girls' first menstruation (menarche) conducted by the Waiwai, an Amazonian tribe. The account was written by the Danish anthropologist, Niels Fock, who lived among the Waiwai during the 1950s.

A Waiwai emasï
wearing her white bead
armbands.

These practices are still continuing. Reading C comes from recent
ethnographic research into girls' experience of adolescence in Britain,
carried out by the British sociologist, Shirley Prendergast.

Can you spot who's wearing the towel?

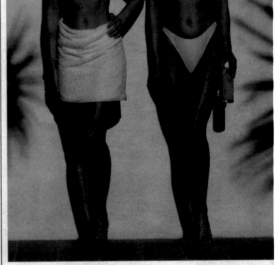

Well spotted. She's the one wearing the towel.

Because however slim and slender sanitary towels may be, they will never be as discreet as Lil-lets.

Nor will they give you the same feeling of security and confidence that Lil-lets give you.

Lil-lets gently expand widthways to fit you perfectly.

So there's no need for any

cover-up, no matter how little you're wearing.

Not even our pack will give you away.

Unwrap it, and it becomes unrecognisable.

All of which explains why Lil-lets are recognised by millions of women as the most

reliable and discreet protection you can wear.

Whether you're wearing a swimsuit, or a business suit. *Lil-lets*

Western women are expected to hide their menstruation.

The description of the significance of menstruation for the Waiwai is in stark contrast to what happens for British schoolgirls, who are expected to carry on their everyday lives as usual when their periods start and most attention is directed at 'managing' their bodies to hide the fact that they are menstruating. Think about the contrast between the British account and the well-ordered ritual that takes place for Waiwai girls (mind you, the views of the Waiwai girls are not known and may not have been elicited!); and how for the Waiwai, the link between menstruation and education and training as a crucial part of attaining adult status is completely differently managed. British girls may feel different once their periods have begun, but although they are teased and victimized by the boys, they aren't regarded or treated particularly differently by the wider (adult) society, they are just expected to carry on as 'normal', as Shirley Prendergast notes in her discussion. In fact, Western social etiquette around menstruation aims to make it as invisible as possible (see the advertisement above).

5.2 Sexuality

Heterosexuality

The topic of young people and sex has become a well-studied field and adolescent fertility rates are the focus of research (and adult concern) around the world. Ann Phoenix, in a study of British teenage mothers, points out that adolescence 'is perceived as a period of preparation for adulthood, adolescents are more likely to be thought of as children rather than adults because they are not generally expected to take part in many adult activities. As such they are conceptualized as needing to be in a state of innocence' (Phoenix, 1991, p. 25).

In Britain, teenage pregnancy is increasingly seen as a social problem.

This has important implications for how young people who are sexually active are perceived by adult society, and there is, generally speaking, in most cultures disapproval of young people who become sexually active 'too young'. However, what counts as 'too young' differs widely among societies and over time. In Britain, teenage pregnancy is seen as a social problem, and banner headlines of newspapers frequently sensationalize stories about teenage or school girl pregnancies, as shown by this example from the *The Times* (published in the UK):

When your baby has a child

The latest case of a 12-year-old girl's pregnancy has caused outrage. But ... it can happen to any family. What can parents do to cope?

When a 12-year-old Rotherham schoolgirl told her parents she was pregnant and that the father could be any of five men she had slept with, it blew the family apart. She had to leave home to live with a relative....

Rotherham, in South Yorkshire, depressed by the decline of the mining industry and the closure of steelworks, has one of the highest rates of teenage pregnancies in Britain. Latest figures show that the conception rate among under-16s is 11.5 conceptions per 1,000, compared with the national average of 8.3.

(Carroll and Rumbelow, 2001)

This girl was twelve at the time of conception and thirteen when the baby was born. The fact that a twelve-year-old can be sexually active seems to be the primary cause for concern – there is a strong idea, as Ann Phoenix's quotation above suggests, that sex is something that these children should not be doing. However, as you have just seen, the Waiwai girls could become sexually active shortly after their initiation rite, illustrating the point about 'too young' being a relative concept.

At the same time, from the point of view of young people themselves, sexual activity may be perceived as being linked to the establishment of an identity separate from that of a dependent, home-centred child. Janet Holland and her colleagues have carried out a series of qualitative research projects with young people in England on their experiences of heterosexual sex and sexual practice (Holland *et al.*, 1998). For many young people, having a boyfriend or a girlfriend, or having lost one's virginity, may be a marker of adult status. For example, Holland *et al.* suggest that for the young men they interviewed:

Heterosexual first sex is an induction into adult masculinity ... in which women, whether sexually experienced or not, play an ambiguous role. ...

First intercourse is generally a consciously critical moment for young people whether they are actively seeking sexual intercourse, allowing the intercourse to happen, or having it thrust upon them. It is also part of a much more general, and less visible, process of induction into the dominance of masculine norms as 'natural'. Significantly, most young women arrive at their first experience of heterosexual intercourse already constituted as 'woman' by the onset of menstruation and the attendant requirements to discipline this bodily disorder... [as you've already seen in the Reading by Prendergast] ... Yet for the young men, puberty has no such exact marker, and first sex is the key act by which they can become a man ...

The issue of 'how was it for her?' is largely irrelevant for the young men, unless they are actively subverting 'normal' masculinity. Their inexperience as adult males is rectified by the act of intercourse, and this in itself constitutes pleasure.

> 'I mean it's the old saying, "you enter the bed a boy and you leave it a man" or words to that effect. I felt the same, I didn't alter physically, but I felt different after that first time. I did definitely feel different.'

(19 year old)

Feeling different is not seen primarily as a private pleasure, but more significantly as having publicly crossed a threshold, making their partner's experience less salient than their own transition to manhood that can be told to others. First sex experiences are also performances in a peer group, events that can be made meaningful by talking about them, thereby bringing them into the public realm and allowing the values of the male peer group into the private and the intimate. In young men's 'performance stories', and their impact on sexual reputations, heterosexuality is reproduced and social meanings are attributed in ways that are difficult to escape. This is particularly marked in the case of young men who become sexually active as young teenagers. One who first had intercourse when he was just fifteen commented:

> 'Like the first time I was like saying, "Oh, God, Yes! Now I've got something to chat about. Yes! Yes!"... I was saying to myself, "now I am a man, I'm a man", sort of thing.'

(16 year old)

(Holland *et al.*, 1998, pp. 179–81)

Here the exclamation 'I am a man!', is about *feeling* adult. While this sixteen-year-old's exclamation does not have the ritual social significance of the Xhosa initiate's similar cry at the point of circumcision, his feelings about the significance of his first experience of heterosexual intercourse also reflect how masculinity and manhood are talked about and socially marked among his peers and in the local community more generally.

Homosexuality

For many years developmental psychological theories (and Western culture more generally) have constructed 'heterosexuality' as the norm and ideal, and homosexuality as deviant. Chris Griffin (1993, p.171) notes that 'the impact of pressures to become heterosexual on young women (and men) have been recognized in some of the feminist youth literature'. Gill Dunne (1997) found that a third of the 60 adult lesbian women she interviewed felt that the process of questioning or reinterpreting their sexuality had extended back into their adolescence. Dunne suggests that women who were not fully convinced that heterosexuality was right for them realized when they were teenagers that the conventional heterosexual route to adulthood, that is, marriage and dependence on their husband's wage, was not an option for them. They tended to be more focused on finding a job that would give them financial independence.

More recently, there has been a growing body of research and literature looking at the experience of gay and lesbian young people and the issues for them around moving into adulthood. The literature includes autobiographical reflections by adults about coming out in their teens, and accounts of self help and mutual support among gay and lesbian young people themselves (Epstein, 1994; Plummer, 1995; Trenchard and Warren, 1984; Watney, 1991). Prendergast, Dunne and Telford (2002) report that two contrasting groups of young gay people in the UK, those who are homeless and those in higher education, had both experienced certain levels of exclusion and hardship because of their sexuality. For example, many of the homeless young people they interviewed felt that their sexuality had been a precipitating or major factor in their homeless crisis. Parental responses for both groups varied from acceptance and support in a few cases to a longer term process of negotiated acceptance, often fraught with conflict, for others. Some young gay people experienced parental rejection and the removal of support. To give one example:

> Alec, aged 22, [when interviewed, described how he] first realised he was gay at secondary school – a rough school where he had been bullied – 'for being posh and for being queer'. He realised his sexuality was a potential source of trouble – to be kept secret – worked hard at school, and did incredibly well in his GCSEs – all A's. During the lower sixth he felt more confident, came out to close friends, explored the gay scene and began his first steady relationship. Just before his A levels, he had a row with his mother and [told her he was gay] ... She was very upset and aggressive, constantly shouting, calling him names like poof and queer. It was horrible and he couldn't concentrate on schoolwork. Although Alec had a university place to read English, she refused to support him, saying she wouldn't give him money to go and would disown him. His dad remained silent.

> Unable to stand the strain, Alec left home, took a supermarket job, and lived in a shared house with his boyfriend. He sat his A levels but had to give up his university place. The two young men have been together ever since. Realising he needed a degree to get on, Alec became increasingly motivated to go to university. Using money that he has saved over the years and a student loan, he is studying accountancy. He continues to have a very difficult relationship with his parents.

> (Prendergast *et al.*, 2002)

Prendergast *et al.* argue that the wider policy changes towards extended dependency (described in Section 2 above) have adversely affected both groups. For instance, the loss of family financial support was a serious threat at a time when students in England and Wales were no longer entitled to grants and fees. While popular culture may have encouraged greater acceptance of diverse sexual identities, it also seems to have provided powerful weapons for others to police these. For example, homophobic bullying in schools may actually be more widespread than it was a decade ago. For the young people in this study, the labels of lesbian and gay were 'both tantalising and horrifying ... most struggled with their suspicions in silent turmoil. Thus, for almost all of the young people in our study, the social frameworks of understanding available to them at a key time of sexual exploration both facilitated gay identification and at the same time signified that it could only be a source of trouble, exclusion and possible danger' (Prendergast *et al.*, 2002). However, on the positive side, this research suggests that young people like Alec also found innovative and imaginative ways of overcoming obstacles.

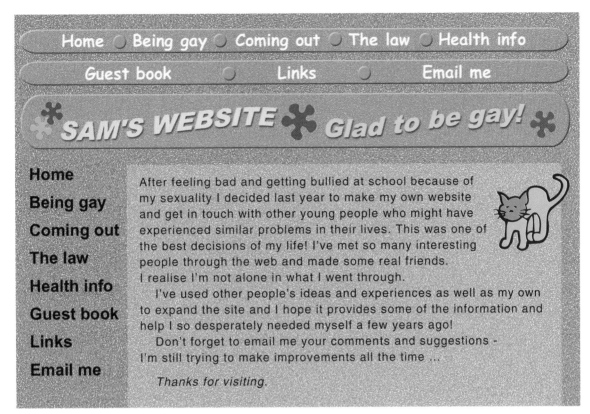

For some young gay people, the web provides ways of making contact with others, gaining confidence, and giving and receiving support.

SUMMARY OF SECTION 5

- The physical changes at puberty are dealt with very differently across different cultures, affecting how they become socially meaningful for the young people involved.

- The transition to adulthood may also involve starting sexual relationships. What this means, and how it is perceived both by individual young people and wider society, differs across cultures.

- The significance of sexuality for young people's identity and their experience of becoming adult is also influenced by prevailing and changing social conditions and cultural values.

6 CONCLUSION

To bring us back full circle to where I began with this chapter, the processes through which the transition to adulthood takes place vary widely. In many affluent societies, puberty is not the marker of anything in particular, in terms of formal culturally marked transitions, though some of the physical processes, for example menstruation, may make young women 'feel' more adult, in a subjective sense. Young men may have sex for the first time in their mid teens, which again, may make them feel more adult. This doesn't mean that they are seen as adults. I've also explored how adulthood in affluent societies is linked with economic independence and particularly involvement in work, and is not necessarily linked to being married or being a parent.

You saw, in the examples from Tanzania and South Africa, that full womanhood and manhood depend on a slightly different range of factors, such as passing through an initiation rite, economic independence and becoming a parent. As the Tanzanian researchers point out, differences between Tanzanian (Swahili) and English conceptualizations of 'child':

> ... complicate the idea of 'puberty', which is often treated in the biological sciences as if it were clearly defined and fixed. In the social sciences, on the other hand, puberty is regarded as a category of shifting meanings, which is not particularly useful for defining the act of sexual maturity, despite almost universal acknowledgement of the physical changes it brings. In the Tanzanian case ... it is *reproductive* (rather than chronological) age that is the crux of the progress from childhood to youth.
>
> (Ahmed *et al.*, 1999, p. 102).

Allow about 30 minutes

ACTIVITY 5 Your personal view

Think back again to your own transitions to adulthood. Note your feelings about the following:

1 In what ways did your own transitions to adulthood echo, or contrast with, the experiences discussed in this chapter?
2 To what extent were your own experiences shaped by factors like ethnicity, class and gender?
3 How far do you feel that you became a 'free' autonomous agent?
4 In what ways were your experiences of becoming adult different from those of your parents' generation?

In summary, how young people are perceived and dealt with, and how the transition to adulthood takes place depend upon cultural and historical context. A wide range of factors has an impact on how the end of childhood is experienced. Some of the ones touched upon in this chapter include gender, social class, ethnic background, religion, dis/ability, sexuality and geographical location. I have also explored the idea that in many industrialized countries, the division between adult and child is not clear cut: the categories child and adult are not least a way of organizing our thought processes, though this has very real consequences. In a manner of speaking, these are merely ideal types, and there are often instances where the ideal type of 'independent' adult versus 'dependent' child doesn't fit the reality of people's lives, and in practice people (older children, young people, adults) may become interdependent as they move through the life course. Family members remain an important source of emotional support for young people, and relationships may become reciprocal. Rites of passage are used to mark the transition to adulthood in many cultures, but these are dynamic and are likely to change according to the socio-cultural environment in which they take place. In many industrialized countries, the transition to adulthood is similarly dynamic and subject to change.

REFERENCES

Abrams, M. (1959) *The Teenage Consumer*, London, London Press Exchange.

Afshar, H. (1995) 'Muslim women in West Yorkshire: growing up with real and imaginary values amidst conflicting views of self and society' in Afshar, H. and Maynard, M. (eds) *The Dynamics of 'Race' and Gender: some feminist interventions*, London, Routledge.

Ahmed, S., Bwana, J., Guga, E., Kitunga, D., Mgulambwa, A., Mtambalike, P., Mtunguja, L., Mwandayi, E., with Sumra, S. and Ennew, J. (1999) *Children in Need of Special Protection Measures: a Tanzanian study*, Dar es Salaam, Tanzania, UNICEF.

Aldridge, J. and Becker, S. (2002) 'Children who care: rights and wrongs in debate and policy on young carers' in Franklin, B. (ed.) (2002) *The New Handbook of Children's Rights*, London, Routledge.

Allatt, P. and Yeandle, S. (1986) 'It's not fair, is it?: youth unemployment, family relations and the social contract' in Allen S., Waton A., Purcell K. and Wood S. (eds) (1986) *The Experience of Unemployment*, Basingstoke, Macmillan.

Bates, I. (1993) 'A job which is 'Right for me'?: social class, gender and individualization' in Bates, I. and Riseborough, G. (1993), *Youth and Inequality*, Milton Keynes, Open University Press.

Beck, U. (1992) *The Risk Society: towards a new modernity*, London, Sage.

Beck, U. (1997) 'Democratisation of the family' *Childhood*, **4**(2), pp. 151–168.

Becker, S. (2000) 'Young carers speak out', press release for *Young Carers in Their Own Words*, (eds) Bibby A. and Becker S., London, Turnaround Publisher Services.

Carroll, H. and Rumbelow, H. (2001) 'When your baby has a child', *The Times*, 14 May.

Council of Europe (1996) *Ages at which Children are Legally Entitled to Carry Out a Series of Acts in Council of Europe Member Countries (Document CDPS 111.8 Obs (96) 1)*, Strasbourg, Council of Europe.

Delamont, S. (2000) *The Anomalous Beasts: hooligans and the sociology of education*, Sociology, **34**(1), pp. 95–111.

Dunne, G. A. (1997) *Lesbian Lifestyles: women's work and the politics of sexuality*, Toronto, University of Toronto Press.

Epstein, D. (ed.) (1994) *Challenging Gay and Lesbian Inequalities in Education*, Buckingham, Open University Press.

Erikson, E. (1968) *Identity: youth and crisis*, New York, Norton.

Furlong, A. and Cartmel, F. (1997) *Young People and Social Change: individualization and risk in late modernity*, Buckingham, Open University Press.

Gennep, van, A. (1909) *Les Rites de Passages*, Paris, Libraire Critique Emile Nourry.

Gillies, V., Ribbens McCarthy, J. and Holland, J. (2001) *Pulling Together, Pulling Apart: the family lives of young people*, London, Joseph Rowntree Foundation/Family Policy Studies Centre.

Griffin, C. (1985) *Typical Girls? Young women from school to the job market*, London, Routledge & Kegan Paul.

Griffin, C. (1993) *Representations of Youth: the study of youth and adolescence in Britain and America*, Cambridge, Polity.

Hall, T. and Montgomery, H. (2000) 'Home and away: "childhood", "youth" and "young people"', *Anthropology Today*, **16**(3), pp. 13–15.

Hockey, J. and James, A. (1993) *Growing Up and Growing Old: ageing and dependency in the life course*, London, Sage Publications.

Holland, J., Ramazanoglu, C., Sharpe, S. and Thomson, R. (1998) *The Male in the Head: young people, heterosexuality and power*, London, The Tufnell Press.

Johnson, A., Wadsworth, J., Wellings, R., Field, J. and Bradshaw, S. (1994) *Sexual Attitudes and Life Styles*, London, Blackwell Scientific Publications.

Jones, G. and Wallace, C., (1992) *Youth, Family and Citizenship*, Milton Keynes, Open University Press.

McDowell, L. (2000) 'Learning to serve? Employment aspirations and attitudes of young working-class men in an era of labour market restructuring', *Gender, Place and Culture*, **7**(4), pp. 389–416.

Mirza, H. (1992) *Young, Female and Black*, London, Routledge.

Morrow, V. (1996) 'Rethinking childhood dependency: children's contributions to the domestic economy', *The Sociological Review*, **44**(1), pp. 58–77.

Morrow, V. and Richards, M. (1996) *Transitions to Adulthood: a family matter?* York, Joseph Rowntree Foundation/York Publishing Services.

Phoenix, A. (1991) *Young Mothers,* Cambridge, Polity Press.

Plummer, K. (1995) *Telling Sexual Stories: power, change and social worlds*, London, Routledge.

Prendergast, S., Dunne, G. A. and Telford, D. (2002) 'A light at the end of the tunnel? Experiences of leaving home for contrasting groups of young lesbian, gay and bisexual people', *Youth and Policy*, **75**, pp. 42–61.

Punch, S. (2002) 'Youth transitions and interdependent adult–child relations in rural Bolivia', *Journal of Rural Studies*, **18**, pp. 123–133.

Riddell, S. (1998) 'The dynamic of transition to adulthood' in Robinson, C. and Stalker, K. (eds) *Growing Up with Disability*, London, Jessica Kingsley.

Trenchard, L. and Warren, H. (1984) *Something to Tell You: the experiences of young lesbians and gay men in London*, London, Gay Teenage Group.

Van Gennep (1909) – see Gennep, van, A.

Watney, S. (1991) 'Ordinary boys' in Spence, J. and Holland, P. (eds) *Family Snaps; the meanings of domestic photography*, London, Virago.

Willis, P. (1977) *Learning to Labour: how working class kids get working class jobs*, London, Saxon House.

Woodhead, M. (2003) 'The child in development' in Woodhead, M. and Montgomery, H. K. (eds) (2003) *Understanding Childhood: an interdisciplinary approach*, Chichester, John Wiley and Sons Ltd/ The Open University (Book 1 of the Open University course U212 *Childhood*).

READING A

Becoming a man

Nelson Mandela

When I was sixteen, the regent decided that it was time that I became a man. In Xhosa tradition, this is achieved through one means only: circumcision. In my tradition, an uncircumcised male cannot be heir to his father's wealth, cannot marry or officiate in tribal rituals. An uncircumcised Xhosa man is a contradiction in terms, for he is not considered a man at all, but a boy. For the Xhosa people, circumcision represents the formal incorporation of males into society. It is not just a surgical procedure, but a lengthy and elaborate ritual in preparation for manhood. As a Xhosa, I count my years as a man from the date of my circumcision.

The traditional ceremony of the circumcision school was arranged principally for Justice. The rest of us, twenty-six in all, were there mainly to keep him company. Early in the new year, we journeyed to two grass huts in a secluded valley on the banks of the Mbashe River, known as Tyhalarha, the traditional place of circumcision for Thembu kings. The huts were seclusion lodges, where we were to live isolated from society. It was a sacred time; I felt happy and fulfilled taking part in my people's customs and ready to make the transition from boyhood to manhood.

We had moved to Tyhalarha by the river a few days before the actual circumcision ceremony. These last few days of boyhood were spent with the other initiates, and I found the camaraderie enjoyable. The lodge was near the home of Banabakhe Blayi, the wealthiest and most popular boy at the circumcision school. He was an engaging fellow, a champion stick-fighter and a glamour boy, whose many girlfriends kept us all supplied with delicacies. Although he could neither read nor write, he was one of the most intelligent among us. He regaled us with stories of his trips to Johannesburg, a place that none of us had ever been to. He so thrilled us with tales of the mines that he almost persuaded me that to be a miner was more alluring than to be a monarch. Miners had a mystique; to be a miner meant to be strong and daring: the ideal of manhood. Much later, I realized that it was the exaggerated tales of boys like Banabakhe that caused so many young men to run away to work in the mines of Johannesburg, where they often lost their health and their lives. In those days, working in the mines was almost as much of a rite of passage as circumcision school, a myth that helped the mine-owners more than it helped my people.

A custom of circumcision school is that one must perform a daring exploit before the ceremony. In days of old, this might have involved a cattle raid or even a battle, but in our time the deeds were more mischievous than martial. Two nights before we moved to Tyhalarha, we decided to steal a pig. In Mkhekezweni, there was a tribesman with a typical old pig. To avoid making a noise and alarming the farmer, we arranged for the pig to do our work for us. We took handfuls of sediment from home-made African beer, which has a strong scent much favoured by pigs, and placed it upwind of the animal. It was so aroused by the scent that he came out of the kraal, following a trail we had laid and gradually made his way to us, wheezing and snorting, and eating the sediment.

When he got near us, we captured the poor pig, slaughtered it, and then built a fire and ate roast pork underneath the stars. No piece of pork has ever tasted as good before or since.

The night before the circumcision, there was a ceremony near our huts with singing and dancing. Women came from the nearby villages and we danced to their singing and clapping. As the music became faster and louder, our dance turned more frenzied and we forgot for a moment what lay ahead.

At dawn, when the stars were still in the sky, we began our preparations. We were escorted to the river to bathe in its cold waters, a ritual that signified our purification before the ceremony. The ceremony was at midday, and we were commanded to stand in a row in a clearing some distance from the river where a crowd of parents and relatives, including the regent, as well as a handful of chiefs and counsellors, had gathered. We were clad only in our blankets and as the ceremony began, with drums pounding, we were ordered to sit on a blanket on the ground with our legs spread out in front of us. I was tense and anxious, uncertain of how I would react when the critical moment came. Flinching or crying out was a sign of weakness and stigmatized one's manhood. I was determined not to disgrace myself, the group or my guardian. Circumcision is a trial of bravery and stoicism; no anaesthetic is used; a man must suffer in silence.

To the right, out of the corner of my eye, I could see a thin, elderly man emerge from a tent and kneel in front of the first boy. There was excitement in the crowd, and I shuddered slightly, knowing that the ritual was about to begin. The old man was a famous *ingcibi*, a circumcision expert, from Gcalekaland, who would use his assegai to change us from boys to men with a single blow.

Suddenly I heard the first boy cry out '*Ndiyindoda!*' ('I am a man!'), which we had been trained to say at the moment of circumcision. Seconds later, I heard Justice's strangled voice pronounce the same phrase. There were now two boys before the *ingcibi* reached me, and my mind must have gone blank because, before I knew it, the old man was kneeling in front of me. I looked directly into his eyes. He was pale, and though the day was cold, his face was shining with perspiration. His hands moved so fast they seemed to be controlled by an otherwordly force. Without a word, he took my foreskin, pulled it forward, and then, in a single motion, brought down his assegai. I felt as if fire was shooting through my veins; the pain was so intense that I buried my chin in my chest. Many seconds seemed to pass before I remembered the cry, and then I recovered and called out, '*Ndiyindoda!*'

I looked down and saw a perfect cut, clean and round like a ring. But I felt ashamed because the other boys seemed much stronger and firmer than I had been; they had called out more promptly than I had. I was distressed that I had been disabled, however briefly, by the pain, and I did my best to hide my agony. A boy may cry; a man conceals his pain.

I had now taken the essential step in the life of every Xhosa man. Now I might marry, set up my own home and plough my own field. I could now be admitted to the councils of the community; my words would be taken seriously. At the ceremony, I was given my circumcision name, Dalibhunga, meaning 'Founder of the Bungha', the traditional ruling body of the Transkei. To Xhosa traditionalists, this name is more acceptable than either of my two previous given names, Rolihlahla or Nelson, and I was proud to hear my new name pronounced: Dalibhunga.

Immediately after the blow had been delivered, an assistant who followed the circumcision master took the foreskin that was on the ground and tied it to a corner of our blankets. Our wounds were then dressed with a healing plant, the leaves of which were thorny on the outside but smooth on the inside, which absorbed the blood and other secretions.

At the conclusion of the ceremony, we returned to our huts, where a fire was burning with wet wood that cast off clouds of smoke, which was thought to promote healing. We were ordered to lie on our backs in the smoky huts, with one leg flat, and one leg bent. We were now *abakwetha*, initiates into the world of manhood. We were looked after by an *amakhankatha*, or guardian, who explained the rules we had to follow if we were to enter manhood properly. The first chore of the *amakhankatha* was to paint our naked and shaved bodies from head to foot in white ochre, turning us into ghosts. The white chalk symbolized our purity, and I still recall how stiff the dried clay felt on my body.

That first night, at midnight, an attendant, or *ikhankatha*, crept around the hut, gently waking each of us. We were then instructed to leave the hut and go tramping through the night to bury our foreskins. The traditional reason for this practice was so that our foreskins would be hidden before wizards could use them for evil purposes, but, symbolically, we were also burying our youth. I did not want to leave the warm hut and wander through the bush in the darkness, but I walked into the trees and, after a few minutes, untied my foreskin and buried it in the earth. I felt as though I had now discarded the last remnant of my childhood.

We lived in our two huts - thirteen in each - while our wounds healed. When outside the huts, we were covered in blankets, for we were not allowed to be seen by women. It was a period of quietude, a kind of spiritual preparation for the trials of manhood that lay ahead. On the day of our re-emergence, we went down to the river early in the morning to wash away the white ochre in the waters of the Mbashe. Once we were clean and dry, we were coated in red ochre. The tradition was that one should sleep with a woman, who later might become one's wife, and she rubs off the pigment with her body. In my case, however, the ochre was removed with a mixture of fat and lard.

At the end of our seclusion, the lodges and all their contents were burned, destroying our last links to childhood, and a great ceremony was held to welcome us as men to society. Our families, friends and local chiefs gathered for speeches, songs and gift-giving. I was given two heifers and four sheep, and felt far richer than I ever had before. I, who had never owned anything, suddenly possessed property. It was a heady feeling, even though my gifts were paltry next to those of Justice, who inherited an entire herd. I was not jealous of Justice's gifts. He was the son of a king; I was merely destined to be a counsellor to a king. I felt strong and proud that day. I remember walking differently on that day, straighter, taller, firmer. I was hopeful, and thinking that I might some day have wealth, property and status.

The main speaker of the day was Chief Meligqili, the son of Dalindyebo, and after listening to him, my gaily coloured dreams suddenly darkened.

He began conventionally, remarking how fine it was that we were
continuing a tradition that had been going on for as long as anyone could
remember. Then he turned to us and his tone suddenly changed. 'There sit
our sons,' he said, 'young, healthy and handsome, the flower of the Xhosa
tribe, the pride of our nation. We have just circumcised them in a ritual that
promises them manhood, but I am here to tell you that it is an empty,
illusory promise, a promise that can never be fulfilled. For we Xhosas, and
all black South Africans, are a conquered people. We are slaves in our own
country. We are tenants on our own soil. We have no strength, no power,
no control over our own destiny in the land of our birth. They will go to
cities where they will live in shacks and drink cheap alcohol, all because
we have no land to give them where they could prosper and multiply.
They will cough their lungs out deep in the bowels of the white man's
mines, destroying their health, never seeing the sun, so that the white man
can live a life of unequalled prosperity. Among these young men are chiefs
who will never rule because we have no power to govern ourselves;
soldiers who will never fight for we have no weapons to fight with;
scholars who will never teach because we have no place for them to study.
The abilities, the intelligence, the promise of these young men will be
squandered in their attempt to eke out a living doing the simplest, most
mindless chores for the white man. These gifts today are naught, for we
cannot give them the greatest gift of all, which is freedom and
independence. I know well that Qamata [God] is all-seeing and never
sleeps, but I have a suspicion that Qamata may in fact be dozing. If this is
the case, the sooner I die the better, because then I can meet him and
shake him awake and tell him that the children of Ngubengcuka, the
flower of the Xhosa nation, are dying.'

The audience had become more and more quiet as Chief Meligqili
spoke and, I think, more and more angry. No one wanted to hear the
words that he spoke that day. I know that I myself did not want to hear
them. I was cross rather than aroused by the chief's remarks, dismissing his
words as the abusive comments of an ignorant man who was unable to
appreciate the value of the education and benefits that the white man had
brought to our country. At the time, I looked on the white man not as an
oppressor but as a benefactor, and I thought the chief was enormously
ungrateful. This upstart chief was ruining my day, spoiling the proud
feeling with wrong-headed remarks.

But without exactly understanding why, his words soon began to work
on me. He had sown a seed, and though I let that seed lie dormant for a
long season, it eventually began to grow. Later I realized that the ignorant
man that day was not the chief but myself.

After the ceremony, I walked back to the river and watched it meander
on its way to where, many miles distant, it emptied into the Indian Ocean. I
had never crossed that river, and I knew little or nothing of the world
beyond it, a world that beckoned me that day. It was almost sunset and I
hurried on to where our seclusion lodges had been. Though it was
forbidden to look back while the lodges were burning, I could not resist.
When I reached the area, all that remained were two pyramids of ashes by
a large mimosa tree. In these ashes lay a lost and delightful world, the
world of my childhood, the world of sweet and irresponsible days at Qunu
and Mqhekezweni. Now I was a man, and I would never again play *thinti*,

or steal maize, or drink milk from a cow's udder. I was already in mourning for my own youth. Looking back, I know that I was not a man that day and would not truly become one for many years.

Source

Mandela, N. (1994) Long Walk to Freedom, *London, Little, Brown and Company.*

READING B

Waiwai menstruation huts, Amazonia

Niels Fock

As soon as the first menstruation takes place, the young girl informs her mother or the female head of her eta. The girl is at once told to sit down without anything in her hands and without touching anything. She is given an old mat or in some cases a kind of woven hood or cap ... specially made for the purpose, which she must hold over her head at all times and thus not be able to look up towards the sky. All this is done in order that she may not infect her surroundings by her weakness. The mother will at once ... cut off all the girl's hair ... and remove all ornaments, leaving her only her apron. This is done so that she may not in the future become lazy, for the seat of laziness is in the hair and the ornaments. In the meantime the father of the girl starts building the initiation hut, wayapa ... The wayapa can be a screened-off enclosure in the communal house itself, but most often ... it is an individual hut, which differs from others in that it possesses no door ...

As soon as the hut is finished the girl enters it by pushing aside the leaves. Seclusion lasts, as a rule, for about two months ... During her long stay in solitude the girl's main occupation is the spinning of cotton brought to her by her mother. She must leave the hut only for necessary errands to the woods. In such cases she must take great care to have the old mat or hood over her head, as it is believed that the sky will fall down and crush houses, trees and everything should she look up at it ... Here the idea presumably is ... that the girl's weakness infects her surroundings. If the girl manages to see only a small part of the sky, the result may be only a heavy shower of rain ...

Even though an adolescent girl may see people, she will never talk to, much less answer, them. Only if it is imperative will she announce herself in a whisper. Only the father and mother (or their possible deputies) can enter her hut, but even they will limit themselves to saying: 'Here is your food' or something of that kind, whilst the girl merely mumbles 'mh' in reply ... She ... has her hammock for the night, but as opposed to later menstruations, uses no menstruation mat by day. On the other hand she must sit on an old piece of light, white tree trunk. The blood must sink into the ground, as it is thought she will develop dark skin on her posterior if she uses the menstruation mat during the first menstruation. If she sits on a piece of heavy hard wood during her seclusion, it is feared that her reactions will be too slow when later asked to perform a service ...

[...]

When the girl has passed the prescribed two months (approximately) in the wayapa, the mother comes to the hut one day with a long bow. She sticks the bow through the side of the hut and says to the girl: 'Hold on'. The girl does not reply but seizes the bow and by it is pulled out of the hut. This is done so that 'she should not rot before she dies', or in other words, so that she will become very old and will stay strong to the last ... The custom of drawing out by the bow, which marks a violent change in status and in the form of existence, can be regarded as a 'rite de passage'.

When the girl has come out, the mother gives her a little gourd which she must [at] once push up between her legs in order for the cervix uteri not to sink and become visible ... The mother then places an ant belt on various parts of the girl's body, which is to stop her being lazy in the future. Finally, the mother instructs her in six basic rules: 1) To refrain for some time from eating meat and drinking tapioca. 2) Never to answer angrily or pertly an elder relative when asked to perform a service. 3) If an elder relative says: 'Go and fetch water' you must answer ... 'Very well'. 4) Never to be lazy. 5) To rise up quickly when asked to perform a service. 6) Never to steal cotton or anything else from her sisters, 'for if you do they will blow magic on you and you will die'.

[...]

After this teaching the girl can again put on some of her ornaments... Most important, however, after initiation the girl obtains for the first time her ... upper arm bands of white bead strings. These are regarded as a sign of maturity for both sexes. As a rule about a month will pass before the girl has sexual relations.

[...]

For about two years around initiation (i.e. about 11–13 years of age) the adolescent girl is called emasï. The whole of this period is stamped by hard work, the older women trying continually to keep the emasï employed. It was often noticed that the emasï had to do household work even when the other members of the family were assembled for a common meal.

[...]

There is no initiation for Waiwai men corresponding to the seclusion of girls.

Source

Fock, N. (1963) Waiwai: religion and society of an Amazonian tribe, *Copenhagen, Nationalmuseets Skrifter, Etnografisk Raekke, VIII, The National Museum.*

READING C

Girls' experience of menstruation in school: some findings from the research

Shirley Prendergast

> 'I'd say periods are totally a disadvantage. It's all the trauma of getting used to it at first, the pain and embarrassment and everybody finding out. It's worse at first, but it does stay with you. It changes everything, you are limited in what you can do, you limit your actions, stops you doing things.'
>
> (5th-year student)

School offers an interesting way of exploring the role of social context in shaping the experience of puberty. It is a place where young people must spend their 15,000 hours, where, quite unlike the privacy and individuality of home, there are standardized formal rules, obligations and lessons concerning the body. Unlike home, too, where one lives with people at different stages of development, school provides a consistent public location where changes to the body are learned about, experienced and managed in the company of others of the same age. For many, school provides the only formal learning about bodily events and sexuality that they will ever have (Allen, 1987).

Over the course of a recent study about 70 girls between the ages of 13 and 15 spoke in great detail about their experiences of menarche and early menstruation, and about how they learned about it and 'managed' in the context of school (Prendergast, 1987, 1994). A number of key narratives, or story themes, were particularly marked within these interviews. They can be summarized as follows:

(1) Stories about own private, personal experiences, mostly about physiological effects, emotions and feelings.

(2) Revelation stories about accidents, mistakes – things that went publicly wrong.

(3) Stories about male gaze, about teasing and harassment.

(4) Stories about coping in school – practical facilities and school rules etc.

(5) Stories about lessons and classroom teaching.

(1) Stories about own private, personal experiences, mostly about physiological effects, emotions and feelings

> 'I had pains from my stomach downwards, really sharp pains, and I couldn't walk, and the only thing that stopped it was bending over. Then I got a headache and had to lie down. I couldn't get dressed because there was so much heavy bleeding and that.'
>
> (5th-year student)

The first set of stories accentuated both the private and the personal nature of menarche and menstruation, and a kind of fatalism, the key articulation of which was the sense of being 'taken over' by the experience. All the girls could remember exact details of the onset of their first period: where it first happened, who they were with, who they went to for help, and their feelings about it. Their accounts were dominated by a terminology of shock and accident: of being 'taken over', 'knocked out', 'a blow', being 'thrown off balance', 'clobbered', lucky or unlucky in their experience.

Later experiences of menstruation also took girls over but compared to the earlier experiences later ones were related to physical and emotional effects of the cycle. They spoke of being 'crippled' or 'dragged down' by pain, 'flaring up', 'lashing out' with irritability, uncontrollably weeping or depressed. Irregular periods and heavy bleeding were allied to images of the body as 'flooding', 'leaking', 'staining', threatening to breach some unspecified but significant boundary of self. Girls seemed to feel that there was little that they or anybody else can do to alleviate these effects, and rarely discussed them with other girls.

(2) Revelation stories about accidents, mistakes – things that went publicly wrong

> 'Oh God, I'm always thinking what if it happens to me now. And then I'm worried when I'm on, and if it's leaked. That's always a worry for me ... and if I feel I am sweating, I think, oh no, I've leaked and better go to the loo.'

> (3rd-year student)

In contrast the second set of stories were often embarrassing and sometimes funny. They were about the consequences when what girls dreaded - the breaching bodily boundaries - actually happened, when private knowledge and experience was made public. They were expressed as a series of anxieties:

- about staining clothes
- having to ask for emergency help in school
- about feeling ill in class, missing an event
- about boys discovering their 'stuff' (towels and tampons)
- about carrying supplies around in school
- doing games, taking notes, having showers, feeling ill.

Thus girls worried that if they did not carry 'stuff' (spare towels and tampons) around with them all the time, they may begin their period unexpectedly and have no way of coping. They worried that the male games teacher would disbelieve a letter from home and ask personal questions. They worried that boys would turn out their school bags, looking for stuff, and throw them around the classroom. They worried that unless they constantly changed towels or tampons they would stain their clothes.

These were not unreasonable things to worry about, indeed they happened all the time. However, unlike the first set of stories, where the body took over and there was little that girls could do to mediate or relieve the effects, these were incidents which might, with extreme watchfulness, monitoring and advance planning, be avoided. They relate to the practical day-to-day management of menstruation, particularly in keeping knowledge of it away from boys. Constant surveillance on many fronts was necessary to manage menstruation with proper discreetness - in essence total invisibility - in school, and girls blamed themselves if they failed.

(3) Stories about male gaze, about teasing and harassment

'At my last school there was a girl, and the boys found things and tampax in her bag, and they were chucking it round the classroom and kicking it down the corridor. And she was just crying and really they didn't care, they don't really feel or anything.'

(3rd-year student)

The third set of stories concerned boys, and reached a peak in the second and third years of secondary school. Certain groups of boys appeared to delight in using their often new-found knowledge of menstruation to tease and torment girls. In all the mixed schools this had been the case. They watched to see if a girl took her bag to the toilet or missed games. They went into girls' toilets and wrote things on the walls, called girls names, pretended that they had stained their skirts in lessons. Boys turned out girls' school bags, hung towels and tampons around the playground, and threw them in the classroom.

There was a great deal of group hostility from boys, often combined with physical harassment, in which girls were touched, pushed and squeezed. Girls were furious about such things, but rarely if ever spoke to a teacher. They responded with as much dignity as they could muster. In practice this often meant avoiding boys, never letting go of their school bags, wearing special clothes on certain days.

(4) Stories about coping in school – practical facilities and school rules etc.

'Oh God, the toilets! They are awful! Sometimes when I am dying to go, I would sooner wait until I can go home because they are so disgusting, they really are. There's no machines to get towels out of, the toilet paper is really hard. Nobody pulls the chain and there are towels on the floor.'

(5th-year student)

The fourth set of stories concerned the ways in which school facilities, school rules and procedures influenced the ways in which girls were enabled to practically cope and adequately care for themselves in school. One true story: Amy described how the teacher would not let her leave the classroom to use the toilets. Amy bled heavily each period. By the end of the lesson the blood had soaked through her skirt on to the chair, and she was terrified of getting up to leave. She burst into tears and inevitably other pupils noticed. The boys called her Bloody Mary, a name that had stuck for the 18 months that had elapsed before she was interviewed in school.

In these stories girls described the sometimes almost total lack of practical provision in schools necessary to deal with menstruation in a civilized and dignified fashion. For example, whole toilet blocks were often locked during lesson time. It could be hard to get permission to go to the toilet, often involving a lengthy and humiliating search for a teacher with a key. Even the most basic facilities such as soap and toilet paper were not reliably available, disposal bins, paper towels or hand dryers and locks on doors were variable, while vending machines for emergency supplies totally unavailable. Girls described waiting to use lavatories out of school at dinner time, having to change while they blocked the lavatory door closed with one foot, taking away used towels wrapped in paper to dispose of elsewhere, and the disgust they felt at not being able to keep clean or wash their hands.

(5) Stories about lessons and classroom teaching

'And all the boys and girls were together in the first year, and the boys just started laughing whenever we said something [about menstruation] so we laughed back. We didn't really learn anything. We had heard something at primary school, but the boys didn't know anything.'

(5th-year student)

The final set of stories concerned teaching in the formal curriculum. Girls described the ways in which sex education lessons were dominated by boys' behaviour and responses. For example, ... they spoke of boys' laughter and crude comments about women's bodies as they watched many of the videos and films. This was exacerbated because much of the official content of sex education focuses on reproduction rather than sexuality, and therefore is dominated by references to and images of women's reproductive cycle. While the biology of reproduction must refer to the erect penis, and therefore to some notion of male desire and pleasure, there may be little to suggest an active, positive female sexuality. The onset of maturity for boys is marked, it seems, with wet dreams: for girls it is menstruation.

In summary we can say that the average girl who wished successfully to manage menstruation in school must keep a number of issues in mind when she has her period:

- She must know in advance that her period is likely to start that day and be prepared with appropriate supplies (towels, tampons, tissue, painkillers, etc.).

- She must keep these in a safe place so that they are both readily accessible but not likely to be found deliberately or accidentally by boys.

- She must judge the appropriate time to change in order that blood does not leak on to her clothes, and co-ordinate this with lesson breaks, and find a toilet that has the facilities (disposal bin, lock, lavatory paper, soap, hand towels etc.) that she needs.

- She must assess how she is likely to feel in the day, and be appropriately prepared for headache or period pain, for example. She must try to stay alert in lessons, and manage feeling sleepy, irritable or unwell so that other people do not notice.

- She must have considered the day's lessons, and brought a note from home if she wishes to be excused from any of them.

It is against this framework that schools promote the idea of menstruation as a perfectly 'normal and natural thing'.

References

Allen, I. (1987) *Education in Sex and Personal Relationships.* Policy Studies Institute Research Report No. 655. Dorset: Blackmore Press.

Prendergast, S. (1987) Girls' experience of menstruation in school. In L. Holly (ed.) *Girls and Sexuality, Teaching and Learning.* Milton Keynes: Open University Press.

Prendergast, S. (1994) *This is the Time to Grow Up. Girls' experience of Menstruation in School.* London: FPA.

Source

Prendergast, S. (1995) '"With Gender on my mind": menstruation and embodiment at adolescence' in Holland, J. and Blair, M. with Sheldon, S. (eds) *Debates and Issues in Feminist Research and Pedagogy,* Clevedon, Multilingual Matters/The Open University.

ACKNOWLEDGEMENTS

Grateful acknowledgement is made to the following sources for permission to reproduce material in this book.

Chapter 1

Text

Reading A: Murphy, Y. and Murphy, R. F. (1974) *Women of the Forest*, copyright © Columbia University Press, reprinted with the permission of the publisher; *Reading B:* extract from *Out of Place: a memoir* by Edward W. Said, copyright © 1999 by Edward W. Said, used by permission of Alfred A. Knopf, a division of Random House, Inc.

Tables

Table 1: Schaffer, H. R. (1996) *Social Development*, Blackwell Publishers Ltd. Copyright © H. Rudolph Schaffer 1996.

Photographs

p. 4 (bottom): Martin Woodhead; *p. 5 (centre):* Rachel Burr; *p. 9:* courtesy of Yolande Murphy; *p. 13:* Denise Hager/Bubbles; *p. 18 (top):* Professor Jean Briggs, Memorial University of Newfoundland; *p. 18 (bottom):* Jennie Woodcock/Bubbles; *p. 23, p. 24 (top and bottom):* Dr Samantha Punch.

Chapter 2

Text

Reading A: Stacey, J. (1996) 'Virtual social science and the politics of family values in the United States', *In the Name of the Family: rethinking family values in a postmodern age*, Beacon Press; Reading B: Rivière, P. (1985) 'Unscrambling parenthood: the Warnock Report', *Anthropology Today*, **1**(4), August 1985, Royal Anthropological Institute of Great Britain and Ireland; *Reading C:* from *All Our Kin* by Carol Stack, copyright © 1983 by Carol Stack, reprinted by permission of Basic Books, a member of Perseus Books, L.L.C.

Photographs

p.39: Martin Woodhead; *p. 41:* copyright © Popperfoto; *p. 44 (top, bottom left, bottom right):* copyright © Pitt Rivers Museum, University of Oxford; *p. 45:* copyright © Matthias Breiter/Oxford Scientific Films Ltd; *p. 51 (top left):* Gloria Upchurch; *(centre):* Christopher Walker; *(bottom):* Martin Woodhead; *p. 59:* copyright © Government Printing Office/State Library of New South Wales; *p. 61:* Christopher Walker; *p. 64 (top):* copyright © The Children's Society; *p. 64 (bottom):* copyright © The Children's Society/Ed Freeman; *p. 65:* courtesy of John Bowlby.

Chapter 3

Text

Reading A: Schrumpf, E. (1997) 'From full-time to part-time: working children in Norway from the nineteenth to the twentieth century', in de Coninck-Smith, N., Sandin, B. and Schrumpf, E. (eds) *Industrious Children: work and childhood in the Nordic countries 1850–1990*, Odense University Press, copyright © Ellen Schrumpf and Odense University Press 1997; *Reading B:* pp. 64–72 and 239–241 from Pricing the Priceless Child: the changing social value of children by Viviana A. Zelizer, copyright © 1985 by Basic Books, Inc., reprinted by permission of Basic Books, a member of Perseus Books, L.L.C.; *Reading C:* Gardner, P. (1991) ' "Our schools", "their schools". The case of Eliza Duckworth and John Stevenson', *History of Education*, **20**(3), September 1991, Taylor and Francis Ltd.

Photographs

p. 81: Hilton Archive; *p. 83, p. 85 (bottom):* from *Child Labour in Historical Perspective – 1800–1985: case studies from Europe, Japan and Columbia*, edited by Hugh Cunningham and Pier Paolo Viazzo, copyright © UNICEF 1996; *p. 85 (top):* copyright © High Wycombe Reference and Business Library; *p. 87:* copyright © Oldham Local Studies and Archives; *p. 88:* copyright © Mary Evans Picture Library; *p. 93:* O. Vaering Eftf. AS, Eilert Sundts gate 32, Oslo, Norway; *pp. 96 and 98:* copyright © Mary Evans Picture Library; *p. 99:* copyright © Liverpool Record Office, Liverpool Libraries; *p. 100:* courtesy of Bolton Libraries; *pp. 104 and 107:* copyright © Hulton Archive; *p. 106:* copyright © Popperfoto/CPL; *p. 108:* copyright © The Guide Association.

Chapter 4

Photographs

p. 132 (top): Rex Features Ltd; *p. 132 (middle):* Shout Pictures; *p. 132 (bottom), p. 133 (top):* Still Pictures; *p. 133 (top middle):* John Walmsley Photography; *p. 133 (bottom middle):* Link Picture Library; *p. 133 (bottom):* Topham Picturepoint; *p. 151:* Sally and Richard Greenhill; *p. 160 (top and bottom):* Hulton Getty Picture Library.

Chapter 5

Text

Reading A: Woodhead, M. (1999) 'Combatting child labour – listen to what the children say', *Childhood*, **6**(1), Sage Publications Ltd.

Photographs

p.173: Martin Woodhead; *p. 178:* Giacomo Pirozzi/Panos Pictures; *p. 179 (top):* Jim Holmes/Panos Pictures; *p. 179 (middle):* Copyright © Steps Towards Development; *p. 179 (bottom):* Richard A. Brooks/Pink Picture Library; *p. 180:* Shout Pictures; *p.184 (all):* Copyright © Steps Towards Development; *p. 186 (top):* Mark Edwards/Still Pictures; *p. 186 (bottom):* Ron Giling/Still Pictures; *p. 191:* Jorgen Schytte/Still Pictures; *p. 199:* Kim Naylor/Link Picture Library; *p. 200:* Jeremy Horner/Panos Pictures; *p. 206:* Martin Woodhead.

Chapter 6

Photographs/illustrations

p. 224 (top and bottom): Lēwisham Local Studies Centre; *p. 226 (top):* Illustrated London News; *p. 226 (bottom):* Education Photos; *p. 231 (top and bottom):* Martin Woodhead; *p. 232:* copyright © Perssdram Ltd 1999, reproduced by permission/Private Eye (photograph: The British Library); *p. 239:* material from Te Whariki is reproduced by permission of the publishers Learning Media Limited, PO Box 3293, Wellington, New Zealand, copyright © Crown 1996; *p. 244 and 247:* from *The Hundred Languages of Children – catalogue of the exhibition*, copyright © 1996 Municipality of Reggio Emilia, Infant-Toddler Centers and Preschools, published by Reggio Children.

Figures

Figure 1: QCA (2000) *Investing in Our Future: curriculum guidance for the foundation stage*, Qualifications and Curriculum Authority and DfEE.

Text

Box 1: Grace, P. (1987) 'Butterflies', *Electric City and Other Stories*, Penguin Books NZ Ltd; *p. 245:* poem 'No way. The hundred is there' from *The Hundred Languages of Children – catalogue of the exhibition*, copyright © 1996 Municipality of Reggio Emilia, Infant-Toddler Centers and Preschools, published by Reggio Children; *Reading A:* Anning, A. and Edwards, A. (1999) *Promoting Children's Learning from Birth to Five: developing the new early years professional*, Open University Press; *Reading B:* Carr, M. and May, H. (2000) 'Te Whariki: curriculum voices' in Penn, H. (ed.) *Early Childhood Services: theory, policy and practice*, Open University Press; *Reading C:* New, R. (1990) 'Excellent early education: a city in Italy has it', *Young Children*, September, 4–12, National Association for the Education of Young Children, copyright © Rebecca New.

Chapter 7

Photographs/illustrations

p267: David MacGregor; *p. 269:* John Birdsall Photography; *p. 271:* David MacGregor; *p. 278:* John Callan/www.shoutpictures.com; *p. 281:* John Callan/ www.shoutpictures.com; *p. 283:* John Callan/www.shoutpictures.com; *p. 284:* Paul Baldasare/Photofusion; *p. 286:* Paul Doyle/Photofusion; *p. 291:* Copyright © National Museum of Denmark, Department of Ethnography. Photographer: Jens Yde; *p. 292:* The Advertising Archive Ltd; *p. 293:* Frans Rombout/Bubbles;

Text

Box 1: Gillies, V., Ribbens McCarthy, J. and Holland, J. (2001) *Pulling Together, Pulling Apart: The Family Lives of Young People*, Family Policy Studies Centre/ Joseph Rowntree Foundation. Copyright © FPSC/JRF 2001; *Reading A:* From *Long Walk to Freedom* by Nelson Mandela. Copyright © 1994 by Nelson Rolihlahla Mandela. By permission of Little, Brown and Company, (Inc.) and Time Warner Books UK; *Reading B:* Fock, N. (1963) *Waiwai – religion and society of an Amazonian tribe*, The National Museum of Denmark, Department of Ethnography;

Cover and title page photographs

top: copyright © 1996 PhotoDisc, Inc.; *centre:* Martin Woodhead; *bottom:* copyright © 1996 PhotoDisc, Inc.

Every effort has been made to trace all copyright owners, but if any has been inadvertently overlooked, the publishers will be pleased to make the necessary arrangements at the first opportunity.

INDEX